Cross-border claims to cultural objects

Cross-border claims to cultural objects

Property or heritage?

E. Campfens

eleven

This research was supported by the Ministry of Education, Culture and Science of the Netherlands.

Omslagontwerp: Primo!Studio, Delft
Opmaak binnenwerk: Anne-Marie Krens – Tekstbeeld – Oegstgeest

ISBN 978-94-6236-250-5
ISBN 978-94-5189-189-8 (e-book)
NUR 828

www.elevenpub.com

For Dimitri

Σα βγεις στον πηγαιμό για την Ιθάκη, να εύχεσαι να 'ναι μακρύς
ο δρόμος, γεμάτος περιπέτειες, γεμάτος γνώσεις.
Κ. Καβάφης

As you set out for Ithaka may your road be a long one,
full of adventure, full of discovery.
C. Cavafy

Preface / acknowledgments

The seed for this dissertation was planted while I was living in Greece and became intrigued by the conflict over the Parthenon Marbles: what rules existed for such claims? Later, in my capacity as general secretary to the Dutch Restitutions Committee, I was involved in the research and procedures in relation to claims to Nazi-looted art. This provided me with insights into the prevailing interests and approaches to the topic of looted art in various countries. I also became acquainted with the problems that may arise when there is an absence of clear standards. In 2016, my long-held idea to write a PhD on the topic became possible thanks to the support for this research from the Dutch Ministry of Education, Culture and Science. This gave me the opportunity to investigate whether claims to involuntarily lost cultural objects can be seen as a matter of justice and the law.

The support, inspiration and motivation of numerous people was key to this project, many more than I can mention here. Special thanks go to my *promotores* Nico Schrijver and Wouter Veraart for their enthusiasm from the moment I approached them. Their guidance and patience were essential in making it to this final stage. It truly was a learning process. I am also grateful to the members of the promotion committee Alex Geert Castermans, Helen Duffy, Francesco Francioni, Hildegard Schneider, and Amy Strecker for their time and efforts, and for their valuable comments on the May version of this dissertation.

Colleagues from the Grotius Centre made me feel welcome in Leiden and impressed me by their commitment to international law as a means to a better world. In particular, I thank Sergey Vasiliev and my fellow PhD students. The staff of the Meijers Institute were most supportive at various stages.

Inspiration and insights came from many encounters over the years, notably during discussions with colleagues from the Cultural Heritage Committee of the International Law Association, the Ethical Committee of the Dutch Museums Association and the Centre for Global Heritage and Environment. Furthermore, I thank Jos van Beurden and Charlotte van Rappard for their support over the years, and I thank Pieter ter Keurs and my colleagues at the Museums, Collections and Society research group and the Leiden University Centre for the Arts in Society for their support during the final stage of this project.

This dissertation is based on journal articles. I am indebted to the anonymous reviewers, and to the respective journal editors Ruth Redmond-Cooper,

Andrzej Jakubowski, Alexander Bauer and Anna Meijkecht for their comments and help. Irina Tarsis, Ulrike Schmiegelt and Jinyoung Choi were indispensable in my research of Ukrainian, German, and Korean cases discussed in Chapter 3. Irina also gave feedback on an earlier draft. With regard to Chapter 4, I thank Sergey Vassiliev and Patricia Kennedy Grimsted for their comments on an earlier version, and Roos Hoek for her research assistance. Chapter 5 on colonial looting could not have been written if Earl Sullivan had not introduced me to Chief Taku whom I thank for introducing me to a history of Western Africa of which I had no knowledge before. With regard to Chapter 6, I thank Margot Llompart who made my attendance at meetings of UNESCO's 'Restitution Committee' (the ICPRCP) possible; Alessandro Chechi and Karolina Kuprecht for their feedback on an initial conference paper; and Meng Yu for her help in my research into Chinese cases discussed. Furthermore, I thank Lucas Lixinski and Sophie Starrenburg for their comments on an earlier version of this chapter. Last, but certainly not least I am indebted to Marie Duflot, Wendy Rodger, Fiona Herron and Anne-Marie Krens for their editing work. Quality is in the details.

Many others supported me and acted as touchstones over the years by reading drafts, lending an ear without getting tired of me (or at least not showing it!), or distracting me at exactly the right moment. Keeping to the Leiden tradition, I will not even start to list them. My family and close friends kept me going. I hope they realise, even without naming them personally, how much their support meant to me.

Amsterdam, 8 September 2021

Table of contents

TABLE OF ABBREVIATIONS XV

1 INTRODUCTION 1

1 Introduction 1
2 Background to the research 3
2.1 Competing interests and fragmentation of the law 4
2.2 A private law approach: Lost possessions 5
2.2.1 The problem illustrated 6
2.2.2 Attempts at harmonisation 8
2.3 The topic in public international law: Protected heritage 10
2.3.1 Criminal accountability 12
2.3.2 Return obligations 14
2.3.3 The issue of time 17
2.3.4 Another perspective: A human rights approach 18
2.4 Soft law: Evolving law? 20
2.5 Concluding remark: Different models 24
3 Central research question 25
4 Issues of terminology 26
4.1 International cultural heritage law 26
4.2 Cultural objects, cultural heritage or cultural property? 27
4.3 Return and restitution 29
4.4 Former owners, (mis)appropiation and looting 29
5 Methodology 30
5.1 Legal pluralism 31
5.2 A case-based approach 33
5.3 Sources and research methods 33
6 Structure 35

2 PRIVATE TITLE CLAIMS 37

Abstract 37

Restitution of looted art: What about access to justice? 39

1 Introduction 39
2 The legal setting 40
2.1 The international level 40

2.2 Different national approaches 42
2.3 Appraisal of the legal framework 49
3 The ethical model 51
3.1 Soft-law instruments 51
3.2 Alternative dispute resolution 55
3.2.1 Arbitration 56
3.2.2 Mediation and negotiated settlements 56
3.2.3 Government advisory panels for Nazi-looted art 57
3.2.4 Two examples of institutionalised ADR procedures 58
3.2.4.1 The binding expert opinion procedure by the Dutch Restitutions Committee 59
3.2.4.2 The Court of Arbitration for Art 61
4 Developments: From a property framework towards a human rights frame-work 63
5 Final observations 66

3 THE INTERSTATE MODEL 69

Abstract 69

Whose cultural heritage? Crimean treasures at the crossroads of politics, law and ethics 71

1 Introduction 71
2 Background 72
2.1 The artefacts 72
2.2 Loan agreements and export licences 73
2.3 Geopolitical events 74
2.4 Competing claims 75
2.5 Immunity from seizure? 76
3 The 2016 Amsterdam District Court ruling 77
3.1 The arguments 72
3.2 Contractual obligations in the loan agreement 78
3.3 Title to the artefacts 78
3.4 The 1970 UNESCO Convention 80
3.4.1 Unlawful transfer? 81
3.4.2 Return claim? 83
3.5 The verdict 84
4 Discussion of alternative approaches 84
4.1 The 1954 Hague Convention 84
4.1.1 2013 Dutch return of Cypriot icons 86
4.2 Interests beyond the national state: A 'genuine link'? 87
4.2.1 Territoriality and cultural-historical link 88
4.2.2 Case examples 89
4.3 Alternative dispute resolution 91
5 Conclusion 93
6 Addendum (April 2021): interlocutory judgment Amsterdam Courts of Appeals 94

4 CLAIMS TO NAZI-LOOTED ART 95

Abstract 95

Nazi-looted art: A note in favour of clear standards and neutral procedures 97

1 Introduction 97
2 Post-war restitution system 99
2.1 The system of the Inter-Allied Declaration 99
2.2 Internal restitution: A matter of human rights law 101
2.3 Developments since the 1950s 103
3 Today's standards for Nazi-looted art claims 104
3.1 Elements of the 'just and fair' rule 105
3.2 Unjustified Nazi looting 107
3.2.1 Forced sales 107
3.2.2 Early sales 109
3.2.3 Sales in neutral countries (*'Fluchtgut'*) 110
3.2.4 Business transactions by art dealers 114
3.3 Concluding remarks on the material norm 118
4 Access to justice 119
4.1 The ethical model in Western Europe: Restitution committees 119
4.2 Access to justice through courts of law 122
4.3 The US approach 124
4.3.1 US jurisdiction and state immunity 125
4.3.2 US jurisdiction over European cases 127
4.4 Concluding remarks on access to justice 130
5 Final observations 131

5 COLONIAL LOOTING AND INDIGENOUS PEOPLES' LOST HERITAGE 133

Abstract 133

The Bangwa Queen: Artefact or heritage? 135

1 Introduction 135
2 The Bangwa Queen and her loss 137
2.1 The sculpture and her meaning 137
2.2 The loss 139
2.3 Subsequent ownership history 143
3 Legal standards 143
3.1 Unlawful taking? 144
3.2 International law standards 145
3.3 Privileged status of objects of spiritual importance 147
3.4 The legal framework for historical claims 148
3.5 Legality of seizure under the laws of war? 149
3.6 Colonial takings a *sui generis* category? 152
3.7 State practice and recent European developments 154

4 New horizons 155
4.1 Soft law instruments: Signs of evolving norms? 156
4.2 International Council of Museums Code and the International Law Association Principles 157
4.3 The right to one's cultural objects as a human right? 159
4.4 The right of access to culture 160
4.5 UNDRIP 161
4.5.1 Defining 'indigenous people' 162
4.5.2 Legal status 163
4.5.3 Access to justice and wider developments 164
4.5.4 Access to justice 165
5 Concluding remarks 168

6 CROSS-BORDER TRADE AND CLAIMS: A SYNTHESIS 171

Abstract 171

Whose cultural objects? Introducing heritage title for cross-border cultural property claims 173

1 Introduction 173
2 Ownership versus heritage 176
2.1 Ownership 176
2.2 Heritage 179
2.2.1 Property of mankind? 180
2.2.2 Preservation and accessibility 182
2.2.3 Preservation and accessibility: For whom? 183
3 International framework for the art trade 185
3.1 A system of 'national treasures' 185
3.1.1 GATT and TFEU 185
3.1.2 UNESCO Convention 186
3.1.3 UNIDROIT Convention 187
3.2 Rules for the art trade in practice 189
3.2.1 Due diligence standards 189
3.2.2 The 1970 watershed rule on provenance 191
4 Blind spots and the rise of soft law 192
4.1 Nationality? 192
4.2 Sub-state right holders 194
4.3 Non-retroactive? 196
5 A human rights approach and heritage title 198
5.1 Humanization of cultural heritage law 198
5.2 A human right to cultural property? 201
5.2.1 The right of access to (one's own) culture 201
5.2.2 The right to (cultural) property 202
5.2.3 Other human rights norms 203
5.2.4 Cultural rights of indigenous peoples 204
5.3 Heritage title 205
5.3.1 Basis for entitlement 206

5.3.2 Classification of objects 206
5.3.3 Rights 207
5.4 Operationalisation of heritage title 208
6 Conclusion

7 CONCLUDING OBSERVATIONS 215
1 Introduction 215
2 Summary of findings 216
2.1 Private title claims 216
2.2 The interstate model 219
2.3 Nazi looting 223
2.4 Colonial looting and indigenous peoples' lost cultural objects 228
2.5 Cross-border trade and claims: A synthesis 233
3 Further considerations and proposals 239
3.1 Beyond ownership 239
3.2 Heritage title 240
3.3 An integrated approach 242
4 In conclusion 244

TABLE OF INSTRUMENTS 247
TABLE OF CASES 257
SELECTED BIBLIOGRAPHY 265
OTHER RESOURCES 277
ANNEX: ORIGINAL SOURCES 283

Table of abbreviations

ADR	Alternative Dispute Resolution
AiA	Authentication in Art Foundation
ARC	Autonomous Republic of Crimea
ARSIWA	Articles on Responsibility of States for Internationally Wrongful Acts
CAfA	Court of Arbitration for Art
CETS	Council of Europe Treaty Series
CIVS	Commission pour l'indemnisation des victimes de spoliations
ECHR	European Convention of Human Rights
ECLI	European Case Law Identifier
ECtHR	European Court of Human Rights
EEC	European Economic Community
ETS	European Treaty Series
EP	European Parliament
ERR	Einstatzstab Reichsleiter Rosenberg
EU	European Union
FSIA	Foreign Sovereign Immunity Act
GATT	General Agreement on Tariffs and Trade
HEAR	Holocaust Expropriated Art Recovery
ICC	International Criminal Court
ICCPR	International Covenant on Civil and Political Rights
ICESCR	International Covenant on Economic, Social and Cultural Rights
ICJ	International Court of Justice
ICOM	International Council of Museums
ICOM-WIPO	International Council of Museums - World Intellectual Property Organization Arbitration and Mediation Center
ICPRCP	Intergovernmental Committee for Promoting the Return of Cultural Property or its Restitution in Case of Illicit Appropriation
IDI	Institut de Droit international
ILA	International Law Association
ILC	International Law Commission
ILM	International Legal Materials
KB	Koninklijk Besluit
MNR	Musées Nationaux Récupération
NAGPRA	Native American Graves Protection and Repatriation Act
NAI	Netherlands Arbitration Institute
NIOD	Netherlands Institute for War Documentation
OCW	Onderwijs Cultuur, Wetenschap
PCA	Permanent Court of Arbitration
RC	(Dutch) Restitutions Committee

SAP	Spoliation Advisory Panel
TFEU	Treaty on the Functioning of the European Union
UDHR	Universal Declaration of Human Rights
UK	United Kingdom
UN	United Nations
UNCLOS	United Nations Convention on the Law of the Sea
UNDRIP	United Nations Declaration on the Rights of Indigenous Peoples
UNESCO	United Nations Educational, Scientific and Cultural Organization
UNGA	United Nations General Assembly
UNHRC	United Nations Human Rights Council
UNIDROIT	International Institute for the Unification of Private Law
UNSC	United Nations Security Council
UNTS	United Nations Treaty Series
US	United States
WIPO	World Intellectual Property Organization
WTO	World Trade Organization

1 | Introduction

1 INTRODUCTION

In 1971, Norton Simon, founder of the Norton Simon Museum of Arts in California, bought two paintings by Lucas Cranach the Elder. In 2007, the heirs of the Dutch Jewish art dealer Jacques Goudstikker filed a lawsuit claiming restitution of these two paintings in the US. They had been part of Goudstikker's trade stock that Nazi official Hermann Göring had acquired in a forced sale in 1940, days after Goudstikker had managed to escape the country. This marked the beginning of twelve years of litigation that eventually was halted and resolved in the US Supreme Court in 2019.[1] However, the legal saga took a new turn in October 2020. This time, the Ukrainian government considered filing a claim to the two Cranachs.[2] In the 1920s, they appear to have been confiscated from a Ukrainian monastery by the Soviet authorities, who sold them at the (infamous) 1931 Berlin Lepke auction to Goudstikker, who subsequently lost them to Göring.[3] The paintings then passed through other hands – including the Dutch government after the Second World War – before making it to California in 1971. In a nutshell, this case highlights the complexities of the field of looted art and a problem this dissertation aims to address: what to do if more than one party claims rights over the same cultural object? Is this merely a matter of ownership and property law? The case may seem extraordinary, but many such stories exist. What to think for example of the Benin Bronze statue brutally pillaged by British colonial forces at the close of the 19th century and acquired by a German Jewish collector shortly after, only to be auctioned at a forced Nazi sale in the 1930s?[4] The 'provenance' or ownership history of cultural objects is an endless source of history and injustice. But this dissertation does not focus on historical injustices or reparation schemes. Rather, it is a quest for standards that define the legal status

---

1 In the sense that the Supreme Court denied to review the case after earlier rulings in favour of the museum. *Von Saher v Norton Simon Museum of Art at Pasadena* (2019) 587 U.S. 18-1057.

2 M. Baranovskaya and O. Klymchuck in 'Ukraine seeks to bring home Renaissance artworks sold under false pretenses' (27 Oct. 2020) *Deutsche Welle*.

3 See Chapter 3, section 1.3.

4 The statue surfaced at an auction house in Germany where a financial settlement was reached between the new owner and the Jewish collector's successors in rights, see <https://www.tribal-art-auktion.de/en/news-and-events/news-detail/revealed-royal-benin-head-from-jewish-art-collection/>.

of cultural objects that were lost in one country and, over time, found their way to another country.

It consists of seven chapters, five of which have been published in journals on international (art and heritage) law. In addition to these publications, the dissertation includes this introduction and concluding observations. The previously published chapters can be considered both separately and as a whole. Their overarching themes and coherence will be clarified in this introductory chapter.

The persistent gap between rhetoric on the need to return looted art to its 'rightful owners' and the legal reality prompted and served as inspiration for this doctoral project.[5] Whilst many people believe that restitution claims in relation to Nazi-looted art, colonial booty, and more recently looted antiquities need to be honoured, often positive private law does not support such claims at all. Although international treaties clearly set the norm that looted cultural objects should be returned, these do not apply to losses that predate their adoption and, besides, depend on implementation on the national level to sort effect. This all adds up to a highly fragmented legal framework that often results in the inadmissibility and denial of claims, most notably in civil law countries. This may be fair in a specific case, given the many interests at stake, but it also seems at odds with today's perception of justice. Moreover, a legal framework that condones the 'laundering' of stolen cultural objects undermines international policy that aims to curb the illicit trade in looted cultural objects.

For the category of Nazi-looted art, an ethical model was developed at the end of the 20th century: claims by victims of Nazi persecution or their heirs to family heirlooms were to be assessed as 'moral claims' through extra-legal procedures, to circumvent obstacles in the law.[6] Besides Nazi-looted art, such an ethical model is increasingly promoted for other categories of looted art as well, such as colonial takings.[7] It would imply that this field does not rely on the rule of law, but on morality instead. From a legal-theoretical perspective, this raises a fundamental question: if we believe that the application of the law leads to injustice, is that law (or the way it is applied) not due for a change? Might the increase of 'soft law' and other informal regulations in this field be a sign of emerging law?[8]

---

5 'Looting' refers to various types of misappropriation. See Chapter 1, section 4.

6 On the basis of the so-called 'Washington Principles', adopted by over 40 governments in 1998. Washington Conference Principles on Nazi-Confiscated Art (US State Department 1999), in J.D. Bindenagel (ed.) *Washington Conference on Holocaust-Era Assets*, 971-972. See Chapter 4.

7 E.g. Van Beurden in his doctoral thesis proposes a translation of the Washington Principles for colonial takings. Van Beurden JM, *Treasures in Trusted Hands: Negotiating the Future of Colonial Cultural Objects* (2017) Sidestone Press.

8 The term 'soft law' covers a variety of not directly binding yet authorative legal instruments, as opposed to binding 'hard law'. See Chapter 1, section 2.4.

This study explores how cross-border claims to cultural objects fit in the wider legal framework, and where blind spots or clashes of norms occur. The aim is to identify new directions that can help develop this field further. To that end, the five substantive chapters of the dissertation analyse the relevant 'hard' as well as the 'soft' law instruments and international practice from different perspectives on the basis of various case studies. This case-based approach was chosen to deal with the problem that the legal framework is highly fragmented: an approach from one specific field of law or one category of contested cultural objects would not provide the intended overview. Whilst the category of Nazi-looted art will be an important case study on account of its long-standing international practice, other categories such as colonial booty and more recently lost antiquities, will also be addressed. In spite of their differences, they have important elements in common. The main commonality identified in this dissertation is that the intangible heritage value of cultural objects, as symbols of an identity, often lies at the core of claims whilst adequate legal tools to address such values are lacking.

The present chapter serves as an introduction. The next section provides an outline of the legal background and identifies problems in need of further analysis. This is followed by sections on the central research question, on issues of terminology, on the methodology, and a final section on the structure of the dissertation. The annex to this chapter provides an overview of the publication status of the five articles that make up the body of this dissertation.

2 Background to the research

The types of cases that are addressed in the five substantive chapters of this dissertation are: private title claims (Chapter 2); interstate return claims (Chapter 3); claims to Nazi-looted art (Chapter 4); claims to colonial takings (Chapter 5); and claims to more recently looted antiquities (Chapter 6). This represents a wide array of cases that may be perceived as fundamentally different given that the circumstances of the loss vary. Indeed, different rules apply to historical losses or present-day losses, mostly because international treaties in this field do not apply retro-actively. Yet, the protection of cultural objects, and their preferential status under the law, did not start or end with these treaties. Moreover, even if the loss of an object itself – and a claim based on that loss – is not covered by 'hard' law rules that support claims to certain present-day takings, increasingly soft law *does* support such claims. Besides, the possession of 'tainted' cultural objects – i.e. objects that do not have a 'clean' ownership history due to an irregular loss in the past – is increasingly being condemned, which implies a shift in focus from the injustice of a loss in the past to the 'lawful' possession of such objects today. At times, this censure is more vehement for historical losses than when it concerns recently looted cultural objects that *are* covered by international treaties.

From that perspective, I will argue that a common normative framework to the various categories is needed and already exists to a certain degree, even though this is not (yet) a homogeneous body of binding law. This section provides a survey of this common background, and identifies problems that arise in the law on various levels.

2.1 Competing interests and fragmentation of the law

Cultural objects have a multifaceted nature. They can be seen as possessions and, as such, can be owned, traded, and are subject to property law regimes. The commodification of cultural objects may be as old as time itself, and is expanding as a result of globalisation.[9] Yet, it is their intangible cultural or heritage value that sets these objects apart from other goods. That intangible value is by no means a static notion: an artefact may be valued by the general public because of its (art) historical or scientific value, but at the same time it may be of spiritual importance to a specific community, symbolic of the cultural identity of a people or nation, or it may be a special family heirloom. This wide variety of interests means that many fields of law interact and sometimes clash.[10] Whereas, in broad terms, private law norms address cultural object as possessions, public law norms address the intangible cultural and heritage interests at stake.

Another commonality, closely related to the former, is that the relevant facts in cases that concern contested cultural objects are often spread out over a period of many years and can involve multiple jurisdictions. Laws and regulations that determine their legal status, however, differ widely in time and place. This means that norms are to be found on many levels: international and national, private and public, hard law as well as soft law norms, they may all influence that legal status. Fragmentation of the law lies at the core of what causes disputes over contested cultural objects to be so complex and unpredictable.

This dissertation focuses on international standards, but the interrelationship and interaction with domestic law will prove crucial. For example, the specific function of an object may have an immediate effect on that object's legal status under national law: as *res extra commercium* a cultural object may be inalienable.[11] In most countries archaeological objects, elements of monu-

---

9 This commodification in its illicit form has recently reached alarming levels, also as a result of possibilities for the (anonymous) trade over the internet. The illicit flow of cultural goods is believed by UNESCO to be the third largest in terms of volume, after drugs and arms, operating largely online via platforms. E.g. E. Ottone Ramirez, Editorial (October 2020) The UNESCO Courier.

10 For an in-depth analysis, Chapter 6, section 2.

11 In some countries all public museum collections are inalienable, e.g. in France, this is codified in Art. L451-5 *Code du patrimoine.*

ments, or religious objects are inalienable. Furthermore, indigenous peoples may perceive certain cultural goods not as objects at all – but perhaps as incarnated ancestors, not susceptible to ownership.[12] Nevertheless, once it is in another cultural setting and in another jurisdiction such an object may well be classified as any other good.

Another reason that national (private) law is often decisive, is that litigation over contested cultural objects generally takes place at the national level in the country where an object is located, at some distance from international law that oversees the protection of cultural heritage of all people. In fact, the only international body that was envisaged to have a role in this field,[13] the UNESCO Intergovernmental Committee for Promoting the Return of Cultural Property to its Countries of Origin or its Restitution in Case of Illicit Appropriation (the ICPRCP), is solely accessible to states and in practice mainly acts as a discussion forum for governments, not as a forum where disputes are resolved.[14]

The distinction between the model for claims in a private law approach and the model under public international law, as introduced below, will be used as a basis to explore the normative framework.

2.2 A private law approach: Lost possessions

Private law is the field that traditionally arranges title disputes over lost possessions. Laws on ownership and property, however, differ widely per jurisdiction, with many variations on the theme of how ownership over a (stolen) good can be transferred to a new possessor. Common law countries accord relatively strong rights to the dispossessed former owner on the basis of the principle that a thief cannot convey good title (the *nemo dat quod non habet* rule), whereas in civil law countries the position of a new possessor is stronger and title over stolen goods can pass after an acquisition in good faith or simply after the lapse of time (acquisitive perscription).[15] In spite of a

12 Futher to be discussed in Chapters 4 and 6.

13 None of the UNESCO Conventions were accompanied with the setting up of a dispute settlement system.

14 Statutes of the Intergovernmental Committee for Promoting the Return of Cultural Property to its Countries of Origin or its Restitution in case of Illicit Appropriation (adopted October-November 1978, amended 2005) UNESCO Doc CLT/CH/INS-2005/21 (ICPRCP). The ICPRCP was set up in 1978 to address issues *not* arranged for by the Convention on the Means of Prohibiting and Preventing the Illicit Import, Export and Transfer of Ownership of Cultural Property (adopted 14 November 1970, entered into force 24 April 1972) 823 UNTS 231 (1970 UNESCO Convention). See Chapter 5, section 4.2.

15 Chapter 2, section 2.2. For a comparative analysis (in Dutch) see L.P.W. van Vliet 'Verjaring en Kunstwerken' in MA Loth and LPW van Vliet 'Recht over tijd. Hoever reikt het privaatrecht in het verleden?' (2018) Preadviezen Nederlandse Vereniging voor Burgerlijk Recht, Zutphen 2018.

choice on the international level for the model where ownership over stolen or looted cultural objects can*not* easily pass, this distinction between national legal systems still proves highly relevant for restitution claims. According to private international law (conflict of law) rules in the majority of states, the law of the place where a property is located determines proprietary rights in movable goods (the *lex rei sitae*).[16] In civil law countries that may well favour new possessors.

2.2.1 *The problem illustrated*

The opposite outcomes reached in very similar Dutch and UK cases regarding Second World War looting may serve as an example. Both cases concerned a title claim with regard to paintings looted in the aftermath of the Second World War from Germany, probably by the Red Army, and both paintings surfaced at auctions in the late 1990s. In both cases, the dispossessed owners – in the Dutch case the state Sachsen and in the English case the city of Gotha – filed claims and both claims were decided in 1998. Whereas in the Netherlands, the *Hoge Raad* (the Dutch Supreme Court) denied the claim to the painting *Cloister in Landscape* by Jan van der Heyden, in its *Land Sachsen* ruling, the High Court of England and Wales in the same year upheld the claim to the painting *The Holy Family* by Joachim Wtewael in the *City of Gotha* case.[17] In the Dutch ruling, the Court held that the absolute limitation period for claims under the applicable Dutch law (30 years at the time) runs from the moment of the loss, irrespective of the good or bad faith of the present possessor. Legal security, in the Court's view, could neither be set aside by the fact that the deprived owner did not know where its painting was located, nor by the possible lack of good faith of a new possessor.[18] The English Court, however, upheld the claim under application of German law. Illustrative for the different views on 'justice' in this regard, is that in the English case, Judge Moses J. observed that he would have invoked the public order exception if the application of German law had necessitated a ruling against the interests of the

16 The domicile of a new possessor or where the acquisition took place (being usually that location). See, for example the German ruling *Oberlandesgericht Frankfurt am Main* of 4 February 2013 (OLG *Frankfurt*, Urt. v. 04.02.2013 - 16 U 161/11, holding that acquisitive prescription as arranged for in German private law governed the matter of ownership of antiquities in possession in Germany and, thus, the lawful ownership title of the new possessor, a priori, stands in the way of the Turkish return claim.

17 *Land Sachsen* (1998) Supreme Court of the Netherlands, ECLI:NL:HR:1998:ZC2644; *City of Gotha and Federal Republic of Germany v Sotheby's and Cobert Finance SA* (1998) No. 1993 C 3428 (QB).

18 Ibid. under 3.5 and 3.6. On Dutch property law see, e.g., A.F. Salomon 'National Report on the Transfer of Ownership of Movables in The Netherlands', in W. Faber, B. Lurger (eds) National Reports on the Transfer of Movables in Europe, Vol. 6 (Sellier, Munich, 2011), p. 17. See also Chapter 2, section 2.2; Chapter 3 section 4.1.1; Chapter 6 section 1; and Chapter 7, section 2.1, n. 1.

deprived owner and in favour of a possessor who was not in good faith.[19] The same contrast surfaces in two rulings that regard Cypriot church relics that were looted in the 1970s. In the US *Goldberg* case, the application of US (Indiana) law to the question of ownership resulted in restitution of the artefacts to the Church,[20] whilst in the Dutch *Lans* case the claim was denied under application of Dutch civil law and the collector was deemed the lawful owner due to acquisitive perscription.[21] As an aside: this controversial outcome – also in the light of the obligations of the Dutch state under the First Protocol to the 1954 UNESCO Convention –[22] was afterwards corrected by acquisition of the icons by the Dutch state and their return to Cyprus.[23]

Arguably, today such an outcome where even a possessor who was (or could be) aware of the tainted provenance upon acquisition gains lawful ownership title, could (or should) be different. For the specific Dutch situation, it is relevant that courts in recent years have developed some 'escape routes' for manifest unjust effects of time limitations.[24] Amongst those is the possibility to regain lost property from a bad faith new possessor (who became the owner due to acquisitive prescription), by awarding compensation of damages in the form of restitution of the property.[25] This would open up the door to claimants to regain their lost artefacts also beyond the (very limited) categories of cultural objects for which the Dutch law already provides exceptions to

---

19 As a 'framework for further debate' he notes in this respect that '[i]t does seem [...] possible to identify, [...], a public policy in England that time is not to run either in favour of the thief nor in favour of any transferee who is not a purchaser in good faith'. In the end, there was no need to invoke the public order exception after it was established the German 30-years' limitation period (of para 221 BGB) had not expired at the time of the claim. *City of Gotha* case, II.4.

20 *Autocephalous Greek-Orthodox Church v. Goldberg & Feldman Fine Arts, Inc.* - 917 F.2d 278 (7th Cir. 1990).

21 *Autocephalous Greek Orthodox Church in Cyprus v. Lans,* Rechtbank (*First Instance Ct*) Rotterdam, 4 February 1999 (NJ 1999, 37); *Autocephalous Greek Orthodox Church in Cyprus v. Lans,* Hof (Ct of Appeal) The Hague, 7 March 2002. NIPR (2002) No 248. Discussion follows in Chapter 3, section 4.1.1.

22 Convention for the Protection of Cultural Property in the Event of Armed Conflict (adopted 14 May 1954, entered into force 7 August 1956) 249 UNTS 240 and First Protocol to the Convention for the Protection of Cultural Property in the Event of Armed Conflict (adopted 14 May 1954, entered into force 7 August 1956) 249 UNTS 358.

23 Discussion follows in Chapter 3, section 4.1.1.

24 In certain (serious) cases reliance on limitation periods to deny a (tort) claim was held unreasonable and unjust, e.g. *Plaintifs v. the Dutch State,* Hof (Ct of Appeal) the Hague, 1 October 2019 (ECLI:NL:GHDHA:2019:2524) concerning a claim for compensation for family of Indonesian men executed during colonial actions in Indonesia in 1947. Ownerhsip claims, however, concern rights *in rem.*

25 *Municipality Heusden v. Plaintifs,* Supreme Court of the Netherlands 24 Feburary 2017 (ECLI: NL:HR:2017:309). I.e. a claim for an unlawful act (ex art 6:162 Dutch Civil Code) after ownership passed duet o acquisitive prescription (art 3:305 Dutch Civil Code).

acquisitive prescription.[26] The question this dissertation should address is whether, from the patchwork of regulations that typifies the legal framework today, general (international law) standards on the lawful possession of looted art may be deducted. If so, domestic courts might apply such standards, also if these are not directly binding law in the specific jurisdiction, by making use of open norms that exist in all legal systems such as 'reasonableness and fairness', 'public policy', 'moral standards of the trade' and the like.[27]

2.2.2 *Attempts at harmonisation*

Although the examples given above may give the impression that in common law jurisdictions claimants stand good chances to reclaim their lost artefacts, many other obstacles exist in a private law approach to regain ownership over looted cultural objects. These are caused by the fact that, as a general rule, foreign public law will not be applied in another jurisdiction. Export restrictions or other public law instruments that render cultural objects inalienable, as touched upon above, however often form the basis of the unlawfulness of a taking in the country of origin.[28] Another obstacle is that foreign forms of (collective) ownership may not be acknowledged by the private law system of the country where the object ended up.[29]

Such complications were addressed in the 1995 UNIDROIT Convention on Stolen or Illegally Exported Cultural Object that aims at harmonisation of these issues in the private law of member states.[30] It introduces a model where ownership title over objects *cannot* (easily) pass if these were stolen or unlaw-

26 Pursuant to Art. 3:86a; 3:86b; 3:87a; 3:310a; 3:310b, and 3:310c of the Dutch Civil Code, exceptions apply if it regards (European) cultural objects claimed on the basis of (i) the EU Directive of 15 May 2014 on the return of cultural objects unlawfully removed from the territory of a Member State and amending Regulation (EU) No. 1024/2012 (Recast) (OJ 2014, L 159); (ii) Dutch cultural heritage that is protected from export from the Netherlands under the Heritage Act (Erfgoedwet); or (iii) objects claimed by States Parties under the 1970 UNESCO Convention lost *after* the implementation of the 1970 Convention in 2009. See also E. Campfens, 'Bridging the Gap between Ethics and Law: The Dutch Framework for Nazi-looted Art' (2020) 25 *Art Antiquity Law* 1, p. 13-16.

27 Discussion follows in Chapter 6 section 1, sections 3.1.2 and 5.4; and Chapter 7, section 2.1.

28 The US case *United States v. McClain* 593 F2d 658 (at 670) held that the Mexican ownership claim, based on its heritage laws, was not expressed 'with sufficient clarity to survive translation into terms understandable and binding upon American citizens'; see also the UK ruling *Attorney General of New Zealand v Ortiz* (1982) 3 All ER 432, holding the denial of New Zealand's claim to (protected) Maori carvings that were acquired in the US by Ortiz.

29 For a Dutch ruling, *Village Communities of Yangchun and Dongpu v Van Overveem, Design & Consultancy BV* (Judgment of 12 December 2018) Amsterdam District Court, No. ECLI:NL:RBAMS:2018:8919; a French ruling: *Association Survival International France v SARL Néret-Minet Tessier Sarrou* (2013) *Tribunal de Grande Instance de Paris*, No RG 13/52880 BF/No 1. See Chapter 2, section 2 and Chapter 6, section 1.

30 UNIDROIT Convention on Stolen or Illegally Exported Cultural Objects (adopted 24 June 1995, entered into force 7 July 1998) 2421 UNTS 457 (1995 UNIDROIT Convention).

fully taken – according to the country of origin's laws – and the introduction of extended limitation periods for claims.[31] Such a preference for the laws of the country of origin (the *lex originis*) over the law of the country where the object was traded or ended up (the *lex rei sitae*), has also been promoted by the *Institut de Droit international*.[32]

The adoption of the 1995 UNIDROIT Convention would enhance a smooth and lawful international art trade in the future. However, 'market countries' (i.e. countries with major art markets or where cultural objects tend to end up in collections) mostly did not accede to the 1995 UNIDROIT Convention[33] and, moreover, today's claims deal with past losses. In other words, even if all states were to accede to the UNIDROIT Convention today, the fragmented situation will continue in as far as it concerns looted or stolen objects that are already circulating.

Complications for former owners to reclaim their lost cultural objects in a private law setting form the subject of Chapter 2 and will be further analysed and set off against the interstate model in Chapter 6. This introduction serves to highlight the need for international standards: not only to ensure a smooth art trade – by setting clear rules to enhance legal security – but also to safeguard the intangible (heritage) interests of people in their lost cultural objects that are found in another jurisdiction. Such international standards exist. They vary from directly binding norms such as UN Security Council resolutions that impose a ban on the trade of antiquities from Syria and Iraq,[34] to treaty obligations that apply to the extent that states have ratified the relevant treaties and implemented those standards in their national (private) law.[35] Furthermore, a wide variety of non-binding resolutions and other informal legal instruments define the status of cultural objects that were lost in one jurisdiction and, over time, made their way to another jurisdiction.

31 The 1995 UNIDROIT Convention, articles 3 and art 5. See also Chapters 2 and 6.

32 See the arts. 2, 3 and 4 of the 1991 IDI Basel Resolution. Institut de Droit International, 'The international Sale of Works of Art from the Angle of the Protection of the Cultural Heritage', Resolution adopted at Basel (1991).

33 Fifty states did so, but excluding Western 'market countries' such as the US, the UK, Germany and France (status 10 April 2021). Although Switzerland and the Netherlands are signatories these countries did *not* ratify.

34 As a matter of peace and security certain UN SC resolutions contain obligations imposed on all states, aimed at the return of objects to the people they came from: UNSC Res. 2199 (2015) UN Doc S/RES/2199; UNSC Res. 1483 (2003) UN Doc S/RES/1483. These are both based on articles 39 and 41 of Chapter VII of the UN Charter. Charter of the United Nations (adopted 26 June 1945, entered into force 24 October 1945) 1 UNTS 16 (UN Charter). See also Chapter 6.

35 Most notably the 1954 UNESCO Convention; the 1970 UNESCO Convention; and the 1995 UNIDROIT Convention.

2.3 The topic in public international law: Protected heritage

Cultural heritage is under special protection in international law, and the prohibition to pillage cultural objects has a long history. It developed through the laws of warfare.[36] Already in the 17th century Hugo Grotius exempts cultural objects from the right to pillage in times of war – in his turn referring to the writings of Polybius and Cicero:

> 'There are some things of that nature, that they can no way contribute either towards the making or maintaining of a war, which things even common reason will have spared during a war. ... Polybius called it an act of extreme madness to destroy those things ... Such are temples, porticos, statues, and all other elegant works and monuments of art. ... Our ancestors used to leave to the conquered, what things were grateful to them, but to us of no great importance.'[37]

The enhanced protection for sacred objects highlights that the *rationale* for this protection is their intangible value for local communities, as symbols of an identity:

> 'But as this maxim ought to be observed in regard to public ornaments, ... so more especially in regard to things dedicated to sacred uses ...'[38]

Although this immunity of cultural objects in times of armed conflict certainly did not always prevail, it did find its way into the first legal instruments on the laws of war. Eventually, it was codified in Article 56 of both the 1899 and 1907 Regulations concerning the Laws and Customs of War on Land, reading:

> 'The property of municipalities, that of institutions dedicated to religion, charity and education, the arts and sciences, even when State property, shall be treated as private property. All seizure of, destruction or wilful damage done to institutions of this character, historic monuments, works of art and science, is forbidden, and should be made the subject of legal proceedings.'[39]

---

36 'Pillage' is the traditional term for the misappropriation of private property during times of war (i.e. constitutes 'looting' as used in this study). See Art. 47 of the Convention (IV) respecting the Laws and Customs of War on Land and its annex: Regulations concerning the Laws and Customs of War on Land (adopted 18 October 1907, entered into force 26 January 1910) 205 CTS 277 (1907 Hague Convention).

37 Usually Grotius is quoted confirming the rights to spoils; however, this is his 'moderation' in Chapter XII of Book III of *De Jure Belli Ac Pacis (On the Law of War and Peace)* (1625), under (V). R. Tuck (ed.) *The Rights of War and Peace,* from the Edition by Jean Barbeyrac (Indianapolis: Liberty Fund, 2005). Vol 3, p. 1466-1467.

38 Ibid., Book III, Chapter XII, under (VI).

39 Convention (II) with Respect to the Laws and Customs of War on Land and its annex: Regulations concerning the Laws and Customs of War on Land (adopted 29 July 1899, entered into force 4 September 1990) 32 Stat. 1803.

After the Second World War, the first dedicated convention on the topic of heritage protection, the UNESCO Convention for the Protection of Cultural Property in the Event of Armed Conflict of 1954, confirmed the protected status of cultural objects in times of war.[40] The 1954 Hague Convention obliges states to respect cultural heritage, and in that regard to 'prohibit, prevent and, if necessary, put a stop to any form of theft, pillage or misappropriation of, and any acts of vandalism directed against, cultural property', and to 'refrain from requisitioning movable cultural property situated in the territory of another High Contracting Party.'[41] The obligation to return cultural objects taken in violation of these provisions was arranged for in a separate Protocol of the same year.[42]

When in the 1990s cultural heritage was deliberately targeted in the Balkan conflicts and the shortcomings of this protective system became clear, in 1999 the Second Protocol to the 1954 Hague Convention was adopted.[43] It extends the protection of cultural heritage to armed conflicts *not* of an international character;[44] clarifies that any transfer of cultural property (including archaeological finds) from occupied territories is prohibited[45] arranges for obligations for states to criminalise and prosecute grave violations;[46] and to adopt measures to supress the 'illicit export or other removal or transfer of ownership of cultural property from occupied territory'.[47] These and other regulations of humanitarian law illustrate the importance attached by the international community to the protection of cultural objects when they are most vulnerable to looting: in times of armed conflict.

With the adoption of the UNESCO Convention on the Means of Prohibiting and Preventing the Illicit Import, Export and Transfer of Ownership of Cultural Property this special protection of cultural object under international law was extended beyond situations of armed conflict. It was an answer by the international community to the one-way flow of cultural objects from culturally rich but economically weak 'source countries' to Western 'market countries',

40 The 1954 Hague Convention. In July 2021, 133 states ratified the Convention

41 Ibid, Art 4.

42 First Protocol to the Convention for the Protection of Cultural Property in the Event of Armed Conflict (adopted 14 May 1954, entered into force 7 August 1956) 249 UNTS 358. In July 2021, 110 states ratified the 1954 Protocol.

43 Second Protocol to the Hague Convention for the Protection of Cultural Property in the Event of Armed Conflict (adopted 26 March 1999, entered into force 9 March 2004) 2253 UNTS 212 (Second Protocol). In July 2021, 84 states ratified the 1999 Protocol. For a history of the UNESCO Conventions see A.F. Vrdoljak and L. Meskell 'Intellectual Cooperation Organisation, Unesco, And The Culture Conventions' in F. Francioni and A.F. Vrdoljak (eds.) *The Oxford Handbook of International Cultural Heritage Law* (OUP, 2020)

44 Second Protocol, Art 22.

45 Ibid, Art 9.

46 Ibid, Art 15-17;

47 Ibid, Art 21 (b).

a process that had been ongoing since colonial times and continues today. The 1970 UNESCO Convention can be considered a milestone in the development of international cultural heritage law by setting the standard that the trade in unlawfully exported or looted cultural objects is illicit.[48]

It was adopted after lengthy negotiations, hindered by opposing interests between source states (favouring protection) and market or holding states (favouring a liberal trade).[49] The defensive US reaction to an earlier draft, that its museums displayed the 'cultural heritage of mankind' and 'deserved encouragement' and 'not the threat of being impeded in this dedicated purpose', as cited by Vrdoljak and Meskel, illustrates these opposing interests that still characterise the field of the illicit trade.[50] The outcome of these negotiations at the time is the 1970 UNESCO Convention. It aims to curb the illicit trade by reliance on a system of protected 'national cultural heritage'; export licenses; and internatonal cooperation on issues of return. Its focus, thus, is on the protection of cultural heritage in source countries, whilst the provisions on return are reknown for their general and, at times, ambiguous wording.[51]

The entry into force of the 1970 Convention – in 1972 – is often considered as the watershed moment: export without the authorisation of the source country after that moment is unlawful, whereas earlier looting practices would not be covered by clear legal standards – and therefore, according to some, lawful. That last point of view is challenged by recent practice, but should also be dismissed on account of the long-standing protected status of cultural heritage in international and national laws.[52]

2.3.1 Criminal accountability

In terms of criminal accountability, the Nuremberg Trials after the Second World War set a precedent in the prosecution of individuals for grave offences

48 On 22 July 2021 141 states are party to the 1970 UNESCO Convention,. Most market states acceded recently.

49 On these developments, e.g. Vrdoljak and Meskell (2020).

50 Means of Prohibiting the Illicit Export, Import and Sale of Cultural Property, Preliminary Report, UNESCO Doc. UNESCO/CUA/123 (1963), 10. As cited in Vrdoljak and Meskell (2020).

51 See also Chapter 3, section 3.4.1 and Chapter 6 section 3.1.2.

52 On this watershed moment, see Chapter 6, section 3. Art 15 of the 1970 UNESCO Convention implicitly acknowledges this by providing that in spite of its non-retroactivity '(n)othing in this Convention shall prevent State Parties thereto from concluding special agreements … regarding the restitution of cultural property removed, whatever the reason, from its territory of origin, before the entry into force of this Convention for the States concerned'. This must have been the compromise after calls for retroactivity so as to cover earlier (colonial) takings failed.

against cultural heritage such as looting and destruction.[53] After the International Criminal Tribunal for the Former Yugoslavia gave impetus to the matter during the 1990s, international law has gradually come to recognise that acts against cultural heritage may amount to war crimes and crimes against humanity.[54] In that sense, in 2016 the International Criminal Court (ICC) in the first case that solely focussed on cultural heritage, convicted Ahmad Al Faqi Al Mahdi for 'intentional attacks against historic monuments and buildings dedicated to religion in Mali'.[55] In response to the wide-scale destruction and looting of heritage sites during the conflicts in Syria and Iraq, in 2017 the UN Security Council unequivocally reiterated that unlawful attacks against sites or historical monuments constitute a war crime for which perpetrators must be brought to justice.[56] Criminal accountability of states or individuals or protection schemes will not be the topic of this study. Instead, it takes as an hypothesis that to 'break the chain' of looting and plundering, apart from the protection of cultural heritage *in situ* and criminalisation of the act of looting, the legal status of cultural objects themselves - the matter of entitlement - deserves our attention.

In that regard, the conflicts in Syria and Iraq brought about a new awareness. Awareness on the scale of the looting and the illicit trade in looted cultural objects, often said to be the largest only after drugs and weapons; on the involvement of terrorist groups and organised crime in their commodification; and on the detrimental effects for source communities who are left without their cultural heritage after looting practices.[57] It prompted the involvement of the UN Security Council and the adoption of directly binding sanction measures, as a matter of peace and security, that introduced a ban on the trade in and possession of cultural objects that were removed from Syrian territories (since 2011) and Iraqi territories (since 1990).[58]

53 E.g. in the case of Rosenberg – the leader of the special unit responsible for looting, the 'Einsatzstab Reichsleiter Rosenberg' (ERR). See also A.M. Carstens 'The Swinging Pendulum of Cultural Heritage Crimes in International Criminal Law' in A.M. Carstens & E. Varner (eds.) *Intersections in International Cultural Heritage Law* (2020) OUP, pp. 109-131. See also Chapter 4, section 2.

54 See F. Lenzerini 'The Role of International and Mixed Criminal Counts in Enforcement of International Norms concerning the Protection of Cultural Heritage', in F. Francioni and J. Gordley (eds.) *Enforcing Cultural Heritage Law* (2013) OUP, pp. 40-59.

55 *Prosecutor v Al Mahdi* (Trial Judgement and Sentence) ICC-01/12-01/15-171 (27 September 2016).

56 UNSC Res. 2347 S/RES/2347 (2017), at 4.

57 See e.g. the International Guidelines for Crime Prevention and Criminal Justice Responses with Respect to Trafficking in Cultural Property and Other Related Offences, adopted by the UN General Assembly in its resolution 69/196, of 18 December 2014. See also the 'red lists' published by ICOM, <https://icom.museum/en/resources/red-lists/>.

58 UNSC Res. 1483 (2003) UN Doc S/RES/1483; UNSC Res. 2199 (2015) UN Doc S/RES/2199; UNSC Res. 2347 (2017) UN Doc S/RES/2347. These are implemented in the EU by means of Regulations (EC) No. 1210/2003 of 7 July 2003 and No. 1332/2013 of 13 December 2013.

This new awareness also instigated a new generation of international instruments that do not only focus on protection *in situ* and criminalisation of destruction and looting, but also on the trade in and possession of looted artefacts. Besides the UN Security Council resolutions, the 2017 Nicosia Council of Europe Convention on Offences relating to Cultural Property – that has yet to enter into force – takes this approach.[59] On the European level, the 2019 EU Import Regulation prohibits the import of unlawfully exported cultural objects and, in a similar way, shifts the focus from the act of looting to the possession of looted cultural objects.[60] Irrespective of whether such regulations apply directly to a particular case – mostly they only cover future losses – it contributes to a setting where the 'clean' provenance of cultural objects (the ownership history) has become a crucial requirement in the art trade. In that sense, measures that prohibit and criminalise the possession, trade, or import of certain categories of looted cultural objects also influence the legal status of objects that already circulate and have an unknown or 'tainted' – but not *per se* unlawful – provenance.

2.3.2 *Return obligations*

The obligation to return looted cultural objects is the logical counterpart of the prohibition to loot or possess looted objects. 'Return' is also referred to as 'restitution', if a legal obligation is implied, or as 'repatriation', which denotes the physical return of an object.[61]

With regard to wartime looting, the legal obligation to return dispersed cultural objects is well established in international law. The Peace Treaties after the Napoleonic Wars in the early part of the 19th century are generally considered the turning point in the development of the law in this respect: on that occasion the European powers considered that restitution on the basis of geographic origin (territoriality) of dispersed heritage was a principle of justice – not merely a matter of 'winners takers'.[62] Eventually, the legal obligation to return cultural objects looted in times of war, further than a general

59 Nicosia Council of Europe Convention on Offences relating to Cultural Property (adopted 3 May 2017) CETS No. 221. The Convention aims to prevent and combat the illicit trafficking and destruction of cultural property, and falls within the Council of Europe's action to fight terrorism and organised crime. It is open to all states and on 9 January 2021 the number of signatures were 10, ratifications 2 (Cyprus and Mexico).

60 Regulation (EU) 2019/880 of 17 April 2019 on the introduction and the import of cultural goods (2019) OJ L 151. Art 3: 'The introduction of cultural goods […] which were removed from the territory of the country where they were created or discovered in breach of the laws and regulations of that country shall be prohibited'. The Regulation introduces a licensing system – for some goods a licence and for others an 'importer statement' is needed – that will gradually become operational. Regulations are binding in their entirety and are directly applicable in all European Union countries.

61 In Chapter 1, section 4, these terms will be further discussed.

62 On this development see Chapter 5, section 3.2.

call for legal proceedings in the 1907 Hague Convention, was codified in the First Protocol to the 1954 Hague Convention.[63]

Beyond situations of armed conflict, the 1970 UNESCO Convention provides for the rule that unlawfully exported designated cultural objects should be returned.[64] Where initially only a few market countries acceded to the 1970 UNESCO Convention, this changed at the beginning of the millennium. Today, 141 states have ratified or acceded to the Convention including market states,[65] and its main principle that the unauthorised export of protected cultural objects ('national cultural property') is unlawful has been recognised as international public policy on several occasions.[66] Nevertheless, the exact scope of this principle in terms of return obligations is far from evident, not in the last place because the 1970 UNESCO Convention itself is not unambiguous on return obligations.[67] The 1995 UNIDROIT Convention, discussed above, aims to further clarify the issue of return and fills some of the lacunae of the 1970 UNESCO Convention, for example by including undocumented (archaeological) cultural objects. However, it is not widely adopted.[68]

Although, today, the obligation to return looted cultural objects for certain categories may be considered to have the status of customary international law – or, at least, as a general principle of international law –, the exact scope of that rule remains unsettled.[69] Does it only cover situations of pillage and looting during armed conflict, or does it extend to the unauthorised export

63 First Protocol to the Convention for the Protection of Cultural Property in the Event of Armed Conflict (adopted 14 May 1954, entered into force 7 August 1956) 249 UNTS 358.

64 For an in-depth discussion, see Chapter 3, section 3.4 and Chapter 6, section 3.1.2.

65 As of 22 July 2021. Amongst these are the major art market states: the US (1983), China (1989), France (1997), the UK (2002), Japan (2002), Switzerland (2003) and Sweden (2003). The Netherlands ratified in 2009.

66 Cf. the Statute of the ICJ, Article 38, general principles of law are subsidiary sources of international law. International customary law pre-supposes an established practice and *opinio juris*. Nevertheless, practice is not unambigious. See Chapter 6, sections 3.1.2 and 5.4.

67 Although the spirit of the 1970 UNESCO Convention may be clear in its stance that looted cultural objects should be returned, the only straighforward return obligation concerns Art 7 (b) regarding 'cultural property stolen from a museum or a religious or secular public monument or similar institution .. after the entry into force of this Convention, provided that such property is *documented* as appearing in the inventory of that institution' under the condition of 'just compensation to an innocent purchaser or to a person who has valid title to that property. Other obligations contained in the articles 7 and 13 are less clear because those depend on consistency with national legislation.

68 On 5 May 2021 the status was 50 contracting states, excluding Western-Eurpean countries such as Germany, UK, France, Switzerland and the Netherlands. See Chapter 2, section 2.1 and Chapter 6, section 3.1.3.

69 See, e.g., F. Francioni, 'The Human Dimension of International Cultural Heritage Law: An Introduction' (2011) 22 EJIL 9, page 14; A. Chechi, *The Settlement of International Cultural Heritage Dispute* (2014) OUP, p. 244-292. Acc. to the Statute of the ICJ, Article 38, international customary law pre-supposes an established practice and *opinio juris*. Practice, however, is not unambigious. See Chapter 6, sections 3.1.2 and 5.4.

irrespective of a situation of war? Another question is whether the return obligation is of a general nature, or only addresses the perpetrator of the norm, such as the individual looter or the occupying state in the event of an armed conflict?[70] This matter is of importance since cultural objects are no longer looted as trophies by the conqueror to be exhibited in public places – as in Roman, Napoleonic, colonial or Nazi times – but as commodities and irrespective of a situation of (official) war. 'Since financial value has been added to the historical, cultural and scientifc aura of cultural objects, creating unlimited monetary value for limited resources, the illicit trade has become their major threat', as observed in a study by the International Council of Museums (ICOM).[71] Objects often surface years after the looting and may do so in any given (public or private) collection. An obligation resting only on the perpetrator of the norm that prohibits looting would therefore be ineffective to address injustices on the object.

The general nature of the duty to return looted cultural objects is certainly strengthened by the UN Security Council resolutions that provide for a full ban on the trade and possession of looted antiquities.[72] In these resolutions, the duty to return looted cultural objects is also incumbent upon third parties. Whereas these measures are limited to objects from a specific place and lost in a specific (recent) time period, this development is supported by a range of other new instruments that criminalise the possession of looted art.

70 (ICRC) Rule 41, Export and Return of Cultural Property in Occupied Territory: *The occupying power must prevent the illicit export of cultural property from occupied territory and must return illicitly exported property to the competent authorities of the occupied territory.*

71 F. Demarais and M.A. Haldiman 'Bids on the Rise, Object on the Go: Are Cultural Objects Commodities Like Any Other? (2014) ICOM News 67, pp. 16. Recently, empirical studies are undertaken that aim at mapping routes and quantifying data regarding the illicit trade; e.g. N. Brodie, D. Yates e.a., *Illicit trade in cultural goods in Europe Characteristics, criminal justice responses and an analysis of the applicability of technologies in the combat against the trade: final report* (2019), European Commission; The German ILLICID Report analyses the trade in ancient cultural objects in Germany over a 24-month period and substantiates fears that the majority of such ojects are traded without documentation of a lawful provenance: B. Hemeier and M. Hilgert 'Transparency, Provenance and Consumer Protection. Facts and Policy Recommendations Concerning the Trade in Ancient Cultural Property in Germany. Findings of the Federal Ministry of Education and Research's Collaborative Project «Analysing the Dark Figure as a Basis for Countering and Preventing Crime Using the Example of Ancient Cultural Property» (ILLICID)' (2020).

72 UNSC Resolution 2199 of 12 February 2015 (n. 58): 'Reaffirms its decision in para 7 of Resolution 1483 (2003) and decides that all member states shall take appropriate steps to prevent the trade in Iraqi and Syrian cultural property […] illegally removed from Iraq', 'thereby allowing for their eventual safe return to the Iraqi and Syrian people […]'. These resolutions are limited in time in the case of Iraq to objects that left the country as of 6 August 1990 and in the case of Syria as of 15 March 2011. Of a more general nature, condemning the illicit trade, UNSC Resolution 2347 (n. 56).

2.3.3 *The issue of time*

In the context of this study, it is of crucial importance that a binding rule that prohibits looting and obliges the return today, does not have direct legal consequences for objects looted in the past. According to the principle of intertemporal law, a juridical fact must be appreciated in the light of the law contemporary with it.[73] For claims that are based on an unlawful loss in the past, the time dimension is important both in a private law approach, as well as in an international law approach.[74]

In accordance with the Articles on Responsibility of States for Internationally Wrongful Acts (ARSIWA) by the International Law Commission (ILC) of 2001,[75] two requirements are of importance in this regard: (1) Was the looting an internationally wrongful act at the time; or (2) Is the denial of the original owner's right a breach of an international obligation with a continuing character? If one of these requirements is fulfilled, reparations by the responsible states should follow.[76] For the fulfilment of the first requirement, it must be established that the specific taking was a breach of international law at the time, which will depend on the specific circumstances at the time. Was the loss, for example, the result of pillage by a foreign (occupying) army at a time when the obligations to return cultural objects attained customary status?[77] Then again, the unlawfulness of the loss at the time is not relevant if the need for reparation would follow from a more recent norm. In that case, it would be needed to establish a rule that entitles former owners to rights in the present. A denial of those rights may then add up to a violation of a norm with a continuing character.[78] If so, the responsibility of a state to repair the situation would extend over the entire period the situation is not in conformity with the obligation.

Given the focus in this study on the legal status of the objects in relation to the people to whom these are meaningful – not *per se* on the injustices of the past – this latter approach seems the better option. On the one hand,

---

73 *Island of Palmas Arbitration*, ICA (1928).

74 For a discussion on the relation between private law and historical claims see (in Dutch) see M.A. Loth 'Houdbaar recht; over de aansprakelijkheid voor historisch onrecht', in M.A. Loth and L.P.W. van Vliet, *Recht over tijd. Hoever reikt het privaatrecht in het verleden?* (2018) Preadviezen Nederlandse Vereniging voor Burgerlijk Recht, Zutphen 2018.

75 ILC, Articles on Responsibility of States for Internationally Wrongful Acts by the International Law Commission (2001) UN Doc A/56/10, 'commended to the attention of governments' by the UNGA: 13 and 14.

76 Under certain conditions, e.g. that there are no conditions precluding the wrongfulness such as consent (Art. 20 ARSIWA) and the right was not lost as a result of acquiescence (Art. 45 ARSIWA).

77 This question will be explored for cultural objects looted in a colonial setting in Chapter 5.

78 Article 14(2) ARSIWA reads: 'The breach of an international obligation by an act of a State having a continuing character extends over the entire period during which the act continues and remains not in conformity with the international obligation.'

because the exact circumstances of a loss in the past are often unknown: for obvious reasons, illicit practices by which cultural objects were removed are not always documented. In practice, therefore, it may be impossible to identify cultural objects as being unlawfully looted.[79] On the other hand, the assessment of historical wrongs such as colonial takings by contemporary standards of international law that for long was biased and unfavourable to non-Western stakeholders, is problematic. It would implicate a critical examination of the origins of international law that exceeds the limits of this study.[80] Apart from the analysis of the post-war legal framework for Nazi-looted art in Chapter 4, and the assessment of the legitimacy under contemporary international law of the looting of an ancestor statue at the close of the 19th century in Chapter 5, the following chapters will therefore focus on the possible existence and evolution of *new* norms in this field. Furthermore, this dissertation will focus on the legal status of cultural objects, not on reparations or compensation schemes for past injustices.

The question is thus: even though the unlawfulness of a specific loss at the time may not be established, and in spite of the fact that ownership title may have passed under domestic private law, might there be other norms that 'link' a cultural object to its former owner or creator?

2.3.4 Another perspective: A human rights approach

In international law, the obligation to return looted cultural objects developed through the laws of war: restitution as the preferred form of reparation after the removal of cultural objects during armed conflict or foreign occupation. Since the adoption of the 1970 UNESCO Convention, this obligation also extends to cultural objects looted in peacetime. The recipient of the rights to restitution in these 'traditional' international law approaches are national states. The question of which party is eventually entitled to (returned) cultural objects in that model is a matter of state sovereignty and domestic (private) law. Complications may arise in such a model when rights of others are at stake, for example an individual or community that no longer feels represented by the government of a state from where the object was removed. Such complications will be explored in Chapter 3 – on the position of communities after a (*de facto*) change of borders – and in Chapter 4 – on the rights of victims of the Nazi regime who mostly emigrated to other countries since the loss.

Increasingly, international law vests rights on cultural objects with individuals and groups such as minorities and indigenous peoples. This is part and parcel of the emergence and evolution of human rights law. Another

79 Provenance (the ownership history of cultural objects) has only recently become a requirement in the trade. See e.g. Chapter 6.

80 Similarly, expropriation by states of their own nationals (e.g. Nazi looting within Germany) traditionally is not covered by international law. See Chapter 4, sections 3.2.3 and 4.3.1.

model in international law is therefore return as a remedy for human rights violations. In such a model, the recipients of rights ('right holders') are not states, but individuals or communities.

For example, according to the UN Principles and Guidelines on the Right to a Remedy and Reparation for Victims of Gross Violations of International Human Rights Law and Serious Violations of International Humanitarian Law, victims of human rights violations are entitled to reparations for harm suffered. This can be effectuated by the restitution of lost possessions.[81] An early example of a human rights' approach to the issue of restitution – the Allied internal restitution programme after the Second World War that made national states (temporarily) adapt their private laws in favour of the persecuted dispossessed former owners – will be discussed in Chapter 4.[82]

Under contemporary international law, individuals and communities such as minorities also enjoy a direct right to culture. This follows from a number of human rights instruments, most notably Article 15(1)(a) of the 1966 International Covenant on Economic, Social and Cultural Rights (ICESCR).[83] According to the 2009 General Comment on the right to culture of the supervisory treaty body of this Covenant, this has come to include 'access to cultural goods'. This implicates that states have an obligation to adopt 'specific measures aimed at achieving respect for the right of everyone ... to have access to their own cultural ... heritage and to that of others'.[84] In other words, access to cultural objects may be seen as an essential dimension of human rights. In that sense, claims to lost cultural objects are not merely a matter of stolen property, but also a matter of lost heritage where it concerns identity values for specific people. Such different approaches activate different norms.

The interrelationship of cultural heritage law and human rights law is illustrated by the active involvement of the UN Human Rights Council in heritage protection and the illicit trade. This heightened involvement coincided with the conflicts in the Middle East, where the detrimental effects for source

81 Principles and Guidelines on the Right to a Remedy and Reparation for Victims of Gross Violations of International Human Rights Law and Serious Violations of International Humanitarian Law, adopted by the United Nations General Assembly Res. 60/147 of 16 December 2005. As remedies for victims are named: (a) access to justice, (b) reparation for harm suffered, and (c) access to information concerning violations and reparation mechanisms.

82 Chapter 4, section 2.1.

83 International Covenant on Economic, Social and Cultural Rights (adopted 16 December 1966, entered into force 3 January 1976) 993 UNTS 3 (ICESCR), Art. 15, para. 1(a): the right of everyone to take part in cultural life. See also Art. 27 of the Universal Declaration of Human Rights (adopted 10 December 1948) UNGA Res. 217 A (III) (UDHR). See also the UN Declaration on the Rights of Indigenous Peoples (UNDRIP), UNGA Res. 61/295 (13 September 2007) UN Doc A/RES/61/295.

84 Committee on Economic, Social and Cultural Rights, General Comment No. 21 (2009), UN Doc E/C.12/GC/21, para 49(d); see also paras 15(b) and 50.

communities[85] of destruction of heritage sites and wide-scale looting became vividly clear. In its 2007 Resolution dedicated to the protection of cultural heritage, the Human Rights Council confirms in this respect that 'cultural heritage is an important component of the cultural identity of communities, groups and individuals, and of social cohesion, so that its intentional destruction may have adverse consequences on human dignity and human rights'.[86] Apart from concerns about looting and destruction, the Council also addressed the illicit trade and the need for measures to ensure the return of looted cultural objects.[87] In other words, people who are left *without* their cultural objects after looting practices may well be affected in their human rights.

In the following chapters, I will evaluate whether a human rights law approach can help develop the field of contested cultural objects further, especially where it concerns older losses. The hypothesis is that it might solve several of the problems identified above. Most importantly, human rights law appears equipped to address the intangible (cultural or heritage) interests at stake, addresses the rights of sub-state actors such as private individuals and communities, and does so by universally accepted notions. The contours of this approach will surface in all chapters, most notably in Chapter 5 in the context of indigenous peoples rights to their cultural heritage, and will be further elaborated upon in Chapter 6.

2.4 Soft law: Evolving law?

Over the last decades, in addition to 'hard' law such as international treaties and other directly binding law, a vast body of informal 'soft' law has emerged on the topic of looted art. From a law-making perspective the term 'soft law' is simply a convenient description for a variety of non-legally binding yet authorative instruments used in contemporary international relations.[88] Its impact in terms of normative force varies and may even equal binding legal instruments. At times, soft law simply operates as a practical solution to a

85 The term 'source communities' in this study refers to communities of origin.

86 UNHRC, Res. 6/11 on Protection of Cultural Heritage as an Important Component of the Promotion and Protection of Cultural Rights (28 September 2007) UN Doc A/HRC/RES/6/11, Preamble.

87 UNHRC, Res. 33/20 on Cultural rights and the protection of cultural heritage (6 October 2016) UN Doc. A/HRC/RES/33/20 at p. 4; repeated in UNHRC Res. 37/17 on Cultural rights and the protection of cultural heritage (9 April 2018) UN Doc A/HRC/RES/37/17 at p. 4: '*Calls for* enhanced international cooperation in preventing and combating the organized looting, smuggling and theft of and illicit trafficking in cultural objects and in restoring stolen, looted or trafficked cultural property to its countries of origin, and invites states to take measures in this regard at the national level'.

88 A. Boyle, 'Soft Law in International Law-making' in M. Evans, *International Law* (4th, 2014) p. 118 et seq.

problem for which existing legal tools are insufficient.[89] Beyond this, soft law may be a forebode of evolving law, clarify vague conventional law, or be a source of law. Particularly in a situation where positive 'hard' law is unclear or in a situation where norms clash, soft law can have normative significance. As will surface in the subsequent chapters, in the present context the unclarity and clash of positive law norms indeed appears to be a reason why soft law has stepped in: to bridge the gaps.[90]

Soft law instruments in the field of looted art vary widely. Some merely condemn looting practices and the illicit trade, whilst others formulate specific rights of former owners with regard to their lost cultural objects and may even set out rules for procedures. In their form soft law instruments in this field also vary and include declarations by international organisations,[91] ad-hoc multilateral declarations (also with the participation of non-state actors),[92] and operational or explanatory guidelines.[93] Apart from such instruments adopted at the interstate level (soft law in the strict sense), ethical codes for professional conduct in the art and museum world also contain international standards. Not seldom, such instruments of transnational private regulation are developed under the auspices of intergovernmental organisations such as UNESCO.[94] For the purpose of this study, therefore, such hybrid instruments are at times also discussed under the sections on soft law.[95] Often, instruments in this field operate in mixed settings of states and non-state actors – not only on the interstate level – and address states, but also institutions (e.g. museums), individuals (e.g. dispossessed private owners or collectors) and communities (e.g. indigenous peoples or other source communities).

89 'Soft law as tools to make the behaviour of those involved predictable for the joint benefit, even without enforceable rules' in H. Hillgenberg, 'A Fresh Look at Soft Law' (1999) 10 EJIL 499.

90 Esp. Chapters 2, 4, and 6.

91 E.g. a multitude of UNESCO, UNGA Declarations, and those by the Human Rights Council, discussed above.

92 E.g., the 1998 Washington Principles undersigned by states but also by non-state actors (n. 6). See Chapters 2 and 4.

93 E.g. Operational Guidelines for the Implementation of the Convention on the Means of Prohibiting and Preventing the Illicit Import, Export and Transfer of Ownership of Cultural Property (adopted at the UNESCO Meeting of States Parties, 18-20 May 2015) C70/15/ 3.MSP/11; Resolution of the Institute de droit international on the International Sale of Works of Art from the Angle of the Protection of the Cultural Heritage (1991), in *Institut of International Law Yearbook* 64 II (1991 IDI Basel Resolution).

94 E.g. the 'ICOM Code of Ethics for Museums', adopted by the 15th General Assembly of the International Council of Museums (4 November 1986, renamed and revised in 2001 and 2004). ICOM is an affiliate of UNESCO. Another example is the UNESCO International Code of Ethics for Dealers in Cultural Property, UNESCO Doc. CLT/CH/INS-06/ 25 REV.

95 Another term could be 'informal international lawmaking'. See J. Pauwelyn 'Informal International Lawmaking: Framing the concept and research questions' in J. Pauwelyn, R.A. Wessel and J. Wouters (eds.) *Informal International Lawmaking* (2012) OUP, p. 13 et seq.

The content of the various soft law instruments varies widely. On the one hand, they take the form of non-specific declarations that looting is 'wrong' – detrimental to peace and security and the sustainable development of societies – and therefore states are urged to cooperate to prevent the trade in looted cultural objects. These are recurring phrases in declarations of international organisations. In fact, the United Nations General Assembly adopted a whole series of resolutions, beginning in 1973, on the subject of restitution and return.[96] Although these resolutions differ in wording, they all encourage international cooperation in the return of cultural objects, urging states to adopt adequate measures to prevent illicit trafficking, raise awareness amongst the public and to strengthen museum due diligence standards.

Others entail specific standards for claims. The UN Declaration on the Rights of Indigenous Peoples (UNDRIP), for example, provides very specific rules for the return of indigenous peoples' lost cultural objects.[97] National or international policy guidelines for museums for claims to Nazi-looted art or colonial takings, increasingly, also set specific substantive and procedural standards for claims.[98] These may be merely aspirational, such as the standard that (since 1986) features in the International Council of Museums (ICOM) ethical code that museums should neither display nor acquire unprovenanced material or material that may have been looted in the past – a standard that is hardly attainable and is certainly not met today.[99] On the other hand, some of these informal regulations set standards that in terms of adherence – and *opinio juris* – sort more effect than binding international conventions.[100]

Nazi-looted art is an example of a category for which the norm is embodied in a non-binding declaration that gained status as *the* prevailing international rule. The 1998 Washington Principles on Nazi-confiscated art, a declaration in which 44 states and 13 non-governmental organisations essentially voiced their intention to promote the identification and return of looted artefacts, form

96 More than twenty, starting with UNGA A/Res/3187 (XXVIII) of 18 December 1973, biannually repeated in similar or (slightly) different wording until recently. For an overview, see the list of General Assembly instruments at the end of this dissertation.

97 See above, n. 83. Discussion in Chapter 5, section 4.3 and Chapter 6, section 5.2.4.

98 See e.g. Dutch National Museum of World Cultures, Principles and Process for addressing claims for the Return of Cultural Objects (2019), see <https://www.volkenkunde.nl/en/about-volkenkunde/press/dutch-national-museum-world-cultures-nmvw-announces-principles-claims>; the UK 'Procedures for claims for the Return of Cultural Objects from Oxford University Museums and Libraries' (2020), see <https://www.glam.ox.ac.uk/procedures-for-return-of-cultural-objects-claims>.

99 The ICOM Ethical Code (n. 71) prescribes that museums should acquire objects only after establishing 'the full history of the item since discovery or production' (in 2.3) and should 'avoid displaying or otherwise using material that has a questionable origin or lacking provenance' (in 4.5).

100 E.g. often provenance research is primarily focused on the identification of Nazi-looted art - not addressed by any formal treaty-, whereas the identification of illegally excavated antiquities – addressed in the 1970 UNESCO Convention - lags behind.

the basis of widespread international practice.[101] The Principles highlight the need for 'just and fair' solutions for heirs of the victims of Nazi looting with regard to confiscated artefacts 'depending on the facts and circumstances surrounding a specific case', and, besides, urge states to 'develop national processes to implement these principles'.[102] Often, the extraordinary circumstances of Nazi looting, as part of genocide, are cited as a reason for the need for a 'moral' approach to such claims. These would justify an extra-legal treatment, i.e. not according to regular private law under which, often, such claims are stale. Through an in-depth analysis of this model in Chapter 4 and a comparison with other looted art cases such as colonial takings – the topic of Chapter 5 – this proposition and the pitfalls of such an 'ethical model' will be further explored.

Also for the category of colonial takings, soft law instruments urge Western states to return cultural objects that were taken from former colonies, amongst which the 2007 UNDRIP on indigenous peoples' cultural rights. As mentioned above, since the era of decolonisation, a series of over twenty UN General Assembly Declarations have been passed on the issue of return.[103] In fact, already in 1979, at the request of UNESCO, ICOM presented a study stating that

> '[t]he reassembly of dispersed heritage through restitution or return of objects which are of major importance for the cultural identity and history of countries having been deprived thereof, is now considered to be an ethical principle recognised and affirmed by the major international organizations.'[104]

It even predicted that this principle would 'soon become an element of *jus cogens* of international relations'.[105] Nevertheless, the political will to follow up on such calls has generally been lacking.

The by now famous 2017 speech of French President Emanuel Macron in which he addressed the rights of Africans to their own cultural heritage, appears to have changed this status quo.[106] It signalled a departure from

101 1998 Washington Principles. See Chapter 4.

102 Ibid. Principle 9: 'If the pre-War owners of art that is found to have been confiscated by the Nazis and not subsequently restituted, or their heirs, can be identified, steps should be taken expeditiously to achieve a just and fair solution, recognizing this may vary according to the facts and circumstances surrounding a specific case.'; Principle 11: 'Nations are encouraged to develop national processes to implement these principles, particularly as they relate to alternative dispute resolution mechanisms for resolving ownership issues.'

103 See above, n. 96.

104 Ad hoc Committee appt. by the Executive Council of ICOM (H. Ganslmayr, H. Landais, G. Lewis, P. Makambila, P. Perrot, J. Pré and J. Vistel), 'Study on the principles, conditions and means for the restitution or return of cultural property in view of reconstituting dispersed heritages' (1979) 31 *Museum International* 62.

105 Ibid. p. 66.

106 E. Macron, President of the French Republic, Speech at the University of Ouagadougou, Burkina Faso (28 November 2017), see: <https://www.youtube.com/watch?v=8I3exI4f9BY&feature=youtu.be>.

'cultural internationalism', the long prevailing school of thought developed and named by John Henry Merryman, and the line taken in the 'Declaration on the Value and Importance of Universal Museums'.[107] In this 2002 Declaration, the main Western encyclopaedic museums argued that cultural treasures from around the world – no matter their provenance and how they were taken – are shown to their best advantage and can be best kept under the care of the big 'universal' museums, and should remain in these institutions. Recent developments in the field of colonial takings are reminiscent of earlier developments in the field of Nazi-looted art since 1998.[108]

That parallel underscores that not the form of an instrument but the willingness of stakeholders, and public awareness that creates the need to act, shape the norms in this field. At the same time, it also underscores the last essential problem in this field: which institution and by which procedure can non-binding soft law standards be implemented, monitored and amended, if necessary? What are the pitfalls of an ethical model where alternative dispute resolution is the sole way to resolve disputes, and what does this mean in terms of access to justice for parties in a dispute?[109] These pitfalls were an incentive to search for solutions *within* the existing legal framework. The human rights model that will surface throughout the following chapters and mostly in Chapter 6, is the result of that search. An advantage is that such a model may overcome the problem of access to justice for non-state 'right holders', which is important in an understanding that culture is not *per se* defined by nationality.

2.5 Concluding remark: Different models

Different models exist for claims to lost cultural objects. Apart from possibilities for former owners to claim lost possessions in a private law setting, public international law caters for the interstate model where restitution is seen as an obligation, or right, of states. Claims may also be seen as a matter of international human rights law. Furthermore, in the 'ethical model' claims by individuals or communities are based on soft law instruments. These models and their interrelation, as well as the question whether such non-binding instruments reflect evolving law in this field, will be explored in this study.

107 J.H. Merryman, 'Cultural Property Internationalism' (2005) 12 *International Journal of Cultural Property* 11. See Chapter 6.2.
108 See Chapters 2, 5, and 6 (section 2.2).
109 To be addressed mainly in Chapters 2 and 4.

3 Central research question

Cultural objects are under special protection in international law and looting and destruction are prohibited. Today, a number of international conventions codify the norm that looted cultural objects should be returned. Nevertheless, they generally do not regard cultural objects that were lost longer ago and already circulate on the market or form part of museum collections. Furthermore, these conventions primarily operate on the interstate level. In contrast, soft law instruments increasingly support the rights of (non-state) former owners to their lost cultural objects, also if these were lost before the adoption of international conventions, and even if ownership title passed to a new possessor under domestic private law. As a consequence, 'grey' categories of tainted cultural objects have emerged that presently can only be 'cleared' through extra-legal (alternative) procedures: the ethical model for title disputes. In such a situation, abidance by the rules depends on the willingness of parties and political pressure, while norms often remain vague. This can give rise to legal insecurity and, at times, injustice.

The central research question in this dissertation is: How could the interests of former owners who involuntarily lost their cultural objects be addressed more effectively? This central question is divided into the following sub-questions per chapter.

Chapter 2 addresses claims to cultural objects in a private law setting by their former owners who lost them in another country. Sub-questions addressed in this chapter are: What are the main difficulties that obstruct restitution claims by former owners, both in civil law and common law jurisdictions? Given the increasing reliance on soft law and alternative dispute resolution (ADR) as the preferred way to solve disputes: how does access to justice work in such an 'ethical' model?

Chapter 3 addresses claims to cultural objects after a loss in another country under the interstate system of the 1954 Hague Convention and the 1970 UNESCO Convention. The following sub-questions are addressed: How does the 'nationality' prong for entitlement to cultural objects in the 1970 UNESCO Convention relate to territoriality and cultural-historical considerations? What is the position in this system of non-state right holders who lost their cultural objects, such as communities or private owners?

Chapter 4 addresses claims to cultural objects that were lost as a result of Nazi looting. In this chapter, the following sub-questions are addressed: How was restitution of Nazi-looted art arranged in the post-War period, and how is it arranged in today's system of the Washington Principles? In addition, what are the consequences of the differences between the 'legal' model in the US and the 'ethical' model in Western Europe?

Next, Chapter 5 addresses claims to cultural objects that were lost as a result of colonial actions at the close of the 19th century. Sub-questions addressed are: How did international law with respect to looting and restitution of cultural objects develop? How were claims to colonial booty in the post-colonial era generally perceived? Can recent soft law and national policy guidelines in this field be seen as a reflection of evolving human rights law, and what is the status of the UNDRIP in this regard?

Chapter 6 elaborates on the insights of Chapters 2, 3, 4, and 5, and develops a model in answer to the main research question of how the interests of former owners with regard to their lost cultural objects could be addressed more effectively. It analyses the international framework for the art trade and how that arranges for the issue of contested cultural objects – including the category of more recently looted artefacts. Sub-questions addressed in this last chapter are: What interests are at stake in cultural heritage protection, on the one hand, and in the art trade, on the other hand? What are the blind spots in this system? It furthermore addresses the question whether international human rights law is equipped to clarify standards in this regard and how such standards can be transposed to a private law setting of title claims.

4 Issues of terminology

4.1 International cultural heritage law

International cultural heritage law is that branch of international law that has as its centre the protection of cultural heritage by an international regime. This regime extends to tangible cultural heritage – artefacts, antiquities, ethnographic objects, and monuments – above[110] and under water,[111] as well as intangible heritage such as traditions and specific ways of life.[112] The present study is limited to tangible, movable cultural heritage for which the neutral term 'cultural object' is used. Obviously, fragments of monuments – parts of immovable cultural heritage – may turn into movable objects after the removal from their original sites. More specifically, this dissertation concerns cultural objects that have been transferred to another country and are contested on account of their specific ownership history.

A useful perspective of this field of law is given by Chechi who introduces the term '*lex culturalis*' for the growing body of rules that aim at the protection of cultural heritage, underlining their status as *lex specialis*.[113] This implicates that cultural objects are subject to special rules and should not be automatically treated as ordinary goods.

110 Most notably: the 1954 Hague Convention; the 1970 UNESCO Convention; and the 1995 UNIDROIT Convention.

111 UNESCO Convention on the Protection of the Underwater Cultural Heritage (adopted 2 November 2001, entered into force on 2 January 2009) 2562 UNTS 3.

112 UNESCO Convention for the Safeguarding of the Intangible Cultural Heritage (adopted 17 October 2003, entered into force 20 April 2006) 2368 UNTS 3.

113 Chechi (2014), p. 246.

4.2 Cultural objects, cultural heritage or cultural property?

The central assumption in this study is that cultural objects are distinct from other goods because they represent intangible values that people identify with.[114] Cultural objects may be of specific interest to an individual, a community or national state, or even to mankind as a whole.[115] From that perspective, and because the intangible value is not a static given, no definition of cultural objects can be strictly limited.

The term 'cultural property' is also often used and features in both the 1954 Hague Convention and the 1970 UNESCO Convention. As a protected category in international law 'cultural property' first appeared in the 1954 Hague Convention. This new concept was supposed to serve as a wide-ranging and synthetic category of objects worth protecting because of their inherent values.[116] It defines cultural property as movable as well as immovable property 'of great importance to the cultural heritage of every people', such as religious and secular monuments, archaeological sites, works of art, manuscripts, books and other objects of artistic, historical, or archaeological interest.[117]

In the 1970 UNESCO Convention, the definition shifts to emphasise not the universal heritage interest of cultural objects to all people, as the 1954 Hague Convention appears to do, but the national interest in preserving its cultural heritage. It defines 'cultural property' as 'property, which, on religious or secular grounds, is specifically designated by each state as being of importance for archaeology, prehistory, history, literature, art or science' and which belongs to one of the eleven categories listed in Article 1.[118] Moreover, Article 4

---

114 That cultural goods cannot be treated as ordinary consumer goods because they are 'vehicles of identity, values and meaning' is, for example, recognized in Art 1 (g) of the UNESCO Convention on the Protection and Promotion of the Diversity of Cultural Expressions (adopted 20 October 2005, entered into force 18 March 2007) 2440 UNTS 311.

115 The preambles of various UNESCO Conventions, such as the 1954 Hague Convention and the 1972 World Heritage Convention, refer to the importance of cultural heritage for all mankind. For a discussion of the notion of 'universal heritage', see Chapter 6.

116 F. Francioni, 'A dynamic Evolution of Concept and Scope: From Cultural Property to Cultural Heritage', in A.A. Yusuf (ed.), *Standard Setting in UNESCO, Vol I: Normative Action in Education, Science and Culture* (2007) Leiden, Martinus Nijhoff, pp. 221-236, 225.

117 1954 Hague Convention, Art. 2. The list is non-exhaustive.

118 These are: Rare collections and specimens of fauna, flora, minerals and anatomy, and objects of paleontological interest; property relating to history, including the history of science and technology and military and social history, to the life of national leaders, thinkers, scientists and artists and to events of national importance; products of archaeological excavations (including regular and clandestine) or of archaeological discoveries; elements of artistic or historical monuments or archaeological sites which have been dismembered; antiquities more than one hundred years old, such as inscriptions, coins and engraved seals; objects of ethnological interest; property of artistic interest, such as pictures, paintings and drawings produced entirely by hand on any support and in any material (excluding industrial designs and manufactured articles decorated by hand); original works of statuary

sets standards for the possible inalienability of cultural objects ('the cultural heritage of each State'), by introducing nationality, in terms of creation and territorial provenance, as a criterion. This aspect – the 'nationality' of objects and the perception of cultural objects as exclusive property of states – will be topic of analysis in the Chapters 3 and 6. The 1995 UNIDROIT Convention, the third important treaty in this field, let go of the nationality prong and deploys the more neutral term 'cultural object' throughout.[119] In a more nuanced way, the UNIDROIT Convention provides a basis for states to reclaim their national patrimony if that is of 'significant cultural importance' to that state.[120]

As this short survey may illustrate, definitions usually take on the prevalent view in a specific time and no term is completely value free. Where in the 1950s the recognition of cultural heritage as a matter of international public policy (for all mankind) was in focus, at the time of the 1970 UNESCO Convention the organisation of a protection scheme to counter the illicit trade (by appointing states as 'proprietors' of that heritage) was in the minds of the drafters. In that respect, today the broader term 'cultural heritage' is preferred over 'cultural property', to express a more holistic view of cultural objects. Indigenous peoples, for example, generally also do not perceive cultural objects in terms of 'property' or individual rights, but in terms of community values and responsibilities.[121]

As the term 'cultural property' suggests exclusive entitlement which touches upon the research question in this study, that term is considered less suitable. In line with the 1995 UNIDROIT Convention (and authors such as Vrdoljak), in this dissertation the more neutral term 'cultural object' will therefore be used for tangible, movable cultural items that are valued for their intangible, symbolic, meaning. The term 'artefact', within the context of this dissertation, is seen as a subcategory of cultural objects, and 'cultural heritage' as the wider category.[122]

---

art and sculpture in any material; original engravings, prints and lithographs; original artistic assemblages and montages in any material;- rare manuscripts and incunabula, old books, documents and publications of special interest (historical, artistic, scientific, literary, etc.) singly or in collections; postage, revenue and similar stamps, singly or in collections; archives, including sound, photographic and cinematographic archives; articles of furniture more than one hundred years old and old musical instruments. NB these categories are mostly used (also in the 1995 UNIDROIT Convention), although the age threshold varies.

119 1995 UNIDROIT Convention, Art. 2: 'Cultural objects are those which, on religious or secular grounds, are of importance for archaeology, prehistory, history, literature, art or science' and which belongs to one of the eleven categories listed in the Annex. This corresponds to the 1970 UNESCO Convention list.

120 1995 UNIDROIT Convention, Art. 5. For a discussion, see Chapter 3, section 4.2, and Chapter 6, sections 3 and 4.

121 K. Kuprecht, *Indigenous Peoples' Cultural Property Claims* (2014) Springer International Publishing, p. 40.

122 I consider the term 'cultural good', used in the 2019 EU Import Regulation, as equivalent to 'cultural object'. For the EU Regulation, supra, n. 60.

4.3 Return and restitution

'Return' is also referred to as 'restitution', if a legal obligation is implied, or as 'repatriation', which implies the physical return home ('patris' being Greek for native community). Much can be said on the difference between the terms 'restitution' and 'return'; in the end, the use of either of the two terms tends to reflect the particular view on whether there is a legal obligation.[123]

The term 'return' in legal instruments was introduced in the 1970s to address colonial takings in museum collections of former colonial powers. With regard to that category, Western-European countries did not want to acknowledge any legal obligation. Hence, claims with regard to pre-1970 losses were to be referred to as 'return' claims, whereas 'restitution' was reserved for post-1970 claims in as far as countries adopted and implemented the Convention. This argumentation lies behind the name of the 'Intergovernmental Committee for Promoting the *Return* of Cultural Property to its Countries of Origin or its *Restitution* in Cases of Illicit Appropriation'. Obviously, differences of opinion on the legitimacy of the continued possession of cultural objects from colonised people existed at the time, however only very recently this outlook is gaining ground in Western holding countries.[124] The development of international law and the double standards in this regard will be addressed in Chapter 5.[125]

Nevertheless, over the last decades the term 'restitution' has become commonly used also for older losses, most notably in the field of Nazi-looted art. Within the context of this study 'return' and 'restitution' are both used: 'return' as a neutral term for the physical return of an object in an original setting, and 'restitution' mostly if transfer of ownership is implied.

4.4 Former owners, (mis)appropiation and looting

Former owners can be individuals, communities or national states. The original title may indeed be based on ownership title under private law, but an original title may also be based on norms (laws or custom) that exempt certain cultural objects from private ownership. In many cultures throughout history that is

---

123 For an overview, see R. Peters, 'Complementary and Alternative Mechanisms beyond Restitution: An Interest-oriented Approach to Resolving International Cultural Heritage Disputes' (Doctoral thesis, European University Institute, Florence, 2011), pp. 40-50.

124 Not in the last place as under influence of claims by countries that had suffered cultural losses and, today, have gained political strength, such as China or Turkey.

125 A legal obligation *was* recognised for objects looted during European wars, e.g. after the Second World War such obligations were based on the 1907 Hague Convention.

the case for objects of religious importance, archaeological finds, or even for family heirlooms.[126]

The involuntary loss in the cases under consideration may have been in the distant or more recent past. As the counterpart of such losses, at times the neutral term 'taking' will be used as well as the term (mis)appropriation. The term 'looting' is commonly used to describe the misappropriation of a cultural object without consent of the owner or local authorities, originally in a setting of armed conflict or foreign occupation.[127] The term is also widely used for the illicit excavation of antiquities irrespective of a situation of war. What exactly, according to present-day standards, constitutes an unlawful taking or looting will be touched upon in the next chapters.

Today, however, the term 'looting' is also widely used to indicate a taking that is seen as unjust, not *per se* a taking that was unlawful at the time. For example, the term 'Nazi looting' is used today for sales that are viewed as the result of general circumstances of persecution – sales that were not unlawful at the time.[128] Such developments may well be an indication of evolving law. Whilst international law first regulated restitution after looting in the specific situation of a formal war under the laws of warfare, with the adoption of the 1970 UNESCO Convention the term 'looting' became mainstream for the unauthorised export of cultural objects and, today, has come to include losses that were the consequence of persecution. In a similar vein, the term 'restitution claim' – traditionally used for a claim for the return of full ownership – at times is also used as a generic term for claims that fall short of a claim for full ownership (e.g. claims to Nazi-looted art for example often take the form of a sharing in the sales proceeds between the present owner and the heirs of the former owner). This may indicate that norms are changing. These thoughts will be recurring in Chapters 2, 4, and 6.

5 Methodology

Fragmentation was identified above as one of the main problems of the normative framework for cross-border disputes over cultural objects: inter-

126 E.g., the concept of 'fidei commissum' e.g. in old German law, where property should be kept to pass on to the next generation.

127 M. Cornu, J. Fromageau, C. Wallaert, (eds.) *Dictionnaire comparé du droit du patrimoine culturel* (2012) CNRS Editions, defines 'looting' as the appropriation of goods by force or by constraint in the event of a national or international armed conflict. However, 'looting' today is also a common word for the illicit excavation of antiquities beyond situations of war.

128 The definition of looting as takings 'offensive to the principles of humanity and dictates of public conscience' is useful here. See UNESCO Draft of the Declaration of Principles Relating to Cultural Objects Displaced in Connection with the Second World War (5 October 2009), principle II. Hereafter, Chapter 4.

national and national, private and public law of different places and times, hard law as well as soft law, may all influence the legal status of cultural objects. Fragmentation obviously is a more general problem of international law,[129] but especially true for cultural heritage law and particularly for the topic of this study. The most obvious reasons for this are that cross-border disputes involve multiple jurisdictions and cultural objects are valued in many different ways. Not only as a commodity or possession, but also for their (art) historical or scientific value, that may be of universal importance, and for their intangible heritage value as symbols of an identity of specific communities, nations or individuals.

This last element underscores that an approach of the issue solely from the perspective of national private law – as title issues over stolen property – would be insufficient. Conversely, to approach the topic of contested cultural objects solely from a public international law perspective would also not do justice to the issue, as private interests – for example those of innocent new possessors – need to be taken into account as well. Moreover, due to the absence on the international level of a specialised court or compliance mechanism in the field of contested cultural objects, adjudication in this field is mainly a matter of national courts and mechanisms for ADR, at some distance from international law.[130] This means that domestic legal doctrines define the contours for dispute resolution in this field, whilst the relevant international norms may not be directly applicable, depending on the domestic legal system, or may simply be unknown.

5.1 Legal pluralism

The methodological problems caused by this fragmentation where rules apply that may be binding, but also non-binding, in a setting where multiple stakeholders operate, was the reason to follow others in cultural heritage studies and to adopt a legal pluralist outlook.[131] Whereas a legal positivist stance would implicate a focus on binding instruments, a legal pluralist approach opens the door to the perception of law as a 'legal order', not as the sum total

---

129 See 'Fragmentation of International Law: Difficulties arising from the diversification and expansion of international law' (2006) Report of the Study Group of the International Law Commission, finalised by M. Koskenniemi (A/CN.4/L.682); D. Shelton, 'International Law and Relative Normativity', in M.D. Evans *International Law* (4th ed., 2014) OUP.

130 See also A. Chechi, 'Some reflections on International Adjudication of Cultural Heritage-related Cases' (2013) 10(5) Transnational Dispute Management.

131 E.g., F. Fiorentini 'A legal pluralist approach to international trade in cultural objects' in JAR Nafziger, RK Paterson (eds) *Handbook on the law of cultural heritage and international trade* (2014), 589-621; K. Kuprecht, *Indigenous Peoples' Cultural Property Claims* (2014) Springer, p. 20 et seq.; F. Francioni, 'Public and Private in the International Protection of Global Cultural Goods' (2012) 23 EJIL 719.

of binding norms that states enact, but as a social structure that is made up of much more than that. As Francioni puts it, law from that perspective consists of a plurality of legal orders that are made 'within, outside and above the state'.[132]

That concept suits the topic. In fact, disputes are often *not* solved by referral to binding legal instruments but to soft law instruments. Moreover, extra-legal methods such as negotiated settlements or cultural diplomacy, not litigation, are the preferred way to solve disputes. As such, the normative framework in this field can be perceived as a 'transnational legal order' where the conduct of a varied set of actors – e.g. states, individuals, communities, museums, and corporations – is informed by a multi-levelled set of norms.[133] These norms are to be found in binding national law (national private law, heritage laws, and import and export regulations); binding international law (such as UN Security Council resolutions, treaties in as far as applicable, and EU Regulations); in non-binding law and declarations (e.g. certain treaty standards that are not directly applicable, UN resolutions, the 1998 Washington Principles on Nazi-Confiscated Art, and the like); and in ethical codes for professional conduct (e.g. the ICOM Code of Ethics and art dealers guidelines).

In terms of methods, this means that whilst this study is a search for international (or transnational) standards, it will not focus on the identification of the traditional sources of international law as provided for in Article 38 of the Statute of the ICJ. These sources are: treaties and conventions; international custom; general principles of law; and as subsidiary sources judicial decisions and legal teachings.[134] Instead, this study has a broader perspective and also takes account of soft law instruments, transnational private regulation, national policies, and other documents in as far as these are perceived as standard-setting in the field. An extra reason for more flexibility in this regard is that norms on the issue of contested heritage are rapidly changing. Where at first, significant alterations of the legal approach occurred in the field of Nazi-looted art – moving away from a strict private law approach – this is presently happening in the field of colonial takings, and also in the wider field of looted antiquities. Depending on one's perspective, this is more or less visible.

132 Referring to Santi Romani's ideas of law as a 'plurality of legal orders'. Francioni (2012), p. 720.
133 See also T.C. Halliday and G. Shaffer, *Transnational Legal Orders* (2015) Cambridge University Press, New York.
134 Cf. the Statute of the ICJ, Article 38. Treaties are only binding on the parties to them, and customary international law pre-supposes an established practice and *opinio juris*.

5.2 A case-based approach

These dynamics and similarities were the reason to not focus solely on one specific category, even though these are often perceived as self-contained areas with specific rules, but instead to compare different categories. The question is, how to limit the scope of this study? In that regard, a case-based approach is chosen for this dissertation: in five separate publications, different types of claims are addressed through the spectrum of case studies. In this way, the research remains focussed on the peculiarities of the legal framework and practices in those specific types of claims, while at the same time insights are gained on similarities, differences, and the effectiveness of the law. Besides, by using case examples, it can be established whether a certain level of consistency of theory and practice exists in the particular category.

That choice, and the decision to write the dissertation in separate publications that stand on their own – instead of writing a monograph – has meant that a certain overlap is unavoidable. Several instruments are relevant to all categories in one way or another and since the aim of this study is to discover common principles, a comparison of categories from the perspective of the given case study is also a recurring theme. Some conclusions turned out similar for different categories, which is fortunate from the perspective of the aim of this study. For the reader of this dissertation as a whole, however, it results in some repetition.

5.3 Sources and research methods

As discussed above (section 2.3), soft law instruments and transnational private regulations in this field are numerous and have considerable normative significance. Whether a normative consistency can be established amongst such instruments and in comparison with hard law rules such as treaties or other binding law, will be explored in the following chapters. Apart from soft law and transnational private regulation, to that end domestic case law and outcomes of ADR procedures or diplomatic negotiations – in as far as possible since such procedures are often confidential – are also taken into account.[135]

Domestic case law from a wide number of jurisdictions is included in this study. An extensive comparative analysis would, however, exceed its scope. Differences between jurisdictions will be addressed by a comparison of jurisprudence in common law countries (such as the US and the UK), and civil law countries (most European countries).[136] But this study will not be limited to those jurisdictions, as this would give a misplaced outlook on the field of colonial takings. Available case law from other regions will therefore be

135 See Chapter 4.
136 See Chapters 2, 3, and 5.

included, though Western-European (mostly Dutch) and US case law will, overall, be the primary focus. The reason for this is pragmatic: familiarity with the Dutch and Western-European situation, and the availability of US case law due to the prominent US position in the international art trade.

The findings in this dissertation are primarily rooted in classical legal research: the study of legal documents, jurisprudence, literature, and other sources such as archives, databases, and policy and news reports. Over the last two decades, an impressive number of monographs, publications and dissertations[137] on the legal framework for (contested) cultural objects saw the light, signalling the proliferation of international cultural heritage law as a distinct branche of international law.[138] The present dissertation builds further on these studies and owes much to their insights.

In conclusion, although this study is ultimately a search for new rules, the main challenge is to identify the rules that already operate on the various levels, and to examine how these are followed up. That search is undertaken for each category in the subsequent chapters. Ideally, this would all add up to an organised 'transnational legal order'. However, due to rapid changes which are not synchronously per country or region, it seems that this ideal is not yet possible.

137 Amongst which the following dissertations: P.S. Sjouke, *Het behoud van cultuurgoederen, twee werelden, twee visies* (1999) Ars Aequi Libri [in Dutch]; A.F. Vrdoljak, *International law, museums and the return of cultural objects* (2006) CUP; K.R.M. Lubina, *Contested Cultural Property. The Return of Nazi Spoliated Art and Human Remains from Public Collections* (2009), Maastricht University; B. Schönenberger, *The Restitution of Cultural Assets* (2009) Eleven; I.A. Stamatoudi, *Cultural Property Law and Restitution. A Commentary to International Conventions and European Union Law* (2011) Elgar; R. Peters, *Complementary and Alternative Mechanisms beyond Restitution: An Interest-oriented Approach to Resolving International Cultural Heritage Disputes* (2011), European University Institute; A. Chechi, *The Settlement of International Cultural Heritage Disputes* (2014) OUP; K. Kuprecht, *Indigenous Peoples' Cultural Property Claims* (2014) Springer; Z. Liu, *Repatriation of cultural objects: The case of China* (2015), UVA-Dare; A. Jakubowski, *State Succession in Cultural Property* (2015) OUP; J.M. Van Beurden, *Treasures in Trusted Hands: Negotiating the Future of Colonial Cultural Objects* (2017) Sidestone Press; V.M. Tünsmeyer, *Repatriation of sacred indigenous cultural heritage and the law: Lessons from the United States and Canada* (2020) Maastricht University. Related Dutch disssertations, e.g.: W.J. Veraart, *Ontrechting en rechtsherstel in Nederland en Frankrijk in de jaren van bezetting en wederopbouw* (2005) Kluwer [in Dutch]; N.A.F. Van Woudenberg, *State immunity and cultural objects on loan* (2012) Martinus Nijhoff; L.P.C. Belder, *The Legal Protection of Cultural Heritage in International Law and Its Implementation in Dutch Law* (2014), Universiteit Utrecht.

138 See, e.g., the OUP series on Cultural Heritage Law and Policy; handbooks such as the 2014 *Handbook on the law of cultural heritage and international trade*, edited by J.A.R. Nafziger and R.K. Paterson (2014, Elgar); the *Oxford Handbook of international cultural heritage law*, edited by F. Francioni and A.F. Vrdoljak (OUP, 2020); commentaries on the various conventions; and edited volumes on the topic of restitution, amongst which, e.g., V. Vadi and H.E.G.S. Schneider (eds), *Art, Cultural Heritage and the Market. Ethical and Legal Issues* (2014) Springer.

6 Structure

The series of five chapters that make up the body of this dissertation address different categories of claims, each from different legal perspectives. These chapters (the publications) can be considered separately – and were all published as such – but they also form a whole as they all add insights to the analysis. The types of disputes that are subsequently addressed are: private title claims (Chapter 2); interstate return claims (Chapter 3), Nazi-looted art (Chapter 4); colonial takings from indigenous peoples (Chapter 5); and more recently looted antiquities (Chapter 6).

The structure is as follows. Chapters 2 and 3 address the legal framework for the two models that currently exist for cross-border claims to cultural objects: as private claims and as interstate claims. Chapter 2 deals with claims by non-state actors to their lost cultural objects – as stolen possessions – for which (international) private law and soft law instruments are key, and specific problems that occur on that level. Chapter 3 addresses the interstate model of the 1954 and 1970 UNESCO Conventions for claims to cultural objects that were removed from the territory of a state – claims to lost national heritage – and specific problems related to that model. Chapters 4 and 5 are in-depth case studies of two types of 'historical' claims, i.e. claims based on a loss that occurred before the adoption of international treaties in this field. Chapter 4 analyses the field of Nazi-looted art, with a focus on private claims by heirs of owners who lost their artefacts as a result of Nazi persecution. Chapter 5 explores the category of 'colonial looting', i.e. title disputes over cultural objects that were taken by Western powers in a colonial setting, with a focus on losses at the close of the 19th century by indigenous peoples. Chapter 6, finally, approaches the topic of contested cultural objects from the wider perspective of heritage protection, the international art trade and the system of the 1970 UNESCO Convention. It analyses the interrelation (and disconnect) between private and public law in this field and puts forward proposals for the notion of 'heritage title' and a human rights law approach as legal tools to bridge gaps. This chapter can be seen as the substantive concluding chapter of the dissertation.

Each chapter aims to add a layer of insight and a different perspective to the questions how cross-border claims to cultural objects fit in the wider legal framework, and how the interests of former owners can be addressed more effectively. These insights then add up to the final observations and a summary of the answers to the research questions in the concluding Chapter 7 as well as the propositions put forward for purposes of the public defence of this doctoral dissertation.

2 Private title claims

ABSTRACT

Chapter 2 addresses claims to cultural objects in a private law setting by their former owners who lost these in another country. Although international conventions clearly establish the rule that misappropriated artefacts should be returned, the legal reality is less straightforward. The question of whose interests are given priority in disputes that regard such losses – those of the former owner or a new possessor – vary per jurisdiction. Moreover, restitution claims with regard to artefacts that were lost longer ago are often inadmissible due to limitation periods for claims or other obstacles in a private law approach. Given this fragmented situation, an increasing number of international soft-law instruments promote an ethical approach and alternative dispute resolution (ADR) to resolve title disputes: apparently to fill the 'gaps' between the law and present-day morality. This chapter analyses what (ADR) procedures are available for parties to settle title disputes over looted cultural objects. A lack of transparent and neutral procedures to implement and clarify standards in European jurisdictions has proven problematic in that regard.

Questions that are addressed in this chapter are: What are the main difficulties that obstruct restitution claims by former owners, both in civil law and in common law jurisdictions? Given the increasing reliance on soft law and Alternative Dispute Resolution (ADR) as the preferred way to solve disputes: what about access to justice in such an 'ethical' model?

*Restitution of looted art: What about access to justice?**

1 INTRODUCTION

'What is stolen should be returned' is probably one of the oldest legal principles.[1] When it comes to the return of artefacts stolen longer ago, the legal reality is less straight-forward. Given the reliance on non-binding soft law in this area and obstacles in the positive legal framework, the question of *how* former owners can have their stolen artefacts returned – in terms of access to justice – deserves further attention. Often, an 'ethical' approach and alternative dispute resolution mechanisms are promoted as the way to resolve such claims. Over the last decades, a body of international soft law and transnational private regulatioin has emerged in support of redress for losses of cultural objects such as Nazi-looting[2] or takings from indigenous peoples.[3] On the other hand, such claims tend not to be supported by positive law, especially in civil law jurisdictions. Thus, grey categories of 'tainted' artefacts have come into existence, where expectations have been raised that 'justice' will be done – expectations that in many countries cannot be fulfilled by relying on regular legal channels. On the practical level this means that certain artefacts cannot be sold or sent on international loans for as long as their title is not 'cleared'. And although market forces have come to fill in some of the gaps in the law, it is questionable whether this is a guarantee for justice. Problematic in this regard is the lack of transparent neutral procedures to implement and clarify the often vague soft-law norms, and a trend where 'big' European restitution cases are brought before US courts (forum-shopping).

---

* This Chapter was originally published in *Santander Art and Culture Law Review* (2/2018 (4): 185-220). To avoid major overlaps with other chapters, some sections were shortened for the purpose of this thesis and some of the discussed ongoing cases were updated.

1 The duty to return objects obtained in violation of the law 'can be found in the oldest known legislation, such as, for example, Eshnunna law going back to the middle of the twenty-third century BC'. W.W. Kowalski, 'Restitution of Works of Art Pursuant to Private and Public International Law' in *Collected courses of the Hague academy of international law*, vol. 288 (2002) Brill, Nijhoff, 28.

2 E.g. the Washington Conference Principles on Nazi-Confiscated Art (3 December 1998) Released in connection with the Washington Conference on Holocaust-Era Assets, Washington, DC (Washington Principles).

3 E.g. the Declaration on the Rights of Indigenous Peoples, UNGA Res. 61/295 (13 September 2007) UN Doc A/RES/61/295 (UNDRIP).

The questions raised here are: why is ADR necessary; what kind of ADR procedures are available; and how this ethical approach guarantees clear standards and neutrality and transparency in the event of disputes? In other words, what about access to justice? This chapter sets out in the first section with an overview of the legal setting; followed by an examination of the ethical model that relies on soft law and ADR procedures in the second section.

2 The legal setting

Artefacts cross borders and are meant to be kept over time, meaning that the laws of different times and places may be relevant to their legal status. Artefacts are also unique and have an intangible quality, although that may differ per setting: the same object that in the hands of a collector or museum is of aesthetic, monetary, or art-historical value, may be held sacred by the former owner, or it may be a symbol of a family history. In consequence, the legal framework based on such a variety of interests is highly fragmented.[4] Moreover, at times, more than one party may have a justified interest in the same artefact. Whose interests are given priority when it comes to ownership claims, however, varies per jurisdiction. What follows is a birds'-eye overview of the legal framework.

2.1 The international level

On the international level a clear choice was made for the principle that 'the possessor of a cultural object which has been stolen shall return it', marking a victory for the interests of dispossessed owners over the interests of subsequent possessors.[5] This echoes and confirms the special status cultural objects have had since the beginning of international law: both the destruction of monuments and looting of cultural objects are prohibited during times of war or foreign occupation.[6] The 1899 Hague Regulations codified this prohibition,[7]

4 The multi-layered and de-centralised structure of cultural property law is well explained in F. Fiorentini, 'A Legal Pluralist Approach to International Trade in Cultural Objects' in J.A.R. Nafziger and R. Kirkwood Paterson (eds) *Handbook on the Law of Cultural Heritage and International Trade* (2014) Edward Elgar Publishing.

5 See e.g. Convention on Stolen or Illegally Exported Cultural Objects (adopted 24 June 1995, entered into force 7 July 1998) 2421 UNTS 457 (1995 UNIDROIT Convention) art 3(1).

6 The terms 'looting' and 'pillage' are used in the cultural heritage field to define misappropriation of cultural goods in the event of an armed conflict, see M. Cornu, C. Wallaert and J. Fromageau, *Dictionnaire comparé du droit du patrimoine culturel* (2012) CNRS Editions. However, in the present context the term 'looting' is used to include takings in a situation beyond an 'armed conflict', such as confiscation as a result of racist legislation.

and after the massive plundering during the Second World War, the 1954 UNESCO Convention for the Protection of Cultural Property in the Event of Armed Conflict and its First Protocol firmly established the norm that looted artefacts should be returned to the place they came from.[8] Since the adoption of the 1970 UNESCO Convention on the Means of Prohibiting and Preventing the Illicit Import, Export and Transfer of Ownership of Cultural Property (the 1970 Convention), this obligation also applies to looting in peacetime.[9] In this conventional framework, states are appointed as 'right holders' to the cultural objects within their territory. The question of ownership, however, is not addressed in these UNESCO treaties but left to the national level.[10] Given that regulation of ownership and property is, generally, considered a matter of state sovereignty, rules on the transfer of ownership title over stolen goods vary widely per jurisdiction.[11] Also within the European Union, for example, Article 345 of the Treaty on the Functioning of the European Union leaves issues of 'property ownership' to Member States.[12]

– *1995 UNIDROIT Convention*

In 1995, the UNIDROIT Convention on Stolen or Illegally Exported Cultural Objects 1995 was adopted that aimed at the harmonisation of national laws in this field. Its main principles include that:

---

7 Regulations Concerning the Laws and Customs of War on Land, Annex to the Convention (II) with Respect to the Laws and Customs of War on Land (adopted 29 July 1899) 32 Stat. 1803 (Hague Regulations) arts 46, 47, 56. For more on the development of the norm, see See E. Campfens, 'The Bangwa Queen: Artefact or Heritage?' (2019) 26 *International Journal of Cultural Property*.

8 Convention for the Protection of Cultural Property in the Event of Armed Conflict (adopted 14 May 1954, entered into force 7 August 1956) 249 UNTS 240 and First Protocol to the Convention for the Protection of Cultural Property in the Event of Armed Conflict (adopted 14 May 1954, entered into force 7 August 1956) 249 UNTS 358.

9 Convention on the Means of Prohibiting and Preventing the Illicit Import, Export and Transfer of Ownership of Cultural Property (adopted 14 November 1970, entered into force 24 April 1972) 823 UNTS 231.

10 At times, this causes tensions, see E. Campfens, 'Whose Cultural Heritage? Crimean Treasures at the Crossroads of Politics, Law and Ethics' (2017) 22 *Art Antiquity and Law* 193; A. Chechi, *The Settlement of International Cultural Heritage Disputes* (2014) Oxford University Press, 138; I.F. Gazzini, *Cultural Property Disputes: The Role of Arbitration in Resolving Non-Contractual Disputes* (2004) Transnational Publishers, 52.

11 With the exception of the human right to property and rights of indigenous peoples to their cultural property regulation is a matter of national legislatioin. See below.

12 Consolidated Version of the Treaty on the Functioning of the European Union (2012) OJ C 326: 'The Treaties shall in no way prejudice the rules in Member States governing the system of property ownership'. Article 36 exempts from free trade 'national treasures possessing artistic, historic or archaeological value', and constitutes the basis for European Parliament and Council Directive 2014/60 on the return of cultural objects unlawfully removed from the territory of a Member State and amending Regulation (EU) No 1024/2012 (Recast) OJ L 1159.

i) Stolen cultural objects should be returned to their owners;[13]
ii) Claims should be brought within three years from the time the location of the artefact and the identity of its possessor are known – with a maximum of 50 years from the time of the theft. No time limitation is set out if it concerns 'a cultural object forming an integral part of an identified monument or archaeological site, or belonging to a public collection' or concerns 'a sacred or communally important cultural object belonging to and used by a tribal or indigenous community as part of its community's traditional or ritual use', although also for these categories states may set limitation periods up to 75 years;[14] and
iii) A new possessor can claim compensation if his or her due diligence at the time of the acquisition can be proven, for which standards are set.[15]

These rules, however important for future restitution claims, only apply insofar as it concerns the loss of an artefact *after* ratification and implementation by states on the national level.[16] The 1995 UNIDROIT Convention, however, has not been widely adopted.[17] This means that many categories of stolen artefacts remain beyond the scope of their application: misappropriated artefacts tend to surface much later and, as a consequence, today's restitution cases deal with takings from the past. The legal situation with regard to such title disputes will be illustrated hereafter by a discussion of some case examples and an appraisal of new developments. A sketch of the ethical framework of soft law and ADR initiatives in this field will follow in the second part.

2.2 Different national approaches

A common denominator in art restitution cases based on a past loss is that the relevant facts are spread out over many years and involve multiple juris-

13 1995 UNIDROIT Convention art 3(1).
14 Ibid. arts 3(3), 3(5), 3(8).
15 Ibid. art 4(4): 'In determining whether the possessor exercised due diligence, regard shall be had to all the circumstances of the acquisition, including the character of the parties, the price paid, whether the possessor consulted any reasonably accessible register of stolen cultural objects, and any other relevant information and documentation which it could reasonably have obtained, and whether the possessor consulted accessible agencies or took any other step that a reasonable person would have taken in the circumstances'.
16 Ibid. art 10(1): 'The provisions of Chapter II shall apply only in respect of a cultural object that is stolen after this Convention enters into force in respect of the State where the claim is brought'.
17 Few Western European States ratified the Convention, see 'UNIDROIT Convention on Stolen or Illegally Exported Cultural Objects (adopted 24 June 1995) – Status', *International Institute for the Unification of Private Law* <https://www.unidroit.org/status-cp> accessed 2 May 2021.

dictions, whereas national ownership laws differ widely.[18] This is at the core of what causes title disputes over looted or stolen artefacts to be so complex and unpredictable.

Common law countries, most notably the US legal system, accord relatively strong rights to the dispossessed former owner on the basis of the principle that a thief cannot convey good title (the *nemo dat* rule), whereas in countries with a civil law tradition (most European countries with the exception of the UK and Ireland), the position of the new possessor is stronger and a valid legal title can be obtained over stolen artefacts if they were acquired in good faith, or even just by the passage of time. Besides, time limitations for ownership claims may either start to run from the moment of the loss of property, or from the moment of discovery of the object (or when one would reasonably have been able to discover it); or – as under New York – from the moment of 'demand and refusal'.[19] These differences may cause tension within the legal framework.

The opposite outcomes reached in very similar Dutch and UK cases regarding Second World War looting may serve as illustration. While the Dutch Supreme Court denied a claim to a painting looted from Dresden in the aftermath of the Second World War by the Red Army in its 1998 *Land Sachsen* ruling, the UK High Court honoured a similar claim in the *City of Gotha* case the same year.[20] The Dutch court argued it had no choice but to apply the absolute (30-year) limitation period for ownership claims, which dated from the moment of the loss and runs irrespective of the good or bad faith of the present possessor. The court in the UK, on the other hand, honoured the claim, observing that it would have invoked the public order exception if German law would have implicated a ruling in favour of a possessor that was not in good faith.[21]

A case concerning Camille Pissarro's 1897 depiction of a Paris street scene, *Rue Saint-Honoré, Après-midi, Effet de Pluie*, at the centre of litigation in the US for almost 14 years, may highlight this point in more depth.[22] Today, the

18 For a general overview of the obstacles to restitution, see B. Schönenberger, *The Restitution of Cultural Assets* (2009) Eleven International Publishing, ch. 4.

19 Ibid. See also Chechi (2014) 89.

20 *Land Sachsen* (1998) Hoge Raad, Case No. 16546, ECLI:NL:HR:1998:ZC2644 (Supreme Court of the Netherlands); *City of Gotha and Federal Republic of Germany v Sotheby's and Cobert Finance SA* (1998) No. 1993 C 3428 (QB). For a similar US case, see *Kunstsammlungen zu Weimar v Elicofon* (1982) United States Court of Appeals for the Second Circuit, 678 F2d 1150.

21 Two expert interpretations were presented on this point and, eventually, there was no need to invoke the public order exception.

22 Claude Cassirer, the grandson of Lilly Cassirer, filed the law suit in 2005 in California. The first rulings confirmed the US Foreign Sovereign Immunity Act's exception to sovereign immunity for lawsuits concerning rights to property taken in violation of international law. Two rulings on appeal confirmed this: *Cassirer v Kingdom of Spain* (2010) United States Court

Pissarro painting is part of the Thyssen-Bornemisza Museum in Madrid. However, it once belonged to Jewish art collector Lilly Cassirer Neubauer, who was forced to sell it just before her escape from Germany in 1939. After the war, it surfaced in the US and changed hands several times before Baron Thyssen-Bornemisza acquired it from a New York dealer in 1976. He brought the Pissarro to Switzerland, after which the Spanish State acquired it as part of the Baron's art collection in 1993. Whereas the first years of the litigation revolved around the question whether a US court had jurisdiction over property of the Spanish State – foreign states' property usually being immune – the next question was which law should apply – Spanish or US law? In its 2015 ruling Judge Walter held that according to conflict rules Spanish law should be applied, which was a (temporary) victory for the museum, inasmuch as the doctrine of acquisitive prescription under Spanish law – as in many European countries – would mean that ownership of the painting passed to the museum.[23] In a July 2017 appellate ruling, the choice of Spanish law was confirmed, however the question was raised whether the museum can be seen as an 'accessory to the theft' (*encubridor*) under Article 1956 of the Spanish Civil Code, which might mean the painting could still be claimed as stolen property.[24] On referral in its 30 April 2019 ruling the district court concluded, albeit very reluctantly, that the Thyssen-Bornemisza Museum acquired lawful ownership according to Spanish law.[25]

Interestingly, Judge Walter advised the parties in an *obiter dictum* in the 2015 ruling, to 'pause, reflect and consider whether it would be appropriate to work towards a mutually agreeable resolution (...) in light of Spain's acceptance of the Washington Conference Principles (...), and its commitment to achieve just and fair solutions for victims of Nazi persecution'.[26] Apparently Spanish law on this point was not considered to be 'just and fair' – hence the advice that the parties consider resolving their dispute in an alternative way.

---

of Appeals for the Ninth Circuit, 616 F. 3d 1019; *Cassirer v Thyssen-Bornemisza Collection Foundation* (2013) United States Court of Appeals for the Ninth Circuit, 737 F. 3d 613.

23 *Cassirer v Thyssen-Bornemisza Collection Foundation* (2015) United States District Court for the Central District of California, 153 F. Supp 3d 1148.

24 According to the verdict, 26 years after acquisition by the Spanish State. *Cassirer v Thyssen-Bornemisza Collection Foundation* (2017) United States Court of Appeals for the Ninth Circuit, 862 F. 3d 951, 29-30.

25 *Cassirer v Thyssen-Bornemisza Collection Foundation* (2019) United States District Court for the Central District of California, No. CV 05-CV-03459. E. Pettersson, 'Spanish Museum Can Keep Nazi-Looted Masterpiece, Judge Rules' (30 April 2019) *Bloomberg News* <https://www.bloomberg.com/news/articles/2019-04-30/spanish-museum-can-keep-nazi-looted-masterpiece-judge-rules>.

26 *Cassirer v Thyssen-Bornemisza Collection Foundation* 2017.

Given the course of the earlier *Altmann* litigation (2001-2004) this may not be surprising.[27] The *Altmann* case dealt with six paintings by Gustav Klimt – amongst them the famous *Lady in Gold* – of the Viennese Jewish Bloch-Bauer family who had been persecuted by the Nazis. The paintings had come into the possession of the Austrian National Gallery, which had refused to return them to the family ever since the Second World War, amongst other reasons because they were protected 'national treasures'. The case is considered seminal because it opened the doors of US courts to claimants seeking redress against foreign states or their institutions, even though foreign states and their acts would normally be exempt from jurisdiction in another state. The implication of the US Supreme Court's 2004 ruling is that, in spite of the immunity provided for by the Foreign Sovereign Immunity Act (FSIA), Nazi confiscations fall under an exception.[28] This exception 'abrogates sovereign immunity in any case where rights in property *taken in violation of international law* are in issue and that property (…) is owned or operated by an agency or instrumentality of the foreign state and that agency or instrumentality is engaged in *a commercial activity* in the United States'.[29] As to this last condition, the availability of a museum catalogue in the US was deemed sufficient. Such a low threshold may illustrate the US courts' readiness to claim jurisdiction over Holocaust-related cases.[30]

In this regard, interesting too is the rejection by the California District Court in 2001 of the plea by Austria that the matter should have been litigated in Austria (the US being a *forum non conveniens*). The court found that: 'Plaintiff's claims, if asserted in Austria, will most likely be barred by the statute of limitations of thirty years. (…) [Then] she would be left without a remedy; clearly, therefore, Austria is not an adequate alternative forum for Plaintiff's claims'.[31] After this victory, the Austrian government agreed to arbitration

27 In this case several court rulings led to two arbitral awards: *Maria V Altmann v Republic of Austria et al* (2001) United States District Court for the Central District of California, 142 F. Supp. 2d 1187; *Maria V Altmann v Republic of Austria et al* (2002) United States Court of Appeals for the Ninth Circuit, 317 F. Supp. 3d 954, as amended 327 F. Supp. 3d 1246 (2003); *Republic of Austria et al v Altmann* (2004) Supreme Court of the United States, 541 US 677. For an overview, see C. Renold and others, 'Case Six Klimt Paintings – Maria Altmann and Austria' (2012) Platform ArThémis, Art-Law Centre, University of Geneva.

28 This was a 'statutory holding' allowing for retroactive application of the exceptions in the FSIA to foreign states' immunity from suit, thus allowing US courts to assume jurisdiction. The parties then agreed on international arbitration.

29 As cited in *David L. de Csepel et al. v Republic of Hungary et al* (Memorandum Opinion, 2016) United States District Court for the District of Columbia, No. 10-1261 (ESH) 28 (emphasis added).

30 B. Schönenberger (*The Restitution of Cultural Assets* (2009) Eleven International Publishing), citing in fn 1102 from a review by G. Cohen of M.J. Bazyler, *Holocaust Justice: The Battle for Restitution in America's Courts* (2003) New York University Press: 'The author (…) posits that the 'real hero' is the American justice system, the only forum in the world where Holocaust claims can be heard today'.

31 *Maria v Altmann v Republic of Austria et al* (2001) (n. 27) 1209.

and eventually returned five of the six Klimt paintings to Maria Altmann, the Bloch-Bauer heir.[32]

A similar clash of laws as in the *Pissarro* case was at issue in the *Malewicz v City of Amsterdam* case.[33] This case revolved around a claim by the heirs of the painter Malewicz to 14 of his paintings in the Amsterdam Stedelijk Museum collection which had been on temporary loan in the US, on the grounds that the painter had been forced to leave them behind in Berlin in 1927 and could not retrieve them as a result of persecution by the Bolsheviks.[34] Two court rulings made it evident that the position of the City of Amsterdam that it was the legitimate owner of the paintings, was not looked upon favourably by the judges in New York. The City of Amsterdam argued that title had passed on grounds of acquisition in good faith of the collection from a relative of Malewicz in 1958, and that even if that sale would not be valid, the absolute prescription periods under Dutch law would render a claim time-barred. Similarly as in the *Altmann* case, the American judge ruled in favour of the former owners and stated that the taking of the paintings without paying compensation to the 'true owner' is a violation of international law – referring to the human right to property – and therefore the facts provided a sufficient basis for jurisdiction by a US court.[35] The *Malewicz* case was also eventually settled out of court, in this instance with the help of a neutral third party who mediated a settlement.[36] Under the settlement, five paintings were returned to the ownership of the heirs, while the heirs acknowledged legal title of the City of Amsterdam to the remainder of the collection in the Stedelijk Museum.[37] The settlement agreement of 2008 acknowledges, on one hand, the circumstances that prevented Malewicz from returning to his artworks and the interests of the heirs while, on the other hand, it aims at keeping 'such a part of the collection together, that in essence it embodies a representation of and homage to Malewicz as one of the major artists of the twentieth century

32 *Maria v Altmann and others v Republic of Austria* (Arbitral Award, 15 January 2004) <http://bslaw.com/altmann/Klimt/award.pdf> accessed 1 April 2019; *Maria v Altmann and others v Republic of Austria* (Arbitral Award) (6 May 2004) <http://bslaw.com/altmann/Zuckerkandl/Decisions/decision.pdf> accessed 1 April 2019.

33 *Malewicz v City of Amsterdam* (2005) United States District Court for the District of Columbia, 362 F. Supp. 2d 298; *Malewicz v City of Amsterdam* (2007) United States District Court for the District of Columbia, 517 F. Supp. 2d 322.

34 A. Chechi, E. Velioglu and M.A. Renold, 'Case Note – 14 Artworks – Malewicz Heirs and City of Amsterdam' (2013) Platform ArThémis, Art-Law Centre, University of Geneva.

35 *Malewicz v City of Amsterdam* (2007) (n. 33) 340. On this point, see also *David L. de Csepel et al v Republic of Hungary et al* (2016) (n. 29) 28.

36 J.M. Boll, at the time a member of the Dutch State Council, in this instance acted in his personal capacity without formal involvement or (financial) ties with the parties. Interview with author (14 August 2018) (on file with the author).

37 Settlement Agreement between the Municipality of Amsterdam and the Malewicz heirs (24 April 2008) (on file with the author).

and as a leading source of modern and contemporary art'.[38] This enabled the continued public exhibition by the Amsterdam Stedelijk Museum of a considerable collection of Malewicz works.

The *Malewicz* case was not the first restitution claim that revolved around paintings that were on a temporary loan in the US: a similar case concerned Egon Schiele's *Portrait of Wally*, seized while on loan from the Leopold Museum in Austria for a temporary exhibition in New York.[39] Anxiety in the museum world that these developments would hinder cross-border loans resulted in the adoption of a law aimed at providing greater security for foreign museums sending their works on loan to the US: the Foreign Cultural Exchange Jurisdictional Immunity Clarification Act.[40] Nevertheless, under this law two exceptions apply. The first exception concerns 'Nazi-era claims', and the second concerns artefacts 'taken in connection with the acts of a foreign government as part of a systematic campaign of coercive confiscation or misappropriation of works from members of a targeted and vulnerable group'. In other words, owing to these exceptions the door of the US judiciary would remain open to cases alleging property takings in the course of human rights violations.[41]

As a last example to illustrate the willingness of US courts to assess Nazi-era restitution claims, the 2016 ruling in *Simon v Republic of Hungary* should be mentioned.[42] In this case the court argued that confiscation of private property by the Hungarian Wartime authorities – in this instance not artefacts – may, in itself, constitute genocide and therefore violates international law. Although this interpretation of the term 'genocide' seems inconsistent with the generally-accepted notion of genocide,[43] the verdict may underline that in the US such

38 Ibid. g, h.

39 *United States v Portrait of Wally* (2009) United States District Court, SD New York, 663 F. Supp. 2d 232. N van Woudenberg and JAR Nafziger, 'The Draft Convention on Immunity from Suit and Seizure for Cultural Objects Temporarily Abroad for Cultural, Educational or Scientific Purpose' (2014) 21 *International Journal of Cultural Property* 481.

40 Foreign Cultural Exchange Jurisdictional Immunity Clarification Act of 2016, PL 114-319.

41 I. Wuerth, 'An Art Museum Amendment to the Foreign Sovereign Immunities Act' (2017) *Lawfare* <https://www.lawfareblog.com/art-museum-amendment-foreign-sovereign-immunities-act>.

42 *Simon v Republic of Hungary* (2016) United States Court of Appeals for the District of Columbia Circuit, No. 14-7082: 'Such takings did more than effectuate genocide or serve as a means of carrying out genocide. Rather, we see the expropriations as themselves genocide'.

43 In its *Genocide* case (2007), the International Court of Justice (ICJ) concluded that: '(...) the destruction of historical, cultural and religious heritage cannot be considered to constitute the deliberate infliction of conditions of life calculated to bring about the physical destruction of the group. Although such destruction may be highly significant inasmuch as it is directed to the elimination of all traces of the cultural or religious presence of a group and contrary to other legal norms, it does not fall within the categories of acts of genocide set out in Article II of the Convention'. *Application of the Convention on the Prevention and Punishment of the Crime of Genocide (Bosnia and Herzegovina v Serbia and Montenegro)* (2007) ICJ Rep 2007. See also Convention on the Prevention and Punishment of the Crime of Genocide (adopted 9 December 1948, entered into force 12 January 1951) 78 UNTS 277.

cases are approached from the perspective of fundamental human rights. In that sense, also Eric Jayme argued that the *Altmann* case should be seen as an example of the retroactive application of human rights.[44]

The above overview highlights the different setting of restitution claims in European civil law jurisdictions, where new possessors of looted artefacts often have a more advantageous position. With respect to Holocaust takings, one reason for this is the expiration of the special restitution laws that were enacted after the Second World War, in an attempt to return looted art to the victims of Nazi-plundering.[45] Such laws often had very short limitation periods and in today's practice mostly lost their meaning. At times these may still apply.[46] In France, for example, the Tribunal de Grande Instance de Paris ruled that the painting *Pea Harvest* by Camille Pissarro should be returned to the grandson of Jewish art collector Bauer, who had lost his collection through confiscation by the Vichy government in 1943 and this ruling was upheld on appeal.[47] Generally speaking however, the 2018 German court ruling that denied a claim to a painting by Max Pechstein from the collection of Jewish art collector Robert Graetz lost as a result of Nazi persecution, seems more representative of legal systems in Europe where claims tend to be inadmissible after a certain period of time.[48] As the German ruling explains: When the law is clear on the matter of ownership and limitation periods for ownership claims, the hands of a judge are tied.

---

44 E. Jayme, 'Human Rights and Restitution of Nazi-Confiscated Artworks from Public Museums: The Altmann Case as a Model for Uniform Rules?' (2006) 11 *Uniform Law Review* 393.

45 For more on post-war restitution laws, see E. Campfens, 'Sources of Inspiration: Old and New Rules for Looted Art' in E. Campfens (ed) *Fair and Just Solutions? Alternatives to Litigation in Nazi-Looted Art Disputes* (2015) Eleven International Publishing, 21-26. In the Netherlands, for example, claims had to be filed before July 1951. Regulation Concerning Article 21 of Law KB E 100 'Koninklijk Besluit Herstel Rechtsverkeer' (1950) 251 Dutch Staatscourant 5.

46 In France courts held claims admissible on the grounds of a 'void' transaction, see the *Gentili di Giuseppe* case (*Gentili di Giuseppe et al v Musée du Louvre* (1999) Court of Appeal of Paris, 1st Division, Section A, No RG 1998/19209) and the *Bauer* case discussed hereafter. In the German *Hans Sachs Poster collection* case, a claim was honoured on grounds that it had been impossible for claimant to meet deadlines earlier (*Hans Sachs Poster Collection* (2012) *Bundesgerichtshof*, V ZR 279/10).

47 *Bauer et al v B and R Toll* (2017) Tribunal de Grande Instance de Paris, No RG 17/58735 No 1/FF; upheld in appeal on 2 October 2018, see V. Noce, 'Paris Court Orders US Collector to Turn Over Pissarro Painting' (3 October 2018) *The Art Newspaper* <https://www.theartnewspaper.com/news/paris-court-orders-us-collector-to-turn-over-pissarro-painting> accessed 30 April 2019. Previously, on 8 November 1945, a Paris court had ruled the confiscation of the painting – from Simon Bauer – to be null and void. See *Bauer et al v B and R Toll* (2017) 4.

48 *Landesgericht Frankfurt am Main Urt,* Judgement of 2 November 2016, Az:2-21 O 251/15; *Oberlandesgericht Frankfurt am Main,* Judgment of 8 February 2018, Az:1 U 196/16.

Obviously, regulations that provide time limits for claims serve a purpose. In the interest of legal certainty, at some point in time the legal reality adapts itself to the prevailing situation. Those who 'sit' on their rights may lose these, and those who acquired an object in good faith may gain valid legal title. The American couple that had acquired the Pissarro from Christie's in New York in 1995 for $800,000 in good faith and had to part from it without compensation, for example, certainly did not agree that the outcome was 'pure justice'. While the verdict was being welcomed with these words by the representative of the family whose heirloom was confiscated by the Nazis, they voiced their discontent by stating that: 'It surely is not up to [us] to compensate Jewish families for the crimes of the Holocaust'.[49] It may illustrate the complexity of finding a 'just' balance between the interests of the original owner against those of a subsequent possessor.

Tension between national private law systems may also arise as a result of cultural differences: unknown forms of (collective) ownership of cultural objects may not be recognised in foreign courts. In December 2018, for example, the Amsterdam District Court denied a claim by two Chinese villages seeking the return of a stolen sacred Buddha statue.[50] The statute was allegedly stolen from a local temple in 1995 and, in 1996, was bought in Hong Kong by a Dutch collector. Without addressing the many substantive issues raised by the case, the claim was dismissed on the grounds that the status of the village committees as a legal entity that owned of the statute was unclear. Similarly, a claim by the Hopi tribe in 2013 French litigation aimed at preventing an auction in Paris of their sacred 'Katsina', masks that represent incarnated spirits of their ancestors, based on their communal and inalienable property rights, was deemed inadmissible and reason for denial by the French courts.[51]

2.3 Appraisal of the legal framework

Claims to artefacts lost in the past are predominantly approached as a matter of stolen property and thus rely on national private law. In terms of national private law, there is a discrepancy between the legal framework in the US and Europe. In the US, the interests of original owners of stolen artworks are traditionally taken more into consideration and courts are willing to assume

49 A. Quinn, 'French Court Orders Return of Pissarro Looted by Vichy Government' (8 November 2017) *The New York Times* <https://www.nytimes.com/2017/11/08/arts/design/french-court-pissarro-looted-nazis.html?searchResultPosition=1> accessed 16 January 2019. According to the representative of the Toll couple, Ron, the contract with Christie's stands redress 'upstream' in the way.

50 Judgment of 12 December 2018, Amsterdam District Court, ECLI:NL:RBAMS:2018:8919.

51 The auction was considered legitimate since their claim has no legal basis in French law. *Association Survival International France v SARL Néret-Minet Tessier Sarrou* (2013) *Tribunal de Grande Instance de Paris*, No RG 13/52880 BF/No 1.

jurisdiction over cases that concern looted art, even if these concern artefacts in European collections.[52] In Europe, the situation is fragmented. At times, national laws offer a loophole in specific cases (as in the *Bauer* case). But often, cases depend on voluntary adherence to soft-law norms, provided that the parties are willing, in accordance with the 'ethical' approach. In such a situation settlements will often depend on the bargaining chips brought to the table by the parties.[53] One of such bargaining chips may be the possibility of taking 'big' cases to the US for costly and lengthy litigation.

In its 2019 resolution on cross-border restitution claims of works of art and cultural goods looted in armed conflicts and wars, the European Parliament has addressed the problems claimants encounter in regaining their lost artefacts (2019 EP Resolution).[54] The resolution calls on the European Commission and Member States to support restitution claims by former owners. As a solution for *future* cases, the Parliament proposes the harmonisation of laws of member states through the adoption of certain elements of the 1995 UNIDROIT Convention.[55] The introduction of due diligence standards as a legal standard indeed would indeed be an important step, as this would prevent the trade in unprovenanced and possibly looted artefacts (i.e. where a history of ownership is not fully documented). Possibilities for 'laundering' stolen or looted artefacts in European civil law countries where new possessors may gain valid ownership title over stolen artefacts, would likewise be diminished. Nevertheless, the implementation of the 1995 UNIDROIT Convention would not solve title disputes regarding artefacts that already circulate and were lost *before* the implementation of the Convention in national private law. These cases would remain in limbo and older, incompatible national norms in European jurisdictions would continue to apply.[56] In other words, due to increased transparency and efforts to enlist potentially looted artefacts in databases, as proposed in the 2019 EP Resolution, more claims will be facilitated, while at the same time the question of *how* to resolve these claims remains unaddressed. In such cases the 2019 EP Resolution proposes the use of alternative dispute resolution mechanisms (ADR): a confirmation of the extra-legal 'ethical model' for restitution claims.[57]

---

52 For a listing, see E. Campfens, 'Nazi-Looted Art: A Note in Favour of Clear Standards and Neutral Procedures' (2017) 22 *Art Antiquity and Law* 339-342.

53 F. Shyllon, 'The Rise of Negotiation (ADR) in Restitution, Return and Repatriation of Cultural Property: Moral Pressure and Power Pressure' (2017) 22 *Art Antiquity and Law* 130-142.

54 European Parliament Resolution on Cross-Border Restitution Claims of Works of Art and Cultural Goods Looted in Armed Conflicts and Wars (17 January 2019) 2017/2023 INI.

55 Ibid. paras 11, 12.

56 1995 UNIDROIT Convention, art 10(1).

57 Ibid. para 15 and further.

3 THE ETHICAL MODEL

Since the end of the last century, the adoption of various soft-law instruments underscores that norms are changing with regard to the possession of looted art, even if artefacts are lawfully owned under private law rules. Ethical codes, professional guidelines, and declarations tend to have a similar pattern, one that focuses on equitable solutions for title disputes that take the interests of former owners into account; and, in the second place, on the use of ADR mechanisms to resolve claims.[58] The following section provides a discussion of such soft-law instruments and their referral to ADR procedures. This is followed by a closer look at two institutionalised procedures in this field – the Binding Opinion Procedure of the Dutch Restitutions Committee, a procedure established by the Dutch government for the assessment of Nazi-looted art claims; and the recently-established international Court of Arbitration for Art, a private initiative.

3.1 Soft-law instruments

Soft law in the field of Nazi-looted art, arguably the most well-known category of restitution claims, follows the above outline promoting equitable solutions by means of ADR in the system of the 1998 Washington Principles.[59] The referral by Judge Walter in the Spanish/US *Pissarro* case mentioned above highlights their impact. With the adoption of the Washington Principles, 40 states agreed to assist parties in finding 'just and fair' solutions to ownership disputes that regard Nazi-confiscated art. The relevant rule reads as follows:

> If the pre-war owners of art that is found to have been confiscated by the Nazis and not subsequently restituted, or their heirs, can be identified, steps should be taken expeditiously to achieve a just and fair solution, recognizing this may vary according to the facts and circumstances surrounding a specific case.[60]

ADR mechanisms are advocated in Principle no. 9: 'Nations are encouraged to develop national processes to implement these principles, particularly as they relate to alternative dispute resolution mechanisms for resolving ownership issues'. Their adoption instigated a practice of settlements and returns, initially restricted to national public collections, but soon followed by the

58 For more co-operative solutions, see M.A. Renold, 'Cultural Co-Ownership: Preventing and Solving Cultural Property Claims' (2015) 22 *International Journal of Cultural Property* 163-176.

59 'Washington Conference Principles on Nazi-Confiscated Art' (n. 2).

60 Ibid. principle 8.

private sector.[61] Today, works that are 'tainted' by a possible history of Nazi-looting are unsaleable on the international art market and cannot be sent on international loans by museums. In other words, the reputation of a work of art and its market value has come to fill a gap where the law is lacking.

While this extra-legal 'ethical' approach can overcome legal obstacles that today are seen as leading to immoral outcomes, given the special circumstances of the loss, such an approach nonetheless has a drawback: the field is hampered by a lack of clear rules and compliance mechanisms.[62] Some believe a 'fair and just solution' means the full restoration of property rights – a straightforward and absolute right on the part of dispossessed owners to restitution of their lost property. Others believe interests of other parties should also weigh in to reach a 'fair and just' solution.[63] Likewise, views on what exactly is 'Nazi-looted art' differ. While it is well-understood that the confiscation of artefacts on basis of racial (Nazi) laws, theft, and forced sales fall under the notion, some argue that sales in neutral countries by Jewish refugees – having an indirect causal relation with the Nazi regime – should also be considered as forced sales.[64] Clearly the norm is widening, and is also applied to wartime losses at the hands of others than the Nazis.[65] The twin-pronged question is: In what direction is it evolving and who is to clarify these rules?

61 E.g. German/US Joint Declaration Concerning the Implementation of the Washington Principles from 1998 (26 November 2018) <https://www.lootedart.com/web_images/pdf2018/2018-11-26-gemeinsame-erklaerung-washingtoner-prinzipien-engl-data.pdf> accessed 6 December 2018: 'Both our governments recognize that the Washington Principles and Terezin Declaration apply to public *and private* collections, although we recognize the latter presents a particular challenge. We therefore call on art auction houses and other private dealers in each of our countries to adhere to the Washington Principles, taking note of positive examples set by some auction houses and art dealers in handling possible Nazi-looted artworks' (emphasis added).

62 Further discussion in E. Campfens (2017), 'Nazi-Looted Art ...'. It has also not been clarified by later international declarations, such as: Council of Europe, Resolution 1205, 'Looted Jewish Cultural Property' (1999) Doc 8563; Vilnius Forum Declaration (2000) <https://www.lootedart.com/MFV7EE39608> accessed 23 April 2019 (signed by 38 governments) and the Terezin Declaration on Holocaust Era Assets and Related Issues (2009) <https://www.lootedartcommission.com/NPNMG484641> accessed 23 April 2019, with 46 signatory states. For an overview of such later instruments, see E. Campfens (2015) 37.

63 See, however, the commotion over a Dutch decision that held that the interest of the museum outweighed the interests of former owners (discussed below). See C. Hickley, 'Dutch Policy on Nazi-Loot Restitutions under Fire' (21 December 2018) *The Art Newspaper* <https://www.lootedart.com/news.php?r=TETJ4L309041> accessed 23 April 2019.

64 Examples in E. Campfens (2017) 'Nazi-Looted Art ...' 23-26.

65 Reports of the Spoliation Advisory Panel Regarding the *Beneventan Missal* (23 March 2005 and 15 September 2010). Dutch Restitutions Committee, Recommendation Regarding Krasicki (2017) RC 1.152.

It has been argued that a similar instrument to the Washington Principles should be developed for restitution claims that concern colonial takings.[66] On the national level – in France, the Netherlands, and Germany – guidelines and declarations of this type have recently indeed been adopted.[67] It demonstrates a political will to act. It should be noted, however, that the Washington Principles themselves are not more specific or legally binding than already existing instruments in other categories.

Insofar as it concerns claims where museums are involved, the 1986 International Code of Ethics adopted by the International Council of Museums (ICOM), an example of transnational private regulation, gives guidance.[68] Most museums are members of ICOM and are expected to adhere to the principles adopted in the ethical code. Similar to the approach outlined above, these guidelines state that with regard to restitution issues, museums should collaborate with source communities. The Code encourages readiness to enter into dialogue, preferably on a non-governmental level. The relevant provisions read as follows:

- Museums should be prepared to initiate dialogues for the return of cultural property to a country or people of origin. This should be undertaken in an impartial manner, based on scientific, professional and humanitarian principles as well as applicable local, national and international legislation, in preference to action at a governmental or political level.
- When a country or people of origin seeks the restitution of an object or specimen that can be demonstrated to have been exported or otherwise transferred in violation of the principles of international law and international conventions, and shown to be part of that country's or people's cultural or natural heritage, the museum concerned should, if legally free to do so, take prompt and responsible steps to co-operate in its return.

---

66 J.M. van Beurden, *Treasures in Trusted Hand: Negotiating the Future of Colonial Cultural Objects* (2017) Sidestone Press; see also H. Parzinger, 'Bauen Wir Museen in Afrika!' (25 January 2018) *Frankfurter Allgemeine Zeitung*.

67 In France, recommendations were presented but not yet policy lines; see 'Remise du Rapport Savoy/Sarr sur la Restitution du Patrimoine Africain' (*Elysée*, 2018) <https://www.elysee.fr/emmanuel-macron/2018/11/23/remise-du-rapport-savoy-sarr-sur-la-restitution-du-patrimoine-africain> accessed 23 April 2019; German: 'Eckpunkte zum Umgang mit Sammlungsgut aus Kolonialen Kontexten' (2019) <https://www.kmk.org/fileadmin/pdf/PresseUnd Aktuelles/2019/2019-03-25_Erste-Eckpunkte-Sammlungsgut-koloniale-Kontexte_final.pdf> accessed 23 April 2019; for the Dutch guideliens, see 'Dutch National Museum of World Cultures Announces Principles Claims Colonial Collections' (*Museum Volkenkunde*, 2019) <https://www.volkenkunde.nl/en/about-volkenkunde/press/dutch-national-museum-world-cultures-nmvw-announces-principles-claims> accessed 23 April 2019.

68 The ICOM Code of Professional Ethics was adopted by the General Assembly of the International Council of Museums on 4 November 1986, retitled 'ICOM Code of Ethics for Museums' in 2001, and revised in 2004. See 'ICOM Code of Ethics for Museums' (2004) <https://icom.museum/wp-content/uploads/2018/07/ICOM-code-En-web.pdf>, ICOM Code 6.2 (Return of Cultural Property), and ICOM Code 6.3 (Restitution of Cultural Property).

Another instrument that provides guidelines is the 2006 Principles for Co-operation in the Mutual Protection and Transfer of Cultural Material.[69] Adopted by the International Law Association, they emphasise a general duty on the part of institutions and governments to enter into 'good-faith negotiations' regarding restitution claims by persons, groups, or states. The principles also list what should be taken into account during those negotiations, namely '(…) the significance of the requested material for the requesting party, the reunification of dispersed cultural material, accessibility to the cultural material in the requesting state, and protection of the cultural material'.[70] Insofar as concerns the outcome, a focus is placed on 'caring and sharing': the alternatives to outright restitution mentioned include loans, production of copies, and shared management and control.[71] Two categories are singled out: Principle 4 sets out the obligation 'to respond in good faith and to recognise claims by indigenous groups or cultural minorities whose demands are not supported by their national governments'; whereas Principle 5 confirms the special status of human remains with a straightforward obligation of repatriation.

Indigenous peoples' cultural property claims form a category that increasingly is acknowledged as a matter of international human rights law. For this category, the adoption in 2007 – after 20 years of negotiations – of the UN Declaration on the Rights of Indigenous Peoples (UNDRIP) is of major importance.[72] The primary obligation is for states to 'provide redress, (…) which may include restitution, with respect to cultural property taken without their free, prior and informed consent'.[73] Beyond emphasising the need for redress, it also obliges states to set up 'fair, transparent and effective mechanisms' to address claims. Given the fact that in many (civil law) jurisdictions new possessors gained valid legal ownership/title over objects lost longer ago, states would seem to have the choice to either (i) arrange by law for expropriation and restitution; or perhaps more feasibly as a first step, to (ii) provide assistance in finding solutions through the setting up of transparent ADR mechanisms.[74]

Apart from these instruments that address right-holders on the sub-state level, numerous UN and UNESCO declarations underline the importance of

69 International Law Association, Report of the Seventy-Second Conference (2006), Annex to J.A.R. Nafziger, 'The Principles for Cooperation in the Mutual Protection and Transfer of Cultural Material' (2007) 8 *Chicago Journal of International Law* 147. Nafziger states that current practice is the jurisprudential basis.

70 Ibid. principle 8.

71 Ibid. principle 3.

72 UNDRIP (n. 3) arts 11(2), 12(2).

73 Ibid.

74 Further discussion in E. Campfens (2019), 'The Bangwa Queen…'.

return of (a representative part of) a country's lost cultural patrimony.[75] In this regard, in 1978 the UNESCO Intergovernmental Committee (ICPRCP) was established to assist Member States with return requests that concern cultural property 'which has a fundamental significance from the point of view of the spiritual values and cultural heritage of the people of a Member State or Associate Member of UNESCO and which has been lost as a result of colonial or foreign occupation or as a result of illicit appropriation'.[76] In various UN Resolutions attention is drawn to the services of the ICPRCP, and, once more, the 2015 Operational Guidelines to the 1970 UNESCO Convention reiterate this.[77] Notwithstanding this appreciation and the introduction of a special mediation procedure, the relatively low number of cases referred to the Committee indicates that the state-centred approach of the ICPRCP creates a political setting that may not *per se* be suitable to resolve these matters.[78] It therefore mostly is used as a forum for best practice examples and for governments to state certain claims.

3.2 Alternative dispute resolution

In the context of cultural property claims, adversarial litigation is generally considered a last option, to be entered into only after good-faith negotiations and ADR mechanisms and procedures have been exhausted.[79] Their specific nature and the complex moral and legal issues that are involved are often cited as reasons. The main reason for resorting to ADR is that positive legal standards

---

75 For an overview of UN Resolutions, see 'Restitution of Cultural Property: Resolutions Adopted by the United Nations General Assembly about Return and Restitution of Cultural Property' (*UNESCO*) <http://www.unesco.org/new/en/culture/themes/restitution-of-cultural-property/resolutions-adopted-by-the-united-nations-general-assembly-about-return-and-restitution-of-cultural-property/> accessed 29 April 2019.

76 Statutes of the Intergovernmental Committee for Promoting the Return of Cultural Property to its Countries of Origin or its Restitution in Case of Illicit Appropriation (adopted 24 October-28 November 1978, amended October 2005) UNESCO Doc CLT/CH/INS-2005/21.

77 See, e.g., UNGA Res. 67/80 (12 December 2012) UN Doc A/RES/67/80 para 80. UNESCO, 'Operational Guidelines for the Implementation of the Convention on the Means of Prohibiting and Preventing the Illicit Import, Export and Transfer of Ownership of Cultural Property' (adopted 18-20 May 2015) C70/15/3.MSP/11 (UNESCO Operational Guidelines).

78 Chechi (2014) 104-106. The General Conference of UNESCO adopted Resolution 44 (UNESCO General Conference, 33rd Session, Paris, 2005) 33 C/Resolution 44, adding mediation and conciliation to the mandate of the Intergovernmental Committee.

79 M. Cornu and M.A. Renold, 'New Developments in the Restitution of Cultural Property: Alternative Means of Dispute Resolution' (2010) 17 *International Journal of Cultural Property* 1, 1-3; ALBandle and S Theurich, 'Alternative Dispute Resolution and Art-Law – A New Research Project of the Geneva Art-Law Centre' (2011) 6 *Journal of International Commercial Law and Technology* 28; N. Palmer, 'Waging and Engaging – Reflections on the Mediation of Art and Antiquity Claims' in A.L. Bandle, A. Chechi and M.A. Renold (eds) *Resolving Disputes in Cultural Property* (2012) Schulthess Verlag, 81.

will not provide the redress promised in soft-law instruments.[80] Consequently, also international organisations such as UNESCO and ICOM promote the use of alternative procedures in cultural property disputes.[81] Below are some comments on specific ADR formats.

3.2.1 *Arbitration*

Arbitration is specifically mentioned in the 1995 UNIDROIT Convention, which provides that: 'The parties may agree to submit the dispute to any court or other competent authority or to arbitration'.[82] In 2003, at a seminar at the Permanent Court of Arbitration (PCA), the idea was launched of creating a special arbitral regime equipped with unique substantive and procedural rules for handling cultural property claims.[83] Whereas arbitration may offer advantages, its value probably mainly lies in the field of contractual claims over authenticity and attribution, due to the confidentiality that it grants.[84] So far, arbitration plays hardly any role in restitution claims.[85] The *Altmann* arbitration, which was instituted after the initial stage of litigation as discussed above, is amongst the few such cases. In the words of Chechi: 'In effect, while negotiation is very common and mediation is becoming increasingly popular, it appears that recourse to arbitration is the exception rather than the rule'.[86]

3.2.2 *Mediation and negotiated settlements*

Mediation, an informal procedure in which a mediator helps parties to settle a dispute by identifying their interests but without imposing a decision, is a method that has gained considerable popularity in cultural property disputes. In the private sector special mediation initiatives have been created, such as

80 As was illustrated by the examples in the first section. See also C. Woodhead, 'Nazi Era Spoliation: Establishing Procedural and Substantive Principles' (2013) 18 *Art Antiquity and Law* 167-192. In the UK, for example, the Spoliation Panel is not an alternative method – it is the sole way to resolve Nazi-era claims on their merits.

81 'Competing claims (…), if they cannot be settled by negotiations between the States or their relevant institutions (…) should be regulated by out of court resolution mechanisms, such as mediation (…) or good offices, or by arbitration'. UNESCO Operational Guidelines (n. 83) 18-20. At the ICOM level, see A. Cummins, 'Promoting the Use of Mediation in Resolution of Disputes over the Ownership of Objects in Museum Collections: Statement by the President of ICOM Alissandra Cummins' (2006).

82 1995 UNIDROIT Convention art 8(2).

83 'Resolution of Cultural Property Disputes', organised in 2003 by the PCA in The Hague. See O.C. Pell, 'Using Arbitral Tribunals to Resolve Disputes Relating to Holocaust-Looted Art' in International Bureau of the Permanent Court of Arbitration (ed) *Resolution of cultural property disputes* (2004) Kluwer Law International, 307-327.

84 Cf. Chechi (2014) 177.

85 Ibid. 181.

86 Ibid.

Art Resolve;[87] and also in the public sector specific mechanisms for cultural property disputes have been set up. In 2011 ICOM established its mediation programme for the museum sector in cooperation with the World Intellectual Property Organization (WIPO).[88] It was presented after positive experiences in the restitution case regarding a *Makonde Mask* stolen from a museum in Tanzania and acquired in 1985 by a Swiss museum, a case that fell outside of any 'hard law' rules obliging restitution, as Switzerland acceded to the UNESCO Convention only much later.[89] The programme/procedure is administered by ICOM-WIPO in Geneva. As regards the question whether only the interests of the parties or soft-law norms are guiding, Article 14(a) of the WIPO-ICOM Mediation Rules states that 'the mediator and the parties shall bear in mind the ICOM Code of Ethics for Museums'. Nevertheless, the implication of these words remains unclear, as in mediation the parties' respective interests are leading, which do not need to coincide with ethical standards. Interestingly, the Guidelines on Dealing with Collections from Colonial Contexts of the German Museum Association of 2018 advise that disputes be solved through mediation, and refer to the ICOM-WIPO procedure.[90]

The usual way to resolve Nazi-looted art claims is by way of mediation or negotiated settlement, with or without the help of auction houses or organisations such as the Art Loss Register. The confidentiality of such procedures, and the leading role of the parties, offer advantages in terms of costs and the quick resolution of claims. On the other hand, confidentiality – however justifiable in a specific case – will not add to the clarification of vague norms. A public debate, legal analysis and development of norms is only possible over public decisions. Moreover, the lack of a 'back-up' neutral procedure with standards of due process in the event the parties cannot agree voluntarily, could hinder the application of soft-law norms in a situation of unequal power relations.

3.2.3 *Government advisory panels for Nazi-looted art*

Whereas Nazi-looted art cases are often settled through confidential settlements, several European States have set up special advisory bodies. Around the year 2000 five of such committees were established: the Spoliation Advisory

87 'Art Resolve' <https://artresolve.org/>.

88 'ICOM-WIPO Art and Cultural Heritage Mediation' (*World Intellectual Property Organization*) <https://www.wipo.int/amc/en/center/specific-sectors/art/icom/>.

89 See S. Slimani and S. Theurich, 'The New ICOM-WIPO Art and Cultural Heritage Mediation Program' in A.L. Bandle, A. Chechi and M.A. Renold (eds) *Resolving Disputes in Cultural Property* (2012) Schulthess Verlag.

90 German Museums Association, 'Guidelines on Dealing with Collections from Colonial Contexts' (2018) 98.

Panel in the UK, the CIVS[91] in France, the Dutch Restitutions Committee in the Netherlands, the Beratende Kommission in Germany, and the Beirat in Austria.[92] These are government-appointed panels to enable the assessment of Nazi-looted art claims on their merits. Over the last decades these panels have dealt with many claims and have fulfilled an important role in terms of offering redress for victims of Nazi-looting.

In establishing these panels, the focus was on the specific national situation of each country. For example, in France and the Netherlands so-called 'heirless art' collections – that consist of artefacts that all have a certain 'war history' and are in custody of these governments since the post-War period – call for specific obligations and solutions, while in Germany museums may have objects acquired directly from their persecuted owners.[93] Their working methods, organisational structure, and recommendations differ, consequently, a great deal. On the other hand, art collections that were forcibly sold by persecuted owners often were dispersed throughout the art market, hence claims in different countries may concern objects from the same collection lost in the exact same way. The different standards applied and outcomes reached in similar cases can sometimes cause confusion. Nevertheless, in terms of (procedural) justice the neutrality and transparency of these procedures obviously are important.[94]

3.2.4 *Two examples of institutionalised ADR procedures*

As examples of institutionalised ADR procedures in the field of restitution claims, this section looks closer at the Binding Opinion Procedure of the Dutch Restitutions Committee – a national claims procedure aimed at the assessment of claims that regard Nazi-looted art – and the recently established international Court of Arbitration for Art – a private initiative aimed at resolving a wide range of disputes in the field of cultural property.

---

91 Commission pour l'indemnisation des victimes de spoliations intervenues du fait de législations antisémites en vigueur pendant l'Occupation.

92 For an overview of the committees, see A. Marck and E. Muller, 'National Panels Advising on Nazi-Looted Art in Austria, France, the United Kingdom, the Netherlands and Germany – a Brief Overview' in E. Campfens (ed) *Fair and Just Solutions? Alternatives to Litigation in Nazi-Looted Art Disputes* (2015) Eleven International Publishing.

93 Futher elaborated on in E. Campfens (2017) 'Nazi looted Art…'.

94 In January 2019, a network was created linking the committees. Commission for the Compensation of Victims of Spoliation, 'Establishment of a Network of European Restitution Committees' (2019) <http://www.civs.gouv.fr/news/establishment-of-a-network-of-european-restitution-committees/> accessed 30 April 2019.

3.2.4.1 The binding expert opinion procedure by the Dutch Restitutions Committee

The Restitutions Committee was established by the Dutch government by a decree dated 16 November 2001.[95] Its task is two-fold: first, to advise the Minister of Culture on decisions to be taken concerning claims for the restitution of artefacts that were lost as a result of Nazi looting which are currently in the possession of the State of the Netherlands. A well-known case in this category is the 2005 *Goudstikker recommendation*, in which the Committee advised the Dutch government to return 202 paintings to the heirs of Jewish art dealer Jacques Goudstikker after denial of the claim by a Dutch court.[96] The Committee's second task is to assess claims that concern non-state Nazi-looted art that are brought before the Committee; such cases can be referred to the Committee, the so-called 'binding expert opinion procedure'. This procedure takes a middle ground between mediation and arbitration and is, as all ADR mechanisms, based on the voluntary decision by the parties to refer their case to the Committee. If they choose this procedure, the parties must agree beforehand to accept the opinion of the Committee as binding upon them. In other words, the binding nature of the Committee's decision is based on a contract between the parties and, obviously, does not have the same strong status of an arbitral award or court ruling.

A distinguishing element of this procedure is the factual research report, which plays a central role.[97] After the parties are given an opportunity to clarify their positions, a neutral investigation into the facts is carried out by researchers based at the Netherlands Institute for War Documentation (NIOD).[98] The relevant information is summarised and cited in a draft investigation report, sent to both parties for comments. Furthermore, the Committee may order further investigations, a hearing, or consultation between the parties at any time. The Committee is guided by 'principles of reasonableness and fairness' in delivering its binding opinions.[99] An overview of the considera-

95 Besluit Adviescommissie Restitutieverzoeken Cultuurgoederen en Tweede Wereldoorlog [Decree Establishing the Advisory Committee on the Assessment of Restitution Applications for Items of Cultural Value and the Second World War] 2001 WJZ/2001/45374(8123) (Establishing Decree). For more information, see the yearly reports and other information published on the website: <https://www.restitutiecommissie.nl/>.

96 While denying the heirs' claim to 31 paintings on the grounds that rights to these works had been relinquished in the post-war period. See Restitutions Committee, Goudstikker, Summary RC 1.15 <https://www.restitutiecommissie.nl/en/summary_rc_115.html> accessed 12 May 2019.

97 The Committtee has drawn up Regulations for this procedure, see <https://www.restitutiecommissie.nl/en/regulations_binding_expert_opinion_procedure.html> (acc. 2 May 2021)

98 'Expertisecentrum Tweede Wereldoorlog En Restitutieverzoeken' (*NIOD*) <https://www.niod.nl/nl/expertisecentrum-restitutie>. The 'Expertisecentrum' at the NIOD was established in 2019.

99 Establishing Decree, arts 2(4), 2(5). The weighing of verious interests this implicates, however, been rejected as being not in accordance with the Washington Principles (see below).

tions the Committee may take into account is given in Article 3 of its regulations, and is summarised below:

- The Washington Principles and other policy guidelines;
- The circumstances of the loss of possession of the work;
- The extent efforts were made earlier to recover the work;
- The circumstances in which the present possessor acquired the work;
- The importance of the work to the claimant;
- The importance of the work to the present possessor;
- The interest of the general public (i.e. public access).

As to the possible solutions or outcomes, Article 11 of the Regulations provides any solution the Committee deems fit, which may be restitution or another solution. Commemoration by means of a plaque has also been recommended.[100]

The positive elements of this procedure are, in my view, neutrality, transparency, and flexibility. Neutral research into the often ambiguous historical circumstances is important from the perspective of truth-finding – to establish if an artefact can be identified as the lost work and was looted – but also from the perspective of procedural justice. The acknowledgement of past injustices in a neutral factual report may, at times, serve as a remedy in its own right (i.e. by telling the story of this injustice). As to transparency, the procedure follows a set sequence and recommendations are published on the Committee's website and may thus serve as precedents. A third positive element is that the procedure is flexible and, given the central role of the research report, also less adversarial than arbitration, which may heighten the chances for creative or cooperative solutions.

An important reason for the initial success of this procedure has been that the Dutch Museum Association had advised its members to refer all Nazi-looted art claims to this procedure as a matter of general policy.[101] Over the last years, however, the Committee has been widely criticised on account of its interpretation of the 'fair and just' rule in its recommendation regarding a claim on the painting *Bild mit Häusern* by Wassily Kandinsky, which had

100 Restitutions Committee, 'Binding Opinion in the Dispute on Restitution of the Painting Entitled Christ and the Samaritan Woman at the Well by Bernardo Strozzi from the Estate of Richard Semmel, Currently Owned by Museum de Fundatie' (2013) RC 3.128; Restitutions Committee, 'Binding Opinion Regarding the Dispute About the Return of the Painting Madonna and Child with Wild Roses by Jan van Scorel from the Collection of Richard Semmel, Currently in the Possession of Utrecht City Council' (2013) RC 3.131.

101 Letter from the State Secretary for Education, Culture and Science to Parliament (22 June 2012).

been sold by its Jewish owner to the Stedelijk Museum in Amsterdam in 1940.[102] The Committee rejected this claim on the argument that the interests of the museum outweighed the interest of the claimant: 'The work has an important art historical value and is an essential link in the limited overview of Kandinsky's work (…) and is included in the [museum's] permanent display'; whereas the claimant had not shown an 'emotional or other intense bond with the work'. Such a balance of interests is – according to the critics – incompatible with the Washington Principles. And indeed, the essential question if the loss should be seen as voluntary or under duress was not clearly addressed by the Committee. If nothing else, it illustrates that the 'fair and just' norm is open to many different interpretations. An appeal of this decision was instigated by the claimants but denied by a Dutch court in December 2020.[103] It must be taken into account, however, that a court of law is bound by positive law and, thus, can only marginally review such outcomes: it will not be able to apply or even explain the soft-law norm in the Washington Principles.

3.2.4.2 The Court of Arbitration for Art

A second example of an institutionalised ADR mechanism is the Court of Arbitration for Art (CAfA). In June 2018, CAfA was launched as a specialised 'tribunal' providing for alternative dispute resolution in the field of art-related disputes.[104] The spectrum of disputes aimed at by the organisation is much wider than the procedure before the Dutch Restitutions Committee described above: these may include authenticity issues, and contract or title disputes.

The CAfA is the result of a cooperation between the Authentication in Art foundation (AiA), founded in 2012 as a platform for stakeholders to promote best practices in art authentication, and the Netherlands Arbitration Institute (NAI). Its base is in The Hague, but proceedings in a case can be held anywhere.[105] The main 'special' feature of the CAfA is the fact that experienced art lawyers are the arbitrators in charge of the assessment of cases. These arbitrators are chosen from a pool made up by the AiA Board and the NAI. In addition, for factual evidence the CAfA relies on (neutral) experts, appointed by the tribunal whenever forensic science (authentication issues) or provenance

---

102 Restitutions Committee, Binding Opinion Regarding the Dispute About Restitution of the Painting with Houses by Wassily Kandinsky, Currently in the Possession of Amsterdam City Council (2018) RC 3.141. For criticism, see, e.g., Hickley (2018).

103 *Claimants (anonymised) v City of Amsterdam et al.*, Amsterdam Disctrict Court 16 December 2020 in the case ECLI:NL:RBAMS:2020:6277.

104 See 'CAfA – Court of Arbitration for Art' (*Authentication in Art*) <https://authenticationinart.org/cafa/>.

105 CAfA Adjunct Arbitration Rules (entered into force 30 April 2018), Explanatory Note (6.2): 'Notwithstanding the seat of arbitration in The Hague, the arbitral tribunal may decide under Art. 21(8) and 25(2) of the NAI Rules to conduct the hearing of factual and/or expert testimony and/or oral argument at any other location in the world'.

issues arise.[106] Like the arbitrators, these experts are chosen from a controlled pool. Evidence offered by a party-appointed expert is only admissible in matters that are *not* 'forensic science or provenance issues'; and even then may not 'compete with or supplement the expert evidence from the arbitral tribunal-appointed expert'.[107] This reliance on neutral expertise appears a valuable element in cases involving provenance issues – i.e. in restitution claims – where the uncertainty about the factual circumstances and weighing of (missing) evidence is often the major challenge.[108]

The parties can either agree on the governing substantive law, or may authorise the arbitral tribunal to decide equitably as *amiable compositeur*.[109] If no choice is made, the CAfA Adjunct Arbitration Rules provide for the law of the principal location of the seller in the case of a sales transaction, and the law of the principal location of the owner of the art object as 'the appropriate choice of law'.[110] In other words, a preference for the owner's national law – which usually will be where the object is located. This choice may be problematic for restitution cases, given that in title disputes the question of who should be seen as the legitimate owner is usually the contentious issue at stake, especially in the light of the differences in approach between common and civil law jurisdictions (as described above).

Furthermore, the CAfA rules highlight one substantive rule: 'Unless agreed otherwise, the tribunal shall (...) respect the applicable periods of limitation, prescription, and repose as well as similar time-bar principles when claims or defences have not been acted on within a reasonable time'.[111] In other words, restitution claims brought long after a work was lost are deemed time-barred, and this is explained by the argumentation that parties should be protected from 'stale' claims or defences which were not pursued with reasonable diligence, and that situations of 'undue prejudice' should be avoided, i.e. where evidence has been lost due to the lengthy passage of time.[112] As has been oft-mentioned above, however, the decisive element for the admissibility of claims with respect to cultural losses are frequently time limits. Abiding by the legal restrictions in this regard, in other words, ignores present-day

106 AiA/NAI CAfA Adjunct Arbitration Rules, Point 4: 'Arbitrators shall in principle be chosen from among those persons listed in the Pools. Only in the event of compelling reasons with the consent of the AiA Board and the administrator may an arbitrator be appointed from outside the Pools'. On expert evidence, Point 10: 'On issues of forensic science or the provenance of an object, the only admissible expert evidence shall be from an expert or experts appointed by the arbitral tribunal. The arbitral tribunal may appoint such experts from within the Expert Pool'.

107 Ibid. Point 10.

108 Ibid. Explanatory Note (2.2).

109 Ibid. Explanatory Note (13.9); art 42 of the NAI Arbitration Rules.

110 Ibid. Explanatory Note (9). Nota bene the question of who is the legitimate 'owner' of the artefact is not a given; but often the contested issue.

111 Ibid. Point 14.

112 Ibid. Explanatory Note (9.3).

soft-law norms, which urge an appraisal of claims 'on their merits'. In fact, it might even be in conflict with laws that lift such time limits for claims, like the US HEAR Act for claims that concern Nazi-looted art.[113]

Apart from arbitration, since January 2019 mediation is also a possibility.[114] As in the procedure for arbitration, the mediators are drawn from a pool composed of mediators with demonstrated experience in art law disputes and/or international mediation. Also similar to the arbitration procedure is that special attention is given to expert advice: a mediator may, with the prior consent of the parties, appoint an expert to provide the parties with neutral third-party advice on specific questions in dispute. On issues of forensic science or the provenance of an art object, only advice from experts from within the controlled 'Expert Pool' is admissible. Such expert advice shall be confidential and non-binding (unless otherwise agreed) and may not be used or referred to outside of the mediation.[115]

Given the absences of a follow-up to the 2003 initiative to give the Permanent Court of Arbitration a central role in the resolution of cultural property disputes exactly 15 years before the launch of the CAfA,[116] one can draw the conclusion that arbitration is not well-suited for dispute resolution in this field. The mediation procedure of the CAfA in combination with the reliance on neutral expert advice, however, might be promising. More generally, the CAfA procedure may be better suited for commercial disputes than for disputes where public interests – or unequal power relations between the parties – are an issue, given the confidentiality of the procedures. This, however, is an observation that with regard to all voluntary ADR procedures: without having a back-up of a regular judicial system to apply norms, it is questionable whether ADR procedures can act as a guardian of 'neutrality, transparency and justice' – as envisaged for example by the 2019 EP Resolution.

4 Developments: From a property framework towards a human rights framework

Whereas the approach to restitution of looted art still mainly relies on the framework for stolen property in national private law, often implicating these are time-barred and inadmissible before regular courts of law, human rights law notions appear to gain importance. This development surfaces in references to the human right to property as the rationale for redress for losses in the course of Nazi persecution in soft-law instruments, (US) court rulings and

113 Holocaust Expropriated Art Recovery Act (2016, 114th Congress, 2nd Session, S.2763).
114 CAfA Mediation Rules (entered into force 1 January 2019) (NAI Mediation Rules and AiA/NAI Adjunct Mediation Rules Combined).
115 Ibid. 5.
116 O. Pell (2004). To my knowledge not one resitution dispute was referred tot he PCA since.

policy instruments. The 2019 EP Resolution, for example, refers to identity values (of societies, communities, and individuals) and the human right to property of Article 1 of Protocol 1 to the European Convention on Human Rights.[117] It is also noticeable in the discussion about cultural objects taken in a colonial context. In this regard, the reference to the right of everyone to have access to one's own culture in recent Western-European instruments is noteworthy. For example, French President Macron, in his November 2017 policy announcement, underlined the need for Africans to be able to access their own culture and, hence, he considered it no longer acceptable that most of it is in European collections.[118] Likewise, the rationale for the 2019 German policy framework is to enable the return of colonial takings so that 'all people should have the possibility to access their rich material culture (…) to connect with it and to pass it on to future generations'.[119] This is reminiscent of the 2009 General Comment on the 'right of everyone to take part in cultural life' of Article 15 (1)a of the International Covenant on Economic, Social and Cultural Rights, stating this has come to include 'access to cultural goods'.[120]

For the time being, the state of the law in this field is unsettled, therefore soft law and ADR remain important to resolve restitution disputes in a way that reflects a new sense of justice. In the meantime, it should also be noted that the term 'restitution' has deviated from its traditional legal meaning on several points. Traditionally, restitution has been the preferred remedy for an unlawful act on the interstate level and has been aimed to restore the previous state of affairs (*restitutio in integrum*).[121] On three levels this approach has undergone changes.

First, within the context of present-day practice that relies on soft law, there is a shift from a state-centred approach towards an approach that focusses on the interests of non-state entities, such as private former owners (families) or (indigenous) communities. In the second place, the unlawfulness of the taking at the time is, in today's restitution cases, not always a given. Often, the losses occurred during times of historical injustice, such as the Holocaust or colonial suppression of indigenous communities. At the core of such claims is a changing notion of justice and legality: In some cases the original taking can indeed be classified as unlawful, but in other cases the loss was legal at

117 Protocol to the European Convention for the Protection of Human Rights and Fundamental Freedoms (adopted 20 March 1952) ETS 9 art 1: 'Every natural or legal person is entitled to the peaceful enjoyment of his possessions. No one shall be deprived of his possessions except in the public interest and subject to the conditions provided for by law and by the general principles of international law'.

118 See E. Macron, Speech at the University of Ouagadougou (28 November 2017) <https://www.elysee.fr/emmanuel-macron/2017/11/28/discours-demmanuel-macron-a-luniversite-de-ouagadougou> accessed 23 April 2019.

119 'Eckpunkte zum Umgang mit Sammlungsgut aus Kolonialen Kontexten' (n. 67).

120 Committee on Economic, Social and Cultural Rights, General Comment No. 21 (2009) UN Doc E/C.12/GC/21.

121 W.W. Kowalski, *Art Treasures and War* (1998) Institute of Art and Law.

the time. For example, a sale by a Jewish owner of an artefact in the years of Nazi-rule was probably lawful at the time; likewise, the confiscation of indigenous peoples' cultural objects may also have been sanctioned by colonial laws at the time. This deviation from the earlier paradigm should be kept in mind. Similarly, the term 'restitution' in the 2018 French Sarr/Savoy report – 'The Restitution of African Cultural Heritage. Toward a New Relational Ethics'[122] – is deliberately used to underline the authors' views on the *injustice* of colonial acquisition practices – not their *unlawfulness*. This term has undergone changes, not unlike the term 'confiscation' as the central element within the context of Nazi-era losses. The sale of artefacts by Jewish collector Curt Glaser in 1933 in Berlin, i.e. before racial laws were enacted by the Nazis, could for example hardly be qualified as a 'confiscation' in the legal sense or even unlawful. Still, the loss *did* qualify for restitution under the soft law system of the Washington Principles.[123] In other words, many of today's restitution cases rely on present-day norms, and not on the unlawfulness of the taking at the time.[124] Such norms provide redress for a continuing injustice and aim to reunite people with objects that have a specific symbolic meaning, like a family heirloom or works that are sacred to a certain community.

A third remark about the evolution of the term 'restitution' is that present-day soft-law norms do not aim *per se* at the restoration of full ownership rights, but may be limited to a lesser right, like a right to an equitable solution – defined as the right to a 'just and fair solution' in the Washington Principles, and as a right of 'redress which may include restitution' in the context of the UNDRIP.

All the above points may underline that changes in this field have legal implications, and that international cultural property law is moving away from a property framework towards a human rights framework. This would mean that the ethical model for (historical) restitution cases – including voluntary ADR procedures without guarantees in terms of due process – may eventually be replaced with a more solid legal model.

---

122 F. Sarr and B. Savoy, 'The Restitution of African Cultural Heritage. Toward a New Relational Ethics' (2018) 29 <http://restitutionreport2018.com/sarr_savoy_en.pdf>.

123 Dutch Restitutions Committee, Recommendation Regarding Glaser (2010) RC 1.99. Also in Germany Glaser's claims were upheld, see 'Stiftung Preußischer Kulturbesitz Findet Erneut Faire Und Gerechte Lösung Mit Den Erben von Prof. Dr. Curt Glaser' (2016) *Stiftung Preußischer Kulturbesitz* <http://www.preussischer-kulturbesitz.de/pressemitteilung/article/2016/04/20/pressemeldung-stiftung-preussischer-kulturbesitz-findet-erneut-faire-und-gerechte-loesung-mit-den-erb.html> accessed 1 April 2019. See also E. Campfens, (2017) 'Nazi-Looted Art, 325.

124 A.F. Vrdoljak, *International Law, Museums and the Return of Cultural Objects* (2006) Cambridge University Press, 2-3.

5 Final observations

In art restitution claims the application of regular property law rules, and the system of conflict of law rules that would normally guide judges to a 'just' outcome, appear to no longer fulfil this aim. A common theme in soft-law instruments and transnational private regulations. that have emerged in this field includes a call for equitable solutions to title disputes, and for alternative methods to settle claims. Such procedures are advocated as being more efficient, less adversarial, and more flexible to culturally sensitive arguments. However, in many jurisdictions alternative procedures are the *only* way to assess claims, because the positive legal framework has not (yet) adapted to the newly emerging standards of morality and justice. Seen in this light, the 'ethical' framework and reliance on extra-legal procedures may be viewed as an intermediate solution in a process of evolving law.

For the time being, most legal systems do not support title claims regarding cultural losses that took place in the past. Grey categories of 'tainted' artefacts have thus emerged, whilst soft law instruments raise expectations that 'justice' will be done. On the practical level this also means that certain artefacts cannot be sold or sent on international loans as long as their title is not cleared. And although market forces have come to fill in some gaps in the law, this does not guarantee justice. Problematic in this regard is the lack of transparent neutral procedures to implement and clarify soft law norms. In the view of the author this institutional vacuum in terms of access to justice in Europe, needs to be addressed. A lack of clarity at both the substantive and the procedural levels – e.g. what is the norm and who will interpret and apply it? – will otherwise aggrevate legal uncertainty. In its 2019 Resolution the European Parliament acknowledged the fragmented situation and advocated for the adoption of the principles of the 1995 UNIDROIT Convention as a roadmap to a transparent, responsible, and ethical global art market in the future, and for an ethical approach and voluntary ADR procedures to address claims of works of art looted in armed conflicts and war in the past.[125] In this regard the establishment of a European claims procedure could be considered. This would also meet the obligation that states have taken upon themselves – by signing instruments like the Washington Principles and the UNDRIP – to develop neutral and accessible procedures to ensure that promises about justice are upheld.

The ethical model and ADR may, at times, indeed be the best setting to resolve disputes in a non-adversarial manner and to foster dialogue, cooperation, and creative solutions. Nevertheless, ultimately these cases are about justice and the role of law should be to provide a framework where similar cases will be dealt with similarly, independent of power-relations. This may not be guaranteed in a legal framework that depends solely on non-binding

125 Above n. 54.

soft law and voluntary ADR procedures. In that respect, developments of international cultural property law from a property framework into a human right framework are promising.

3 The interstate model

ABSTRACT

Chapter 3 analyses the interstate model for claims to lost cultural heritage under the 1954 Hague Convention and the 1970 UNESCO Convention, on the basis of a case example. In the so-called 'Crimean Gold' case 500-or-so archaeological objects from the Crimean Peninsula are at stake that had been sent to the Allard Pierson Museum in Amsterdam for a short-term loan. The period of this exhibition – from February to August of 2014 – coincided with geopolitical events, resulting in the occupation and (de facto) secession of Crimea from the Ukrainian state in March 2014. After the exhibition, the Allard Pierson was confronted with two competing claims to the objects: the Ukrainian state on the one hand and the Crimean museums on the other. Ukraine claims the objects are its national cultural property, whilst the Crimean museums claim return on the basis of the loan agreement and on Crimea being the 'genuine home' of the artefacts. An analysis of the applicable UNESCO treaty system highlights that it does not address issues that are at the heart of the present case, like the division of a country and the cultural-historical interests at the sub-state level. This, because it is based on the notion of a national state as the key 'right holder' to cultural objects. The Crimean Gold case offers a wealth of political, legal and ethical dilemmas. This chapter aims step back from the political context and to focus on aspects relevant to the legal framework for return claims more generally.

The following questions are addressed in this chapter: How does the 'nationality' prong for entitlement to cultural objects in the 1970 UNESCO Convention relate to territoriality and cultural-historical considerations?; and: What is the position in this system of non-state 'right holders' who lost their cultural objects, such as communities or individuals?

*Whose cultural heritage? Crimean treasures at the crossroads of politics, law and ethics**

1 Introduction

Restitution claims concerning cultural objects are often a cause for vivid controversies, where concepts of property and state sovereignty are intertwined with intangible aspects such as a cultural-historical or religious identity. A case which exemplifies this is the so-called 'Crimean Gold' case, currently being litigated in Amsterdam.

At stake are 500-or-so archaeological artefacts from the Crimean Peninsula that had been sent to Amsterdam on a short-term loan by four Crimean museums for the exhibition 'Crimea: Gold and Secrets from the Black Sea' at the Allard Pierson Museum. The period of this exhibition in 2014 coincided with a series of political events, resulting in the Russian annexation of Crimea and its secession in March 2014 from the Ukrainian State of which the Peninsula had been part since 1954. This secession, however, is not recognised by most other states, including the Netherlands, adding a layer of complexity to the case. After the exhibition, the Allard Pierson was confronted with two competing claims to the objects: the Ukrainian State on the one hand and the Crimean museums on the other. Ukraine claims the objects as national patrimony and state property; the Crimean museums seek their return on the basis of guarantees contained in the loan agreement and the argument that Crimea is the 'true home' of the artefacts – having been discovered and preserved there over time. In December 2016, the Amsterdam District Court delivered a first substantive verdict in this case:[1] it found in favour of the Ukrainian State and ordered the return of the objects to Kiev on the basis of the 1970 Convention on the Means of Prohibiting and Preventing the Illicit Import, Export and Transfer of Ownership of Cultural Property.[2]

---

* This chapter in its original version was published in the journal *Art Antiquity and Law* (Vol. XXII, Issue 3/2017) in November 2017. A new section (3.6) was added that takes stock of the preliminary outcome (interlocutory judgement) of the appeals procedure in the Crimean Gold case in 2019.

1 *Rechtbank Amsterdam (Verdict of 14 December 2016) Amsterdam District Court*, C/13/577586/HA ZA 14-1179, ECLI:NL:RBAMS:2016:8264. *NB* see the post scriptum for the 2019 Amsterdam Appeals Court's interlocutory judgement.

2 Convention on the Means of Prohibiting and Preventing the Illicit Import, Export and Transfer of Ownership of Cultural Property (adopted 14 November 1970) 823 UNTS 231 (1970 UNESCO Convention).

The Crimean Gold case presents a wealth of political, legal and ethical dilemmas, sufficient reason for an intermediary report. The present chapter aims to detach from the political context and to focus on the legal and ethical issues, with special attention for the position of right-holders other than nation states (like local communities, indigenous peoples or individuals) in the international legal framework for return requests.

To that end, it sets out with an overview of the factual background information and events leading up to the December ruling (section 2). The legal arguments of the parties – in as far these can be deduced from the ruling[3] – and a summary of the verdict, focusing on the Court's interpretation of the 1970 UNESCO Convention regarding the questions 'what is unlawful transfer?' and 'who can make a claim for their return?' will follow in section 3. Furthermore, section 4 will touch upon aspects not addressed in the verdict, such as the role of the 1954 Hague Convention for the Protection of Cultural Property in the Event of Armed Conflict and its First Protocol;[4] the status of right holders beyond the Nation State; and alternative dispute resolution and its role in cultural heritage disputes.

2 Background

2.1 The artefacts

'Crimea: Gold and Secrets from the Black Sea' at the Allard Pierson Museum in Amsterdam (hereafter also: AP Museum) was the second stage of an international travelling exhibition showing artefacts – jewellery, weapons, decorative objects – from five Ukrainian museums. Four of these were Crimean museums – the Tavrida Central Museum in Simferopol, the Kerch Historical and Cultural Preserve in Kerch, the Bakhchisaray History and Culture State Preserve of the Republic of Crimea in Bakhchisaray and the National Preserve of 'Tauric Chersonesos' in Sabastopol – and there was one museum in Kiev, the National Museum of History.[5] Before travelling to Amsterdam, the exhibition was displayed in the Landesmuseum in Bonn. The exhibition's alternate title, *'The Crimea: Greeks, Scythians and Goths at the Black Sea'*, better

3 N.B.: in the Netherlands, the Parties' procedural documents are not public; the interpretation given here is therefore mainly based on the Court rulings.

4 Hague Convention for the Protection of Cultural Property in the Event of Armed Conflict (adopted 14 May 1954) 249 UNTS 240 (1954 Hague Convention); First Protocol to the Hague Convention for the Protection of Cutlural Property in the Event of Armed Conflict (adopted 14 May 1954) 249 UNTS 358 (1954 Protocol) (ratified by the Netherlands, Ukraine and the Russian Federation).

5 The nineteen objects from the National Museum of History in Kiev were returned to Ukraine after the exhibition ended in August 2014.

characterises the objects. As described in the announcement by the AP Museum the exhibition would:

> reveal the rich history of the peninsula colonised by the Greeks since the seventh century BC. The Crimea and the Black Sea were and remain an important crossroads between Europe and Asia.

The artefacts, in other words, are testimony to the various civilisations the Peninsula has known. One exhibit, a Chinese lacquer box dating from the Han dynasty, for example, attests to Crimea's position as part of the Silk Road.[6]

The present case is often referred to as the 'Scythian Gold case',[7] a cause for confusion as the name 'Scythian Gold' is also used for a well-known collection of antiquities excavated from the territory of the present-day Ukraine preserved in the Russian Hermitage. That *other* collection of Scythian Gold had been the subject of a dispute which arose after the collapse of the Soviet Union in the early 1990s.[8] The artefacts at stake in the dispute in the Netherlands are not the same as the controversial Scythian Gold treasures from the Hermitage. Since the objects from the National Museum of History in Kiev were returned to Ukraine after the exhibition ended in August 2014, the objects at stake in this present dispute are Crimean archaeological artefacts, that, until the loan, were part of four museum collections situated in the Autonomous Republic of Crimea in Ukraine.

2.2 Loan agreements and export licences

To arrange for the loan of the objects from Ukraine to Bonn (from July 2013) and to Amsterdam (from February 2014), agreements were finalised in the spring of 2013. The parties to the agreements were the representatives of the Landesmuseum and the AP Museum on one side, and their counterparts at the five Ukrainian museums – one in Kiev and four in Crimea – on the other. The loan agreements stipulated that the AP Museum would return the loaned materials to each of the five museums in a timely manner 'after the expiration of the term of the temporary storage for the purpose of demonstration'.[9] The interests of Ukraine surface in the loan agreements in the reference to the objects as part of the 'Museum Fund of Ukraine' and a reminder that the parties:

6 For the exhibits, see the Allard Pierson Museum Series. P. Retél and T. Vugts, *De Krim: Goud en geheimen van de Zwarte Zee* (2014) WBooks.

7 E.g. M. Nudelman, 'Who Owns the Scythian Gold? The Legal and Moral Implications of Ukraine and Crimea's Cultural Dispute' (2015) 38 *Fordham International Law Review* 1276, 1261.

8 A. Jakubowski, *State Succession in Cultural Property* (2015) Oxford University Press, 198-235.

9 Verdict (n. 1) 2.2, 2.8.

> realize that the exhibits of the exhibition are the property of Ukraine and world civilization and shall take all possible measures to avoid their loss and damage.[10]

The Ukrainian executive branch of the Government approved the loans by signing export licences in June 2013 and an extension authorisation in January 2014.[11]

2.3 Geopolitical events

The exhibition at the AP Museum coincided with the Ukrainian-Russian political and military crisis with major consequences for the status of the Crimean objects. The Amsterdam court summarised the events as follows:

> On 6 March 2014, the Autonomous Republic of Crimea (ARC) agreed on the secession from Ukraine and accession to the Russian Federation. On 16 March 2014, the ARC held a referendum and voters in Crimea were in favour of accession to the Russian Federation. On 18 March 2014, the ARC and Sevastopol became part of the Russian Federation.[12]

It is beyond the scope of this research (and the expertise of the author) to delve into the history of the region. It is relevant, however, to note that Crimea has its own, turbulent, history. It was under Ottoman rule when it was annexed in 1783 by the Russian Empire, remaining under Russian influence till 1954, when it was transferred by an order of Nikita Khrushchev from the Russian Soviet Federative Socialist Republic to the Ukrainian Soviet Republic (both within the Soviet Union). In 1991, after the dissolution of the Soviet Union, it gained its autonomous status within the newly founded independent Ukrainian State.[13] From 1954 until the secession and Russian annexation in 2014, in other words, the Crimean peninsula was under Ukrainian rule.

The secession of Crimea – the ARC – from the Ukrainian State and the annexation by the Russian Federation in 2014, however, was not recognised by most other nation states, including the Netherlands. Ukraine took the position that Crimea was temporarily occupied rather than permanently

10 Ibid. 3.4; Loan Agreements (2013) art 7(1).
11 Ibid. 2.3, 2.4.
12 Ibid. 2.5.
13 For an overview of Crimea's history, see A. Taylor, 'To Understand Crimea, Take a Look Back at Its Complicated History' (27 February 2014) *The Washington Post* <https://www.washingtonpost.com/news/worldviews/wp/2014/02/27/to-understand-crimea-take-a-look-back-at-its-complicated-history/?utm_term=.d9b8bef3486c>.

annexed,[14] and the General Assembly of the United Nations underlined the territorial integrity of Ukraine by adopting Resolution 68/262 in March 2014.[15]

That the Russian Federation considers Crimea as its territory while the international community regards the annexation as unlawful occupation of Ukrainian territory has international legal consequences. It may suffice in this regard to allude to the difficulties of a situation where the Ukrainian State is considered to be the lawful representative of Crimea but lacks effective control over the territory. Besides, it may be obvious that any official act that could be understood as a *de facto* recognition of the illegal situation – such as the return of cultural objects other than to the Ukrainian State – might cause political problems.

2.4 Competing claims

During the exhibition, the AP Museum was confronted with competing demands for return of the objects that had come from Crimea: Ukraine on the one hand and the Crimean Museums on the other. From March 2014 onwards, the four Crimean museums insisted that the AP Museum return all objects to the lending institutions as stipulated in the loan agreements.[16] That same month, the Ministry of Culture of Ukraine requested an early return of the Crimean treasures to the State of Ukraine, stating that Ukraine was working on the return of all artefacts that belonged to the State Museum Fund as they were 'national treasures and an integral part of the cultural heritage of Ukraine protected by law'.[17]

By July 2014, the AP Museum suspended its obligations under the loan agreement to return the objects to the four Crimean museums, and, instead, adopted a position that it had no interest in the Crimean treasures and simply wanted to return the artefacts to the entitled party, but that it did not want to be held liable for breach of contract or damages claimed by the other party.[18] This position was consistent with the AP Museum's decision to return objects that had been borrowed from the National Museum of History of Ukraine in Kiev after the termination of the exhibition in August 2014.[19]

---

14 Law of Ukraine on Securing the Rights and Freedoms of Citizens and Legal Regime on the Temporarily Occupied Territory of Ukraine (15 April 2014) No 1207-VII. See also Nudelman (2015) 1276, 1283.

15 UNGA Res. 68/262 (27 March 2014) UN Doc A/RES/68/262, adopted by 100 states in favour, 11 agains and 58 abstentions; Resolutions by the Security Council stating the illegality of the events were vetoed by Russia.

16 Verdict (n. 1) 2.9.

17 Ibid. 2.6.

18 Ibid. 2.10, 3.7, 3.8.

19 Ibid. 2.11.

On 19 November 2014, the four Crimean museums commenced legal proceedings against the AP Museum before the District Court of Amsterdam.[20] Ukraine's request to intervene was granted by the Amsterdam District Court a few months later, on 8th April 2015.[21]

At that point, the Dutch State also asked to be admitted as a party to the civil proceedings in order 'to see that its international obligations would not be jeopardised' and to prevent the artefacts from being returned to the Crimean Museums 'unless it would be definitely and irrevocably established the Crimean Museums are the entitled party'.[22] This request was rejected by the Court in its April 2015 verdict on the grounds that the Dutch State lacked a specific interest in the outcome as it had shown no intentions to file an independent claim.

This last point is of interest, as a basis for legal action would seem to exist under the 1954 Protocol to the Convention for the Protection of Cultural Property in the Event of Armed Conflict (hereafter: 1954 Protocol).[23] The Dutch State could (or even should), on this view, have taken the artefacts into custody for safekeeping pending their return to the appropriate party. This issue will be discussed in section 4 as that path was not taken.
The Russian Federation did not enter the debate independently.

2.5 Immunity from seizure?

One may ask, what was the role of immunity arrangements with the Dutch State to avoid litigation over works of art on short-term loan? In the Netherlands, this can be arranged by so-called 'letters of comfort', documents issued by the Ministry of Foreign Affairs that aim to provide some degree of immunity from seizure for cultural property from foreign states in the event of international loans. More specifically, such letters are issued to the borrowing museum to pass on to the lending institutions and explain that:

> the Government of the Netherlands will do everything that is legally within its power to ensure that the art object loaned by the foreign state will not be encumbered at any time while it is located on Dutch territory.[24]

---

20 Ibid. 2.12. Apparently, only two meetings were held in Amsterdam in Sept. and Oct. 2014: one between representatives of the AP and Crimean Museums, and another between the AP and government officials from Ukraine.

21 *Rechtbank Amsterdam* (8 April 2015) Amsterdam District Court, C/13/577586/HA ZA 14-1179, ECLI:NL:RBAMS:2015:2000.

22 Ibid. 4.6, 5.4. According to the Court, the interest of the Dutch State could be better served by the right to a hearing as provided for by art 44 Rv (Dutch Code of Civil Procedure).

23 1954 Protocol.

24 The Dutch system follows the 2004 UN Convention on Jurisdictional Immunities of States and their Property, under which State-owned cultural property enjoys immunity from meas-

In the present case, such letters indeed were issued to the Crimean institutions; however, although such 'letters of comfort' may provide some protection (against attachment by others than the 'foreign state'), they do not provide immunity from lawsuits, at least not in the Dutch situation.[25]

3 The 2016 Amsterdam District Court ruling

The arguments of the three parties – the four Crimean Museums, the Ukrainian State, and the AP Museum – and the Court ruling will be discussed below.[26] In this discussion, the focus will be on the Court's interpretation of the 1970 UNESCO Convention concerning the questions as to what constitutes 'unlawful transfer', and which parties are entitled to make a return claim under the Dutch implementation laws of the UNESCO Conventions.

3.1 The arguments

The opposing parties based their claims for the return of the Crimean objects, summarised (and at points, simplified), on the following arguments. Ukraine claimed legal ownership of the loaned objects on the basis of Ukrainian law, which deems archaeological objects to be state property. In addition, it relied on the 1970 UNESCO Convention and the 1954 Protocol for its international return claim. The Crimean Museums based their claim for the return of the objects on the loan agreement and on their rights of operational management. In their view, this right is stronger than the 'bare' ownership rights Ukraine may have, taking into account the close cultural-historical ties of the objects with the territory and people of Crimea, as well as the principle of the integrity of museum collections. The Crimean institutions, in other words, argued that they are the 'true home' of the archaeological findings as they were discovered and preserved there over time, while Ukraine argued on the basis of its sover-

---

ures of constraint. See 'Temporary Import for Exhibitions' (*Cultural Heritage Inspectorate, Ministry of Education, Culture and Science*) <https://english.inspectie-oe.nl/cultural-goods/temporary-import-of-cultural-goods-for-exhibitions-in-heritage-institutions> accessed 21 April 2017. At some point, the Ukrainian State attached the objects (acc. to 16, pleading notes 5/10/2016 of Mr. P.L. Loeb on behalf of the AP Museum).

25 Cf a US case, *Malewicz v City of Amsterdam* (2007) United States District Court for the District of Columbia, 517 F. Supp. 2d 322, ruling that foreign states lending art to the United States were not *per se* immune from jurisdiction, even if the loaned objects were immune from seizure. In the US in 2016, however, the Foreign Cultural Exchange Jurisdictional Immunity Clarification Act (FCEJICA), or Art Museum Amendment, was passed into law, narrowing the expropriation exception in the FSIA to provide greater immunity from suit for foreign states lending artworks to the United States for temporary exhibit.

26 See n. 3, above.

eign rights over the Crimean territory that the artefacts are part of its national patrimony, protected by international conventional law.

On 14th December 2016, the civil chamber of the Amsterdam District Court held in favour of Ukraine and against the Crimean Museums by relying on the interstate return system as provided for in the 1970 UNESCO Convention. The following issues were discussed in the verdict:

- The obligations imposed by the loan agreement
- Who is legally entitled to the collection(s)?
- How does the 1970 UNESCO Convention and its implementation in the Netherlands apply?

3.2 Contractual obligations in the loan agreement

One of the questions presented to the Court was whether or not the AP Museum was bound by its contractual obligations as to the 'timely return of the exhibits to the museum', given the change in circumstances in Ukraine. The loan agreements clearly spelled out an obligation to return the objects to their specific lending museums. That said, the choice of law clause in the loan agreement made Ukrainian law determinative, and according to Ukrainian Law Article 652 CCU, any agreement can be terminated by the contracting parties in case of a 'material change in circumstances'.[27] A similar provision can be found in Dutch law.

The Dutch Court held that the Crimean annexation was indeed a 'material change in circumstances', justifying the termination of the AP Museum's contractual obligations.[28] The Court – referring as well to its main conclusion that the Ukrainian return request should be honoured (see below, 4.2) – set aside the loan agreement and found that the AP Museum was within its rights not to return the artefacts to the Crimean Museums.

3.3 Title to the artefacts

On the matter of title to the objects, as expected, opinions differ between Ukraine and the Crimean Museums. Ukraine, on the one hand, bases its claim on a Decree of 2nd February 2000 designating the collections of the four Crimean museums as Ukrainian State property.[29] More generally, Ukraine invokes Ukrainian laws vesting ownership of all archaeological finds in the

27 Verdict (n. 1) 4.24, 4.25.
28 Ibid. 4.27.
29 Decree on the Basis of Article 15 Paragraph 13 of the Law of Ukraine on Museum and Museum Affairs (29 June 1995). See Verdict (n. 1) 3.4.

state, one of those being the 2004 Law of Ukraine on Protection of Archaeological Heritage.[30] Underlining this argument is the premise that the secession of Crimea is irrelevant to the legal status of Ukrainian-registered cultural objects.

The Crimean Museums, on the other hand, argue that the matter of title is more complex and the Autonomous Republic of Crimea (ARC), not Ukraine, should be considered to be the owner of the majority of the loaned objects.[31] The ARC has had autonomous status since the foundation of Ukraine as an independent nation in the early 1990s. Moreover, according to the 1996 version of the Ukrainian Constitution, ARC is entitled to autonomously administer its possessions and to keep and use its historical objects. Given that three of the four Crimean Museums were apparently founded by ARC independently, the Crimean Museums believe the ARC should be considered to have title to all the objects other than those from the Sevastopol museum, which was founded by Ukraine. Further, they maintain that Ukraine's 'bare ownership right' over the objects is superseded by the superior rights of the Crimean Museums on the basis of their rights of 'operational management'. Under the previous version of the Ukrainian law, at least until May 2014, the Crimean Museums enjoyed certain *in rem* rights known as 'operational management rights' over the objects in their care. Following the annexation of Crimea, the Ukrainian Ministry of Culture transferred the operational management right over Crimean-based Ukrainian national patrimony to the National Historical Museum of Ukraine.[32] The Crimean Museums contest the legality of this transfer.[33]

Not without significance – and as a reminder that 'national patrimony' is a relative concept – the Russian Federation adopted a law on 4th February 2015, which states that museum collections in Crimea are to be included in the national museum registry of the Russian Federation.[34]

---

30 Under the heading of 'Rights and Duties of Archaeological Researchers' Article 18 reads: 'Finds, received in the result of archaeological research (immovable and movable items, which were connected with the object of archaeological heritage and discovered and documented during archaeological research) are the [sic] state property.' Law of Ukraine on Protection of Archaeological Heritage (Vidomosti of Verkhovna Rada (VVR)) No 26 (2004) 361. UNESCO Database of National Cultural Heritage Laws (*UNESCO*) <http://www.unesco.org/culture/natlaws/media/pdf/ukraine/ua_law_protection_archaelogical_heritage_engtof.pdf> accessed 1 April 2017. Moreover, the Law of Ukraine on Protection of Cultural Heritage (Vidomosti of Verkhovna Rada (VVR)) No 39 (2000) art 17 confirms that all 'archaeological finds' are state property. See UNESCO Database of National Cultural Heritage Laws.

31 Verdict (n. 1) 3.2.

32 Per Order No 292 on Transfer of Museum Objects to the National Historical Museum of Ukraine (13 May 2014). Verdict (n. 1) 2.7.

33 Verdict (n. 1) 3.2.

34 Russian Federal Law on 'Regulation of Relations in the Matter of Culture and Tourism as Related to the Annexation of the Republic of Crimea to the Russian Federation…' (12 February 2015) No 9-FZ. Information provided by Irina Tarsis.

The Court in its December 2016 ruling avoided the issue of ownership. Instead, it limited itself to the question as to whom the AP Museum was obliged to return the objects to on the basis of the Dutch Heritage Act 2016 – the law implementing the 1970 UNESCO Convention in the Netherlands.[35] Questions as to ownership should be decided, according to the Verdict, once these objects have been returned to the state from which they came, as will be elaborated upon below.[36]

3.4 The 1970 UNESCO Convention

Ukraine as well as the Netherlands (and Russia) are States Parties to the 1970 UNESCO Convention and have implemented its principles, albeit in different ways. The Convention is non-self-executing: it needs to be implemented in domestic law, which in the Netherlands took effect with the Implementation Act of 2009 that was replaced by the Dutch Heritage Act 2016.
The aim of the 1970 UNESCO Convention, to which 132 countries are party as of June 2017, was to attain a minimum level of uniform protection against the illicit trafficking of cultural objects and international co-operation and solidarity in doing so.[37] Its rationale, stated in Article 2, is the recognition of the illicit import, export and transfer of ownership of cultural property as 'one of the main causes of the impoverishment of the cultural heritage of the countries of origin'.[38] The Convention's pillars are:

- Adopting protective measures, such as creating national inventories of cultural property (Article 5). (The Museum Fund in Ukraine, for example);
- Control of the movement of cultural property through a system of export certificates and laws prohibiting the import of stolen objects (Articles 6-9). (As Ukraine issued temporary export licences with regard to the Crimean treasures.)
- The interstate return of illicitly transferred cultural property (Articles 3 and 7).

35 The Act Relating to the Combining and Amendment of Rules Regarding Cultural Heritage (9 December 2015) (Dutch Heritage Act) supersedes the earlier Implementation Act of 2009. It applies from 1 July 2016 on; it has not changed regarding the relevant provisions.

36 The court rules that on the basis of Article 1012 RV (Dutch Code of Civil Procedure) legal ownership of a cultural object shall be determined upon return of the cultural object in the country that requested its return by its national laws. Verdict (n. 1) 4.17.

37 I.A. Stamatoudi, *Cultural Property Law and Restitution?: A Commentary to International Conventions and European Union Law* (2011) Edward Elgar Publishing Limited.

38 1970 UNESCO Convention, art 2.

3.4.1 *Unlawful transfer?*

The provisions of the 1970 UNESCO Convention, the product of lengthy negotiations, are very generally, and even, at times, vaguely, phrased. As a consequence, various interpretations can co-exist, such as what exactly falls under the definition of 'illicit' import, export or transfer.[39] This is important, as Ukraine's request for return was based on the argument that the unlawfulness of the situation is created by the non-return of the objects once the export licences had expired, while the way the objects had been sent abroad on a short-term loan and had entered the Netherlands was perfectly legal.

Under Ukraine's implementing legislation for the UNESCO Convention, the expiration of an export licence results in an 'illicit' situation:

> Those cultural values, which were temporarily exported from Ukraine and were not returned in the period provided by the contract, are considered [to have been] unlawfully exported.[40]

The applicable provisions of the Dutch Heritage Act, however, do not provide for the unlawfulness of the situation in case of non-return after a loan abroad. Article 6.7 of the Dutch Heritage Act makes the illicit *import* the sole prerequisite for return:

> The return of cultural property imported into The Netherlands in breach of the prohibition as referred to in Section 6.3 may be claimed [...] by proceedings brought by the State Party from which the property originates or by the party with valid title to such property.[41]

In its December 2016 decision, the Amsterdam District Court concluded on this point that the term 'illicit import' in the Dutch Heritage Act should be interpreted broadly and in such a way as to include a situation where the illegality is created by the non-return after the expiration of the loan contract or export licences. To come to this interpretation, the Court argued that to exclude a situation like the present would be contrary to the aim of the 1970

39 E.g. P.J. O'Keefe, *Protecting Cultural Objects: Before and After 1970* (2017) Institute of Art and Law. See also Stamatoudi (2011) 32-33.

40 Law of Ukraine on Exportation, Importation and Return of Cultural Values (Vidomosti Verkhovna Rada (BBP)) No 48 (1999) art 23: 'Those cultural values, which were temporarily exported from Ukraine and were not returned in the period provided by the contract, are considered unlawfully exported'.

41 Dutch Heritage Act, art 6.7. Article 6.3 reads: 'It is prohibited to import into the Netherlands cultural property which: a) has been removed from the territory of a State Party and is in breach of the provisions adopted by that State Party, in accordance with the objectives of the 1970 UNESCO Convention in respect of the export of cultural property from that State Party or the transfer of ownership of cultural property, or b) has been unlawfully appropriated in a State Party.'

Convention.[42] In addition, the Court drew inspiration from the 2014 European Union Directive on unlawfully removed cultural objects,[43] and the 1995 UNIDROIT Convention,[44] both of which include in their definition of 'unlawfully removed' cultural objects, objects that were not returned at the end of a period of lawful temporary removal. The Court furthermore found it:

> not without importance that according to Ukrainian law [...] objects will be deemed illegally exported if they have not returned after the lapse of time limits mentioned in export licences.[45]

Here the Court implicitly confirmed the view that the *lex originis* should be decisive for the question as to what constitutes 'unlawful transfer' of cultural objects. The country of origin's domestic law governs this matter, with the result that 'illicit export' means that an object which is considered by the country of origin to have been illicitly exported should then be considered to have been 'illicitly imported' if it enters other countries, thereby creating a sufficient basis for return claims under the UNESCO system. For the international protective framework to be successful, recognition of the laws of the country of origin seems a logical precondition. This principle indeed had already been recognised, in 1991 in a Resolution of the *Institut de Droit International*.[46]

For the Crimean case, the District Court found that the non-return of the artefacts after the lapse of the loan agreement – illicit export under Ukrainian

---

42 See 1970 UNESCO Convention, art 2. Note that the 1970 UNESCO itself provides much clarity by stating in Article 7 in very general terms that States Parties undertake, at the request of the States Party of origin, to take appropriate steps to recover and return any such cultural property imported [...]. The Court relied, however, for the interpretation of the 1970 Convention on the scholarly opinion of O'Keefe (2017) and L.P.C. Belder, *The Legal Protection of Cultural Heritage in International Law and Its Implementation in Dutch Law* (Doctoral Thesis, Universiteit Utrecht 2014).

43 European Parliament and Council Directive 2014/60 on the Return of Cultural Objects Unlawfully Removed from the Territory of a Member State and Amending Regulation (EU) No 1024/2012 (Recast, 2014) OJ L 1159, art 2: 'unlawfully removed from the territory of a Member State' means: (a) removed from the territory of a Member State in breach of its rules on the protection of national treasures or in breach of Regulation (EC) No 116/2009; or (b) not returned at the end of a period of lawful temporary removal or any breach of another condition governing such temporary removal.'

44 Convention on Stolen or Illegally Exported Cultural Objects (adopted 24 June 1995) 2421 UNTS 457 (UNIDROIT Convention) art 5.2(2): 'A cultural object which has been temporarily exported from the territory of the requesting State, for purposes such as exhibition, research or restoration, under a permit issued according to its law regulating its export for the purpose of protecting its cultural heritage and not returned in accordance with the terms of that permit shall be deemed to have been illegally exported.'

45 Verdict (n. 1) 4.15.

46 Institut de Droit International, 'Resolution on The International Sale of Works of Art from the Angle of the Protection of the Cultural Heritage' (1991).

law – creates the 'illicit' situation the UNESCO Convention aims to reverse; and the situation of 'illicit import' within the meaning of the Dutch Heritage Act.

3.4.2 *Return claim?*

The next question – of crucial importance in this case – is who can rightfully claim the return of cultural objects that are unlawfully retained in the Netherlands? On this point, Article 6.7 of the Dutch Heritage Act states that return may be claimed by 'the State Party from which the property originates *or* by the party with valid title to such property', seemingly facilitating return claims by states as well as non-State Parties. This possibility for non-state deprived owners 'with a valid title', as laid down in Article 6.7 of the Dutch Heritage Act, arises out of the 1995 UNIDROIT Convention – aimed at harmonisation of the principles laid down in the 1970 UNESCO Convention. Whilst the Netherlands signed but did not ratify the 1995 Convention, the Dutch legislator nevertheless chose to implement some of its principles into Dutch law.[47]

The Dutch Court, on this point, ruled that, in the event of concurring claims between a state that listed the objects as protected cultural patrimony and a third party, the question of ownership will be suspended and the return claim of the state will have priority.[48] The question of title and ownership should be left open and decided upon after their return in the requesting state, in this case Ukraine. For this, the Court invoked Article 1012 of the Dutch Code of Civil Procedure stating that 'ownership of the cultural object that is subject to a return request by a State Party will be decided upon *after* return by the national laws of the state that claimed for its return'.[49]

Prioritising claims of a sovereign state may well be in line with the UNESCO principles – based as they are on a system of protection in national patrimony laws. However, it raises the question what are the possibilities for deprived owners, not being national states, to claim their artefacts. What is the legal force of cultural rights of parties, other than sovereign states, like individuals or communities? This issue will be touched on below in section 4.

47 See the Explanatory Memorandum to the Implementing Act 1970 UNESCO Convention (Parliamentary Documents, Kamerstuk 31255, No 3, 2007-2008).

48 Verdict (n. 1) 4.8, 4.16, 4.17. Conform Dutch scholarly opinion on the relevant provisions, see AIM van Mierlo and CJJC van Nispen, *Tekst & Commentaar, Burgerlijke Rechtsvordering* (2014) Wolters Kluwer.

49 Article 1012 Rv [Dutch Code of Civil Procedure] implements Article 13 of Directive 2014/60/EU (n. 43). However, it differs slightly from the EU provision which reads: 'Ownership of the cultural object after return shall be governed by the law of the requesting Member State.'

3.5 The verdict

In its decision of 14th December 2016, the District Court found in favour of Ukraine and held the following:

- the loan agreement between the Crimean Museums and the AP Museum is dissolved;
- the AP Museum shall transfer the loaned objects to the National Historical Museum of Ukraine in Kiev in its capacity as custodian of the Crimean objects designated by the Ukrainian State;
- pending an appeal, the artefacts shall remain in storage at the AP Museum;
- Ukraine shall pay storage and insurance costs to the AP Museum.[50]

As noted above, in January 2017, the Crimean Museums lodged an appeal.[51]

4 Discussion of alternative approaches

The outcome of the case confirms the view that the system of the 1970 UNESCO Convention for cross-border return claims is an interstate affair, with a focus on the protection of national interests. Might there have been other approaches?

4.1 The 1954 Hague Convention

Surprisingly, the 1954 Hague Convention is not mentioned in the verdict. Given the fact that this Convention and its Protocol are specifically aimed at situations of armed conflict and occupation, Netherlands and Ukraine are both parties and its principles are generally considered as binding customary international law, one may wonder why not.[52]

The central provision is that states 'undertake to prohibit, prevent and, if necessary, put a stop to any form of theft, pillage or misappropriation of,

50 Verdict (n. 1) 4.20, 5.

51 According to the representative of Ukraine, G.J. van den Bergh, the case was scheduled for 'Grieven' (complaint by the Crimean Museums) in the summer of 2017.

52 On the customary international law status, see, for example, W.W. Kowalski, *Art Treasures and War* (1998) Institute of Art and Law; Stamatoudi (2011) 235; A. Chechi, *The Settlement of International Cultural Heritage Disputes* (2014) Oxford University Press, 258; Jakubowski (2015) 265. It is problematic in this context that the Russian Federation does not accept these principles, and adopted the Law on Removed Cultural Property (Federal Law on Cultural Valuables Displaced to the U.S.S.R. as a Result of the Second World War and Located on the Territory of the Russian Federation (1998) No 64-FZ). The Law declares to be the property of the Russian Federation all cultural valuables located in the territory of the Russian Federation that were brought into the USSR following the Second World War by way of exercise of the right of the USSR to compensatory restitution.

and any acts of vandalism directed against, cultural property', and 'shall refrain from requisitioning movable cultural property situated in the territory of another High Contracting Party.'[53] According to the 1954 Protocol, states should take into custody cultural property from occupied territories until the situation has stabilised, with the aim of ensuring its safe return to that territory, and cultural property 'shall never be retained as war reparations'.[54] The reasoning behind this is that cultural objects have a protected status and should not be used as hostages in a conflict. In the much-cited words of Justice Croke in 1813 (by which he released artefacts seized during the Anglo-American war):

> The same law of nations, which prescribes that all property belonging to the enemy shall be liable to confiscation, has likewise its modifications and relaxations of that rule. The arts and sciences are admitted amongst all civilized nations, as forming an exception to the severe rights of warfare, and as entitled to favour and protection. They are considered not as the peculium of this or that nation, but as the property of mankind at large, and as belonging to the common interests of the whole species.[55]

It could be argued that application of the 1954 Protocol would, in the short term, not produce more favourable results for the Crimean institutions. Like the 1970 UNESCO Convention, it creates obligations between sovereign states, leaving entities like the museums or the Crimean Autonomous Republic as outsiders. That said, the Dutch authorities would seem to be in a position to 'help out', by taking the objects in custody for safekeeping with a view to their eventual return upon cessation of hostilities to the territory they came from. Moreover, the Dutch Heritage Act, implementing the 1954 Protocol, prohibits the *possession* of cultural property from occupied territory – implicating that the question whether the object is unlawfully acquired or imported is irrelevant.[56] If 'there is a reasonable suspicion that the prohibition … has been

53 1954 Hague Convention, Art 4.

54 1954 Protocol, art 1(2): 'Each High Contracting Party undertakes to take into its custody cultural property imported into its territory either directly or indirectly from any occupied territory. This shall either be effected automatically upon the importation of the property or, failing this, at the request of the authorities of that territory', art 1(3): 'Each High Contracting Party undertakes to return, at the close of hostilities, to the competent authorities of the territory previously occupied, cultural property which is in its territory, if such property has been exported in contravention of the principle laid down in the first paragraph. Such property shall never be retained as war reparations.'

55 Judge Crook ordered the release of the *Marquis de Somerueles*, a vessel filled with artefacts seized in the war between the US and the UK. *The Marquis de Somerueles*: Vice-Admiralty Court of Halifax, Nova Scotia Stewart's Vice-Admiralty Reports 482 (1813), cited by J.H. Merryman, 'Note on The Marquis de Somerueles' (1996) 5 *International Journal of Cultural Property* 321.

56 In this way, no proof is necessary as to the unlawful *acquisition* by the current possessor. Any acquisition before 2007 (the year the 1954 Protocol was implemented in the Nether-

contravened, our Minister shall take into custody the cultural property concerned.'[57]

In fact, this is what happened (after some detours), in a case concerning the return of four Cypriot icons by the Netherlands to Cyprus in 2013.

4.1.1 2013 Dutch return of Cypriot icons

The icons, removed from the Greek Orthodox church of Christ Antiphonitis in Lefkosia in Northern Cyprus, were found in the possession of a Dutch private collector, who had bought them in 1975, shortly after the occupation of Northern Cyprus and their disappearance from the Church. The icons were attached by the Church upon discovery in 1995; however, at that point a civil action seeking their return before the Dutch courts was unsuccessful.[58]

The main reason for this was that the 1954 Hague Protocol which, although ratified by the Netherlands in 1958, had never been implemented in Dutch law. As a consequence, the ownership claim by the Church was time-barred under regular Dutch property law, as that law provides for a general limitation period for any right of action of twenty years.[59] And although concerns were raised about the collector's good-faith on acquiring the icons, the Appeal Court did not deal with those, stating that even if it was proven that the collector was in bad faith,[60] such a circumstance would not affect the outcome. The absolute twenty-year term, according to the Court, runs independently of the possible bad faith of the holder,[61] and since the icons had disappeared in March 1975 the claim was time-barred just months before their attachment

lands) may well have been legitimate. A discussion of those rules can be found in n. 59, below.

57 Dutch Heritage Act, sections 6.10, 6.11. Section 6.11: 'Where there is a reasonable suspicion that the prohibition in Section 6.10 has been contravened, Our Minister shall take into custody the cultural property concerned [..] at his own volition at the time of the importation [...]; or at the request of the authorities of the relevant occupied territory or previously occupied territory.' In case of competing return claims based on the 1970 Convention and on the 1954 Protocol, the return claim based on the 1954 Protocol would seem to have priority, a view based on Article 24 of the 1954 Hague Convention. See Explanatory Memorandum to the Implementing Act 1970 UNESCO Convention.

58 *Autocephalous Greek Orthodox Church in Cyprus v Lans* (2002) Court of Appeal of the Hague, Case No. 99/693.

59 Dutch 'regular' law is far-reaching in its protection of new possessors of stolen goods, as a result of provisions on title transfer following a *bona fide* acquisition (Dutch Civil Code 3:86), and relatively short limitation periods for ownership claims: Article 3:306 DCC provides for a general limitation period of twenty years for all rights of action, also for a right based on ownership (revindication), moreover, after that period a possessor will gain ownership title irrespective of his or her good faith (DCC 3:105).

60 Something that would not easily be assumed, as appears from the earlier District Court's verdict in the case; NJK 1999, 37: Rb. Rotterdam (1999) No 44053/HA ZA 96-2403.

61 For this Dutch stance on losses predating the 2007 and 2009 Implementation Acts of the 1954 Protocol and 1970 Convention, see also *Land Sachsen* (1998) HR, Case No. 16546, C97/025 (Dutch Supreme Court).

in 1995. This controversial outcome – in the light of the fact the Netherlands signed the 1954 Protocol as early as 1958 – was one of the factors for the Dutch Government to speed up implementation.

Following that implementation in 2007 and an official request for their return from the Cypriot authorities in 2011, the Dutch authorities arranged for the acquisition of the icons from the collector (as discussed above, the legitimate owner under Dutch law) and their return to Cyprus in September 2013.[62] Two points are of interest within the present context. Their restitution to the Government of the recognised Republic of Cyprus was on the understanding that they would eventually return to the Church in Lefkosia: in the words of the Cypriot statement upon the presentation of the case at UNESCO headquarters 'their journey will only end when they finally occupy their original and rightful place in the iconostasis of the Church of Antiphonitis'.[63] Another point of interest is that the icons were returned through diplomatic channels after the initial failure of civil litigation. The first point – interests beyond those of a national state – will be touched upon in section 2, and the second point – as to what procedures are available – in section 3.

4.2 Interests beyond the national state: a 'genuine link'?

Returning to the Crimean Gold case: the 2016 Amsterdam District Court ruling highlights that the international legal framework does not address issues that are at the heart of this case, such as partition of a country or disconnect between the territorial or cultural-historical link of the object to (groups of) people(s). That framework, based on the UNESCO Conventions, provides for a system of interstate co-operation and is based on the premise that national states are key 'right holders' to cultural heritage. In the majority of cases, this will work efficiently but, on occasion, it may be to the detriment of other interests, including groups who do not believe themselves to be represented by their former national government.[64] A question that surfaces in this regard

62 According to the mutual presentation of the return case at the 10th meeting of the High Contracting Parties to the Hague Convention on 16 December 2013 in Paris, the case was the first return in the world under application of the First Protocol, see 'Mutual Presentation of Cyprus and the Netherlands on the Return of 4 Icons from the Netherlands to Cyprus under the Protocol of the Hague Convention of 1954', 10th meeting of the High Contracting Parties to the Hague Convention (16 December 2013) <http://www.unesco.org/culture/laws/1954/NL-Cyprus-4icons_en>.

63 Ibid.

64 Perhaps exactly because of this 'gap' in the legal framework, a parallel system of soft-law signals a trend that confirms the rights of communities or individuals – i.e. non-state actors – to *their* cultural heritage. Two well-defined categories would be: (i) rights of indigenous peoples to their lost cultural heritage – as included in the United Nations Declaration on the Rights of Indigenous Peoples; and (ii) rights of deprived private owners of Nazi-con-

is what elements could create a 'genuine link' to prioritise interests in cultural objects.

4.2.1 *Territoriality and cultural-historical link*

In that regard, it is worthwhile to reflect first of all on the meaning and scope of the notion of 'country of origin' in the UNESCO conventions. Article 4 of the 1970 Convention sets out five categories of objects that can qualify as protected national cultural objects,[65] all with a clear hint to territoriality as a necessary link between the object and national protection.[66] Archaeological objects like the Crimean treasures would logically fall under Article 4(b), as these are objects that form an integral part of the state's soil.[67] Arguably, this would mean that protection may be granted only to objects emanating from soil within the national borders over which the state has effective control.[68] That, however, is precisely the problem in the dispute under review; effective control over the Crimean territory is presently not with the Ukrainian State, and, moreover, historically it had not been so either.

In 1991 the Institute of International Law clarified the question of what should be understood as the 'country of origin' in return requests. For the purpose of protection of cultural heritage 'The country of origin of a work of art means the country with which the property is most closely linked from the cultural point of view'.[69] Return claims based on the national patrimony argument should, in other words, be seen in relation to a genuine link from a cultural-historical point of view. Obviously, a case like the Crimean Gold case, where national borders are contested and still unclear, pose a challenge to the UNESCO system; a system where protection is based on interstate co-

fiscated art – based on the Washington Conference Principles of 1998, promoting 'fair and just' solutions to ownership claims.

65 1970 UNESCO Convention, art 4: 'property which belongs to the following categories forms part of the cultural heritage of each State: (a) cultural property created by the individual or collective genius of nationals of the State concerned, and cultural property of importance to the State concerned created within its territory of that State by foreign nationals or stateless persons resident within such territory; (b) cultural property found within the national territory.' Categories in sections (c)-(e) furthermore name objects acquired or exchanged with the consent of the country of origin.

66 Stamatoudi (2011) 38. See also M. Cornu and M.A. Renold, 'New Developments in the Restitution of Cultural Property: Alternative Means of Dispute Resolution' (2010) 17 *International Journal of Cultural Property* 1, 16-17, giving examples such as historical archives, objects of sacred or symbolic value, objects found in archaeological excavations, elements removed from monuments. See also Jakubowski (2015); Chechi (2014).

67 Stamatoudi (2011) 39.

68 Unless of course those objects were earlier acquired by the claiming state in accordance with the provisions of Article 4(c)-(d) of the 1970 Convention.

69 In its 'Resolution on The International Sale of Works of Art from the Angle of the Protection of the Cultural Heritage' (n. 46).

operation. The just outcome of such cases will obviously, ultimately, depend on political will, as can be illustrated by the following case example.

4.2.2 *Case examples*

– *Pechory Treasure*

A case with similarities to the Crimean Gold case is the return of the so-called Pechory Treasure to a Russian-Orthodox monastery in May 1973.[70] The story behind it is that of the return 'home' of the treasures of the Orthodox Pskovo-Pechersky Dormition Monastery in Pechory ('Petserin' in Estonian and 'Petschur' in German), in Russia, in an area that borders Estonia. It used to be under independent Estonian rule, however had been under Russian control since 1945. The Treasure – ecclesiastical objects and secular objects related to the history of the Monastery – was taken by Nazi officials in 1945 in anticipation of the advancing Russian army. It was discovered in the early 1970s, having been kept for decades in the storage area of a German museum, away from the public eye, by a German researcher.[71] At that point, a return claim was voiced by the Monastery (as well as by the Estonian World Council in exile). After lengthy discussions on the legal implications of the case with a focus on the Baltic question (the non-recognition of Soviet rule over Estonian and other Baltic territory by Western European nations), the Treasure was returned directly to the Monastery by the authorities of the German Federal Republic. This, after the formal consent by Soviet authorities, in effective control over the territory, constituted an acknowledgement that the Treasure would remain in the Monastery.[72]

In that sense, the return may be compared to the present dispute as in both instances the implicit recognition of an unrecognised state loomed around the corner as an unwanted side-effect of any act of restitution. In the German-Estonian-Soviet case of the Pechory Treasure a solution was found – and the politically sensitive issue of the 'Baltic question' was avoided – by the restitution of the objects directly to the Monastery. This, thanks perhaps to a moment of *détente* in international relations.

---

70 I am much indebted to Ulrike Schmiegelt for bringing the case up in her paper 'A Hostage of the Cold War? The Return of the Monastery Treasure of Pechory' at the conference 'From Refugees to Restitution: The History of Nazi Looted Art in the UK in Transnational Perspective' (Cambridge, May 2017), and for her efforts and time to assist me in the archival research. I refer to her paper for general information on the case.

71 Report of the German Consul in Leningrad Following the Ceremonial Return (1973) Political Archive of the German Foreign Ministry, B 86, Bd 1596.

72 Ibid. According to a report by the Max Planck Institute for International Law in Heidelberg in this file, the Soviet Union was legally entitled to the Treasure, irrespective of the (non)-recognition of the annexation of Estonian territory by the Soviet Union. The official transfer, however, was in a deed signed by German and Church authorities. A claim by the Estonian Council in exile was denied; written consent had been given by Soviet authorities that the objects would remain in the Monastery.

– *Peace treaties*

State practice honouring the cultural-historical link principle can also be found in various bilateral or multilateral peace treaties.[73] The Treaty of Saint-Germain of 1919, for example, arranging for the division of the Austrian Empire, enabled the return of objects that were to be considered 'intellectual patrimony' of a given territory, to 'their districts of origin'.[74] Another famous example is the return of the leaves of the triptych of the *Mystic Lamb* by the Van Eyck brothers to Belgium after the First World War, taken by Germany in what appears to have been a perfectly legal transaction, as arranged for in the Treaty of Versailles.[75]

– *Intrastate returns*

Contemporary examples of intrastate returns are, for example, the UK/Scottish disagreement regarding the *Lewis Chess Men case* – A longstanding debate over where the figures, most of which are in the British Museum in London, belong[76] – and the *Ancient manuscripts and Globe case* between Saint Gall and Zurich in Switzerland.[77] In this last case, a creative solution was found honouring the cultural-historical link – not focusing on the ownership issue –, by means of a long-term loan and the production of a replica of the Globe for the other location.

– *Korean Buseok Temple Case (2017)*

A last example that is worth mentioning is a case presently under litigation in South Korea. It concerns contesting claims to a fourteenth-century bronze statue that was stolen from a Buddhist temple on the Japanese island of Tsushima in 2012, however originating from a Korean temple. As Japan and

73 Nudelman (2015) 1285-1290 discusses this point and names many examples. See also Jakubowski (2015); Kowalski (1998). P.S. Goodwin, 'Mapping the Limits of Repatriable Cultural Heritage: A Case Study of Stolen Flemish Art in French Museums' (2008) 157 *University of Pennsylvania Law Review* 673.

74 Treaty of Peace Between the Principal Allied and Associated Powers and Austria Together With Protocol and Declarations, Saint-Germain-en-Laye (adopted 10 September 1919, entered into force 8 November 1921) 226 CTS 8, art 196: 'objects of artistic, archaeological, scientific or historic character forming part of the [imperial] collections' could 'form part of the intellectual patrimony of the ceded districts', and 'may be returned to their districts of origin'. A.F. Vrdoljak, 'Enforcement of Restitution of Cultural Heritage through Peace Agreements' in F. Francioni and J. Gordley (eds) *Enforcing International Cultural Heritage Law* (2013) Oxford University Press, 35.

75 Treaty of Versailles (adopted 28 June 1919) 225 CTS 188, art 247.

76 About the long-term loan of six of the Lewis Chessman, see 'Lewis Chessmen' (*The British Museum*) <https://www.britishmuseum.org/about_us/news_and_press/statements/the_lewis_chessmen.aspx> accessed 8 August 2017.

77 A settlement regarding manuscripts looted during the religious wars in eighteenth-century Switzerland. A.L. Bandle, R. Contel and M.A. Renold, 'Case Note – Ancient Manuscripts and Globe – Saint-Gall and Zurich' (2012) Platform ArThémis, Art-Law Centre, University of Geneva.

South Korea both ratified and implemented the 1970 UNESCO Convention, a return claim by Japan regarding the other artefacts that were part of the same theft from Tsushima, *was* honoured in 2013. Pending the claim from Japan for the return of the specific bronze statue, however, the South-Korean Buseok Temple also filed a claim for its return. The statue apparently originated from the Buseok Temple from where it had disappeared centuries ago.[78] In its January 2017 ruling the South-Korean Daejon District Court decided that that statue should indeed be returned not to Japan but to the Buseok Temple 'considering the historical and religious value of the statue'. The Court found it sufficiently proven that the statue originated from the Temple – given a historic document inside the statue which mentioned its origin -, while it was common knowledge that the territory had been invaded by Japanese military in the fourteenth century.[79] Similarly to the Dutch Crimean case but from a different angle, this case highlights questions that are not answered with the 1970 UNESCO Convention.

Although at points different from the Crimean case, in all these examples the cultural interests of (public) entities other than the national state – such as monasteries, churches or communities – were at stake.

4.3 Alternative dispute resolution

A further question is how to resolve disputes by finding lasting solutions that can take account of the cultural interests that are at stake. Within the context of cultural heritage claims, adversarial litigation procedures are generally considered a last option, to be entered into only after good-faith negotiations and alternative dispute resolution (ADR) methods failed. This, precisely because certain interests are not covered by the present legal regime.

In that sense, the Operational Guidelines to the 1970 UNESCO Convention, adopted in May 2015, recognise that the Convention does not always provide answers, and suggest ADR to settle claims:

> The Convention does not attempt to establish priorities where more than one state may regard a cultural object as part of its cultural heritage. Competing claims to such items, if they cannot be settled by negotiations between the states or their relevant institutions [...], should be regulated by out of court resolution mechanisms,

78 Report by E.A. Heath, 'Korean Court Rules Statue Stolen from Japan Can Remain in the Country (January 26, 2017)' (2017) *American Society of International Law* <https://www.asil.org/blogs/korean-court-rules-statue-stolen-japan-can-remain-country-january-26-2017> accessed 10 August 2017.

79 *Daejeon District Court, 2017.1.26 Judgment 2016Ga* Hap102119 'Transfer of physical movables'. See Section II. My colleague Jinyoung Choi from Leiden University kindly translated the relevant parts for me.

> such as mediation [...] or good offices, or by arbitration. There is no strong tradition for the judicial settlement of such differences in cultural matters. State practice would suggest a preference for mechanisms that allow consideration for legal, as well as cultural, historical and other relevant factors.[80]

In 2009, also the International Law Association promoted ADR methods for resolving cultural heritage disputes in the 'Principles for Cooperation in the Mutual Protection and Transfer of Cultural Material'.[81] Similarly, in his draft for 'Guiding Principles Relating to the Succession of States in Respect of Tangible Cultural Heritage', Jakubowski proposes ADR methods to resolve claims on the basis of his analysis of state practice, legal doctrine and the tendencies detected.[82] In these draft Principles the use of equitable principles and alternative dispute resolution is promoted with regard to the settlement of disputes that result from a change of borders of a national state, for example as a result of dissolution of a state or war:[83]

> In case of disagreement, the states ... are encouraged to bring their disputes before impartial arbitration or mediation commissions. The expert assistance of UNESCO is strongly recommended.

Obviously, ADR in all forms should not be seen as a *panacea* for complicated legal issues. Negotiation or mediation procedures are generally guided by party interests and not by principles of justice and the outcome of such procedures, as Shyllon points out, will depend on the bargaining chips brought to the table by parties that may not be equally powerful.[84] The role of lawyers, therefore, remains to find 'just' solutions based on the interpretation of existing legal

---

80 'Operational Guidelines for the Implementation of the Convention on the Means of Prohibiting and Preventing the Illicit Import, Export and Transfer of Ownership of Cultural Property (UNESCO, Paris, 1970)' (2015) 2015) C70/15/3.MSP/11 (UNESCO Operational Guidelines) para 19.

81 As reproduced in J.A.R. Nafziger, 'The Principles for Cooperation in the Mutual Protection and Transfer of Cultural Material' (2007) 8 *Chicago Journal of International Law* 147.

82 Jakubowski (2015) Annex, 321. The draft principles can be seen as an analysis of state practice and relevant legal doctrine and the 'promising tendencies' detected by Jakubowski in his extensive research of state practice.

83 In the first Principle the scope is defined as 'to provide general guidance for bilateral or multilateral interstate negotiations in order to facilitate the conclusion of agreements related to movable and immovable cultural property, following succession of States.' Under 1(d) this is further refined by stating that it aims at situations like the present, being 'the property, which is situated in the territory to which the succession of States relates, or having originated from said territory, was displaced to a different location by the predecessor State'.

84 F. Shyllon, 'The Rise of Negotiation (ADR) in Restitution, Return and Repatriation of Cultural Property: Moral Pressure and Power Pressure' (2017) 22 *Art Antiquity and Law* 130-142.

rules or developing new ones, as well as on the development of neutral and transparent alternative procedures if litigation would be considered inadequate.

5 Conclusion

In the 2016 verdict, the Dutch Court held, unsurprisingly perhaps, that the Allard Pierson Museum should return the artefacts to Ukraine and not to the Crimean Museums. The ruling confirms that the international legal framework – based on the UNESCO Conventions – is still firmly anchored in the idea that national states are the main right holders of cultural heritage. Consequently, it is up to national authorities to pass the objects on to other possible stake-holders. Usually that will work adequately. In cases where a national government is not in a position (or not willing) to represent the interest of such right holders, however, tensions in that framework will be noticeable, as in the present case.

Where, one may wonder, does this leave the rights and interests of non-state actors like local communities, minorities or individual victims of human rights violations, to 'their' cultural heritage? The principle of territoriality – over nationality – seems on itself an accepted notion in cultural heritage law and could benefit sub-state right holders. Such rights, however, are also increasingly acknowledged in soft law instruments – such as the UNDRIP recognising indigenous peoples' rights to cultural heritage, and the Washington Principles recognising rights of individual former owners to Nazi-confiscated art. This development may even signal the coming into existence of a right for former owners to 'their' cultural objects under international (human rights) law.[85] Although the content of that right may be far from clear as yet, an important point is the acknowledgement of the intangible interests of cultural heritage for certain (groups of) people, beyond being a commodity or state property.[86]

A non-formalistic approach – alternative procedures – to settle such disputes, as advocated in various soft law instruments to bridge this 'gap' in the international legal framework, was a path *not* taken yet in the Crimean Gold case. Neither was the path taken as set out in the 1954 Hague Protocol to take the objects in custody for safekeeping – with an eye at their return to Crimea after cessation of hostilities. Perhaps those paths are still open. A solution similar to that in the Pechory case might be an example of a solution that proved effective under similar conditions. In that case, upon their return a

85 International Covenant on Economic, Social and Cultural Rights (adopted 16 December 1966) 993 UNTS 3, art 15 para 1(a).

86 See e.g. F. Shaheed, 'Report of the Independent Expert in the Field of Cultural Rights, Submitted Pursuant to Resolution 10/23 of the Human Rights Council' (22 March 2010) UN Doc A/HRC/14/36.

guarantee was given by the (non-recognised) Soviet authorities that controlled the area *de facto* at the time, that the Pechory treasure would remain *in situ* at the Monastery in Estonia, as the place with the closest cultural-historical ties. Admittedly, given the political context, this might be a challenge in the current time frame.

6 Addendum (April 2021): Interlocutory Judgment Amsterdam Courts of Appeals

On 16 July 2019, the Amsterdam Court of Appeals gave an interlocutory judgment in the appeals procedure.[87] In this ruling, the court rejected the opinion of the District Court that the 1970 UNESCO Convention covers the dispute. In the view of the Court of Appeals the failure to return the Crimean treasures cannot be qualified as unlawful behaviour the 1970 UNESCO Convention aims to address, and neither does the Dutch implementation law allow for such an extensive interpretation.[88] Instead, it qualified the case as a matter of title and private law.

According to Dutch international private law rules, Ukrainian law should be applied to clarify the matter which party is entitled to the objects, the Ukrainian State or the Crimean museums. In that context, the court asked the parties to provide further information to clarify the claim to ownership title by the Ukrainian State and entitlement to the objects by the Crimean museums in terms of their rights to 'operational management' under Ukrainian law.[89]

The court did not (yet) confirm the District Court's view that the loan contracts are void. Nevertheless, it ruled that, pending the outcome of the appeal the AP Museum is within its rights not to return the artefacts to the Crimean Museums. The appeal verdict is pending at the time of writing.[90]

87 *The Travida Central Museum, the Kerch Historical and Cultural Preserve, the Bakhchisaray History and Cultural State Preserve of the Republic of Crimea, the National Preserve of 'Tauric Chersonesos' v the State of Ukraine v University of Amsterdam* (Judgment of 16 July 2019) Amsterdam Court of Appeal, Case No. 200.212.377/01, ECLI:NL:GHAMS:2019:2427 (2019 Ruling).

88 Overruling the legal opinion of Patrick O'Keefe. See 2019 Ruling (n. 87) 4.13-4.32.

89 2019 Ruling (n. 87), ad 4.44.

90 January 2021.

4 Claims to Nazi-looted art

ABSTRACT

Over the last two decades, rules that support restitution of artefacts lost as a result of Nazi looting have gained impetus. In that regard, the 1998 Washington Principles on Nazi-Confiscated Art set the international standard that: 'if the pre-war owners of art that is found to have been confiscated by the Nazis and not subsequently restituted, or their heirs, can be identified, steps should be taken expeditiously to achieve a just and fair solution, recognising this may vary according to the facts and circumstances surrounding a specific case'. Positive law, however, is often not in line with such soft-law standards: post-War restitution laws have mostly expired; national ownership regulations vary widely and usually do not support claims based on a loss so long ago; and, besides, treaties aimed at harmonisation are non-retroactive. As a result, parties looking for 'justice' before a court of law often find themselves in a position where claims are inadmissible. In a reaction to the Washington Principles, several European countries installed advisory committees to deal with claims to Nazi-looted art, each with its own approach but often with a limited mandate. In the meantime, an increasing number of cases are being brought before American courts. Taking account of this 'institutional vacuum' in most European jurisdictions, this chapter argues in favour of a cross-border solution.

Questions addressed in this chapter are: How was restitution of Nazi-looted art arranged in the post-War period, and how is it arranged in today's system of the Washington Principles? In addition, what are the consequences of the differences between the 'legal' model in the US and the 'ethical' model in Western Europe?

*Nazi-looted art: A note in favour of clear standards and neutral procedures**

1 Introduction

In November 2017 the Paris Tribunal de Grande Instance held that the painting *La Cueillette des Pois* ('Pea Harvest') by Camille Pissarro, in the possession of an American couple who had sent it on a short-term loan to Paris, was to be returned in ownership to the heirs of the Jewish art collector Simon Bauer whose collection had been confiscated in 1943.[1] They welcomed the verdict as pure justice: 'I think the French court has applied the natural law.'[2] The American collector, however, had acquired the Pissarro a Christie's in 1995, reportedly for $800,000, unaware of its wartime history. Their discontent with the outcome was voiced as: 'It surely is not up to [us] to compensate Jewish families for the crimes of the Holocaust'.[3] This case may illustrate the clash of interests that may be at stake in cases that concern Nazi-looted art that no longer is in the hands of the 'perpetrator'. Usually, such cases are *not* settled in a court of law but in extra-legal procedures. This chapter will analyse the question how this field is regulated: what are the international standards for Nazi-looted art?[4]

Such standards exist at the interstate level: the obligation to return cultural objects taken during armed conflict to the state from which they came from

* In its original form this Chapter was published in *Art Antiquity and Law*, Vol. XXII, Issue 4/2017, in January 2018. For the purpose of this dissertation, it has been slightly amended, mostly to take account of new developments and new rulings in ongoing cases.

1 *Bauer et al v B and R Toll* (2017) Tribunal de Grande Instance de Paris, No RG 17/58735 No 1/FF ; confirmed by the Cour de Cassation (2019), No B 18-25.695. In 2020, the representative of the US owners announced the case was brought before the ECtHR for infringement of their right to property, see <https://www.theartnewspaper.com/news/pissarro-european-court>.

2 A. Quinn, 'French Court Orders Return of Pissarro Looted by Vichy Government' (8 November 2017) *The New York Times* <https://www.nytimes.com/2017/11/08/arts/design/french-court-pissarro-looted-nazis.html?searchResultPosition=1> accessed 16 January 2019.

3 Ibid. Words of parties' representatives (Ron Soffer for defendants, Cedric Fischer for claimants) as cited in the New York Times article.

4 NB The term 'Nazi-looted art' can be used for various types of losses of cultural objects during the Second World War, see section 2, below.

is well-accepted under international law.[5] The focus of this chapter, however, will not be on interstate claims, but on the position of private (non-sate) parties. This position was addressed in the 1998 Washington Conference Principles on Nazi-confiscated Art, a non-binding declaration signed by over 40 governments that introduced the standard that former owners or their heirs are entitled to a 'just and fair solution', 'depending on the circumstances' with regard to Nazi-confiscated art that had not been restituted to them earlier.[6] Whilst in 1998 the focus was primarily on claims by family members of Jewish Holocaust victims to unclaimed confiscated artefacts that were found in museum or state collections, today the array has grown much wider. Nazi-looted art may surface in any collection, and claims are also no longer limited to art that was confiscated by the Nazis. They may concern artefacts lost to others than the Nazis, or sold by refugees in a neutral country: so-called *Fluchtgut* ('escape-goods'). These developments are an indication that norms are evolving. The question is, in what direction?

International practice today is typified by inconsistent outcomes and untransparent procedures. Often cases are settled – works are 'cleared' – in (confidential) agreements. However understandable from the perspective of the parties, a lack of publicly available argued decisions hinders the development of a consistent, predictable and understandable set of norms. It is desirable for similar cases to be treated similarly (and different cases differently), but in order to do so one must agree on which relevant circumstances need to be similar. The soft-law norm prescribing 'just and fair' solutions is open and still unsettled, which means that there is a need for precedents to further develop that norm. Parties looking for 'justice' before a court of law, however, will often find that claims are inadmissible: the expiration of post-War restitution laws, limitation periods for claims or adverse possession, are reasons for this.[7] Whilst several Western European countries have established special committees to advise on these claims, their mandate is limited.[8] That leaves

5 Interstate restitution as reparations for violations of the laws of war. On the development of this norm, see A.F. Vrdoljak, 'Enforcement of Restitution of Cultural Heritage through Peace Agreements' in F. Francioni and J. Gordley (eds) *Enforcing International Cultural Heritage Law* (2013) Oxford University Press. See section 2, below.

6 Washington Conference Principles on Nazi-Confiscated Art (3 December 1998) Released in connection with the Washington Conference on Holocaust-Era Assets, Washington, DC (Washington Principles) Principle VIII. See citation in section 3.1, below.

7 On post-war restitution laws, E. Campfens, 'Sources of Inspiration: Old and New Rules for Looted Art' in E. Campfens (ed) *Fair and Just Solutions? Alternatives to Litigation in Nazi-Looted Art Disputes* (2015) Eleven International Publishing, 16-27. For the Dutch post-war restitution system, see L. van Vliet, 'The Dutch Postwar Restoration of Rights Regime Regarding Movable Property' (2019) 87 Legal History Review, 651. For an overview of obstacles to restitution, see B. Schönenberger, *The Restitution of Cultural Assets* (2009) Eleven International Publishing, ch 4.

8 See section 4, below.

the second important question open: who is to monitor compliance and explain the norm as propagated since 1998?

This chapter is structured as follows. For a better understanding of the legal setting section 2 starts with an overview of the post-War efforts to restore dispossessed owners in their rights. The third section proceeds to address the material norm and its rationale as it is applied in today's practice based on the Washington Principles, with a focus on the question what qualifies as unjustified Nazi-looting. For that, a closer look at the notion of a 'forced sale' in international practice in various jurisdictions is needed: what is at the heart of this notion and what are its limits? The fourth section analyses the question how compliance with the norm is arranged. The Washington Principles, along with later soft-law instruments in the field, highlight the importance of an extra-legal 'moral' approach and alternative dispute resolution (ADR) to settle claims. However, what (alternative) procedures are available? In this regard, differences between the US and Western European jurisdictions will be addressed. The last section of this chapter contains a recommendation on how the institutional vacuum in Western Europe in terms of access to justice could be addressed.

2 Post-War restitution system

That the Nazi government looted works of art on a vast and systematic scale arguably lies at the base of the special treatment of Nazi-looted art claims. Nazi policy differed from country to country, but the overall objective was to obtain as much 'desirable' art as possible to reinforce the hegemony of the Third Reich. The methods of acquiring artefacts can be divided in (i) seizure or acquisition of private collections in the context of racial persecution, from own citizens as well as in occupied territories (i.e. this mostly concerned Jewish art collections); (ii) pillage of public art collections in occupied territories, mostly in Eastern European countries, and (iii) acquisition of artefacts on the art market in western 'Aryan' neighbouring countries.[9]

2.1 The system of the Inter-Allied Declaration

Already at an early stage of the War, the Allied forces became aware that the Nazis were removing valuable objects from the areas they were occupying on a large scale. In response, they adopted the Inter-Allied Declaration against Acts of Dispossession committed in Territories under Enemy Occupation or

9 See L. Nicholas, *The Rape of Europe* (1994) New York, Alfred Knopf; and the proceedings of the trial against A. Rosenberg in International Military Tribunal, *Trials of the Major War Criminals Before the International Military Tribunal*, vol. 22 (1948) Nuremberg.

Control of 5 January 1943.[10] With respect to property that originated from the occupied areas, they declared to 'reserve their rights to annul transfers or dealings which took the form of open looting or plunder as well as seemingly good faith transactions', making specific mention of the 'stealing and forced purchase of works of art'. It was a formal warning to the German occupiers but also to those who profited from such practices, that transactions could be reversed. The signatories to the Declaration solemnly recorded their solidarity in this matter. These principles were reaffirmed and elaborated upon in various instruments covering restitution, including Resolution VI of the Final Act of the Bretton Woods conferences after the War, and post-War restitution laws.[11] They are the basis of the post-war restitution system that relied on the following pillars:

- Tracing the objects that were taken from the occupied territories;
- Restitution ('external') to the government of the country from which they had last been transferred during the war on the basis of governmental claims;
- 'Internal' restitution to individual owners who had lost their artefacts as a result of confiscation or forced sales at the local (national) level.[12]

In as far 'external restitution' was concerned, international law provided a solid basis for return to the country it had been taken from. Both the destruction of monuments and looting[13] of cultural objects are prohibited during times of war, and this prohibition was codified in the 1907 Hague Convention.[14] The obligation to return artefacts looted in contravention of this prohi-

10 Inter-Allied Declaration against Acts of Dispossession Committed in Territories under Enemy Occupation and Control (5 January 1943) London, in *The Department of State Bulletin*, vol. 8 (1943) US Government Printing Office, Washington (Inter-Allied Declaration).

11 Final Act of the United Nations Monetary and Financial Conference (signed at Bretton Woods on 22 July 1944). 1977, *Tractatenblad van het Koninkrijk der Nederlanden*, No. 40. See also A.F. Vrdoljak, 'Gross Violations of Human Rights and Restitution: Learning from Holocaust Claims' in L.V. Prott, *Realising Cultural Heritage Law: Festschrift for Patrick O'Keefe* (2013) Institute of Art & Law, 167.

12 L.V. Prott, 'Responding to WWII Art Looting' in International bureau of the Permanent Court of Arbitration (ed) *Resolution of Cultural Property Disputes* (2004) Kluwer Law International.

13 The terms 'looting' and 'pillage' are used in the cultural heritage field to define misappropriation of cultural goods in the event of a national or international armed conflict, see M. Cornu, C. Wallaert and J. Fromageau, *Dictionnaire comparé du droit du patrimoine culturel* (2012) CNRS Editions. In the present context, the term 'looting' is used to include takings in a situation beyond an 'armed conflict' such as confiscation as a result of racist legislation in Nazi Germany.

14 Convention (IV) Respecting the Laws and Customs of War on Land and its annex: Regulations Concerning the Laws and Customs of War on Land (adopted 18 October 1907, entered into force 26 January 1910) 205 CTS 277, arts 46, 47, 56.

bition was widely considered to have customary status under international law at the time.[15]

To enable the last important step in the post-war restitution system, the return of lost possessions to their rightful owners, individual states were to enact special restitution laws ('internal restitution'). These laws were to ensure the rights of individual victims of dispossession due to persecution.[16] Such special legislation was mostly needed in civil law countries (i.e. in most European jurisdictions) where new possessors could otherwise rely on the passing of title to looted artefacts following a *bona fide* acquisition, a sale at a public auction, or just by the passage of time.

2.2 Internal restitution: A matter of human rights law

The internal restitution process in Germany came under the remit of occupying authorities. Strictly speaking the special restitution laws, issued for that purpose, were not covered by traditional international law. Restitution here did not aim to reverse the looting in occupied territories but the systematic dispossession by a government of its own citizens. In that sense, the post-War internal restitution programme was a novelty: it was an intervention by the international community in private law relations within a state, traditionally a matter of state sovereignty. The reason was that the dispossession had been part of genocide and persecution, notions covered by the (at the time) emerging field of international human rights law.[17] In the words of Bentwich the aim of such laws was: 'to remedy wrongs caused by the failure of a government to observe minimum international standards for the treatment of human beings'.[18] Accordingly, the preamble and first article of the Restitution Law

15 E.g., W.W. Kowalski, *Art Treasures and War* (1998) Institute of Art and Law 88; and A. Chechi, *The Settlement of International Cultural Heritage Disputes* (2014) Oxford University Press 270 (and note 135 referring for his conclusion on the customary status to authors as Francioni and Siehr). However, Russia takes the position that 'restitution in kind' is also permitted; on this basis, the Russians took and retained as war booty cultural objects which they found in the Russian zone of Germany in the post-war period.

16 A comparison of national restitution laws in N. Robinson, 'War Damage Compensation and Restitution in Foreign Countries' (1951) 16 Law and Contemporary Problems 347; See also Prott (2004) and Campfens (2015).

17 The term 'persecution' was developed in this period; in the Charter of the International Military Tribunal (adopted 8 August 1945, 82 UNTS 279) it fell under Article art 6 (c), covering crimes against humanity, which included: 'persecution of racial, religious, and cultural groups following the installation of the Nazi regime in 1933'.

18 N. Bentwich, 'International Aspects of Restitution and Compensation for Victims of the Nazis' in *BYIL (1955/1956)* Oxford University Press. A.F. Vrdoljak, 'Genocide and Restitution: Ensuring Each Group's Contribution to Humanity' (2011) 22 European Journal of International Law 17.

for the American zone in Germany (Law 59) echoed the definition of crimes against humanity in the London Charter (Nuremberg Tribunal):[19]

> 'It shall be the purpose of this Law to effect to the largest extent possible the speedy restitution of identifiable property [...] to persons who were wrongfully deprived of such property within the period from 30 January 1933 to 8 May 1945 for reasons of race, religion, nationality, ideology or political opposition to National Socialism.'[20]

Law 59 provided that title over looted possessions could not pass to a new possessor.[21] Another noteworthy element surfaces in Article 19, providing that with regard to goods that were acquired in the course of an ordinary business transaction, a right to restitution by the deprived owner would only exist if it concerns private property of artistic, scientific or sentimental personal value.[22]

In many European countries similar restitution laws were adopted, also in neutral countries such as Switzerland where looted artefacts had come on the market.[23] They suspended, for a limited period of time, regular private law to prevent that subsequent possessors – also if they were in good faith – would gain lawful title, and allowed for the restitution of property to the victims of dispossession. Such laws would typically render void *ab initio* confiscations which directly resulted from racial (Nazi) laws, while forced sales would be *voidable* upon a valid claim being made.[24] This difference is of

19 Charter of the International Military Tribunal (n. 17).

20 Art. 1 (1) 'Law No. 59, Restitution of Identifiable Property' of the Military Government for Germany, US in United States Courts of the Allied High Commission for Germany, *Court of Restitution Appeals Reports* (1951) 499-536.

21 Ibid., Art. 1 (2): 'Property shall be restored to its former owner or to his successor in interest [...] even though the interests of other persons who had no knowledge of the wrongful taking must be subordinated. Provisions of law for the protection of purchasers of good faith, which would defeat restitution, shall be disregarded except where this Law provides otherwise.'

22 Ibid. Art. 19: '(...) tangible personal property shall not be subject to restitution if the present owner or his predecessor in interest acquired it in the course of an ordinary and usual business transaction in an establishment normally dealing in that type of property. However, the provisions of the Article shall not apply to *religious objects* or to *property which has been acquired from private ownership if such property is of an unusual artistic, scientific, or sentimental personal value,* or was acquired at an auction or at a private sale in an establishment engaged mainly in the business of disposing property the subject of an unjust deprivation'. The provision mirrors Art. 15 of the UK restitution law for the British zone, and reflects elements of the Dutch Law (*Besluit Herstel Rechtsverkeer* (17 Sept. 1944) Staatsblad E100, art. 27 (2)) *[futher elaborated in E. Campfens, 'The Dutch Framework for Nazi-looted Art' (2020) Art Antiquity and Law, Vol XXV, 1, p 1-24; p 10].*

23 *Bundesratbeschluss betreffend die Klagen auf Ruekgabe in kriegsbesetzten Gebieten weggenommener Vermoegenswerte* (10 December 1945) 15 Bundesblatt 391, also known as the Booty Decree. See also E. Campfens (2015).

24 See Prott (2004); Campfens (2015), 21-26.

importance since claim possibilities to claim lost possession ended with the lapse of the often very short limitation periods in the special national restitution laws, whilst the rule that a loss of ownership was void (i.e. never occurred) may still sort effect today. The French Bauer case mentioned in the introduction illustrates this: in that case the transfer of ownership – as a result of confiscation in 1943 under the Vichy regime in Paris – was declared null and void in the post-War period and this lies at the base of the ruling by the Paris court that the Pissarro was to be restored in full ownership to the heirs of the pre-War Jewish owner.[25]

As Vrdoljak explains, in the post-War period legal scholars struggled to rationalise the ground-breaking aspects of the restitution programme within the existing legal framework.[26] According to a contemporary legal scholar, the rationale for these special laws should be found in new principles of international law and in the 'more comprehensive, interstate notion of justice'.[27] In other words, it was a matter of international human rights law that was emerging at the time.

2.3 Developments since the 1950s

In spite of the efforts to reverse the Nazi looting in the post-War period, the enthusiasm appeared short-lived. The national restitution laws soon expired, and many works found their way into collections all over the world before they could be returned.[28] Moreover, in the 1950s the signatory states to the *Convention on the Settlement of Matters Arising out of the War and the Occupation* seem to have made a choice to 'clear' looted artefacts in the hands of third parties by providing for a sunset clause for private restitution claims, set at 1956.[29] Under that system, dispossessed owners who could prove their arte-

25 *Bauer et al v B and R Toll* (n. 1) 4.

26 As was the case with the concept 'crimes against humanity'. Vrdoljak (2013) 'Gross Violations of Human Rights and Restitution' (n. 11).

27 'De Bundesratbeschluss hilft mit durch unseren Verzicht auf erworbene Rechte, und zwar (und darin liegt der wesentliche Unterschied ...), durch Verzicht auf Rechte, die unserer Gesetzgebungsbefugnis unterstehen, einer umfassenderen, einer instersaatlichten Rechtsidee zu dienen'. G. Weiss, 'Beutegueter aus besetztend Laendern. Die privatrechtlichte Stellund des schweizerischen Erwerbens' (1946) 42 Schweizerische Juristen-Zeitiung, p. 274.

28 L.V. Prott (2004) 114.

29 '[..] Any person who, or whose predecessor in title, during the occupation of a territory, has been dispossessed of his property by larceny or by duress (with or without violence) by the forces or authorities of Germany or its Allies, or their individual members (whether or not pursuant to orders), shall have a claim against the present possessor of such property for its restitution. [..] *No such claim shall exist if the present possessor has possessed the property bona fide for ten years or until 8 May 1956, whichever is later.*' Convention on the Settlement of Matters Arising out of the War and the Occupation (adopted 26 May 1952), as amended by Protocol on the Termination of the Occupation Regime in the Federal Republic of Germany

facts had been taken to Germany, would instead be able to claim compensation from the German State in the event that their looted artefacts were not located before that date.[30]

Obviously, this chapter was all but over as became clear at the end of the 1990s. Paintings on the walls of museums that had once belonged to Jewish families turned into tangible symbols of the injustices of the past. Amidst a renewed historical awareness of Nazi looting and scandals concerning other assets of perished Jewish owners that were never returned to their heirs, the artefacts came at the centre of public debate. Against this background, in 1998, the Washington Principles on Nazi-Confiscated Art were adopted.

3 TODAY'S STANDARDS FOR NAZI-LOOTED ART CLAIMS

Similar to the post-war internal restitution laws, the return to individual owners is at stake in the present-day system of the Washington Principles for claims to Nazi-looted art. This means that although another model for the restitution of Nazi-looted art exists – the interstate model under public international law under which states may claim artefacts that were transferred from occupied territories – this should not be confused with the model for 'Nazi looting' as addressed in the Washington Principles. The latter creates rights, albeit of a non-binding nature, for individual victims of looting or their heirs to their lost artefacts without the intervention of a victim's national government. At times, these two models for claims to Nazi-looted art (for states and on the other hand for private individuals) may clash, but this will not be further addressed hereafter.[31] The next section addresses the rights of private claimants to their lost possessions under the soft law system of the Washington Principles. In that regard, the 'just and fair' norm introduced in 1998 in Washington prescribes that:

> If the pre-war owners of art that is found to have been confiscated by the Nazis and not subsequently restituted, or their heirs, can be identified, steps should be taken expeditiously to achieve a just and fair solution, recognizing this may vary according to the facts and circumstances surrounding a specific case.[32]

(adopted 23 Oct. 1954, entered into force 5 May 1955) 49 American Journal of International Law 69-83 (Settlement Convention) ch. 5, Art. 3 (1).

30 Ibid. ch 5 art 4. And a loss at the hands of the Vichy Government in France would be compensated by the French Government.

31 See P.K. Grimsted, 'Nazi-Looted Art from East and West in East Prussia: Initial Findings on the Erich Koch Collection' (2015) 22 International Journal of Cultural Property 7. Grimsted's research deals with artefacts held in Russian or Polish museums that were confiscated from persecuted individuals in western territories and were taken to these countries as 'war booty' in the post-war period. Neither Poland nor Russia implemented the Washington Principles. On the position of the Russian Federation regarding 'war booty', see n. 15.

32 Washington Principles, principle VIII.

This is an abstract norm which has not been clarified much by later declarations.[33] In the Terezín Declaration of 2009, signed by 46 states, the 'just and fair' rule was rephrased as follows:

> [W]e urge all stakeholders to ensure that their legal systems or alternative processes, while taking into account the different legal traditions, facilitate just and fair solutions with regard to Nazi-confiscated and looted art, and to make certain that claims to *recover* such are resolved expeditiously and based on the facts and the merits of the claims [...].[34]

The focus in most instruments is on Holocaust-related losses by Jewish owners.[35] The Terezín Declaration allows for a somewhat wider notion as it addresses 'victims of the Holocaust' as well as 'other victims of Nazi-persecution by the Nazis, the Fascists and their collaborators'.[36] Another instrument is the 2009 UNESCO Draft Declaration of Principles Relating to Cultural Objects Displaced in Connection with the Second World War.[37] Although this draft was never adopted and therefore has no practical importance, it introduced a more inclusive and neutral definition, aiming at losses under 'circumstances deemed offensive to the principles of humanity and dictates of public conscience'.

At issue in the following section is the question of what makes a loss of an artefact during the Nazi era qualify for preferential treatment – transcending regular standards for stolen property.

3.1 Elements of the 'just and fair' rule

The soft-law rule prescribes that in the case of Nazi-confiscated art a just and fair solution should be reached on the merits of the case. Although this rule is unspecific, certain elements may be distinguished.

---

33 In short: Council of Europe, Resolution 1205, 'Looted Jewish Cultural Property' (1999) Doc 8563; Vilnius Forum Declaration (2000) <https://www.lootedart.com/MFV7EE39608> (signed by 38 governments and the Parliamentary Assembly of the Council of Europe); W. CEH De Clercq, Report on a Legal Framework for Free Movement Within the Internal Market of Goods Whose Ownership is Likely to Be Contested (2003) A5-0408/2003; Terezín Declaration on Holocaust Era Assets and Related Issues (2009) <https://www.lootedartcom mission.com/NPNMG484641> (Terezín Declaration), with 46 signatory states. For an overview see E Campfens (2015) 37.

34 Terezín Declaration, 4-5.

35 In the Washington Principles: 'Pre-war owners of art confiscated by the Nazis or their heirs'; Resolution 1205, repeated in the Vilnius Forum Declaration; the Terezín Declaration has a focus on Holocaust victims.

36 Terezín Declaration, 4.

37 See UNESCO, Draft of the Declaration of Principles Relating to Cultural Objects Displaced in Connection with the Second World War (2009), 35 C/24, principle II. See also section 4.2, below.

That the rule was created specifically for *art* supports the view that its rationale should be found in the intangible quality of artefacts; the ability of cultural objects to symbolise a family history appears a reason for special treatment, beyond the regular rules for stolen property, even where many years have passed. As seen above, also in the Post-War restitution laws personal attachment to a specific object was a reason for special treatment.[38] A second element of the rule is that it is aimed at a 'just and fair solution' implying that it is not *per se* about the restitution of full ownership rights (restoration of the *status quo ante*). International practice supports the view that the interests of good faith new possessors also deserve a place in a 'just and fair' outcome, meaning that it is a matter of finding a fair balance between various interests – not solely a matter of establishing ownership title of the dispossessed owner.[39] A third element is that such a 'just and fair' outcome depends on the merits of a case, the 'facts and circumstances surrounding a specific case'. What, however, are those circumstances?

The following is a non-exhaustive list of circumstances that appear to determine the outcome of present-day restitution cases:[40]

- The identification of the artefact as property of the claimant's predecessor in right at the time of looting (the original title);
- The circumstances of the loss by 'Nazi looting';
- Previous post-war compensations and settlements;
- The extent to which the owner made efforts to recover the work over time;
- The circumstances in which the present possessor acquired the work and the provenance research carried out prior to acquiring it;
- The specific interest of the parties in the artefact (e.g. the intangible interest or monetary value);

An analysis of all these circumstances exceeds the scope of this chapter. The first two elements – identification as former property and loss through looting – could, however, be classified as the basic requirements for the admissibility of a claim. If a specific work of art can be identified as being owned by the claimant's predecessor in rights at the moment of loss, and was lost through Nazi-looting, a claim can be considered (i.e. a right exists); if not, no claim arises under the soft law norm. Whereas identification of a work is a matter of factual research and interpretation of that research, the second

38 Section 2.2.

39 Numerous (confidential) financial settlements to claims to Nazi-looted that are concluded in the realm of the art trade (i.e. mostly when private owners are at stake) support that view. See also Dutch Restitutions Committte 'Binding Advice on Dispute Over the Painting Road to Calvary' (2010) RC 3.95. In that case, the sale proceeds were to be shared between the former and the present possessor. On the position of the new possessor in the Dutch post-War restitution practice, that also confirms this, see Campfens (2015) 27-30, 233.

40 This is a tentative list based on research and personal experience.

element is a matter of legal definition: when can a loss be defined as 'Nazi looting' in the sense of the Washington Principles?

3.2 Unjustified Nazi looting

The just and fair rule addresses losses where there is a causal relationship with persecution. A controversial issue, which will be the focus of the remainder of this section, is how direct and proximate the causal link with persecution should be. Clearly, thefts, confiscations and seizures by Nazi organisations – resulting from the so-called '*Möbel-Aktion*' or seizures by *Einsatzstab Reichsleiter Rosenberg* (ERR) – qualify, as do the forced so-called *Judenauktionen* ('Jewish auctions') set in motion by the Nazis.[41] In short, all losses that were directly based on racial legislation qualify.[42] Nazi acquisition policies were, however, often more subtle. Hence, also 'sales under duress' qualify as Nazi-confiscation under the just and fair rule – as they would under post-War restitution laws discussed above. But what are the limits to the notion of a forced sale? The next section will consider the question of forced sales.

3.2.1 *Forced sales*

At one end of the spectrum lies the typical 'gun-to-the-head' situation: a Jewish owner being forced to sell his or her artefacts to Nazi authorities under threat of reprisals. A loss occurring in the owner's absence (i.e. without the will or initiative on the part of the owner), because he or she had been forced into hiding or managed to escape the Nazis would similarly add up to a forced sale. A sale by an owner at an undervalue in order to keep himself alive while in hiding generally also qualifies, as dealt with in the first report of the UK Spoliation Panel and many similar cases by the Dutch Restitutions Commit-

---

41 E.g. the various *Gentili di Giuseppe* cases, in France (*Gentili di Giuseppe et al v Musée du Louvre* (1999) Court of Appeal of Paris, 1st Division, Section A, No RG 1998/19209) and the US. See for the forfeiture action in the US of a work from the same collection on loan from Italy: L. Bursey, E. Velioglu Yildizci and M.A. Renold, 'Case Christ Carrying the Cross Dragged by a Rascal – Gentili Di Giuseppe Heirs v Italy' (2015) Platform ArThémis, Art-Law Centre, University of Geneva.

42 See, e.g. Dutch Recommendation Regarding a Sculpture from Fritz Gutmann's Collection Confiscated by the ERR in Paris (2011) RC 1.114-B; the 1996 US *Gutmann* case (*Goodman v Searle* (1996) United States District Court for the Northern District of Illinois, No. 96C-6459) concerned a Degas painting that was part of the same group of artefacts confiscated by the ERR in Paris. Litigation ended by a settlement. Another example is the Altmann case, litigated in the US and settled by arbitration (*Republic of Austria et al v Altmann* (2004) Supreme Court of the United States, 541 US 677).

tee.[43] However, the circumstances are not always as clear-cut as this. Difficult categories include early sales, sales by art dealers and so-called *'Fluchtgut'* sales; these will be discussed below. Under post-war restitution laws, decisive elements in determining whether a sale should be classified as forced included:[44]

- a fair purchase price (or conversely: disparity between value and selling price);
- the time of the loss of possession (before or after the racial laws of 1935 in Germany, with different periods applying to each occupied state);
- own initiative on the part of the owner; and
- the identity of the acquiring party (was it a Nazi-official?).

These elements resurface in present-day recommendations by the respective European restitution committees and in US case law.[45] In view of the fact that these losses occurred a long time ago, in today's cases value is also attached to contemporary declarations and actions (or a lack thereof) by former owners on the involuntary nature of a sale. Post-War statements and documents can validate (or invalidate) claims by the owners that a sale should be considered to have been forced. In this sense, for example, the Dutch Restitutions Committee considered the lack of action in the post-war period a circumstance of importance in its 2012 Recommendation regarding the loss of two statues under unclear circumstances at an unknown moment after 1934 in Berlin:

> If the exchange had been involuntary, it would have been obvious for Max Von Goldschmidt-Rothschild's private secretary [...] to have mentioned this in his letter of 6 July 1946 [writing about the artefacts at stake]. He did not do so, however. It would also be logical that if the exchange had been involuntary in nature, the Von Goldschmidt-Rothschild family would have submitted an application for restitution of or compensation for the sculptures after the War, as they did for the works of art that were sold in 1938 under the pressure of the Nazi authorities.[46]

43 Report of the Spoliation Advisory Panel in Respect of a Painting Now in the Possession of the Tate Gallery (18 January 2001). All reports of the SAP are available online: <https://www.gov.uk/government/groups/spoliation-advisory-panel#panel-reports>. Dutch examples: e.g. Dutch Restitutions Committee, Recommendation RC 1.28 (2006) or Dutch Restitutions Committee, Recommendation RC 1.37 (2007). All recommendations of the Dutch Restitutions Committee online <https://www.restitutiecommissie.nl/en/recommendations>.

44 N. Robinson (1951); E. Campfens (2015) 21-26.

45 The term 'European Restitution Committees' signifies special panels tasked with the adjudication of Nazi-looted art claims, discussed below. In Germany, the focus is on a 'fair market price' (see the 'Guidelines' from the *Beratende Kommission* (annex V b), under 3); litigated cases obviously have a different character and usually revolve around 'technical' legal issues such as statutes of limitation, jurisdictional matters and conflict of law issues.

46 Dutch Restitutions Committee, Recommendation Regarding von Goldschmidt-Rothschild (2012) RC 1.110. Other examples with considerations as to this point: e.g. the US Glaser litigation: *Matter of Peters v Sotheby's Inc* (14 September 2006) Appellate Divission of the Supreme Court of New York, First Department, NY Slip Op 6480 (34 AD3d 29).

Clear efforts to recuperate a lost work in the post-War period, on the other hand, may strengthen a claim.[47]

3.2.2 *Early sales*

An 'early sale' can be defined as a sale that occurred before racial laws were in force. Because such laws were often introduced gradually, such general conditions vary from country to country. Allied restitution laws for Germany, for example, made a distinction between a sale before or after the Nuremberg Race Laws of September 1935, and this resurfaces in present-day German decisions. Similarly, one can distinguish between periods of increasingly threatening general conditions, for example in the Netherlands or France.

An observation with regard to the category of 'early sales' is that there is no consistent approach amongst the European restitution committees. US courts, then again, seem to have predominantly dismissed such cases on the basis of 'technical defences' (i.e. statute of limitations or lack of jurisdiction),[48] and cases were also settled before judgment.[49] The inconsistency is illustrated by the conflicting outcomes in the various claims relating to the Glaser collection in the UK, the United States, the Netherlands, Germany and Switzerland.

In its 2009 *Report in Respect of Eight Drawings now in the Possession of the Samuel Courtauld Trust*, the UK Spoliation Panel denied the claim of the Glaser heirs.[50] Curt Glaser, a prominent Jewish art historian, lost his job and house almost immediately after Hitler came to power in January 1933 and auctioned his art collection in May 1933 in Berlin to start a new life abroad. The Panel considered that, although Nazi persecution was the main reason for the sale, Glaser had obtained reasonable market prices ('reflecting the general market in such objects and [the prices were] not depressed by circumstances attributable to the Nazi regime'). Besides, it argued, his widow was awarded compensation under an agreed and conclusive settlement with the awarding

---

47 See e.g. Dutch Restitution Committee, Recommendation RC 1.28 (2006).

48 See for example *Schoeps et al v Freistaat Bayern* (Summary Order, 2015) United States Court of Appeals for the Second Circuit, No. 14-2739: the claim based on a loss through the sale of a Picasso by Mendelssohn-Bartholdy in 1934 was dismissed on grounds of lack of jurisdiction over German property. This can be contrasted to rulings where clear confiscation was at stake and jurisdiction was accepted, for example in the *Altmann* case dealing with paintings located in an Austrian museum (*Republic of Austria et al v Altmann* (n. 42)).

49 E.g. *Schoeps et al v The Museum of Modern Art and The Solomon R Guggenheim Foundation* (Memorandum Order, 2009) United States District Court for the Southern District of New York, No. 07 Civ 11074 (JSR) on what seems an early loss of two Picasso paintings (unclear facts). The case was settled on the eve of the trial. Interestingly, Judge Rakoff explicitly voiced his discontent with the confidentiality of the settlement as being: against public interest (*Schoeps et al v The Museum of Modern Art and The Solomon R Guggenheim Foundation* 4-6).

50 Report of the Spoliation Advisory Panel in Respect of Eight Drawings Now in the Possession of the Samuel Courtauld Trust (24 June 2009) HC 757.

authorities. The Panel denied the claim but recommended that the Courtauld display alongside the drawings an account of their history and provenance during and since the Nazi era.

A New York court had previously also denied a claim by the Glaser heirs in the US in 2006 in respect of a painting by Munch, sold by Curt Glaser's brother after Glaser himself had left the country. In line with the UK Panel's decision, the New York court relied on a contemporaneous letter from Glaser himself, reasoning that:

> If Professor Glaser did not treat the painting as stolen in 1936, his wife's estate will not be heard to speculate, some 70 years after the fact, that it might have been misappropriated and that its acquisition at auction [..] was therefore tainted.[51]

Both in the Netherlands and in Germany, however, claims relating to Glaser works sold at the same auction – meaning they were lost under exactly the same circumstances – *were* upheld shortly after. The recommendation by the Dutch Restitutions Committee relied on the view that the loss was involuntary as a direct result of the Nazi regime, and on the consideration that sale proceeds shall not to be taken into account if these were 'used in an attempt to leave the country or go into hiding'.[52] In Germany several other claims by the Glaser heirs were successful, resulting in financial settlements.[53] Furthermore, in March 2020, 12 years after a first rejection, also the Kunstmuseum Basel in Switzerland honoured a claim by the Glaser heirs to works sold at the same 1933 auction.[54]

3.2.3 *Sales in neutral countries ('Fluchtgut')*

Sales in neutral countries during the Nazi era are at the far end of the spectrum of what some consider a 'forced sale'.[55] These could be sales in Switzerland by Jewish owners on their way to freedom, or sales that took place in other countries prior to occupation. In other words, sales concluded outside the direct

51 *Matter of Peters v Sotheby's Inc* (n. 46) 6.

52 Dutch Restitutions Committee, Recommendation regarding Glaser (2010) RC 1.99.

53 E.g. the settlement with the Stiftung Preusssischer Kulturbesitz, that, in the words of SPK's chairman should be considered against a special background, namely: 'In acknowledgment of Prof. Glaser's persecution by the Nazi Regime and in honour of his great achievements for the museums in Berlin'. Hermann Parzinger (Speech, 27 November 2015) <https://www.preussischer-kulturbesitz.de/fileadmin/user_upload/documents/presse/news/2015/151128_Provenienzforschung_Rede-P-final-korr.pdf>.

54 See <https://www.nytimes.com/2020/03/27/arts/design/swiss-nazi-era-art-claim-settled.html>, acc. 5 May 2021.

55 This proposition is supported by Andrew Adler. A. Adler, 'Expanding the Scope of Museums' Ethical Guidelines with Respect to Nazi-Looted Art: Incorporating Restitution Claims Based on Private Sales Made as a Direct Result of Persecution' (2007) 14 *International Journal of Cultural Property* 57.

influence of Nazi rule: so-called *'Fluchtgut'* cases. Although the reason for such sales may well have been persecution – the owner flees the country and therefore needs money to survive – there is no direct causal link between the loss and persecution. Under the post-war restitution laws, such cases would not qualify for restitution.[56] These laws were limited in place and time, and claims were restricted to losses in territories under Nazi rule.[57] However, in current practice it is less clear how *'Fluchtgut'* should be classified.[58]

In fact, the first recommendation of the *Beratende Kommission* allowed such a claim in the *Julius Freund* case, however an argumentation was lacking.[59] As Matthias Weller observes in this regard: 'The recommendation [...] does not [...] explain why the principle of justice laid down in Military Law No. 59 should apply to sales outside Germany in safe states.'[60] In a later *'Fluchtgut'* case concerning the sale in London in 1934 by the German art dealer Flechtheim, the *Beratende Kommission* explained its position by stating that:

> If an art dealer and collector persecuted by the Nazis sold a painting on the regular art market or at auction in a safe country abroad, there would have to be very specific reasons to recognize such a sale as a loss of property as the result of Nazi persecution. In the case of Flechtheim and the painting 'Violon et encrier', no such reasons are apparent. For this reason as well, the Advisory Commission cannot recommend the restitution desired by the Flechtheim heirs.[61]

A similar approach to *'Fluchtgut'* – i.e. a hesitant rejection of the claim – was adopted in 2012 by the UK Spoliation Advisory Panel (SAP) in a case regarding fourteen clocks and watches that had been sold by a refugee in London in 1939,[62] and in two Dutch opinions regarding the sale by the German-Jewish

---

56 To this author's knowledge there is no case law, legislation or literature in support of such an extensive interpretation. See also Robinson (1951).

57 Namely, in the case of Germany to the period of Nazi rule (1933-1945), and in neutral countries the period starting with the outbreak of the War in 1939.

58 Arguments were made by the President of the World Jewish Congress, Ronald Lauder, to treat Fluchtgut in the same way as looted art. See his remarks in Zürich (2 February 2016)<https://www.worldjewishcongress.org/en/news/remarks-by-ronald-s-lauder-in-zurich-a-crime-committed-80-years-ago-continues-to-stain-the-world-of-art-today-2-2-2016>.

59 *Beratende Kommission*, First Recommendation (12 January 2005) Nr. 19/05.

60 M. Weller, 'Key Elements of Just and Fair Solutions: The Case for a Restatement of Restitution Principles' in E. Campfens (ed) *Fair and Just Solutions? Alternatives to Litigation in Nazi-Looted Art Disputes* (2015) Eleven International Publishing) 205.

61 *Beratende Kommission*, Recommendation of the Advisory Commission in the Matter of the Heirs of Alfred Flechtheim v Stiftung Kunstsammlung Nordrhein-Westfalen, Düsseldorf (21 March 2016).

62 Report of the Spoliation Advisory Panel in Respect of Fourteen Clocks and Watches Now in the Possession of the British Museum (7 March 2012) HC 1839.

businessman Semmel in the Netherlands in 1933.[63] The SAP in its 2012 report considered that, although the sale by a Jewish refugee of a collection of clocks and watches in London in 1939 was 'forced' – in the sense that the items would not have been sold had the Nazis not come to power –, this particular sale was:

> at the lower end of any scale of gravity for such sales. It is very different from those cases where valuable paintings were sold, for example, in occupied Belgium to pay for food or where all assets had to be sold in Germany in the late 1930s to pay extortionate taxes. The sale was not compelled by any need to purchase freedom or to sustain the necessities of life. Furthermore, the sale was arranged by a prominent English auction house with […] no cause to question the seller's reasons for selling.[64]

Interestingly, in this case the SAP introduced a 'scale of gravity' whereby restitution or compensation could be recommended if the sale was at the 'high end' rather than the 'low end' of the scale. The SAP dismissed the restitution claim but found an alternative solution in 'the display alongside the objects, or any of them whenever they are displayed, of their history and provenance during and since the Nazi era.'[65]

The Dutch Restitutions Committee followed this line of reasoning in the two Semmel cases – i.e. rejecting the claims in spite of the assessment that the loss was involuntary and recommending instead the display of its provenance in the museums alongside the exhibited objects.[66] Nevertheless, in two other claims concerning objects from the same Semmel collection sold at the same auction the Dutch Restitutions Committee *did* recommend a return. In one case, the reason may be that the painting was part of the NK-collection – for which a more lenient policy applies that does not allow for the

63 Dutch Restitution Committee, Binding opinion in the dispute on restitution of the painting entitled Christ and the Samaritan Woman at the Well by Bernardo Strozzi (2013) RC 3.128, and Dutch Restitutions Committee, Binding opinion regarding the dispute about the return of the painting Madonna and Child with Wild Roses by Jan van Scorel (2013) RC 3.131. On 19 April 2021 in the case regarding the Strozzi painting in (RC 3.128) Museum De Fundatie, however, paid the Semmel heirs 200.000 euro to settle the ongoing dispute, in spite of this outcome. See <https://www.nrc.nl/nieuws/2021/04/19/museum-de-fundatie-betaalt-200000-euro-aan-erfgenamen-nazi-roofkunst-a4040357>.

64 Report of the Spoliation Advisory Panel in Respect of Fourteen Clocks and Watches Now in the Possession of the British Museum (2012) 19-21, 27.

65 In the SAP Glaser case, concerning an early sale in 1933 in Germany, stemming 'from mixed motives', the SAP introduced a similar approach: '[W]e consider that the claimants' moral claim is insufficiently strong to warrant a recommendation that the drawings should be transferred to them. We also consider that, whenever any of the drawings is on show, the Courtauld should display alongside it a brief account of its history and provenance [...]'. *Report in Respect of Eight Drawings now in the Possession of the Samuel Courtauld Trust* (2009) 34, 47.

66 RC 3.128 as well as RC 3.131.

weighing of interests of the present owner –,[67] and in the other instance the reasoning was that the painting was of no particular interest to the museum.[68] This approach was heavily criticised, especially after the Committee's 2018 recommendation concerning the sale of a Kandinsky painting in 1940 in the Netherlands (i.e. not a 'Fluchtgut' case).[69] The Committee rejected that claim by arguing that the interests of the Museum outweighed the interest of the claimant; such a balance of interests is, according to the decision's critics, incompatible with the Washington Principles. And indeed, while it appears from the recommendation that the Committee was of the opinion the loss did not qualify as a forced sale, that question was not clearly addressed.

In the United States, the question of whether *'Fluchtgut'* qualifies as 'unlawful looting' was addressed in a ruling by an Ohio court regarding the sale of a Gauguin painting by Martha Nathan, a Jewish refugee, in Switzerland in 1938. The court ruled in favour of the Toledo Museum and held that:

> In short, this sale occurred outside Germany by and between private individuals who were familiar with each other. The painting was not confiscated or looted by the Nazis; the sale was not at the direction of, nor did the proceeds benefit, the Nazi regime.[70]

In a similar US case, regarding a claim by the Nathan heirs to a Van Gogh painting in the Detroit Institute of Arts, which was sold by Martha Nathan in Switzerland in 1938 as well, a Michigan court also ruled against the claimants.[71] A more recent US Fluchgut case – again, a denial on the ground of the equitable latches defence – involves the 1938 sale of Picasso's The Actor by the German Jewish couple Paul and Alice Leffmann to non-Nazi buyers outside Germany.[72]

---

67 Dutch Restitutions Committee (2009) RC 1.75.

68 Dutch Restitutions Committee, Binding opinion in the dispute on restitution of the painting The Landing Stage by van Maarten Fransz. van der Hulst from the estate of Richard Semmel, currently owned by Stichting Kunstbezit en Oudheden Groninger Museum (2013) RC 3.126.

69 Dutch Resttitutions Committee, Binding Opinion Regarding the Dispute About Restitution of the Painting with Houses by Wassily Kandinsky, Currently in the Possession of Amsterdam City Council (2018) RC 3.141.

70 *Toledo Museum of Art v Claude George Ullin et al* (2006) United States District Court for the Northern District of Ohio, No. 3:06 CV 7031, 7. Concluding: 'Defendants [the Nathan heirs, EC] can prove no set of facts that entitle them to relief.'

71 *Detroit Institute of Arts v Ullin*, Slip Copy (2007) United States District Court for the Eastern District of Michigan, No. 06-10333. For a pending US *'Fluchtgut'* case, see *Zuckerman v The Metropolitan Museum of Art* (Complaint, 2016), No. 1:16-cv-07665.

72 *Zuckerman v. Metropolitan Museum of Art* (2018) United States District Court for the Southern District of New York No. 1:16-cv-07665, aff'd, No. 18-634 (2d Cir. N.Y. 26 June 2019), cert. denied, No. 19-942 (U.S. 2 March 2020). For a discussion of the case in relation to the HEAR Act, see S Drawdy 'Claims for the Return of Holocaust Art: the Scope and Legacy of the HEAR Act' (2020) 25 AAL 79.

On the whole, '*Fluchtgut*' cases appear not to be fully supported by European restitution committees – although increasingly they seem to be honoured –,[73] and much less so by US courts. However, the line of reasoning by European panels in such cases is inconsistent. In the view of the present author, bringing such sales in neutral countries within the notion of 'Nazi-loot' over-stretches the definition.

3.2.4 *Business transactions by art dealers*

Artefacts often fall into a category of personal possessions with emotional or spiritual value, valued for their beauty and handed down through generations.[74] Sales by art dealers often lack this intangible aspect and therefore also could be considered to be a special category. The objects are, in this context, commodities and any sale would normally possess the nature of a business transaction. In other words, the special personal, spiritual or cultural-historical interest in the artefact is not a given. If one takes this intangible heritage value of the artefact as a basic element of the just and fair rule, as put forward in section 3.1 above, sales by art dealers stand out. Another difference is that the objective of an art dealer is to buy and sell artefacts and a sale by a dealer cannot automatically be presumed to be involuntary.

The Dutch Restitutions Committee has dealt with a number of cases concerning works of art sold by Jewish art dealers. The background to this is that the art market in the Netherlands flourished during the Nazi occupation after years of depression. Although trading with the Germans was prohibited,[75] this did not prevent art from being traded on a wide scale by Dutch dealers, both Jewish and non-Jewish, during the early stages of the occupation.[76] In light of this, the present-day Dutch restitution policy makes a distinction between private owners and art dealers with the following rationale: 'That the art trade's objective is to sell the trading stock so that the majority of the transactions even by Jewish art dealers in principle constituted ordinary

73 E.g. *Beratende Kommission*, Recommendation of the Advisory Commission in the case of the heirs of Kurt and Else Grawi vs. Landeshauptstadt Düsseldorf (2021), honouring a claim to a painting sold in 1940 in New York. See also the 2021 voluntary settlement in the Dutch Semmel case (RC 3.128), mentioned above (n. 63).

74 See also the Conference on Jewish Material Claims Against Germany (Claims Conference): 'Looted Art and Cultural Property Initiative' (*Claims Conference/WJRO*) <http://art.claimscon.org/home-new/looted-art-cultural-property-initiative/>.

75 The prohibition was enacted by Law A6 adopted by the Dutch Government in exile (Koninklijk Besluit A6 'Besluit Rechtsverkeer in Oorlogstijd' (7 June 1940)).

76 F. Kunert and A. Marck, 'The Dutch Art Market 1930-1945 and Dutch Restitution Policy Regarding Art Dealers' in E. Blimlinger and M. Mayer (eds) *Kunst sammeln, Kunst handeln: Beiträge des Internationalen Symposiums in Wien* (2012) Böhlau Verlag; see also E. Muller and H. Schretlen, *Betwist Bezit* (2002) Waanders, 25-30.

sales'.[77] Whereas private sales by Jewish owners during the Nazi rule benefit from the presumption of a forced sale, the same is not true for art dealers. On these grounds, the Committee denied, for example, claims by the heirs of the Jewish art dealers Katz regarding objects they had sold during this period.[78]

However, this does not mean all sales by Jewish art dealers are deemed by the Dutch Restitutions Committee to have been voluntary.[79] This is demonstrated by its two recommendations concerning the Mogrobi art dealership: a first claim, regarding thirteen artefacts, was allowed as it concerned sales from 1942 onwards while the owner was persecuted and in hiding (RC 1.37), but a later claim that concerned sales by the same art dealer in the early years of the Nazi occupation was rejected (RC 1.145).[80] The latter claim was rejected on the grounds that:

> (a) The purchaser [..] was a museum director who later became involved in the resistance during the War. The earlier recommendation concerned German buyers, primarily German museums.
>
> (b) The dates on which the currently claimed items were sold were 1 February 1941 and a day in March 1942. The sales involved in the earlier recommendation took place in 1942 and in 1943.[81]

In the *Van Lier* Case (RC 1.87) regarding artefacts sold by the Jewish art dealer Van Lier, the Dutch Committee rejected all but one claim, concerning an ivory horn. The grounds were that this particular object was of special value for the family since Van Lier himself is depicted blowing this horn in a portrait dating from around 1930. In the words of the Committee 'this photograph provides a salient image of their forefather and of an art object that was of unique value to him, thus giving the object an emotional value to the family.'[82] Here we can see that the specific intangible heritage value of an artefact is being recognised.

The German *Beratende Kommission* has also dealt with art dealer cases, for example, in its two *Flechtheim* cases. These concerned the art collection of the prominent Jewish Berlin dealer in modern ('degenerate') art. In its 2013 recom-

77 Ekkart Committee's Recommendations Regarding the Art Trade (2003) <https://zoek.officielebekendmakingen.nl/kst-25839-34.html>.

78 Dutch Restitutions Committee, Recommendation regarding Katz (2009) RC 1.90-A. The case is complicated by the fact that the dealers acted as an intermediate in sales, i.e. they did not necessarily own the artefacts.

79 E.g. the Dutch *Stern* case (RC 1.96) concerning a sale in Germany after 1935.

80 Dutch Restitutions Committee, Recommendation Regarding Kunsthandel Mozes Mogrobi (2007) RC 1.37, and Dutch Restitutions Committee, Recommendation Regarding Mogrobi II (2015) RC 1.145.

81 Recommendation Regarding Mogrobi II (2015) RC 1.145.

82 Dutch Restitutions Committee, Recommendation regarding Van Lier (2009) RC 1.87.

mendation, restitution of a painting sold in 1934 in Germany was granted on the grounds that: 'The loss of ownership was directly connected to the closing of the Galerie Alfred Flechtheim in Düsseldorf which was forced by the political circumstances.'[83] However, not all losses by Flechtheim were under the same circumstances as is illustrated by other *Flechtheim* cases in Germany and the US.[84]

Another case dealt with by the *Beratende Kommission* concerns the sale in 1935 of the so-called *Welfenschatz* ('Guelph Treasure') to the Dresdner Bank by a consortium of Jewish art dealers. In its recommendation, the Commission held that the sale in 1935 cannot be seen as a forced sale:

> According to the findings of the Commission, the art dealers had been trying to resell the *Welfenschatz* since its acquisition in 1929. Although the Commission is aware of the difficult fate of the art dealers and of their persecution during the Nazi period, there is no indication in the case under consideration by the Advisory Commission that points to the art dealers and their business partners having been pressured during negotiations [...]. Furthermore, the effects of the world economic crisis were still being felt in 1934/1935. [...] Moreover, there is no evidence to suggest that the art dealers and their business partners were not free to dispose of the proceeds.[85]

After this rejection in Germany, the *Welfenschatz* claim was brought before a US court.[86]

Another well-known art dealer case concerns the trading stock of Jacques Goudstikker, a prominent Jewish art dealer who escaped Amsterdam on the arrival of the Nazis, leaving behind more than 1,000 works of art. These were bought (fell prey) to German art lovers Aloïs Miedl and Nazi chief Hermann

83 *Beratende Kommission,* Recommendation of the Advisory Commission on the Return of Cultural Property Seized as a Result of Nazi Persecution, Press Release (9 April 2013) <https://www.kulturgutverluste.de> para 4. All recommendations of the Beratende Kommission are available on this website.

84 *Beratende Kommission,* Recommendation of the Advisory Commission in the Matter of the Heirs of Alfred Flechtheim v Stiftung Kunstsammlung Nordrhein-Westfalen, Düsseldorf (21 March 2016). This claim was denied, see above. In the US, a Flechtheim claim concerning paintings in the possession of a Munich museum has been pending since Dec. 2016. In that case the Museum argues that the works were sold before Hitler came to power (*Hulton et al v Bayerische Gemäldesammlungen* (2016) United States District Court for the Southern District of New York, No. 16-CV-9360).

85 *Beratende Kommission,* Recommendation of the Advisory Commission regarding the Welfenschatz (2014).

86 *Philipp et al v Federal Republic of Germany et al* (2015) United States District Court for the District of Columbia, No. 1:15-CV-00266. On 3 February 2021, the US Supreme Court, in a 'writ for certiorari' (No. 19-351) ruled in favour of Germany and the Berlin Museums. See section 4.3 below.

Goering.[87] After the War many of these works returned to the Netherlands – leading to a post-war settlement and, eventually, the return in 2005 by the Dutch Government of 202 paintings.[88] However, many of those works did not return to the Netherlands after the war and, hence, resurface elsewhere. In the United States, the case of *Von Saher v Norton Simon Art Foundation*, concerning a claim by the Goudstikker heir to two paintings by Cranach that were part of the trading stock of Goudstikker, took twelve years of litigation to eventually be halted in the US Supreme Court in 2019.[89] The specific 'art-dealership element' is demonstrated by the fact that Goudstikker bought the Cranach paintings at a 1931 Berlin auction of artefacts that had been confiscated by the Soviet Government from the aristocracy and others. As stated in the 2016 US ruling:

> On or about May 11, 1931, Jacques, on the Firm's behalf, purchased the Cranachs from the Soviet Union at the Lepke auction house in Berlin. Although the auction was entitled the 'Stroganoff Collection' and featured artworks that the Soviet Union had forcibly seized from the Stroganoff family, it also included other artworks, such as the Cranachs, that were never owned by the Stroganoff family but rather that were seized from churches and other institutions.[90]

This provenance was well known at the time and the auction aroused protest.[91] It appears that the Cranachs had been seized in Ukraine in the 1920s.[92] Many people bought artefacts at this auction and Goudstikker, as a dealer,

87 That the sale was 'forced' seems beyond doubt. The Dutch Restitution Committee in its Recommendation Regarding the Application by the Amsterdamse Negotiatie Compagnie NV in Liquidation (2005) RC 1.15, as well as US courts considered the sale as forced. See, for example, the 2016 US ruling (*Von Saher v Norton Simon Museum of Art at Pasadena et al* (2016) United States District Court for the Central District of California, No. 2:07-cv-02866-JFW) 2: 'In July 1940, after the Goudstikkers escaped, Nazi Reichsmarschall Herman Göring, and his cohort, Aloïs Miedl, acquired the Firm's assets through two involuntary 'forced sales'.'; A complication in this case is that in the post-war period a settlement agreement was signed between the Dutch State and the widow of Jacques Goudstikker, Desi Goudstikker, see RC 1.15.

88 As published in the Decision by Secretary of Culture by letter of 6 February 2006, see Parliamentary Documents, Kamerstuk 25839, No 38, Vergaderjaar 2005-2006.

89 The Supreme Court denied to review the case after earlier rulings in favour of the museum. *Von Saher v Norton Simon Museum of Art at Pasadena* (2019) 587 U.S. 18-1057. Litigation iniated in 2007.

90 *Von Saher v Norton Simon Museum of Art at Pasadena et al* (n. 87) 2.

91 A letter of protest by the Stroganoff family, whose collection was auctioned, was published in the New York Herald Tribune of 13 May 1931, at 15: 'The Soviet Republic has taken possession of this collection in a way that sets at defiance every principle of international law', see *Stroganoff-Scherbatoff v Weldon* (1976) United States District Court for the Southern District of New York, 420 F. Supp 18.

92 The argument supporting the paintings' Ukrainian provenance is presented (in Ukrainian) on <http://lostart.org.ua/ua/research/61.html>, and was previously mentioned in N.H. Yeide, K. Akinsha and A.M. Walsh, *The AAM Guide to Provenance Research* (2001) American Association of Museums, 135.

bought the paintings with the intention of reselling them. Claims challenging Soviet seizures of art works have been brought before US, French and English courts, but have in all cases proved unsuccessful as the courts have invoked the Act of State doctrine (unlike certain claims in respect of Nazi confiscations, as to which see part 3, below).[93] Nevertheless, in the context of the ethical framework of the Washington Principles, the question is whose interests in such cases should have priority: a museum that bought the paintings in the 1970s on the regular art market; heirs of the art dealer that acquired the confiscated works in 1931 and lost them as the result of the Nazi-regime in 1940; or perhaps even an unknown third party in Ukraine that lost the works as the result of confiscation in the early 1920s?

3.3 Concluding remarks on the material norm

Inconsistencies in outcomes, as seen in the categories of 'early sales', 'sales by art dealers' and '*Fluchtgut*' sales, illustrate that no clear definition exists of what is considered an unjustified taking ('Nazi looting'). In addition to establishing what constitutes a 'forced sale' – and the limits of that concept – many other difficulties surface in determining what is a 'just and fair solution'. How, for example, to deal with the interests of a new possessor, who may have acquired the artefact for a considerable sum of money and in good faith (as in the French Pissarro case noted in the introduction)? Furthermore, how should earlier compensation or settlements regarding the artefact influence the outcome of claims now?

On another note: is it justifiable to take stock of the interests of the general public in cases involving important works of art in museums, in line with the internationalist (or 'universalist') point of view in the wider restitution debate?[94] How to see, for example, the disappearance of an iconic painting like the Klimt portrait of Adele Bloch Bauer II from public display?[95] If the interest of the general public are considered relevant, that would amount to an argument against the return of such works to private ownership, and

93 For the US case: *Stroganoff-Scherbatoff v Weldon* (n. 91); the UK case is *Princess Paley Olga v Weisz* (1929) Court of Appeal, 1 KB 718; and the French case, in part denied on the basis of the Act of State doctrine: *De Keller v Maison de la Pensée Française* (1954) 82 Journal du Droit International (Clunet) 119 (Civil Tribunal of Seine).

94 'Cultural property internationalism is shorthand for the proposition that everyone has an interest in the preservation and enjoyment of cultural property', an argument formulated by Merryman and often used against the restitution of artefacts to source countries and in support of the idea that major (western) public museums are the best place for important works of art. See J.H. Merryman, 'Cultural Property Internationalism' (2005) 12 *International Journal of Cultural Property* 11.

95 K. Kazakina, 'Oprah Said to Snag $150 Million Selling Klimt to Chinese Buyer' (8 February 2017) *Bloomberg News* <https://www.bloomberg.com/news/articles/2017-02-08/oprah-said-to-snag-150-million-selling-klimt-to-chinese-buyer>.

perhaps in favour of a financial settlement over restitution. This in turn raises another question: what exactly is the *rationale* of the present-day norm? Is it compensation for injustices of the past by a government that may be held responsible in some way, or is it about restoring families in their rights with regard to specific artefacts (i.e. re-uniting families with their heirlooms)?

Every case is different and, as such, alternative procedures, with the flexibility to accommodate creative and fact-specific solutions, may be an efficient way to resolve claims. This also requires the availability of mechanisms to further develop the fair and just norm. However, at a procedural level, there appears to be a discrepancy between the approach in the US, where cases are litigated, and the 'ethical approach in Europe, where cases depend on ADR methods, as illustrated in the next section.

4 Access to justice

The next section addresses access to justice and the extent to which claims may be assessed on their individual merits. The issue here is whether parties have a neutral forum to turn to for clarification of the just and fair rule, and whether compliance to the norm is overseen by a public body. The Washington Principles, along with later soft-law instruments, stress the importance of a non-legalistic approach. In these Principles, the signatory states agreed to 'develop national processes [..], particularly as they relate to ADR mechanisms for resolving ownership issues.'[96] But what neutral ADR procedures are available for a neutral assessment and interpretation of facts – fact that often are ambiguous?

4.1 The ethical model in Western Europe: Restitution committees

At the turn of the 21st century, a number of Western European governments set up alternative procedures for dealing with Nazi-looted art claims: the Spoliation Advisory Panel in the UK, the *CIVS*[97] in France, the Dutch Restitutions Committee in the Netherlands, the *Beratende Kommission* in Germany and the Advisory Board in Austria.[98] These government-appointed committees

96 Washington Principles, principle XI.

97 Commission pour l'indemnisation des victimes de spoliations intervenues du fait de législations antisémites en vigueur pendant l'Occupation (CIVS). See <http://www.civs.gouv.fr/home/>.

98 For an overview of the committees, see A. Marck and E. Muller, 'National Panels advising on Nazi-Looted Art in Austria, France, the United Kingdom, the Netherlands and Germany – A brief Overview' in E. Campfens (ed) *Fair and Just Solutions? Alternatives to Litigation in Nazi-Looted Art Disputes* (2015) Eleven International Publishing.

specialise in out-of-court adjudication or mediation of Holocaust-related art claims. To summarise a few notable characteristics of these committees:

- The role of the Advisory Board of the Commission for Provenance Research in Austria ('*Beirat*'), established under the Art Restitution Act of 1998,[99] is to investigate and decide on the basis of systematic provenance research whether works of art in federal collections should be considered for restitution, regardless of whether or not an individual has brought a claim. This can also apply to items that were originally restituted after Second World War, but subsequently became state property in the course of post-war proceedings on the basis of protective rules for works that were considered national patrimony. At the time of writing, the Commission has issued 337 opinions.[100]
- The French CIVS, established in 1999, is charged with examining individual claims presented by the victims or their heirs to make reparations for damage resulting from spoliations of property that occurred in France under the responsibility of the Vichy authorities.[101] In practice this can result in a situation whereby a claimant has a compensation claim in France for the loss of an item alongside a claim for restitution of that same item from a museum in another country. In June 2017, the CIVS had dealt with 3,259 cases involving personal property, of which 287 involved works of art.[102] Restitution was advised in only a few of these cases, concerning works belonging to the Musées Nationaux Récupération ('MNR') collection of heirless art.
- The UK Spoliation Advisory Panel (SAP), which had dealt with nineteen cases at the time of writing, was established in February 2000 in order to provide an alternative process to litigation and resolve claims relating to art in collections in the UK, lost during the Nazi-era. As stated in its terms of reference, the Panel's function is to achieve a solution which is fair and just to both the claimant and the institution and it may take into account non-legal obligations such as the moral strength of a claim.[103] Claimants can submit claims against institutions to the Panel unilaterally or, in the case of a private collection, at the joint request of the claimant and owner.[104]

---

99 Federal Law on the Restitution of Works of Art from the Austrian Federal Museums and Collections (1998) Federal Law Gazette I No. 181/1998 <http://www.provenienzforschung.gv.at/en/empfehlungen-des-beirats/gesetze/kunstruckgabegesetze/>.

100 *Kommission für Provenienzforschung*, <https://www.provenienzforschung.gv.at/en/empfehlungen-des-beirats/beschluesse/beschluesse-alphabetisch/?decisions-letter=T> accessed 6 November 2017.

101 Marck and Muller (2015) 59.

102 See CIVS, 'Key Figures' (2017) <http://www.civs.gouv.fr/images/pdf/thecivs/key_figures_june_2017.pdf>.

103 The terms of reference of the Spoliation Panel are available at: <https://www.gov.uk/government/groups/spoliation-advisory-panel#terms-of-reference>.

104 Ibid. para 6.

- The Dutch Restitutions Committee, established in 2001, has since dealt with 182 cases regarding 1,617 objects.[105] Most of these objects were part of the Dutch State collection, more specifically belonging to the so-called NK-collection[106] of 'heirless art' – a term used to describe art collections left in the custody of a government and not returned to their pre-war owners. All claims involving works in the Dutch state collection are referred to the Restitutions Committee as a matter of general policy, while claims with regard to other collections can be voluntarily submitted if both parties agree. The Committee's task is to find a 'fair and reasonable' solution for these cases. Dutch Museums generally refer claims involving works of art to the Committee.
- Germany's Advisory Commission on the return of cultural property seized as a result of Nazi persecution (*Beratende Kommission*), initiated in 2003, mediates between current possessors and former owners or their heirs. A request for advice can be laid before the Commission provided that at least one party is a public institution and all the parties involved approve. The Commission seeks to find a just and fair solution in accordance with the Washington Principles and the policies laid out in the so-called *Gemeinsame Erklärung* ('Common Statement'). As of November 2017, the Commission had issued fifteen recommendations.[107]

The mandates, working methods and number of cases dealt with by these committees vary considerably. Charlotte Woodhead notes in relation to the situation in the United Kingdom, that 'in reality the Spoliation Panel's jurisdiction is the *only* method of formal dispute resolution rather than an *alternative* method'.[108] This is an important observation and similarly applies in most other countries. For disputes regarding objects which do not fall within the mandate of these special panels, often no neutral claims procedure is in place to fall back on – with the exception of the US, or in the few cases that still fall under the post-War restitution laws (as in the Bauer case mentioned in the introduction). However, the Gurlitt case in Germany – where a large number of artefacts were found in possession of the son of one of Hitler's main art

105 Dutch Restitution Committee, Two Tasks <https://www.restitutiecommissie.nl/en/two_tasks.html> accessed 6 November 2017. Information on the numbers kindly provided by the Committee on 17 February 2020.

106 *Nederlands Kunstbezit-collectie.*

107 German Lost Art Foundation, Previous Recommendations of the Advisory Commission <https://www.beratende-kommission.de/Webs_BK/EN/Recommendations/Index.html>.

108 C. Woodhead, 'Nazi Era Spoliation: Establishing Procedural and Substantive Principles' (2013) 18 *Art Antiquity and Law* 167.

dealers – is one of the many examples of how problems are *not* limited to public collections.[109]

4.2 Access to justice through courts of law

Parties looking for just and fair solutions to their disputes through regular litigation may find themselves in a legal labyrinth. A common denominator in Nazi-looted art cases is that relevant facts are spread out over a period of some 70-80 years and involve multiple jurisdictions. Property law, moreover, differs from country to country and in the US, from state to state, as well as over time. In common law countries like the UK and US, the position of the dispossessed owner is relatively strong based on the underlying principle that a thief cannot convey good title (the *nemo dat* rule).[110] In countries with a civil law tradition, like most European countries, the position of the current possessor is stronger as a good-faith acquisition, or even the passage of time (adverse possession), may convey to a new possessor a perfectly valid legal title over artefacts that were stolen.[111] All jurisdictions, nevertheless, have in common that possibilities for a court to assess a property claim on its merits are subject to time limits. At a certain moment, the law adjusts itself to reality for the sake of legal certainty, though the moment it does so varies widely.[112]

As explained above, while after the War special restitution laws were enacted in Europe, mostly these laws lost their effect as a result of limitation

109 C. Hickley, *The Munich Art Hoard: Hitler's Dealer and His Secret Legacy* (2015) Thames and Hudson; N Palmer, 'Unclaimed art and the duty of active pursuit: Cornelius Gurlitt and the hidden hoard' (2014) 19 *Art Antiquity and Law* 41.

110 In the words of J. Holmes: 'Throughout the course of human history, the perpetration of evil has inevitably resulted in the suffering of the innocent, and those who act in good faith. And the principle has been basic in the law that a thief conveys no title as against the true owner.' *Silsbury v McCoon* (1850) New York Court of Appeals, 3 NY 379, 383-384, cited in *Menzel v List* (1966) Supreme Court, New York County, 267 NYS 2d 804.

111 For opposite outcomes in similar cases on Second World War looting the Dutch Land Sachsen ruling denying a claim on a painting looted from Dresden applying the limitation period from the moment of the loss (*Land Sachsen* (1998) Hoge Raad, Case No. 16546, ECLI:NL:HR:1998:ZC2644), versus UK and US similar cases that were upheld: (England and Wales): *City of Gotha and Federal Republic of Germany v Sotheby's and Cobert Finance SA* (1998) No. 1993 C 3428 (QB); (US): *Kunstsammlungen zu Weimar v Elicofon* (1982) United States Court of Appeals for the Second Circuit, 678 F2d 1150). For a German denial of a claim regarding Nazi-loss on the basis of the 30-year limitation period, see *Landgericht Frankfurt am Main Urt* (2016) Az: 2-21 O 251/15. See also, on the clash between legal approaches, *Malewicz v City of Amsterdam* (2005) United States District Court for the District of Columbia, 362 F. Supp2d 298, 302-304, in this case Dutch law vs. US (NY) law.

112 E.g. Chechi (2014) 89.

periods laid down therein for filing claims.[113] Since 1954, international conventions were adopted that address looting of cultural objects and their return to countries of origin or former owners.[114] However, these conventions must be implemented into national law and, more importantly in the present context, do not apply retroactively. Also these convention therefor are of no avail in this field.

Several of the international declarations, signed by the international community as a follow-up to the 1998 Washington Principles, include recommendations to proceed with legislative reforms.[115] These recommendations, however, are mostly characterised by non-committal wording. The Terezín Declaration on Holocaust Era and Related Issues 2009, for example declared that:

> Governments should consider all relevant issues when applying various legal provisions that may impede the restitution of art and cultural property, in order to achieve just and fair solutions, as well as alternative dispute resolution, where appropriate under the law.[116]

Attempts by the EU and UNESCO to harmonise rules, or develop dispute resolution methods, have so far remained unsuccessful. The 2009 UNESCO Draft Declaration of Principles Relating to Cultural Objects Displaced in Connection with the Second World War, which relies on interstate co-operation and return as in the post-war Inter-Allied model for 'external restitution', was never adopted.[117] This was primarily due to conflicting views on the issue of 'restitution in kind' – i.e. on the legality of holding on to artefacts taken from

113 At times judges may find a 'loophole', mostly if it concerned a loss by clear confiscation, either on grounds of a 'void' transaction (France) or on grounds that it had been impossible for claimants to meet deadlines set in restitution laws. See the German *Hans Sachs Poster Collection* (2012) Bundesgerichtshof, V ZR 279/10; in France, the 2017 *Bauer* case (n. 1) and the *Gentili di Giuseppe et al v Musée du Louvre* (n. 41).

114 E.g. Convention for the Protection of Cultural Property in the Event of Armed Conflict (adopted 14 May 1954) 249 UNTS 240 and First Protocol to the Convention for the Protection of Cultural Property in the Event of Armed Conflict (adopted 14 May 1954) 249 UNTS 358; Convention on the Means of Prohibiting and Preventing the Illicit Import, Export and Transfer of Ownership of Cultural Property (adopted 14 November 1970) 823 UNTS 231; Convention on Stolen or Illegally Exported Cultural Objects (adopted 24 June 1995) 2421 UNTS 457.

115 The 1999 Council of Europe Resolution 1205 being most firm in recommending (13): 'It may be necessary to facilitate restitution by providing for legislative change with particular regard being paid to: (i) Extending or removing statutory limitation periods; (ii) removing restrictions on inalienability [...] (iv) Waiving export controls [emphasis added, the word 'may' is noncommittal].

116 Terezin Declaration; this is obviously not a firm obligation as it depends on national views if it is 'appropriate'.

117 Section 2, above.

the territory of Germany by the Red Army as War reparations.[118] With regard to such an interstate system and its (in)efficiency in respect of ensuring rights of individual former owners, it should be considered that the persecuted and dispossessed families, today often are no longer nationals of the country where the looting took place.

At a European Union level, in 2003 the European Parliament adopted a resolution on artefacts looted during the Second World War.[119] In this Resolution, which was never followed up, the lack of legal certainty, transparency and coherent approach was highlighted. It therefore called upon the European Commission to launch an investigation into the development of a 'transparent remedial structure' for disputes.[120] The resolution emphasised that this 'should not only contribute to a more consistent and predictable internal market in art works, they should also improve access to justice and respect the rule of law'. Since 2014, the European Parliament has further considered the issue and has worked on a resolution that calls for legislation on the subject of provenance research, and the creation of databases that would document ownership information to enhance due diligence in the art trade.[121] In other words, the objective of such legislation would be to facilitate claims by making information more accessible.

4.3 The US approach

Title claims to Nazi-looted art pose major challenges for former owners and, often, are not supported by private law regulations. The US legal system is an exception. Claimants have more success in litigating Nazi-looted art cases and courts, particularly in California and New York, are more willing to exercise jurisdiction. In this regard, as early as 1966 a claim by Erna Menzel, a Jewish art collector, to a Chagall painting found in possession of Alfred List was upheld by the New York Supreme Court.[122] The painting had been confiscated in 1941 in Brussels and she had been looking for it ever since:

> The court has found that [...] it was pillaged and plundered by the Nazis. No title could have been conveyed by them as against the rightful owners. The law stands

118 Annex IV to the UNESCO Draft of the Declaration of Principles Relating to Cultural Objects Displaced in Connection with the Second World War (n. 37). See also Campfens (2015) 35-36.

119 See n. 33, above.

120 Ibid.

121 European Parliament Resolution of 17 January 2019 on Cross-border Claims of Works of Art and Cultural Goods Looted in Armed Conflicts and Wars, 2017/2023 INI.

122 *Menzel v List* (n. 110).

> as a bulwark against the handiwork of evil, to guard to rightful owners the fruits of their labors.[123]

As a point of interest, in the *Menzel v List* case, List was awarded damages in a third-party action amounting to the value of the painting, payable by the art dealer who had sold him the Chagall (i.e. redress 'upstream').[124] Such liability, however, seems to be often excluded by auction houses today.

4.3.1 US jurisdiction and state immunity

The Act of State Doctrine would normally require a court to refrain from examining the validity of acts by foreign governments (like seizures or post-war restitution decisions), and is for example a reason for courts – in the US and elsewhere – to dismiss claims regarding artefacts confiscated and nationalised in the 1920s by the Soviet authorities.[125] In the case of Holocaust takings, however, this doctrine does not always apply in the US as it never recognised the Third Reich as a sovereign state.[126]

Following the *Altmann* litigation (2001-2004), US courts have considered Nazi-looted art cases concerning artefacts not physically in the US, even where post-war acts by recognised states are involved for example post-war restitution decisions.[127] The *Altmann* litigation dealt with six paintings by Gustav Klimt, amongst them the famous *Lady in Gold,* which had belonged to the Jewish Bloch-Bauer family, and were confiscated during the Nazi era in Vienna. The Austrian National Gallery came into the possession of the paintings and refused to return them to the heir – by then living in the US – after the War. The case is considered seminal because it opened the doors of the US courts to claimants of Nazi-looted art seeking redress against foreign nations or institutions, in spite of the rule stating that foreign states and their acts are normally exempt from jurisdiction in another state. The implication of the Supreme Court's 2004 ruling is that, in spite of such immunity as provided for in the US by the Foreign Sovereign Immunity Act (FSIA), claims based on

---

123 Ibid.

124 The value of the painting at the time of trial, awarded on the basis of a breach of an implied warranty: *Menzel v List and Perls* (1969) New York Court of Appeals, No. 298 NYS 2d 979. Similarly, in the case *Rosenberg v Seattle Art Museum and Knoedler-Modarco* the Knoedler Gallery in the US was held liable to compensate the museum for its loss of a Matisse painting (L'Odalisque) after restitution to the heirs of Rosenberg, who lost possession of the Matisse painting by confiscation in Paris in 1941. See <https://plone.unige.ch/art-adr/cases-affaires/odalisque-painting-2013-paul-rosenberg-heirs-and-seattle-art-museum>.

125 See the cases in n. 93, above, an accompanying text. The Soviet Government was recognised by the US in 1933. For a recent case concerning Bolshevik takings see *Konowaloff v The Metropolitan Museum of Art* (2012) United States Court of Appeals for the Second Circuit, No. 11-4338.

126 *Menzel v List* (n. 110).

127 *Republic of Austria et al v Altmann* (n. 42).

Nazi takings may be the exception.[128] This exception 'abrogates sovereign immunity in any case where rights in property taken in violation of international law are in issue and that property is owned or operated by an agency or instrumentality of the foreign state and that agency or instrumentality is engaged in a commercial activity in the United States.'[129] As to this last condition of 'commercial activity', the *Altmann* case made it clear that the availability of a museum catalogue in the US is sufficient. Such a low threshold illustrates the readiness of US courts to take jurisdiction in Holocaust-related cases.[130] In this regard the Californian District Court in the *Altmann* case in 2001 rejected the plea by Austria that the matter should have been litigated in Austria on the ground that the US court was forum *non conveniens*:

> Plaintiff's claims, if asserted in Austria, will most likely be barred by the statute of limitations of thirty years. [...] If Plaintiff's claims are barred by the statute of limitations, she would be left without a remedy; clearly, therefore, Austria is not an adequate alternative forum for Plaintiff's claims.[131]

This trend, of US courts being willing to hear Holocaust-related art claims, is expected to get a boost with the enactment of two pieces of legislation. In the first place, in 2016 the so-called HEAR Act was adopted.[132] It establishes a federal limitation period of six years for claims to Nazi-confiscated art after the actual discovery of the objects, to 'ensure that claims to Nazi-confiscated art are adjudicated in accordance with United States policy as expressed in the Washington Conference Principles on Nazi-Confiscated Art, the Holocaust Victims Redress Act, and the Terezín Declaration.' The extension of limitation periods is found in section 5(a): 'This bill will allow civil claims or causes of action for the recovery of artwork or certain other property lost between January 1, 1933, and December 31, 1945, because of Nazi persecution to be

128 Ibid. It was a 'Statutory Holding' allowing retroactive application of the exceptions in the FSIA to foreign states' immunity from suit and by doing so, allowing for US courts to take on jurisdiction. After this ruling, the parties then agreed on international arbitration.

129 As cited in de *Csepel et al v Republic of Hungary et al* (Memorandum Opinion, 2016) United States District Court of the District of Columbia, No 10-1261 (ESH), 28.

130 Schönenberger (2007) 213, citing in fn 1102 from a review by G. Cohen of M.J. Bazyler, *Holocaust Justice: The Battle for Restitution in America's Courts* (2003) New York University Press: 'The author [...] posits that the 'real hero' is the American justice system, the only forum in the world where Holocaust claims can be heard today'.

131 *Altmann v Republic of Austria et al* (2001) United States District Court for the Central District of California, 142 F. Supp2d 1187, 1209.

132 Holocaust Expropriated Art Recovery Act of 2016 (114th Congress, 2nd Session, S.2763) (HEAR Act). See N.M. O'Donnell, 'The Holocaust Expropriated Art Recovery Act. A Sea Change in US Law of Restitution' (2017) 22 Art Antiquity and Law 273. See also (in Dutch) L.P.W. Van Vliet 'Verjaring en kunstvoorwerpen' in: Loth M.A., Van Vliet L.P.W., *Recht over tijd. Hoever reikt het privaatrecht in het verleden? Preadviezen Nederlandse Vereniging voor Burgerlijk Recht* (2018), Zutphen 2018, p. 128-132.

commenced within six years after the claimant's actual discovery.' A 'sunset' clause is set for 2029.

The second legal change in 2016 concerns the Foreign Cultural Exchange Jurisdictional Immunity Clarification Act.[133] Initially this legislation was aimed at providing greater security exceptions that may have the opposite effect. The first exception is 'Nazi-era claims', and the second exception concerns artefacts 'taken in connection with the acts of a foreign government as part of a systematic campaign of coercive confiscation or misappropriation of works from members of a targeted and vulnerable group.' Thus, artefacts owned by foreign states or their agents on loan in the US that are allegedly lost under these circumstances, appear not to be barred from litigation in the US.

A third development is that in a 2016 ruling in the case *Simon v Republic of Hungary* – that on itself does not concern artefacts – the court held that confiscation of private property can, in itself, constitute genocide.[134] Leaving aside the matter of whether this interpretation of 'genocide' is consistent with the generally accepted notion of the term,[135] it may be a sign that US courts are willing to adjudicate cases involving Holocaust losses (in this case, confiscations by the Hungarian Wartime authorities). This notion was confirmed in the *Herzog* verdict later in 2016 that does concern confiscated artefacts.[136]

4.3.2 *US jurisdiction over European cases*

Possibilities to litigate Holocaust-related art claims in the US would seem to be a positive development in terms of ensuring access to justice. Moreover, it facilitates the clarification of standards by US courts. From a European perspective, however, it may have undesirable consequences, namely that cases that concern European collections and European parties, are being brought before US courts.[137] Some examples will be given below.

---

133 Foreign Cultural Exchange Jurisdictional Immunity Clarification Act of 2016 (114th Congress, HR 6477). See I. Wuerth, 'An Art Museum Amendment to the Foreign Sovereign Immunities Act' (2017) Lawfare <https://www.lawfareblog.com/art-museum-amendment-foreign-sovereign-immunities-act>.

134 *Simon v Republic of Hungary* (2016) United States Court of Appeals for the District of Columbia Circuit, No. 14-7082: 'Such takings, did more than effectuate genocide or serve as a means of carrying out genocide. Rather, we see the expropriations as themselves genocide.'

135 Convention on the Prevention and Punishment of the Crime of Genocide (adopted 9 December 1948, entered into force 12 January 1951) UNGA Res 260 A (III).

136 *De Csepel et al v Republic of Hungary, et al* (n. 129) 112.

137 See, on the expected favourable consequences of this act for claimants: W.D. Cohan, 'A Suit Over Schiele Drawings Invokes New Law on Nazi-Looted Art' (27 February 2017) *The New York Times* <https://www.nytimes.com/2017/02/27/arts/design/a-suit-over-schiele-drawings-invokes-new-law-on-nazi-looted-art-html>. See also O'Donnell (2017).

The *Altmann* case, concerning six Klimt paintings as discussed above, is perhaps the most well-known example.[138] Although the claim was later settled by international arbitration in 2006, this was enabled by the fact that Altmann was authorised by the US Supreme Court in 2004 to proceed with a civil action against Austria.[139]

The litigation regarding Egon Schiele's *Portrait of Wally* in Vienna's Leopold Museum collection, which ran from 1998 to 2010, is another well-known example.[140] The case was initiated while *Portrait of Wally* was on loan in New York in 1998, and eventually ended after the parties agreed to settle their dispute by way of payment of US $19 million to the heirs of the former owners.[141]

As in the Schiele case, the case of *Malewicz v City of Amsterdam* concerned a collection on a temporary loan to the US, this time a collection of Malewicz paintings from the Stedelijk Museum in Amsterdam.[142] Although Nazi-looting was not the issue, the initial loss by Malevicz of his artefacts occurred within the context of the Nazi-period. The district court rulings in 2005 and 2007 enabled jurisdiction by a US court, even though immunity for seizure arrangements had been in place. It held that immunity for seizure does not mean immunity from suit.[143] Also in this case, the *Malewicz* case was settled out of court in favour of the heirs.[144]

Another well-known example that centres around Nazi-looted art held by a European museum is the case *Cassirer v Thyssen-Bornemisza Collection Foundation*, subject to litigation from 2005 till 2019.[145] It concerns the painting *Street Scene* by Pissarro that had been part of the pre-War collection of the Jewish Cassirer family, had been lost in Germany in 1939, and had eventually been bought by baron Thyssen-Bornemisza bought at a New York gallery in 1976. The 2015 district court verdict, rendered under Spanish law, found in favour of the Spanish museum. Nevertheless, the judge urged the museum to: 'pause, reflect and consider whether it would be appropriate to work towards a mutually agreeable resolution of this action, in light of Spain's

138 Section 4.3.1, above.

139 *Republic of Austria et al v Altmann* (n. 42).

140 *United States v Portrait of Wally* (2009) United States District Court for the Southern District of New York, 663 F. Supp 2d 232.

141 Stipulation and Order of Settlement and Discontinuance of 19 July 2010. Ibid.

142 *Malewicz v City of Amsterdam* (2007) United States District Court for the District of Columbia, 517 F. Supp 2d 322: foreign states lending art to the United States are not *per se* immune from jurisdiction, even if the loaned objects were precluded from seizure under the Immunity From Seizure Act (IFSA).

143 This case was the reason for the amendment of the IFSA, see Wuerth (n. 133). A Chechi, E Velioglu and MA Renold, 'Case Note – 14 Artworks – Malewicz Heirs and City of Amsterdam' (2013) Platform ArThémis, Art-Law Centre, University of Geneva.

144 Chechi, Velioglu and Renold (2013).

145 *Cassirer v Thyssen-Bornemisza Collection Foundation* (2015) United States District Court for the Central District of California, 153 F. Supp 3d 1148.

acceptance of the Washington Conference Principles and the Terezín Declaration, and, specifically, its commitment to achieve 'just and fair solutions' for victims of Nazi persecution.'[146]

Another (ongoing) case concerns the so-called *'Welfenschatz'* ('Guelph Treasure') – a hoard of medieval treasures originating from Brunswick Cathedral in Germany.[147] In 2014, the German *Beratende Kommission* denied this claim, according to the committee because it did not meet the criteria defining a forced sale. Subsequently, a claim against the Berlin Museum Foundation (SPK) and the German Government was filed in the US.[148] The suit was filed on behalf of the heirs of the two art dealers who had acquired the Guelph Treasure from the Duke of Brunswick in 1929 and who in 1935 had sold most of the objects to the Dresdner Bank. In March 2017, the District Court ruled in favour of US jurisdiction, under reference to the HEAR Act: 'Congress specifically recognized and did not foreclose the use of litigation as a means to resolve claims to recover Nazi-confiscated art'.[149] In February 2021, however, the US Surpreme Court ruled in favour of the German State by limiting jurisdiction over claims to Nazi looted art to takings 'in violation of international law'.[150] Since that ruling did not shut de door for jurisdiction by a US court over this case, litigation is expected to continue in lower courts

Furthermore, in December 2016 the Bavarian *Staatsgemäldesammlungen* and the Bavarian State were sued in a New York court by the heirs of Flechtheim, a Jewish art dealer from Berlin, over eight paintings by Beckmann, Klee and Gris in a Munich museum.[151] As seen above in section 3.3.1.2, previously two *Flechtheim* cases had been considered by the German *Beratende Kommission.* The first claim was upheld, while the second was dismissed.[152]

Likewise, in March 2017, litigation was initiated in New York over Kandinsky's *Das Bunte Leben* in the Munich Lenbachhaus Museum, a painting

146 After appeal the district court confirmed that the Thyssen-Bornemisza Museum acquired lawful ownership according to Spanish law. See *Cassirer v Thyssen-Bornemisza Collection Foundation* (2019) United States District Court for the Central District of California, No. CV 05-CV-03459.

147 See section 3.2.4, above.

148 *Philipp et al v Federal Republic of Germany et al* (n. 86).

149 Ibid. See also O'Donnell (2017) 277.

150 In its ruling of 3 February 2021 the Supreme Court confirmed (revived?) the 'domestic takings' doctrine that implicates that the expropriation by foreign governments of their own nationals are off-limit to US courts, by ruling that the expropriation exception in the FSIA ('in violation of international law') is limited to the expropriation of *non*-nationals (those being covered by international law) (n. 86). See <https://www.lawfareblog.com/recent-supreme-court-rulings-foreign-sovereign-immunities-act> (acc. 28 April 2021).

151 *Hulton et al. v Bayerische Gemäldesammlungen* (n. 84).

152 Recommendation of the Advisory Commission on the Return of Cultural Property Seized as a Result of Nazi Persecution (n. 83); Recommendation in the Matter of the Heirs of Alfred Flechtheim v Stiftung Kunstsammlung Nordrhein-Westfalen, Düsseldorf (n. 61).

owned by a German bank.[153] The painting had been owned by the Dutch Lewenstein family, and the claim that is filed on behalf of the heirs seeks damages for the value of the painting, stated in the complaint as US$ 80 million.[154] The case is related to a claim to another Kandinsky painting that also had been owned by the Lewenstein family and that, today, is in the collection of the Amsterdam Stedelijk Museum (mentioned above in section 3.2.3). Although that last claim was denied before the Dutch Restitutions Committee in 2018, and the Amsterdam District Court did not see any reason to reverse this outcome, it may well be reversed in the light of (political) pressure to reconsider the claim.[155]

4.4 Concluding remarks on access to justice

The current legal framework is highly fragmented as to the possibilities of getting claims resolved by a neutral forum. There is a discrepancy between the US and European jurisdictions. In the US, where the interests of original owners of stolen artworks are traditionally taken more into consideration, courts are willing to take jurisdiction over works that were looted by the Nazis, also in cases that concern works in Europe or are under an immunity for seizure arrangement whilst on loan in the US. This does not mean however that the ADR model as propagated in the Washington Principles has been abandoned in the US, particularly given the following statement in the HEAR Act:

> While litigation may be used to resolve claims to recover Nazi-confiscated art, it is the sense of Congress that the private resolution of claims by parties involved, on the merits and through the use of alternative dispute resolution such as mediation panels established for this purpose with the aid of experts in provenance research and history, will yield just and fair resolutions in a more efficient and predictable manner.[156]

In other words, the existence of a European ADR system with certain guarantees as to due process might reduce the need to take cases overseas. In Europe, however, the present situation is fragmented. In some European states, the

153 *Lewenstein et al v Bayerische Landesbank* (2017) No 17-CV-0160 (United States District Court for the Southern District of New York).

154 Ibid., at 22.

155 Binding Advice in the case Bild mit Häusern by Wassily Kandinsky (2018) RC 3.141, *Plaintiffs v. Municipality of Amsterdam*, ECLI:NL:RBAMS:2020:6277 (District Court Amsterdam, 16 December 2020). On the political pressure to reverse this outcome, see the Letter of the Mayor and Aldermen to the Amsterdam Municipal Council, https://amsterdam.raadsinformatie.nl/modules/1/Berichten%20uit%20het%20college/651069 (acc. 15 May 2021).

156 HEAR Act, section 8.

Washington Principles appear not to be implemented at all.[157] In some Western-European countries, certain claims can be referred to national committees. Other cases are settled in confidential agreements – provided the parties are willing: the 'moral' approach. Such settlements will obviously depend on the bargaining chips brought to the table.[158] One such bargaining chip might well be the possibility of taking a case to the United States for costly and lengthy litigation.

5 Final observations

Although the looting of cultural objects by the Nazis obviously has moral and ethical implications, the conclusion of this chapter is that a legal approach is also needed. The role of law in this regard should be to set clear, consistent and transparent standards to ensure cases are treated equally and outcomes are just and fair.

The findings in the preceding sections highlight a lack of clarity of today's standards in the ethical model. The opinion was put forward that the rule in the Washington Principles, prescribing 'fair and just solutions, according to the circumstances of a case' for title claims to Nazi-looted art, is based on two pillars. First, the intangible quality of artefacts, and their ability to be symbolic for lost family histories, is reason for special treatment: these claims are not merely about stolen possessions but about family heirlooms. Furthermore, the rule aims at redress for involuntary losses with a direct causal link between the persecution of the owner, such as a confiscation, theft or sale under duress. If that link cannot be established and it concerns a voluntary transaction, then the 'just and fair' rule should not apply as it does not concern 'Nazi-looted art'. The 2009 Draft UNESCO Declaration – that was never adopted but nevertheless may serve as inspiration – defines Nazi-looting as takings that are 'offensive to the principles of humanity and dictates of public conscience'.

Another finding was that access to justice in the ethical framework is limited. The Washington Principles, along with other non-binding instruments in this field, stress the importance of alternative dispute resolution for resolving ownership issues. And indeed, parties searching for just and fair solutions on the merits of a case often *need* alternative procedures as most legal systems do not support ownership claims regarding losses that took place so many years ago. Increased possibilities to litigate Holocaust-related cases in the United States, however, raise the question as to how this trend will have an

157 See W.A. Fisher and R. Weinberger, 'Holocaust-Era Looted Art: A Current World-Wide Overview' (2014) <https://www.lootedart.com/QTV75V817471>.

158 F. Shyllon, 'The Rise of Negotiation (ADR) in Restitution, Return and Repatriation of Cultural Property: Moral Pressure and Power Pressure' (2017) 22 Art Antiquity and Law 130.

impact on European cases. This institutional vacuum in terms of a lack of access to justice in Europe needs to be addressed. A lack of clarity at both a material and a procedural level – what is the norm and who can clarify it? – may result in legal insecurity, inconsistent outcomes and injustice. Or, as the European Parliament put it as early as 2003: 'the current situation lacks legal certainty, transparency and a coherent approach. This is a cross-border issue calling for a cross-border solution'.[159]

To fill this 'vacuum', the establishment of a European claims procedure could be considered. States which have signed instruments like the Washington Principles and the Terezín Declaration, would in that way meet their promise to develop mechanisms to ensure that the 'just and fair' norm is upheld. The late Professor Norman Palmer voiced this idea as follows:

> [T]he formation of a body [...] to which nations and individuals might refer claims. Either on an *ad hoc* basis or on the basis of a formal agreement. [It] might offer a variety of approaches to claims: arbitration, mediation and conciliation, expert neutral appraisal, binding expert opinion, or the straightforward process of recommendation and moral assessment that lies at the heart of the English regime in this field.[160]

It is a separate matter where such an organisation would fit in – e.g. the European Union or the Council of Europe. It would also be premature to delve into the question of whether such a process should be voluntary or semi-obligatory – for example by including a declaration of intent in the codes of conduct of museums and art dealer associations, or incorporating in the general terms of art fairs and auction houses the requirement that disputes be referred to the body in question. The paramount issue would be the neutrality and transparency of procedures, and the authority of its working methods. With regard to this, a pragmatic argument in conclusion. Recognition of the rights of victims of the Holocaust to their lost cultural objects has triggered broader awareness and discussion on the legitimacy of possession of 'tainted' cultural objects. A proactive and international approach might help structure that wider field. Whilst the historical background of looting practices may be specific to a certain place and time, the effects of such looting practices can be felt in any country in the world with an art market, art collectors or museums, and at any moment in time.

---

159 See n. 33 and section 4.2 above.

160 The thought builds on the 2003 Resolution of the European Parliament and was supported by a recent study: M.A. Renold and ArThemis, 'Cross-Border Restitution Claims of Art Looted in Armed Conflicts and Wars and Alternatives to Court Litigations' (2016) <http://publications.europa.eu/resource/cellar/f600d443-20a9-11e6-86d0-01aa75ed71a1.0001.03/DOC_1>.

5 Colonial looting and indigenous peoples' lost heritage

ABSTRACT

Chapter 5 deals with claims by former owners to cultural objects lost as a result of colonial looting practices. This is a category which recently received much attention. A common response to such claims by holding states has been that the takings were lawful at the time and, therefore, not a legal but (merely) an ethical issue. But is that so? It is argued that it is not a lack of legal norms that explains this (belated) attention for colonial looting but, rather, the asymmetrical application of norms. Moreover, a human rights law approach, focusing on the heritage aspect of cultural objects for people today – instead of a sole focus on ownership – offers useful tools to structure this field. To illustrate these points, a case concerning an African ancestral sculpture today known as the 'Bangwa Queen' will be assessed on its merits under international law. The Bangwa Queen is of spiritual importance to the Bangwa, a people indigenous to the western part of Cameroon. She was taken as part of a collection of so-called *lefem* figures and other artefacts by German colonisers in 1899 and is currently part of a French museum collection.

Questions addressed in this chapter are: How did international law on looting and restitution of cultural objects develop? How were claims to colonial booty in the post-colonial era generally perceived? Can recent soft law in this field be seen as a reflection of evolving law, and what is the status of the United Nations Declaration on the Rights of Indigenous Peoples in this regard?

The Bangwa Queen, photographed sometime in the 1950s or 1960s when the Bangwa Queen was in the United States. Reproduced from Robert Brain and Adam Pollock, *Bangwa Funerary Sculpture* (Gerald Duckworth & Company Limited 1971) 125.

*The Bangwa Queen: Artefact or heritage?**

'One of the most noble incarnations of a people's genius is its cultural heritage. The vicissitudes of history have nevertheless robbed many peoples of this inheritance. They ... have not only been despoiled of ... masterpieces but (were) also robbed of a memory. ... These men and women have the right to recover these cultural assets which are part of their being.'[1]

1 Introduction

Forty years after this plea and some 20 United Nations (UN) Resolutions later, the lingering discussion about colonial takings in Western museums seems to have entered a new phase.[2] In November 2017, President Emmanuel Macron of France set the stage by announcing a policy of restitution of African artefacts from French museums.[3] This change in attitude is not limited to France, as illustrated by the presentation in Germany in March 2019 of new government policy to enable the return of colonial takings, and guidelines of a group of ethnological museums in the Netherlands.[4] In France this was followed by President Macron's decision to return statutes and regalia that were taken as

---

* This chapter was originally published in the *International Journal of Cultural Property* (26 (1): 75-110) in April 2019. In the text for this thesis, a few corrections have been made.

1 A.M. M'Bow, 'A Plea for the Return of an Irreplaceable Cultural Heritage to Those Who Created It' (1978) <http://www.unesco.org/culture/laws/pdf/PealforReturn_DG_1978.pdf>.

2 For an overview, see 'Restitution of Cultural Property: Resolutions Adopted by the United Nations General Assembly about Return and Restitution of Cultural Property' (*UNESCO*) <http://www.unesco.org/new/en/culture/themes/restitution-of-cultural-property/united-nations/>.

3 E. Macron, 'Discours d'Emmanuel Macron à l'université de Ouagadougou' (Burkina Faso, 2017) <https://www.elysee.fr/emmanuel-macron/2017/11/28/discours-demmanuel-macron-a-luniversite-de-ouagadougou> accessed 18 March 2019.

4 See the German 'Eckpunkte zum Umgang mit Sammlungsgut aus Kolonialen Kontexten', Standing Conference of the Ministers of Education and Cultural Affairs of the Länder in the Federal Republic of Germany, Anlage II z. NS 1. Kultur-MK (2019) <https://www.kmk.org/fileadmin/pdf/PresseUndAktuelles/2019/2019-03-25_Erste-Eckpunkte-Sammlungsgut-koloniale-Kontexte_final.pdf> accessed 19 April 2019; for the Dutch guidelines, see 'Dutch National Museum of World Cultures Announces Principles Claims Colonial Collections' (*Museum Volkenkunde*, 2019) <https://www.volkenkunde.nl/en/about-volkenkunde/press/dutch-national-museum-world-cultures-nmvw-announces-principles-claims> accessed 19 April 2019.

war booty during a punitive colonial expedition in 1892 from the Kingdom of Dahomey to Benin,[5] a claim that had been rejected not long before.[6] And in May 2018, the German Prussian Cultural Heritage Foundation – one of the main 'universal' museums[7] – returned artefacts with the argumentation that these were 'taken without the consent of the Alaska Natives and were therefore removed [...] unlawfully.'[8] These are remarkable developments given that a common response to such claims is that they lack legal grounds. In this chapter, the view is taken that it is not a lack of legal norms that explains this belated discussion but, rather, the asymmetrical application of such norms. Furthermore, it is suggested that a human rights law approach as taken in the 2007 United Nations Declaration on the Rights of Indigenous Peoples (UNDRIP), offers useful tools to structure this field.[9] As a case example, it will evaluate a claim regarding an African ancestral sculpture known as the 'Bangwa Queen' (Figure 1) on its merits under international law.

The Bangwa Queen is a wooden ancestor sculpture of spiritual importance to the Bangwa, a people indigenous to the western part of Cameroon. She[10] was lost during an expedition by German colonisers who invaded the Bangwa territory in the latter years of the nineteenth century and, today, is part of a French museum collection. She was recognised in 2014 by a Bangwa chief, and, in 2017, their representative contacted the museum.[11] The background and factual circumstances of this case are discussed in the first section of the article. An overview of international standards relevant to this case will follow in the second and third sections. An analysis of the traditional legal framework in the next section will illustrate that norms that protect cultural objects from pillage and destruction have always existed throughout history. At some point, these evolved into (customary) international law under the rules of warfare.

---

5 'Remise du Rapport Savoy/Sarr sur la Restitution du Patrimoine Africain' (*Elysée*, 2018) <https://www.elysee.fr/emmanuel-macron/2018/11/23/remise-du-rapport-savoy-sarr-sur-la-restitution-du-patrimoine-africain>.

6 P. Dagen, 'La Restitution d'Œuvres d'Art?: «?Une Question de Dignité?»' (17 August 2017) *Le Monde* <https://www.lemonde.fr/festival/article/2017/08/17/la-restitution-d-uvres-d-art-une-question-de-dignite_5173397_4415198.html>.

7 In 2002, eighteen Western museums had taken a stance for 'retention' and against restitution of colonial takings in the so-called Declaration on the Importance and Value of Universal Museums. This declaration can still be found on the website of the Hermitage: <http://www.hermitagemuseum.org/wps/portal/hermitage/news/news-item/news/1999_2013/hm11_1_93/?lng=> accessed 31 March 2019.

8 Objects are grave goods from Chenega Island: 'Press Release: Ethnologisches Museum Returns Objects to Alaska Natives' (2018) <http://www.preussischer-kulturbesitz.de/fileadmin/user_upload_SPK/documents/presse/pressemitteilungen/2018/180516_Restitution-Chugach-Ceremony_EN.pdf>.

9 Declaration on the Rights of Indigenous Peoples, UNGA Res. 61/295 (13 September 2007) UN Doc A/RES/61/295 (UNDRIP).

10 Given the meaning of the statue to the Bangwa, the personal pronoun 'she' will be used.

11 Letters by the legal representative of Fon Fontem Assabaton and the Bangwa People of the Fontem Kingdom (8 June 2017, 24 July 2017) (on file with the author).

Therefore, certain acquisitions that occurred at the close of the nineteenth century might well be characterised as unlawful under contemporary international law, notwithstanding Western justifications. Not seldom, though, the exact circumstances of a loss are unclear. Besides, even if it can be argued that a loss was unlawful, a number of legal hurdles may implicate that claims, based on events in a distant past, today are 'stale.'

On the other hand, the rights of former owners to their involuntarily lost artefacts are increasingly acknowledged in soft law instruments, even if a loss predates treaties that specifically arrange for the return of looted artefacts, and regardless of whose hands the objects are found in today. Although such instruments usually take the form of non-binding governmental declarations or private voluntary codes, they seem to reflect evolving international (human rights) law norms. This will be the topic of the third section of this chapter. In this regard, the UNDRIP is important when it comes to the category of artefacts lost as a result of colonial rule. It formulates the rights of indigenous peoples regarding their lost cultural heritage, ranging from a right to access, use, and control to repatriation. Its relevance for the African Bangwa case will be dealt with in the third section. What follows, in short, is a proposition for a legal approach to claims that are often set aside as merely 'moral' in nature.

2 The Bangwa Queen and her loss

2.1 The sculpture and her meaning

Today, the wooden sculpture known as the Bangwa Queen is part of the collection of the Dapper Foundation exhibited in the Musée du Quai Branly Jacques Chirac in Paris.[12] Since her transfer to Berlin in the latter years of the nineteenth century, and her subsequent acquisition by collector Arthur Speyer in 1926, she gained fame as a major work of art.[13] She was featured in a series of photos taken by Man Ray in the 1930s and was part of several important exhibitions such as the 1935 African Negro Art exhibition in New York and, most recently, the 2011 Heroic Africans: Legendary Leaders, Iconic Sculptures exhibition of the Metropolitan Museum of Art. Her 'iconic' import-

12 A picture of the Bangwa Queen was until recently shown on the website of the Dapper Foundation: 'Présentation' (*Fondation Dapper*) <http://www.dapper.fr/en/foundation-presentation.php> accessed 18 March 2019. Musée Dapper, Paris. Inv. no. 3343. In May 2017, the Fondation Dapper announced it was closing a museum. It announced it would continue exhibiting its collection in other museums.

13 B. Von Lintig, 'On the Bangwa Collection Formed by Gustav Conrau' (2017) 86 *Tribal Art* 94.

ance is illustrated by the fact that the Musée Dapper reportedly set a record for the purchase of African art by paying US $3.4 million for her in 1990.[14]

To her creators, the Bangwa people, who are indigenous to the grasslands region of present-day Cameroon,[15] the Bangwa Queen is not a work of art but, rather, is sacred.[16] She is a so-called *lefem* figure, personifying a special ancestor.[17] In Bangwa tradition, individuals may own artefacts, but once a statue is carved as a symbol of authority, it must be presented to the king and, through a series of traditional procedures, is transformed into a religious symbol of authority of the chief.[18] According to Bangwa representatives, this custom is still revered. The Bangwa Queen was such a statue, and she was meant to be kept in the royal shrine for praying and consultation purposes by the reigning king of the Bangwa kingdom Lebang, Fon Asonganyi, the belief being that lefem statues render the ancestor present.[19] This connotation is confirmed by the Metropolitan Museum of Art, which is home to her counterpart, a male ancestral figure seemingly with the same provenance:

> Because of their important status, memorial figures are honoured and well cared for while being housed in a secure place within the king's palace. This work was assembled with other portrait figures from previous generations, including representations of other chiefs, as well as queen mothers, princesses, titled brothers, and favourite wives. The assembly served as a concentrated symbol of dynastic power and continuity, a visual record of family history that inspired deference and obedience. During the ceremonies that surround a chief's funeral and the installation

14 J.L. DeFabo, 'The Bangwa Queen: Interpretations, Constructions, and Appropriations of Meaning of the Esteemed Ancestress Figure from the Cameroon Grassfields' (2014) Senior Projects Spring Paper 14 1, 59 <https://digitalcommons.bard.edu/senproj_s2014/14/>. See S. Muchnic, '$3.4-Million Sculpture Sale Sets Record for African Art' (22 April 1990) *Los Angeles Times* <https://www.latimes.com/archives/la-xpm-1990-04-22-mn-392-story.html>.

15 The name 'Bangwa' is not used consistently. Bangwa territory consists of nine chiefdom, while Fontem is the name of the chief and main village of the most populated kingdom. R. Brain, *The Bangwa of West Cameroon: A Brief Account of Their History and Culture* (1967) London University College, 1. V. Lockhart, 'A Social-Historical Study of Social Change among the Bangwa of Cameroon' (1994) Occasional Papers No 52, 9.

16 For an object to be defined as 'sacred,' the definition used in the NAGPRA is useful: 'Objects that were devoted to a traditional religious ceremony or ritual and which have religious significance or function in the continued observance or renewal of such ceremony.' Native American Graves Protection and Repatriation Act (16 November 1990) 25 USC (NAGPRA) paras 3001-13.

17 At times also referred to as a 'Njuindem,' a woman who has birthed twins and acts as a priestess of the earth. R. Brain and A. Pollock, *Bangwa Funerary Sculpture* (1971) Gerald Duckworth & Company Limited, fig 58. According to A. Schlothauer, 'Gustav Conrau's Cameroon Collection in the Berlin Ethnological Museum' (2015) 9 Kunst & Kontext Humboldt-Forum 20, this is a mistake.

18 Statement of Chief Taku, Bangwa representative (on file with the author).

19 G. Atem, 'Account on the Looting of the Bangwa King and Queen by the Germans', Statement (2017) (on file with the author); Lockhart (1994) 17; Brain and Pollock (1971) 118.

> of his successor, his lefem is exhibited publicly, again as a means to maintain social and political continuity as well as to encourage faith in the strength of royal ancestral power.[20]

To the religious Bangwa people, this spiritual meaning did not extinguish upon the loss of these statues but continues today; misfortunes that have hit the kingdom since the loss are attributed to the absence from the shrine of the lefem figures like the Bangwa Queen.[21] Moreover, she symbolises the lost lives and injustices that occurred at the time.[22]

Her meaning thus varies in different settings and to different people: from an ancestral portrait in between the human and spiritual world in her original African context, to an exotic ethnographic specimen for European scientists at the turn of the nineteenth century, to a famous work of art that has inspired artists and a commodity for Western collectors.[23] As the Bangwa have largely maintained their religious practices and social-cultural structure, this connotation of the Bangwa Queen continues to exist. Several years ago, the late fontem was informed that the Bangwa Queen was in the Metropolitan Museum of Art in New York, presumably on the occasion of the 2011 Heroic Africans exhibition. He visited the United States to ascertain that this was true and recognised the Bangwa Queen.[24] In late 2017, contact was established with the Dapper Foundation, which, however, did not lead to a meeting or dialogue.[25]

2.2 The loss

Bangwa historical accounts report that the Bangwa Queen, together with other lefem figures, were looted by German soldiers when they invaded the palace of the then ruling Fontem Asonganyi (Figure 2) during their conquest of the Bangwa region in 1899/1900.[26] While his quarters were invaded and

---

20 Commemorative Figure (Lefem) from Cameroon, Grassfields Region, Account No 1978.412. 576 <https://www.metmuseum.org/art/collection/search/311037> accessed 18 March 2019. It appears a total of 71 Bangwa objects were delivered to the Berlin Ethnological Museum by Gustav Conrau. See Schlothauer (2015) 24. Von Lintig (2017) 94 concludes that five of these were 'deaccesioned' in the late 1920s and, today, are in private or institutional collections (amongst them, the Bangwa Queen).

21 Atem (2017).

22 A.F. Vrdoljak, *International Law, Museums and the Return of Cultural Objects* (2006) Cambridge University Press, 299: '[F]or colonized peoples, the removal of these cultural objects represented the dispossession of their lands, autonomy and identity.' Bangwa representatives estimate the Bangwa population at 148,000 in 2017 (on file with the author).

23 For details on the provenance of the Bangwa Queen, see DeFabo (2014).

24 Atem (2017).

25 Correspondence between representative of the Bangwa and Dapper Foundation (2017-18) (on file with the author.

26 Atem (2017); affirmed by Brain and Pollock (1971) 118; Lockhart (1994) 29.

plundered, Fontem Asonganyi escaped.[27] After years in hiding, he turned himself in to stop the punitive German military campaign.[28] The Bangwa consider a voluntary transfer of the statues by Fontem Asonganyi unthinkable as that would mean a relinquishment of his spiritual and political powers.[29]

Where Bangwa sources cast no doubt on the loss of the lefem figures by pillage, research by Andreas Shlothauer and Bettina von Lintig indicates that a German named Gustav Conrau acquired these statues between June and September 1899 for the Ethnological Museum in Berlin – just before the punitive military actions that started in December 1899.[30] Conrau's letters from that period to the director of the Berlin museum mention his 'secret' acquisition of 'quite beautiful fetishes' that were 'carefully hidden.' Conrau hints in his letter that the acquisition was with the consent of Fontem Asonganyi.[31] And whilst Shlothauer characterises the acquisition as peaceful trading, Von Lintig leaves that conclusion open.[32] Obviously, 'consent' in these circumstances is a matter of interpretation.[33]

Notwithstanding the uncertainty concerning the exact circumstances of the loss and diverging views on its voluntary nature,[34] the following circumstances are certain. First, the Bangwa Queen was part of a collection of Bangwa statues taken by Germans in the last year of the nineteenth century and dispatched to the Museum für Völkerkunde (Ethnological Museum) in Berlin.

27 Looting of the palace is confirmed by E.M. Chilver, 'The Bangwa and the Germans: A Tailpiece' (1967) 4 Journal of the Historical Society of Nigeria 156 under reference to German colonial archives: 'Von Pavell's force reached Tinto on November 5th 1901. ... achieving little except the capture of some prisoners and much booty.'

28 Atem (2017); confirmed, for example, Ibid. 157.

29 H. Cadman, 'An Assessment Report on the Bangwa Tribal Area in the Mamfe Division of the Cameroon Province', Buea Archive File No. Af.13 (1922) <http://lebialem.info/page/> accessed 18 March 2019: 'The Clan Chief ... has power over all the Chiefs under him, since he alone has the power to commune with or propitiate the spirit of their ancestors.'

30 Schlothauer (2015); Von Lintig (2017). On the punitive actions against the Bangwa, see Chilver (1967) 155, referring also to German colonial archives and the memoirs of Von Puttkamer, the German governor.

31 Gustav Conrau, Letters to Felix von Luschan (11 June and 1 October 1899) *Acta Africa*, vol 21, file E1015/99-49, cited by Schlothauer (2015) 26.

32 Schlothauer (2015) 27: 'The acquisition from the Bangwa can only have been by consensus [...] Theft or the use of force would have been fatal for Conrau.' However, the expedition was fatal for Conrau. Von Lintig (2017) 104.

33 For an impression on colonial acquisition tactics in Africa, see Michel Leiris's diary of a French scientific expedition. M. Leiris, *Phantom Africa* (Seagull Books 2017), translated by Brent Hayes Edwards from the original Michel Leiris, *L'Afrique fantôme* (Gallimard 1934).

34 Sarr and Savoy recommend restitution of 'any objects taken by force or presumed to be acquired through inequitable conditions,' including acquisitions by 'active administrators' or 'through scientific expeditions prior to 1960.' F. Sarr and B. Savoy, 'The Restitution of African Cultural Heritage. Toward a New Relational Ethics' (2018) 61 <http://restitutionreport2018.com/sarr_savoy_en.pdf>. In the field of Nazi-looted art, a sale by a Jewish owner to a Nazi official is considered a 'forced sale'. E. Campfens, 'Nazi-Looted Art: A Note in Favour of Clear Standards and Neutral Procedures' (2017) 22 Art Antiquity and Law 315.

This was shortly after the colonial powers had arranged for the division of Africa at the Berlin Conference on West Africa in 1884-85, justifying the appropriation of land and resources by relying on the *terra nullius* argumentation[35] and their religious duty to spread the 'blessings of civilization.'[36]

By introducing the principle of 'effective control' as a base for territorial claims by European powers, this instigated a period of conquest of African territories by expeditions to hitherto unknown territories in the following years.[37] Germany had claimed the Bangwa territory at the Berlin Conference as part of the territory they named 'Kamerun,' having had a port colony at Douala since 1884. In this context, the expeditions into the Bangwa territory should be seen as being military and political in nature.[38]

Second, Gustav Conrau had a central role in the transaction relating to the Bangwa Queen. Conrau, a 'recruiter, collector on commission, elephant-hunter, researcher and businessman,' also had a role in the German colonial organisation.[39] He seems to have been the first European to be in contact with the Bangwa in 1898.[40] At the time, he held a position at the German concession company Gesellschaft Nordwest-Kamerun.[41] Indicators of his role as a colonial agent are that he recruited laborers to work at plantations along the coast and that he asked Fontem Asonganyi to raise the German flag during his stay with the Bangwa in 1899.[42] Conrau died on his third visit to the Bangwa in December 1899, reportedly by killing himself to avoid being

35 Scholars like 18th century Emer de Vattel argued that cultivation of the land is a natural duty of humankind, and, therefore, European peoples had the right to occupy, colonise, and thereby organise the land that was of no special need to 'wild peoples' who did not properly use the land. De Vattel, *Le droit des gens, ou Principes de la loi naturelle, Appliqués à la conduite et aux affaires des Nations et des Souverains* (1758) paras 81, 209, cited by K. Kuprecht, *Indigenous Peoples' Cultural Property Claims* (2014) Springer International Publishing, 24.

36 General Act of the Berlin Conference on West Africa 1885 art 6: 'All the Powers ... bind themselves ... to care for the improvement of the conditions of their moral and material well-being. ... They shall ... protect and favour all religious, scientific or charitable institutions and undertakings ... which aim at instructing the natives and bringing home to them the blessings of civilization. Christian missionaries, scientists and explorers, with their followers, property and collections, shall likewise be the objects of especial protection.'

37 Ibid. art 35: 'The Signatory Powers of the present Act recognize the obligation to insure the establishment of authority in the regions occupied by them.'

38 E. Dunstan, 'A Bangwa Account of Early Encounters with the German Colonial Administration' (1965) 3 Journal of the Historical Society of Nigeria 403; see also Cadman (1922) on the political and military nature of the German expeditions in the first years; Von Lintig (2017).

39 See, e.g., Von Lintig (2017) 101: '[I]t is reasonable to assume that this journey was undertaken in consultation with the governor of Cameroon.' See Schlothauer (2015) 25, 28: Schlothauer's conclusion is that Conrau was at most a temporary colonial agent.

40 Confirmed by many sources. See, e.g., Chilver (1967); Schlothauer (2015); Cadman (1922).

41 Chilver (1967) 155.

42 Cadman (1922) 36: 'This German ... again took up his quarters in FONTEM. Chief FONTEM was now given a German flag to fly.'

captured by the Bangwa.[43] The cause of the incident leading to his death appears to have been that Fontem Asonganyi had provided Conrau with a number of Bangwa men on his earlier expedition in the expectation that these men would return.[44] Instead, they did not return, and it can be assumed that they were used or sold as forced laborers on rubber plantations in the coastal region.[45]

In other words, the Bangwa's initial friendly attitude toward Conrau changed after the purpose of the expedition emerged: the recruitment of forced laborers and the collection of valuables. As noted by Elizabeth M. Chilver on the basis of German colonial archival records, '[t]he north-west hinterland – Bangwa territory – was increasingly viewed as a labour reservoir rather than as an outlet for trade-goods or as a producer of raw materials.'[46] In an account in which the lefem figures, which included the Bangwa Queen, were handed to Conrau with the permission of Fontem Asonganyi, as hinted to by Conrau in his letters to the director of the Berlin museum, a misunderstanding similar to the 'lending' of the Bangwa men may have occurred. Indeed, one source notes that the conflict between Fontem Asonganyi and Conrau arose over the missing 'secret' objects.[47]

The German colonial army dispatched several military punitive expeditions after the death of Conrau from late December 1899 on, causing the death of many Bangwa and the destruction of Fontem Asonganyi's palace.[48] Fontem Asonganyi was eventually caught and sent into exile; however, after the area came under British colonial rule (1915-61), he was able to return.[49] Regarding the German colonial period, a study notes:

> Of all the major social changes experienced in the Bangwa area the German colonial period was perhaps the most sudden and violent. The population was conscripted into forced labour both on the plantations and in the building of a road which

43 The Deutsche Kolonialzeitung vol 17 n 6 (8 February 1900) reported on the suicide: '*Er war von den Bangwa...gefangen, unternahm einen Fluchtversuch, wurde dabei durch einen Speerwurf verwundet und erschoss sich selbst, um nicht wehrlos in die Hände der Feinde zu fallen.*' Cited by Dunstan (1965) 403.

44 Chilver (1967) 154: 'Conrau died in December, 1899. According to the Governors' official report Conrau had 'some months before' brought down fifty labourers from Fontem to work for the Victoria plantation company. He had been despatched by Governor von Puttkamer to the relief of von Queis in Rio del Rey.'

45 Interview with Chief Taku, July 2017. See Dunstan (1965); Brain and Pollock (1971); Schlothauer (2015).

46 Chilver (1967) 155. Confirmed by Conrau. See Von Lintig (2017).

47 However, this account is dismissed by Von Lintig (2017) 105.

48 Dunstan (1965) 405-6; Chilver (1967) 155-56; Lockhart (1994) 27.

49 On charges, amongst others, of (1) 'depriving Conrau of his freedom and causing him to commit suicide' and (2) 'tough resistance to the expeditions.' Chilver (1967) 157.

linked the grasslands and the lower forest area, following the traditional trade route. Many Bangwa died in these ventures.[50]

2.3 Subsequent ownership history

In summary, it can be concluded that the Bangwa Queen was taken as part of a bigger collection of Bangwa figures during the annexation of the Bangwa territory, most likely in 1899 by a German named Conrau. While many objects remained in Berlin,[51] the Bangwa Queen was sold and changed hands many times between her arrival at the Museum für Völkerkunde in Berlin in 1899 and the acquisition by the French Dapper Foundation in 1990. Her history of ownership is well documented; she was in the Ethnological Museum in Berlin until 1926, after which she was subsequently owned by collectors Arthur Speyer, Charles Ratton, Helena Rubinstein, and Harry A. Franklin before the Musée Dapper acquired her at an auction in 1990.[52]

3 Legal standards

The Bangwa people wish to bring home the Bangwa Queen since she is sacred for them and personifies the ancestors of their epic Chief Fontem Asonganyi. Moreover, she symbolises the injustices of colonial rule. For an analysis of such a claim under international law, what needs to be assessed is: (1) the unlawfulness of the acquisition according to international law at the time or (2) the existence of a subsequent rule of international law that entitles the Bangwa to rights with regard to their lost cultural property. What follows is, first, an overview of the traditional legal framework for restitution claims, with the aim of achieving clarity on the question of the legality of the taking at the time, whereas new rules that may entitle the Bangwa to rights concerning their lost cultural property will be addressed in Section 3.

---

50 Lockhart (1998) 28. Cadman (1922) 49-56 confirms the German rule that 'plantation labourers had to be supplied (sometimes as often as three times a year)' as well as many other malpractices.

51 It appears a total of 71 Bangwa objects were delivered to the Berlin Ethnological Museum by Gustav Conrau. See Schlothauer (2015) 24. See Von Lintig (2017) 94: Von Lintig concludes that five of these were 'deaccesioned' in the late 1920s and, today, are in private or institutional collections – among those, the Bangwa Queen.

52 DeFabo (2014); Von Lintig (2017) figs 4, 7 and 8.

3.1 Unlawful taking?

It is often said that the looting of cultural objects occurred throughout history and was lawful at the time. This statement, however, depends on the perspective taken: that of the Bangwa, the conquerors, or international law? From the perspective of the Bangwa's customs and laws, the appropriation of a lefem figure was not allowed. It may suffice here to recall the special status of the Bangwa Queen: she was sacred and was to be kept by the ruling fontem in his shrine for praying purposes and as a symbol of his power and of his ancestors.[53] On the other hand, such foreign customs or laws under which certain objects are inalienable are often not recognised in other jurisdictions.[54] In France, for example, litigation on behalf of the Hopi Native Americans to stop the auction of their lost sacred 'Katsina,' referred to as 'friends' that represent incarnated spirits of their ancestors, was soon stranded in court proceedings in 2013.[55] The auction was considered legitimate by the French court since the claim by the Hopi that these Katsina were their communal and inalienable patrimony has no legal basis in French law.[56] Then again, if the Katsina were held by a US museum, the situation would be different given that the 1990 American Graves Protection and Repatriation Act (NAGPRA) recognises the inalienability of cultural objects with an 'ongoing historical, traditional or cultural importance central to the Native American Group.'[57] This is a path-breaking approach to tackle such cultural differences. However, for the Bangwa Queen – or even her counterpart in New York –, this law is of no avail or direct relevance since the NAGPRA only applies to the cultural objects of Native American communities in the United States.

Leaving the particularities of local laws aside, the question raised in this chapter is how such claims fit in the international legal framework. After a general sketch of that legal framework, the question how historical claims fit in will be assessed, after which this section ends with some words on specific problems relating to colonial takings as a *sui generis* category.

---

53 F. Shyllon, 'Collective Cultural Rights as Human Rights Simpliciter: The African and African Charter Example' in A. Jakubowski (ed) *Cultural Rights as Collective Rights, An International Law Perspective* (2016) Brill, 205: 'In African customary law corporate ownership has always attached to sacred objects, ancestral altart, shrines, sacred groves and other objects, tangible and intangible, of material culture that we now call cultural heritage or cultural property.'

54 Inalienability indicates that the object is so important that it cannot be transferred.

55 *Association Survival International France v SARL Néret-Minet Tessier Sarrou* (2013) *Tribunal de Grande Instance de Paris*, No RG 13/52880 BF/No 1.

56 Kuprecht (2014) 111; L. Nicolazzi, A. Chechi and M.A. Renold, 'Case Hopi Masks – Hopi Tribe v Néret-Minet and Estimations & Ventes Aux Enchères' (2015) Platform ArThémis, Art-Law Centre, University of Geneva.

57 NAGPRA. On 'cultural affiliation', see K. Kuprecht, 'The Concept of 'Cultural Affiliation' in NAGPRA: Its Potential and Limits in the Global Protection of Indigenous Cultural Property Rights' (2012) 19 International Journal of Cultural Property 33.

3.2 International law standards

Cultural objects have a protected status in international law because of their intangible 'heritage' value to people: as symbols of their identity. It is precisely this identity that is often targeted in looting and plundering practices. The Arch of Titus in Rome, depicting the spoils taken after the sacking of the Temple in Jerusalem, is a textbook example of this scenario.[58] Identity was at stake in Nazi-looting practices and, similarly, in the colonial context. European powers, for example, justified their presence in Africa by referring to their religious duty to bring to the 'natives' the 'blessings of civilization.'[59]

That being so, it is remarkable how old the notion is that harming other people's cultural objects is uncivilised. Cicero, in his speeches on the case against the Gaius Verres, argues that an honorable Roman should show respect for the culture of conquered people; while pillage was allowed (*ius praedae*), one should not appropriate religious and historical items of special importance to their owners.[60] Early examples of Hindu, Muslim, precolonial African, and Japanese rules protecting sites and objects of spiritual and cultural significance illustrate its global nature.[61] In the European setting, this rule gained legal importance through the writings of the founders of international law like Hugo Grotius and Emer de Vattel. To cite Grotius,

> [t]here are some things of such a nature, as to contribute, no way, to the support and prolongation of war. ... Polybius calls it brutal rage and madness to destroy things, the destruction of which does not in the least tend to impair an enemy's strength, nor to increase that of the destroyer. Such are porticos, temples, statues, and all other elegant works and monuments of art. Cicero commends Marcellus for sparing the public and private edifices of Syracuse, as if he had come with his army to protect them rather than to take the place by storm.[62]

The obligation to respect cultural objects implicates a prohibition to take them away. The corollary of this rule is a duty to return (restitute) pillaged artefacts:

---

58 M.M. Miles, 'Cicero's Prosecution of Gaius Verres: A Roman View of the Ethics of Acquisition of Art' (2002) 11 International Journal of Cultural Property 28.

59 General Act of the Berlin Conference on West Africa art 6.

60 Miles (2002) 31. Cicero made a distinction between ordinary booty and objects that should not be seized – those dedicated to gods or belonging to a sanctuary, temple, or shrine. Interesting is also Cicero's distinction between 'good' uses of art (public, commemorative, and religious) and 'bad' uses of art (private, consumptive, and decadent).

61 Referred to by F. Bugnion, 'The Origins and Development of the Legal Protection of Cultural Property in the Event of Armed Conflict' (2004), Speech at the Fiftieth Anniversary of the 1954 Hague Convention for the Protection of Cultural Property in the Event of Armed Conflict, Geneva; Vrdoljak (2006) 64; Shyllon (2016) 205. See hereafter for the 'special' protected status of religious objects.

62 Usually Grotius is quoted with regard to his confirmation on the rights to spoils; however, this is his 'moderation' in the footsteps of Polybius and Cicero. H. Grotius, *De Jure Belli Ac Pacis (On the Law of War and Peace)* (1625) Book III chapter 12.

'[W]hat is stolen should be returned.'[63] Over time, the obligation to return looted artefacts gained force as the international standard. In this development, the 1815 Congress of Vienna is often quoted as a turning point; at that moment, the European powers agreed, as a principle of justice, on the obligation to restitute artefacts that had been looted by Napoleon.[64] During the negotiations, Viscount Castlereagh, on behalf of the British delegation, stated that it was a legal duty to return the spoils of war taken by Napoleon to their place of origin in order to 'effectuate what justice and policy require.'[65] In other words, not winners takers and reparation for war damages but, rather, restitution as the legal standard for looted artefacts. And, indeed, the duty to return looted artefacts was what Judge Croke, in the much-cited *Marquis de Sommerueles* case, held in 1813 to be part of the 'Law of Nations, as practiced by all civilized countries.'[66]

The protected status of cultural objects was codified in the first multilateral treaty on the laws of war, the 1899 Hague Regulations Concerning the Laws and Customs of War on Land.[67] Eventually, after the massive looting during World War II, specific treaties on the protection of cultural objects were concluded: the 1954 Hague Convention for the Protection of Cultural Property in the Event of Armed Conflict and its Protocols, the 1970 UNESCO Convention on the Means of Prohibiting and Preventing the Illicit Import, Export and Transfer of Ownership of Cultural Property (1970 UNESCO Convention), and the 1995 UNIDROIT Convention on Stolen or Illegally Exported Cultural Objects (1995 UNIDROIT Convention).[68] To summarise, in broad terms, the norm in these treaties is that cultural objects enjoy special protection, both in times

63 E.g., W.W. Kowalski, 'Restitution of Works of Art Pursuant to Private and Public International Law' in *Collected courses of the Hague academy of international law*, vol. 288 (2002) Brill Nijhoff, 28 (the duty to return stolen objects can be found in the oldest known legislation, for example, Eshnunna law going back to the middle of the twenty-third century BC).

64 E.g., A.F. Vrdoljak, 'Reparations for Cultural Loss' in F. Lenzerini (ed) *Reparations for Indigenous Peoples: International and Comparative Perspectives* (2008) Oxford University Press, 26.

65 'Note Delivered by Viscount Castlerough to the Allied Ministers, and Placed upon their Protocol, Respecting the Restitution of the Works of Art' (Paris, 11 September 1815). 'Parliamentary Debates from the Year 1803 to the Present Time' (1816) 32 Hansard 297.

66 Ordering the restitution of artefacts, captured by a British vessel, on the argumentation that these are not the property of 'this or that nation, but of mankind at large.' *The Marquis de Somerueles* case [1813] Stewart's Vice-Admiralty Reports 482, cited by Vrdoljak (2008) 28.

67 Convention (II) with Respect to the Laws and Customs of War on Land (adopted 29 July 1899, entered into force (also for Germany) 4 September 1900) 187 CTS 227 (Hague Regulations) art 56.

68 Convention for the Protection of Cultural Property in the Event of Armed Conflict (adopted 14 May 1954) 249 UNTS 240; Convention on the Means of Prohibiting and Preventing the Illicit Import, Export and Transfer of Ownership of Cultural Property (adopted 14 November 1970) 823 UNTS 231 (1970 UNESCO Convention); Convention on Stolen or Illegally Exported Cultural Objects (adopted 24 June 1995) 2421 UNTS 457 (1995 UNIDROIT Convention).

of war and peace; the transfer of cultural objects during foreign occupation is prohibited; and works of art exported in violation of this prohibition should be returned. Under certain conditions, a good faith new possessor in whose hands the object is found may be entitled to compensation on its return. Such treaty rules, however, are non-retroative and need implementation on the national level to have effect.

3.3 Privileged status of objects of spiritual importance

Under these standards, objects of spiritual or religious importance have a privileged position. In the view of Grotius:

> '... there is still greater reason why it [the protective rule, EC] should be obeyed in respect to things devoted to the purposes of religion. Thucydides says that it was a law among the Greeks of his time, in all their invasions of each other's territories, to forbear touching the edifices of religion: and Livy likewise observes that, upon the destruction of Alba by the Romans, the temples of the Gods were spared.'[69]

In many cultures, such objects are commonly owned or inalienable and form a special category of property as *res extra commercium*.[70] For today's cases, even John Merryman, the proponent of a liberal art trade, makes an exception for 'objects of ritual or religious importance to living cultures' that should 'remain with or be returned to those cultures.'[71] As an example, Merryman cites the case of the Afo-a-Kom, a statue that embodies the 'spiritual, political and religious essence' of the people of the Kom kingdom in Cameroon, which was found in the hands of a US collector in the 1970s.[72]

Given the holistic and spiritual vision of life by indigenous peoples, based on common material and spiritual, intergenerational values, this distinction is of significance in the context of colonial takings from local (indigenous)

69 Grotius (1625) bk II ch 12 VI.

70 The idea that cultural objects in general should not be subject to normal property law is proposed at times by various scholars. See, e.g., P.T. Stoll, 'Where Should Nefertiti Go? Reflections on International Cultural Law' in H.P. Hestermeyer and others (eds) *Coexistence, Cooperation and Solidarity* (2012) Martinus Nijhoff.

71 J.H. Merryman, 'Cultural Property Internationalism' (2005) 12 International Journal of Cultural Property 11-39.

72 Ibid. 13, n. 9, 10. *Nota Bene*, the Afo-A-Kom was returned after compensation of the new possessor for his expenses. See A.L. Bandle, A. Chechi and M.A. Renold, 'Case Afo-A-Kom – Furman Gallery and Kom People' (2012) Platform ArThémis, Art-Law Centre, University of Geneva <https://plone.unige.ch/art-adr/cases-affaires/afo-a-kom-2013-furman-gallery-and-kom-people>.

peoples.[73] Legal instruments in the field of indigenous peoples' rights, like NAGPRA and the UNDRIP, make this distinction and will be discussed in the third section of this chapter. This privileged status is also confirmed in Article 5(3) of the 1995 UNIDROIT Convention, which holds that arrangements should be made for the return of a cultural object 'if the ... removal of the object ... significantly impairs ... the traditional or ritual use of the object by a tribal or indigenous community.'[74]

3.4 The legal framework for historical claims

Claims to artefacts lost during the colonial era fall within the category of 'historic claims.' In the present context, such claims include those that are based on a loss that predates international conventions that arrange for restitution. The 1995 UNIDROIT Convention's provision mentioned above regarding objects of ritual importance, for example, applies to losses after the Convention entered into force in the relevant states.[75] Here, the Operational Guidelines to the 1970 UNESCO Convention, which were adopted in May 2015, are instructive:

> The general rule of public international law embodied in Article 28 of the Vienna Convention on the Law of Treaties does not provide for retroactive application of treaties. ... However, the Convention *does not in any way legitimize any illicit transaction of whatever nature which has taken place before the entry into force of this Convention* nor limit any right of a State or other person to make a claim under specific procedures or legal remedies available outside the framework of this Convention for the restitution or return of a cultural object stolen or illegally exported before the entry into force of this Convention.[76]

---

73 F. Lenzerini, 'Reparations for Wrongs against Indigenous Peoples' Cultural Heritage' in A. Xanthaki and others (eds) *Indigenous Peoples' Cultural Property Claims* (2017) Brill, 327-28; Vrdoljak (2008) 199 on Indigenous peoples' culture: 'a holistic conceptualization ... which covers land, immoviable and movable heritage, tangible and intangible elements.' See also the Study of the Expert Mechanism on the Rights of Indigenous Peoples (2012) UN Doc A/HRC/21/53 para 52.

74 1995 UNIDROIT Convention.

75 Ibid. art 10(2).

76 Operational Guidelines for the implementation of the 1970 Convention on the Means of Prohibiting and Preventing the Illicit Import, Export and Transfer of Ownership of Cultural Property (adopted at 3d Meeting of States Parties held 18-20 May 2015 by Resolution 3.MSP 11), 100-1 (emphasis added). The 1995 UNIDROIT Convention (n. 68), art 10(3), has a similar wording: 'This Convention does not in any way legitimise any illegal transaction of whatever nature which has taken place before the entry into force of this Convention.'

In other words, codification should not be understood as a cut-off line.[77] The legality of a loss should be assessed on the basis of the law in force at the time – the concept of intertemporal law under international law.[78] A first observation, if we revisit the evolution of the law in this field, is that the protected status of (sacred) cultural objects was recognised in various cultures and by early scholars, and was included in early peace agreements and international instruments.

3.5 Legality of seizure under the laws of war?

The question of whether the loss of the Bangwa Queen was unlawful according to contemporary standards depends, first, on how to qualify colonial conquest and rule; can it be compared with a situation of an armed conquest, war, and belligerent occupation? In the Bangwa case, this question can be limited to an evaluation of the character of the 1899 expedition of Conrau and subsequent military actions, as it remains unclear exactly how the Bangwa Queen was lost.

At the time of the Berlin Conference on West Africa in 1885, the division of African territories amongst European nations – and the appropriation of resources – was justified by relying on the *terra nullius* argumentation and the 'religious duty' to bring civilization to Africa.[79] Moreover, indigenous peoples in Africa were excluded from the 'family of civilized nations' and from protection of international law well into the twentieth century.[80] Although such views may explain historic events, they cannot be invoked to justify their legality and certainly not if such acts have a continuing effect today.[81] In the 1975 *Western Sahara* case, the International Court of Justice rejected the notion of *terra nullius* for inhabited territories altogether.[82] The correct perspective, as argued by Mamadou Hébié, is that colonial sovereign rule in Western Africa

77 As the '1970 threshold' is often used. See, e.g., the Association of Art Museum Directors Guidelines on the Acquisition of Archaeological Material and Ancient Art (revised 2013): 'Member museums normally should not acquire a Work unless provenance research substantiates that the Work was outside its country of probable modern discovery before 1970 or was legally exported from its probable country of modern discovery after 1970.'

78 As developed in *Island of Palmas (The Netherlands v USA)* [1928] Arbitral Tribunal Award, reprinted in (1949) 2 United Nations Reports of International Arbitral Awards 829.

79 See n. 35, above.

80 Vrdoljak (2006).

81 The legality or illegality of historical events must be judged according to the law in force at the time in question, but the continuing effects of these events can be judged by more recent standards. Institut de Droit International, 'The Inter-Temporal Problem in Public International Law', Resolution from the Session of Wiesbaden (1975) 537; D Shelton, 'Reparations for Indigenous Peoples: The Present Value of Past Wrongs' in F Lenzerini (ed) *Reparations for Indigenous Peoples: International and Comparative Perspectives* (2008) Oxford University Press 2008, 62-63.

82 *Western Sahara* (Advisory Opinion) ICJ Rep 1975, 12.

in the event of opposition from local rulers, as in the Bangwa territory, was established by means of conquest.[83] In other words, this is a situation that, by all means, can be compared to an armed conflict.

The lawfulness of the appropriation of cultural objects would then depend on what (general) contemporary international law has to say on this subject. For that, we have to revert to the rules of warfare. With respect to those, the 1863 Lieber Code is usually quoted as the first document to codify the laws of war; it provides an exemption of cultural objects from appropriation by parties in a conflict.[84] This special status was repeated in both the Brussels Declaration of 1864 and the Oxford Manual on the Laws of War on Land of 1880.[85] Although none of these are binding treaties, they are considered to reflect customary international law at the time. In fact, the provisions regarding cultural objects have almost the same wording and, afterwards, soon found their way into the Hague Regulations of 1899 and 1907, which were binding.[86] The Hague Regulations read:

> The property of municipalities, that of institutions dedicated to religion, charity and education, the arts and sciences, even when State property, shall be treated as private property. All seizure of, destruction or wilful damage done to institutions of this character, historic monuments, works of art and science, is forbidden, and should be made the subject of legal proceedings.[87]

At what exact moment the prohibition of looting and the ensuing obligation to return looted objects gained customary status is a matter of legal debate.[88]

---

83 M. Hébié, 'The Role of the Agreements Concluded with Local Political Entities in the Course of French Colonial Expansion in West Africa' (2016) 85 British Yearbook of International Law 21.

84 Instructions for the Government of Armies of the United States in the Field, General Orders No. 100 (adopted 24 April 1863) <https://archive.org/stream/pdfy-NG4E2nsEimXkB5mU/The Lieber Code Of 1863_djvu.txt> accessed 18 November 2017 (Lieber Code) art 36: 'If such works of art. ... The ultimate ownership is to be settled by the ensuing treaty of peace. In no case shall they be sold or given away, if captured by the armies of the United States, nor shall they ever be privately appropriated or wantonly destroyed or injured.' It was prepared by Prussian Francis Lieber who, before emigrating to the United States, had surveyed Waterloo. Miles (2002) 44.

85 The Lieber Code of 1863 is seen as reflecting customary law of the time and, with the Brussels Declaration (1874) and the Oxford Manual on the Laws of War on Land (adopted 9 September 1880) (Oxford Manual), it followed the approach that influenced the Hague Peace Conference of 1899 and 1907, where the rules of the protection of cultural property in armed conflict were codified. R. Wolfrum, 'Cultural Property, Protection in Armed Conflict' (2010) Max Planck Encyclopedia of Public International Law.

86 Hague Regulations.

87 Convention (VIII) Relative to the Laying of Automatic Submarine Contact Mines (adopted 18 October 1907) 205 CTS 331 art 56. The Hague Regulations have the same wording.

88 K. Siehr, 'International Art Trade and the Law' in The Hague Academy of International Law (ed) *Collected Courses of The Hague Academy of International Law*, vol 243 (1993) 131: 'It has now been well established that for 150 years any kind of pillage, capture or acquisi-

It is well accepted, however, that at the time of the codification of the 1899 Hague Regulations this was the case. For example, Woljciech Kowalski concludes:

> Through time, a ban on looting works of art became customary international law, and eventually, found its way into regulations of the codified law of war. The obligation of the restitution of a looted work of art correlates with the ban on pillaging. As early as the nineteenth century, it was based on the principle of identification, ... as well as on the principle of territoriality, according to which an item is returned to the place from which it was taken. In many cases, when claims were examined, the period of time that had passed since the loss of the object was not taken into account. ... All the principles relating to the restitution of works of art were fully recognized and developed in the peace treaties signed after World War I.[89]

As to the legality of punitive military actions, the 1880 Oxford Manual is instructive:

> Impositions in kind (requisitions) demanded from communes or inhabitants should be in proportion to the necessities of war as generally recognized, and in proportion to the resources of the country. Requisitions can only be made on the authority of the commander in the locality occupied.[90]

In other words, if the Bangwa Queen was taken by seizure or theft during the annexation of the Bangwa area in 1899, such an appropriation would

tion of works of art as booty during times of war, armistice or occupation is prohibited by public international law. Still open, however, is the question as to how works of art have to be allocated in cases of succession of States' (159). Zhang, on the basis of an intertemporal law analysis concludes that the rule against plunder was founded in the laws and customs of war in the eighteenth century, became well established in the nineteenth century, and further developed in the twentieth century. Generally, scholars argue on an emerging customary rule in the nineteenth century: de Visscher, *International Protection of Works of Art and Historic Monuments* (1949) Washington, DC: Department of State, Division of Publications, Office of Public Affairs ('accepted by all nations during the two Hague Conventions in 1899 and 1907'); Merryman (2005) ('since the late 19th century'); W. Sandholtz, *Prohibiting Plunder: How Norms Change* (2007) Oxford University Press, 39-45 ('emerges after 1815 and was transmitted into general international norms at the end of the 19th century'); S.E. Nahlik, 'International Law and the Protection of Cultural Property in Armed Conflicts' (1976) 27 Hastings Law Journal 1071-72 ('the rules regarding protection of cultural property, already firmly established in practice and in doctrine, and thus in customary law, have appeared, since the middle of the 19th century, in all the consecutive stages of the codification of the laws of war'). See Y. Zhang, 'Customary International Law and the Rule Against Taking Cultural Property as Spoils of War' (2018) 17 Chinese Journal of International Law 944-45. The main problem in proving a well settled practice and *opinion juris* is exactly that this rule was not applied with regard to colonial takings (see discussion later in this article).

89 W.W. Kowalski, *Art Treasures and War* (1998) Institute of Art and Law, 80.

90 Oxford Manual (n. 85) art 56.

arguably be unlawful in contemporary international law. As noted above, the German annexation of the Bangwa area commenced with the expeditions of Conrau, illustrated by the fact that he carried the German flag.[91] Article 1 of the 1899 Hague Regulations states in this regard that the laws apply not only to the military but also to others with 'a fixed distinctive emblem recognizable at a distance.'[92] Notwithstanding justifications at the time, one would expect that such standards under today's inter-temporal law standards would apply to European takings in Africa in 1899-1901.

3.6 Colonial takings a *sui generis* category?

Although the seizure of artefacts in the course of a military action at the close of the nineteenth century may well be unlawful under the laws of warfare, not all acquisitions can be seen in that light. Often, the exact circumstances are unclear, as in the Bangwa case. As Ana Filipa Vrdoljak and Andrzej Jakubowski propose, the return of cultural objects after decolonization may therefore better fit in with the concepts of state succession or the right of self-determination – the restitution of dispersed cultural objects after a period of foreign rule or changes in territorial sovereign rule.[93] After the dissolution of the Austrian-Hungarian Empire in Europe, for example, a legal framework was set up by which cultural objects were redistributed to successor states on the basis of territoriality and the 'reconstruction of artistic and historic patrimony.'[94]

After World War II, such a general legal obligation to return cultural property on the basis of territoriality – understood as a bond between an object, land, and people – was confirmed. For example, the 1947 Peace Treaty with Italy provided for the return of cultural objects to Yugoslavia that were also taken in the period before World War II on the basis of territoriality, and the Allied restitution system, likewise, arranged for the return of artefacts taken by the Nazis from occupied territories, irrespective how such objects had been

91 Cadman (1922) 36: 'This German … again took up his quarters in FONTEM. Chief FONTEM was now given a German flag to fly.'

92 Hague Regulations, art 1 (the laws, rights, and duties of war apply not only to armies but also to militia and volunteer corps if that person 'has a fixed distinctive emblem recognizable at a distance').

93 Vrdoljak (2006) 2: 'From the Congress of Vienna in 1815 to the mid twentieth century, victorious European powers sanctioned the restitution of cultural objects to territories restored following the collapse of empires. However, this recognition of the need to return 'spoliations appertaining to those territories' following independence did not extend necessarily to the dismantling of their own empires in the late twentieth century.' A. Jakubowski, *State Succession in Cultural Property* (2015) Oxford University Press.

94 Jakubowski (2015) 6, citing De Visscher (1949).

removed and notwithstanding later acquisition by good faith new possessors.[95] In fact, such state practice convinced scholars such as Woljciech Kowalski that restitution of dispersed cultural patrimony on the basis of territoriality was a customary rule of international law.[96]

And, indeed, in the period after decolonization, the 1973 UN General Assembly resolution 'on restitution of works of art to countries victim of expropriation' was promising for former colonies.[97] It linked the return of cultural objects to independence, being a necessary element of the cultural development of new states.[98] A 1975 Dutch-Indonesian agreement to return objects 'directly linked with persons of major historical and cultural importance or with crucial historical events' may be seen in this context.[99] Noteworthy, but exceptional in its acknowledgement of a legal duty, is the return to Libya of the Venus of Cyrene by Italy, after the Italian Supreme Administrative Court ruled that the right of self-determination of former colonies implicates that cultural objects should be returned.[100]

On the whole, however, colonial collections were not returned. Hence, a separation between two scenarios of restitution of dispersed cultural objects became the legal reality. Colonial takings were to be discussed as a matter of 'return' on moral grounds – in the setting of the UNESCO Intergovernmental Committee for Promoting the Return of Cultural Property to its Countries of

95 See Treaty of Peace with Italy (signed 10 February 1947) 49 UNTS 3 art 12. Vrdoljak (2006) 140–50: Vrdoljak discusses the 1943 Interallied Declaration; see also E. Campfens, 'Sources of Inspiration: Old and New Rules for Looted Art' in E. Campfens (ed) *Fair and Just Solutions? Alternatives to Litigation in Nazi-Looted Art Disputes* (2015) Eleven International Publishing, 20-21 <https://www.restitutiecommissie.nl/bestanden/fair_and_just_solutions.html>.

96 Jakubowski (2015); Kowalski (1998).

97 UNGA Res. 3187 (XXVIII) (18 December 1973). See 'Restitution of Cultural Property: Resolutions Adopted by the United Nations General Assembly about Return and Restitution of Cultural Property' (n. 2).

98 A. Chechi, *The Settlement of International Cultural Heritage Disputes* (2014) Oxford University Press, 273: '[T]he return of cultural assets still encounters the resistance of current possessors, though it is generally recognized that the return of objects vital to the cultural collective identity of formerly subjugated peoples is essential to the realization of their right of self-determination and full political emancipation.'

99 J.M. van Beurden, *Treasures in Trusted Hand: Negotiating the Future of Colonial Cultural Objects* (2017) Sidestone Press, 123-53 (on the difficult negotiations leading up to this agreement). P.H. Pott and M.A. Sutaarga, 'Arrangements Concluded or in Progress for the Return of Objects: The Netherlands-Indonesia' (1979) 31 Museum International 38.

100 *Consiglio di Stato* (23 June 2008) No 3154. On the verdict, the Consiglio di Stato stated that the principle of self-determination of peoples had come to include the cultural identity as well as the cultural heritage linked either to the territory of a sovereign state or to peoples subject to a foreign government. A. Chechi, 'The Return of Cultural Objects Removed in Times of Colonial Domination and International Law: The Case of the Venus of Cyrene' (2008) 18 Italian Yearbook of International Law 159.

Origin or Its Restitution in Case of Illicit Appropriation (ICPRCP)[101] – as opposed to restitution on legal grounds in the European context. Vrdoljak provides insight into a process where former colonial states came to act on the basis of the paradigm that it is in the best interest of civilization for them to remain custodians of the material culture of their former colonies.[102] The 2002 Declaration on the Value and Importance of Universal Museums may be seen in this light.[103]

3.7 State practice and recent European developments

Increasingly, former colonial powers do honour claims for the return of colonial takings on an *ad hoc* basis. Such returns are usually portrayed as exceptions to the general rule under which Western states have gained ownership and a matter of 'cultural diplomacy.' For example, in France in 2002 the mortal remains of Saartjie Baartman were repatriated to South Africa;[104] in 2010, a *mokomokai*, a mummified tattooed Maori human head, was returned to the New Zealand Te Papa Tongarewa Museum;[105] and, in 2011, historically important manuscripts were returned to Korea on the basis of a renewable five-year loan agreement.[106] The 2018 decision to return statues and regalia from the Kingdom of Dahomey to Benin in 2018, mentioned in the introduction, might well be the first example of a return of important cultural objects – beyond the category of human remains – to an African country based on a wider policy.[107] In their November 2018 report to the French president, Felwine Sarr and Bénédicte Savoy recommend a generous French policy of restitution of

101 Its task is to assist member states with repatriation requests that concern cultural property of 'fundamental significance from the point of view of the spiritual values and cultural heritage' of their people and was 'lost as a result of colonial or foreign occupation or as a result of illicit appropriation.' Statutes of the Intergovernmental Committee for Promoting the Return of Cultural Property to its Countries of Origin or its Restitution in Case of Illicit Appropriation (28 November 1978) UNESCO Doc CLT/CH/INS-2005/21 (Statutes on the Return of Cultural Property).

102 E.g., Vrdoljak (2006) 302.

103 A declaration by eighteen major Western museums stating their collections, however acquired, are best seen and exhibited in the setting of encyclopedic museums. See n. 7.

104 French State Law No 2002-323 (6 March 2002); see also Sarr and Savoy (2018) 73.

105 French State Law No 2010-501 (18 May 2010) <https://www.legifrance.gouv.fr/affichTexte.do?cidTexte=JORFTEXT000022227321> accessed 25 April 2019.

106 Décret No 2011-527 Portant publication de l'accord entre le Gouvernement de la République Française et le Gouvernement de la République de Corée relatif aux manuscrits royaux de la Dynastie Joseon (Ensemble une Annexe) (7 February 2011) <https://www.legifrance.gouv.fr/eli/decret/2011/5/16/MAEJ1111118D/jo> accessed 18 March 2019.

107 'Remise du Rapport Savoy/Sarr sur la Restitution du Patrimoine Africain' (n. 5).

> any objects taken by force or presumed to be acquired through inequitable conditions from Africa over the last 150 years, including objects taken 'through military aggressions, whether these pieces went on directly to France or whether passed through the international art market before finding their way into French collections' as well as objects taken by 'active administrators' or through 'scientific expeditions prior to 1960.[108]

Whether and how these recommendations will be implemented in France remains to be seen, as well if a future policy framework will affect a private collection like the Dapper Foundation.[109] In Germany, both the 2018 Museum Association's Guidelines as well as the 2019 governmental policy framework underline the importance of research, dialogue and cooperation with source communities.[110] The governmental policy framework explicitly also aims to enable the return of cultural objects that were acquired in a way that 'by today's legal or ethical standards is not justifiable.'[111] The return of grave finds by the Berlin Museums Foundation (SPK), mentioned in the introduction, on the grounds that the loss was 'unlawful' in this regard may be an example of a change in moving toward a more structured legal framework.

4 New horizons

For cases like the Bangwa Queen, a traditional legal approach provides no ready solutions. In addition to the challenge of establishing the legality or illegality of a loss so long ago, hurdles arise in terms of accountability and access to justice. If the appropriation of the Bangwa Queen could be held to be unlawful under customary international law, and is attributable to the state, this would amount to an international law obligation by the state responsible

108 Sarr and Savoy (2018) 61.

109 Interestingly, the March 2019 German Policy Framework – setting standards for a proactive stance toward claims regarding colonial takings – requires also non-state institutions, collectors, and the art trade to act in the spirit of the guidelines: 'Wir fordern alle öffentlichen Träger von Einrichtungen und Organisationen, in deren Beständen sich Sammlungsgut aus kolonialen Kontexten befinden, aber auch nichtstaatliche Museen, Sammlerinnen und Sammler sowie den Kunsthandel dazu auf, im Sinne dieser Eckpunkte an der Aufarbeitung der Herkunftsgeschichte von Sammlungsgut aus kolonialen Kontexten aktiv mitzuwirken und die jeweils erforderlichen Maßnahmen hierfür zu ergreifen.'

110 'Guidelines on Dealing with Collections from Colonial Contexts' (July 2018) 63-71, 94-100 <https://www.museumsbund.de/publikationen/guidelines-on-dealing-with-collections-from-colonial-contexts-2/> accessed 18 March 2019. The guidelines focus on research, transparency, mediation, and alternatives to restitution such as loans or joint research projects. See also the Government policy framework ('Eckpunkte zum Umgang mit Sammlungsgut aus Kolonialen Kontexten' (n. 4)).

111 See the seventh principle in 'Eckpunkte zum Umgang mit Sammlungsgut aus Kolonialen Kontexten' (n. 4) 4.

for the looting.[112] This is relevant for Bangwa figures that are still in Berlin; however, the Bangwa Queen is not in possession of the state responsible for the taking but, rather, in the hands of a third party, the Dapper Foundation. Another hurdle is access to justice: which court assumes jurisdiction over such a claim? Claims based on a loss of property that occurred so long ago will most likely be held inadmissible *ratione temporis*.[113] In other words, an approach that focuses on the unlawfulness of the loss at the time will most likely lead to the conclusion that historic claims are stale. This state of affairs is increasingly being challenged by 'softer' legal norms that address the intangible value of artefacts for people today and the continuing injustice of remaining deprived of certain objects.

4.1 Soft law instruments: Signs of evolving norms?

Since the end of last century, the adoption of soft law instruments has illustrated a need to find solutions for restitution claims that are time barred under positive law. Governmental declarations and private ethical codes of conduct tend to have a similar pattern and focus on (1) good faith negotiations with source communities or former owners (dialogue) and (2) equitable solutions for title disputes that honour the interests of former owners as well as the interests of new (innocent) possessors.[114]

For example, the 1998 Washington Conference Principles on Nazi-Confiscated Art (Washington Principles) follow this outline.[115] This document concerns a set of principles signed by over 40 states and underlines the importance of finding 'fair and just solutions' for title claims to works of art that were confiscated by the Nazis or sold under duress by former owners in a setting

---

112 A breach of an international norm that is attributable to a state leads up to the obligation for that state to make reparations. See *Factory of Chorzow (Germany v Poland)* (Merits) [1928] PCIJ Series A No 17, 47; International Law Commission, 'Draft Articles on Responsibility of States for Internationally Wrongful Act' (2001) UN Doc A/56/10.

113 As the European Court of Human Rights did it in a claim regarding the Parthenon Marbles in 2016. *Syllogos ton Athinaion against the United Kingdom* [2016] Application No 48259/15; see also *Certain Property (Liechtenstein v Germany)* (Judgment) ICJ Reports 2005, 6, in which the International Court of Justice denied a claim on a painting confiscated in the post-World War II period.

114 On equitable (cooperative) solutions, see M.A. Renold, 'Cultural Co-Ownership: Preventing and Solving Cultural Property Claims' (2015) 22 International Journal of Cultural Property 163.

115 'Washington Conference Principles on Nazi-Confiscated Art' (1998) <https://www.state.gov/p/eur/rt/hlcst/270431.htm> accessed 18 March 2019 (Washington Principles) (released in connection with the Washington Conference on Holocaust Era Assets, Washington, DC).

of persecution.[116] This instigated a practice of settlements and returns, initially restricted to national public collections but soon followed by the private sector, notwithstanding legal obstacles under positive law. Today, works that are 'tainted' by a possible history of Nazi looting are unsalable on the international art market. The reputation of a work of art and its market value has come to fill in a gap where the law is lacking. In some European countries, government committees were installed to act as mediators. This extra-legal 'ethical' approach, however, does have a drawback: the field is hampered by a lack of clear rules and compliance mechanisms.[117] It has been suggested that a similar instrument to the Washington Principles should be developed for colonial takings, which would, indeed, underline a political will to act.[118] It should be noted, however, that the Washington Principles themselves are not more specific or legally binding as other existing informal instruments in the field. Some examples are provided below, while the most relevant instrument in this field, the UNDRIP, will be discussed later in this article.

4.2 International Council of Museums Code and the International Law Association Principles

Museums are expected to adhere to the ethical principles as adopted in the 1986 International Code of Ethics by the International Council of Museums (ICOM), an instrument of transnational private regulation.[119] Similar to the approach outlined above, these guidelines state that museums, with regard to restitution issues, should collaborate with source communities. Insofar as this concerns claims, the provisions implicate a cooperative stand, preferably on a non-governmental level. The relevant provisions read:

> Museums should be prepared to initiate dialogues for the return of cultural property to a country or people of origin. This should be undertaken in an impartial manner, based on scientific, professional and humanitarian principles as well as applicable

---

116 Ibid. principle 8: 'If the pre-war owners of art that is found to have been confiscated by the Nazis and not subsequently restituted, or their heirs, can be identified, steps should be taken expeditiously to achieve a just and fair solution, recognizing this may vary according to the facts and circumstances surrounding a specific case.'

117 E. Campfens, 'Nazi-Looted Art: A Note in Favour of Clear Standards and Neutral Procedures' (2017) 22 Art Antiquity and Law 315.

118 Van Beurden (2017). See also H. Parzinger, 'Bauen Wir Museen in Afrika!' (25 January 2018) *Frankfurter Allgemeine Zeitung*.

119 The ICOM Code of Professional Ethics was adopted by the General Assembly of the International Council of Museums on 4 November 1986, retitled 'ICOM Code of Ethics for Museums' in 2001, and revised in 2004. See 'ICOM Code of Ethics for Museums' (2004) <https://icom.museum/wp-content/uploads/2018/07/ICOM-code-En-web.pdf>, ICOM Code 6.2 (Return of Cultural Property), and ICOM Code 6.3 (Restitution of Cultural Property).

> local, national and international legislation, in preference to action at a governmental or political level.
>
> When a country or people of origin seeks the restitution of an object or specimen that can be demonstrated to have been exported or otherwise transferred in violation of the principles of international law and international conventions, and shown to be part of that country's or people's cultural or natural heritage, the museum concerned should, if legally free to do so, take prompt and responsible steps to cooperate in its return.

The 2006 Principles for Cooperation in the Mutual Protection and Transfer of Cultural Material, adopted by the International Law Association (ILA), also emphasise a general duty of institutions and governments to enter into 'good-faith negotiations' regarding restitution claims by persons, groups or states.[120] The principles also list what should be taken into account during those negotiations: '[T]he significance of the requested material for the requesting party, the reunification of dispersed cultural material, accessibility to the cultural material in the requesting state, and protection of the cultural material.'[121] In as far as it concerns the outcome, the focus is on 'caring and sharing' and, as alternatives to restitution, the principles mention loans, the production of copies, and shared management and control.[122] Two categories are singled out: Principle 4 sets the obligation 'to respond in good faith and to recognize claims by indigenous groups or cultural minorities whose demands are not supported by their national governments,' whereas Principle 5 confirms the special status of human remains with a straightforward obligation of repatriation.

Apart from such guidelines of an operational character, numerous UN and UNESCO soft law declarations on the interstate level have been adopted that underline the importance of the return of a representative part of a country's lost cultural patrimony.[123] In this regard, the ICPRCP was established in 1978 to assist member states with return requests that concern cultural property 'which has a fundamental significance from the point of view of the spiritual values and cultural heritage of the people of a Member State or Associate Member of UNESCO and which has been lost as a result of colonial or foreign occupation or as a result of illicit appropriation.'[124] In various UN resolutions,

---

120 'Principles for Cooperation in the Mutual Protection and Transfer of Cultural Material', Report of the International Law Association Seventy-second Conference (2006) Annex (Principles of Cooperation), reprinted in JAR Nafziger, 'The Principles for Cooperation in the Mutual Protection and Transfer of Cultural Material' (2007) 8 Chicago Journal of International Law 147. Nafziger states that current practice is the jurisprudential basis.

121 Ibid. principle 8.

122 Ibid. principle 3.

123 'Restitution of Cultural Property: Resolutions Adopted by the United Nations General Assembly about Return and Restitution of Cultural Property' (n. 2).

124 Statutes on the Return of Cultural Property (n. 101) art 2.

attention is drawn to the services of the ICPRCP, and the 2015 Operational Guidelines to the 1970 UNESCO Convention repeat this concern.[125] Notwithstanding this appreciation and the development of a special mediation procedure, the relatively low number of cases referred to the committee implies that the state-centric approach of the ICPRCP creates a (political) setting that is not *per se* suitable to solve these matters.[126] It therefore mainly acts as a forum for best practice examples and for governments to state certain claims.

4.3 The right to one's cultural objects as a human right?

Whereas return claims that concern colonial takings are still usually set aside as a matter of ethics, not the law, the wider legal framework for cultural objects has undergone changes. This 'humanization' of cultural heritage law may be understood as the increased attention for the intangible and social aspects of artefacts, as opposed to property and preservation, and a shift in focus from state interests to the interest of communities.[127] The relevance of this change for the present case surfaces in the approach taken in the UNDRIP, but, first, what follows is a short introduction to such changing notions on the intersection of human rights and cultural property law.

A clear example can be found in the Council of Europe's Framework Convention on the Value of Cultural Heritage for Society (Faro Convention). It quotes in its preamble 'the need to put people and human values at the centre of an enlarged and cross-disciplinary concept of cultural heritage' and defines cultural heritage as a 'group of resources inherited from the past which people identify, *independently of ownership*, as a reflection and expression of their constantly evolving values, beliefs, knowledge and traditions.'[128] As right holders to cultural heritage, the Faro Convention introduces 'heritage

125 UNGA Res. 67/80 (12 December 2012) 18. Operational Guidelines for the Implementation of the Convention on the Means of Prohibiting and Preventing the Illicit Import, Export and Transfer of Ownership of Cultural Property (n. 76).

126 Chechi (2014) 104-6. The General Conference of the United Nations Educational, Scientific, and Cultural Organization (UNESCO) adopted, at its thirty-third session, adding mediation and conciliation to the mandate of the Intergovernmental Committee, Doc 33 C/Resolution 44 (October 2005).

127 As opposed to the state-centered property approach of cultural objects in the UNESCO conventional system. On this, see, e.g., F. Francioni, 'The Human Dimension of International Cultural Heritage Law: An Introduction' (2011) 22 European Journal of International Law 9: '[B]ringing the focus from the protection of the cultural object to the social structures and cultural processes that have created and developed the 'intangible' heritage. States remain the contracting parties to the convention but the substantive addressees are the cultural communities and human groups, including minorities, whose cultural traditions are the real object of the safeguarding under international law.'

128 Framework Convention on the Value of Cultural Heritage for Society (adopted 27 October 2005) CETS No 199 (Faro Convention) (emphasis added). As of 13 February 2019, there were 10 signatories (France is not amongst them).

communities.'[129] These are 'people who value specific aspects of cultural heritage which they wish, within the framework of public action, to sustain and transmit to future generations.' This concept facilitates the acceptance of a collective title to cultural objects by communities and is reminiscent of the 'cultural affiliation' concept adopted in NAGPRA that links objects to communities as a title for rights to cultural objects.[130] Furthermore, in as far as it concerns competing claims to cultural heritage, the Convention requires states to 'establish processes for conciliation to deal equitably with situations where contradictory values are placed on the same cultural heritage by different communities.'[131] This is in line with the obligation to enter into a dialogue – good faith negotiations – in the soft law instruments discussed above. Although the Faro Convention does not create enforceable rights, but, rather, voices policy aims for governments, it opens the door to a new understanding of cultural objects and their title holders.[132]

4.4 The right of access to culture

In the quest for a legal framework for cases like the Bangwa Queen, of key importance is the evolution of a right of 'access to one's culture' as developed from the right to culture in the International Covenant on Economic, Social and Cultural Rights (ICESCR).[133] According to General Comment no. 21 on the 'right of everyone to take part in cultural life' of Article 15(1)a of the ICESCR,[134] the right to take part in cultural life has come to include 'access to cultural goods.'[135] Moreover, this obliges states to adopt 'specific measures aimed at achieving respect for the right of everyone … to have access to their own cultural ... heritage and to that of others.'[136] The 2011 report of the independent expert in the field of cultural rights, Farida Shaheed, gives a further explanation of this right and concludes that

> [t]he right of access to and enjoyment of cultural heritage forms part of international human rights law, finding its legal basis, in particular, in the right to take part in cultural life, the right of members of minorities to enjoy their own culture, and

---

129 Ibid. art 2(b).

130 Kuprecht (2012). Further discussion of NAGPRA later in this article.

131 Faro Convention (n. 128) art 7(b).

132 E.g., the Netherlands is not signatory, but it did introduce the Faro Convention's definition of cultural heritage in art 1(1) of its new Heritage Act Relating to the Combining and Amendment of Rules Regarding Cultural Heritage (2015).

133 International Covenant on Economic, Social and Cultural Rights (adopted 16 December 1966) 993 UNTS 3 (ICESCR) art 15 para 1(a).

134 Committee on Economic, Social and Cultural Rights, General Comment No 21 (2009) E/C.12/GC/21.

135 Ibid. para 15.

136 Ibid. paras 49(d), 50.

the right of indigenous peoples to self-determination and to maintain, control, protect and develop cultural heritage.[137]

Similar to the concept of 'heritage communities' in the Faro Convention, Shaheed notes that 'varying degrees of access and enjoyment may be recognized, taking into consideration the diverse interests of individuals and groups according to their relationship with specific cultural heritages.' She notes the following hierarchy:

- 'source communities,' people who are keeping cultural heritage alive and/ or have taken responsibility for it;
- individuals and communities, including local communities, who consider the cultural heritage in question an integral part of the life of the community, but may not be actively involved in its maintenance;
- scientists and artists; and
- members of the general public accessing the cultural heritage of others.[138]

This would implicate, in the event of disputes, a weighing of interests that different right holders may have in the same object.

In this regard, the reference to a right of everyone to have access to one's own culture in recent Western-European policy instruments is noteworthy. French President Macron, in his November 2017 policy announcement, for example, underlined the need that Africans have to be able to access their own culture and, hence, it cannot be accepted that most of that is in European collections. Likewise, and even more poignant, the German policy framework of March 2019 gives as rationale for this new policy that 'all people should have the possibility to access their rich material culture [...] to connect with it and to pass it on to future generations.'[139] It mirrors the development of 'humanisation' of cultural property law, described above.

4.5 UNDRIP

While the right of 'access to culture' in the binding ICESCR may seem vague and unspecified,[140] the non-binding UNDRIP is clear and specific in its obligations. Since its provisions can be seen as an interpretation of the right of access

---

137 Human Rights Council, 'Report of the Independent Expert in the Field of Cultural Rights (Farida Shaheed)' (2010) Doc A/HRC/14/36.

138 Ibid. 16 para 62.

139 'Eckpunkte zum Umgang mit Sammlungsgut aus Kolonialen Kontexten' (n. 4).

140 Cultural rights are said not to lay any concrete obligation on states but, rather, to impose political commitments. A. Jakubowski, 'Cultural Heritage and the Collective Dimension of Cultural Rights in the Jurisprudence of the European Court of Human Rights' in A. Jakubowski (ed) *Cultural Rights as Collective Rights, An International Law Perspective* (2016) Brill, 157.

to culture in as far as it concerns indigenous peoples' cultural heritage, this is an important instrument.[141]

Already the International Labour Organization (ILO) Convention Concerning Indigenous and Tribal Peoples in Independent Countries of 1989 entitled indigenous peoples to rights with regard to their cultural heritage,[142] however UNDRIP extends this to specific rights with regard to lost cultural objects.

In Article 11(2) of UNDRIP, this is defined as a right of 'redress through effective mechanisms, which may include restitution, developed in conjunction with indigenous peoples, with respect to their cultural, intellectual, religious and spiritual property taken without their free, prior and informed consent or in violation of their laws, traditions and customs.'[143] Article 12 deals with rights to objects of special importance – namely, a right to 'use and control' where it concerns lost ceremonial objects, while for human remains a straightforward right to repatriation applies.[144] Since the loss of the Bangwa Queen appears to have been 'in violation of the Bangwa laws, traditions and customs,' and it concerns a ceremonial figure, this loss would fall under the definition of Article 12 of the UNDRIP, resulting in certain rights to 'use and control.'

4.5.1 Defining 'indigenous people'

The UNDRIP deliberately abstains from defining indigenous peoples, following the advice of Special Rapporteur Erica-Irene Daes who suggested that 'justice would best be served by allowing the scope of this concept to evolve flexibly over time, through practice.'[145] In 2010, the following criteria were suggested by the ILA's Working Committee on Indigenous Peoples' Rights:

- *self-identification*: self-identification as both indigenous and as a people;
- *historical continuity*: common ancestry and historical continuity with pre-colonial and/or pre-settler societies;

141 According to General Comment No 21 (n. 134): the right of 'access to culture' includes the rights as listed in the UNDRIP (see paras 7 and 37). See also A. Xanthaki, 'Culture: Articles 11(1), 12, 13(1), 15, and 34', *The UN Declaration on the Rights of Indigenous Peoples: A Commentary* (2018) Oxford University Press, 275.

142 See also International Labour Organization (ILO) Convention No 169 Concerning Indigenous and Tribal Peoples in Independent Countries (adopted 27 June 1989) 28 ILM 1382 (Convention No 169) art 4. It requests states to take special measures to 'safeguard' the cultures of indigenous peoples.

143 UNDRIP (n. 9) art 11(2).

144 Ibid. art 12(1): 'Indigenous peoples have the right to manifest, practice, develop and teach their spiritual and religious traditions, customs and ceremonies; … the right to the use and control of their ceremonial objects; and the right to the repatriation of their human remains. (2) States shall seek to enable the access and/or repatriation of ceremonial objects and human remains in their possession through fair, transparent and effective mechanisms developed in conjunction with indigenous peoples concerned.'

145 Commission on Human Rights, Subcommission on Prevention of Discrimination and Protection of Minorities, 'Discrimination against Indigenous Peoples: Protection of the Heritage of Indigenous People', Final Report (1995) Doc E/Cn.4.2/1995/26.

- *special relationship with ancestral lands*: having a strong and special link with the territories occupied by their ancestors before colonial domination and surrounding natural resources. Such a link will often form the basis of the cultural distinctiveness of indigenous peoples;
- *distinctiveness*: having distinct social, economic or political systems; having distinct language, culture, beliefs and customary law;
- *non-dominance*: forming non-dominant groups within the current society;
- *perpetuation*: perseverance to maintain and reproduce their ancestral environments, social and legal systems and culture as distinct peoples and communities.[146]

Within the context of a complaint by the Endorois people from Kenya, the African Commission on Human and Peoples' Rights gave its view on this matter in 2009 and noted that indigenous communities can be distinguished by the link between people, their land and culture, and self-identification as a distinct community.[147] The commission agreed that the Endorois 'considered themselves to be a distinct people, sharing a common history, culture and religion' and, therefore, were entitled to the protection of their collective rights under the African Charter.[148] Given the fact that the Bangwa identify themselves as an indigenous people,[149] and would seem to meet the ILA criteria, there is no reason to assume they would not be entitled to the special protective framework of the UNDRIP.

4.5.2 *Legal status*

The UNDRIP was adopted after 20 years of negotiations.[150] France voted in favour it at the adoption. In May 2016, Canada officially removed its objector status, while the other three objectors have also, to various degrees, changed their vote.[151] While it is not binding as a UN General Assembly declaration, the UNDRIP's strong status follows from the reference to it in General Comment

146 International Law Association, 'Rights of Indigenous Peoples', Interim Report (2010) 7.

147 *Centre for Minority Rights Development (Kenya) and Minority Rights Group International (on Behalf of Endorois Welfare Council) v Kenya* (2010) Communication No 276/2003; see also A.F. Vrdoljak, 'Standing and Collective Cultural Rights' in A. Jakubowski (ed) *Cultural Rights as Collective Rights, An International Law Perspective* (2016) Brill 281.

148 Ibid. African Charter on Human and Peoples' Rights (adopted 27 June 1981) 21 ILM 58 (African Charter).

149 Communication with the author (on file with the author).

150 By a majority of 144 states in favor, four votes against (Australia, Canada, New Zealand, and the United States), and 11 abstentions (Azerbaijan, Bangladesh, Bhutan, Burundi, Colombia, Georgia, Kenya, Nigeria, Russian Federation, Samoa and Ukraine).

151 On 3 April 2009, Australia's government endorsed the UNDRIP. On 19 April 2010, New Zealand's support became official. On 16 December 2010, President Barack Obama declared that the United States would 'lend its support' to the declaration. In 2016, Canada officially adopted the declaration and promised to implement it fully.

no. 21 as forming part of the right of access to culture.[152] According to authors like Frederico Lenzerini, the right of indigenous peoples to reparation for the loss of their cultural heritage has, today, crystallised into a principle of customary international law.[153] For the time being, however, this still contrasts with European practice, as the outcome in the 2013 and 2014 French Hopi Katsina cases illustrates.[154] Irrespective of its binding status as customary law, states that have adopted the UNDRIP are under an obligation to work towards fulfilling its aims.[155] This means that states are expected to assist indigenous peoples in providing 'redress through effective mechanisms' and to 'enable the access and/or repatriation of ceremonial objects and human remains in their possession through fair, transparent and effective mechanisms developed in conjunction with indigenous peoples concerned.'

Interestingly, from a 2015 study by the Expert Mechanism on the Rights of Indigenous Peoples, it appears that the UNDRIP is aimed not only at state collections but also at private collections: 'While the role of public authorities is crucial to ensuring such repatriation, the repatriation of ceremonial objects and human remains requires the cooperation of the places where the objects and remains are stored, such as museums and auction houses.'[156] Such efforts could lead to a similar pattern as occurred in the field of Nazi-looted art claims; while the Washington Principles were initially thought to be aimed and implemented at state-controlled collections, they soon had their effect on the private sector.

4.5.3 Access to justice and wider developments

In several settler states, policies or laws have been adopted in response to indigenous peoples' cultural property claims that follow an approach in line with the UNDRIP. The United States took a pioneering step in this regard with the adoption of NAGPRA, introducing the 'cultural affiliation' prong to allocate rights to (indigenous) cultural objects on the basis of (1) a shared group identity and (2) the (continued) existence of an identifiable indigenous group for

152 General Comment No 21 (n. 134).

153 Lenzerini (2017) 343; W van Genugten and F Lenzerini, 'Legal Implementation and International Cooperation and Assistance: Articles 37-42' in J. Hohmann and M. Weller (eds) *The UN Declaration on the Rights of Indigenous Peoples: A Commentary* (2018) Oxford University Press.

154 And the fact these claims are seen as merely 'moral.' E.g., see the reference to the UNDRIP as non-binding in the German Museum Association, Guidelines on Dealing with Collections from Colonial Contexts (n. 110) 70-71.

155 If the UNDRIP could be viewed as a first step toward a binding instrument. See Vienna Convention on the Law of Treaties (adopted 23 May 1969) 1155 UNTS 331 art 18.

156 Study by the Expert Mechanism on the Rights of Indigenous Peoples on the 'Promotion and Protection of the Rights of Indigenous Peoples with Respect to Their Cultural Heritage' (2015) UN Doc A/HRC/30/53 (Study by the Expert Mechanism) 72.

property claims.[157] Where NAGPRA is effective only within the domestic US territory and applies to federal institutions, other settler states have adopted policies to pursue repatriation claims of objects containing human remains on behalf of their indigenous peoples from abroad.[158] A 2019 draft Canadian bill on the subject, the Indigenous Human Remains and Cultural Property Act, planned to take things one step further. It promotes the return of indigenous human remains as well as cultural property, *wherever situated*, to the indigenous peoples of Canada.[159] If this Bill would become law in the future, it would implicate that Canadian authorities will actively pursue the international repatriation of indigenous Canadian cultural objects.

The fact that a human rights law approach is not restricted to indigenous peoples' cultural property claims may be illustrated furthermore by China, which publicly invoked in April 2018 the 'cultural rights of the Chinese people' in a claim to artefacts seized from the Old Summer Palace in the nineteenth century that were on auction in the United Kingdom.[160] Although the request was to no avail, in this instance, the influential role and active stance of the Chinese government in its efforts to reclaim lost cultural objects makes this claim noteworthy.

4.5.4 Access to justice

For African communities like the Bangwa who are not supported by strong governments, access to justice poses an additional obstacle. What forum could evaluate a human rights claim based on the argument that the continued deprivation of sacred cultural objects is an infringement of the right to 'access to culture' and the UNDRIP? Since 2013, the Optional Protocol to the ICESCR offers a complaints procedure. This procedure, however, appears to be limited

157 Kuprecht (2014) 55-56.

158 In New Zealand in 2003, a repatriation policy was developed of ancestral remains on behalf of Maori and Moriori. The National Te Papa Museum has, since then until 1 May 2017, repatriated 420 ancestral remains from overseas institutions. Furthermore, in 2011, the Australian government adopted a policy to facilitate the repatriation of ancestral remains. See also Study by the Expert Mechanism (n. 156).

159 Bill C-391 on the Canadian Indigenous Human Remains and Cultural Property Act (February 2019) <http://www.parl.ca/DocumentViewer/en/42-1/bill/C-391/third-reading> (accessed 15 January 2021). After publication of this article in IJCP, in September 2019, this bill had not become law. Acc. to information kindly provided by the Department of Canadian Heritage, it remains to be seen whether the issue will be taken up in the future.

160 On 10 April 2018, China's National Cultural Heritage Administration (NCHA, formerly SACK) called on the auction house to 'abide by the spirit of international agreements and code of professional ethics, as well as respecting the cultural rights and national feelings of the Chinese people.' See the website of the National Cultural Heritage Administration, an administrative agency of the Ministry of Culture and Tourism of the People's Republic of China (in Chinese) <http://www.sach.gov.cn/art/2018/4/10/art_722_148344.html> accessed 30 October 2018. I thank Maud Yu for her assistance finding and translating this source.

to nationals or groups in the state responsible for the alleged violation.[161] In the Bangwa case, it concerns an African community claiming an object from a French foundation.

What about developments in the regional human rights systems? With respect to the European human rights system, one stumbling block may be that the European Convention on Human Rights does not include a right to culture.[162] The right (of access) to tangible cultural objects has been addressed in case law but always from the perspective of the right to property of Article 1 of the First Protocol.[163] In the *Nowakowski* case, for example, the European Court of Human Rights (ECtHR) did acknowledge the 'sentimental' value of a cultural object to a certain person – in this case, a collection of fire arms that had been confiscated by Polish authorities – and gave that interest preference over other (public) interests.[164] Whether the ECtHR would be ready to acknowledge historical claims remains to be seen. In its rejection of a claim brought by an Athenian organization for the return of the Parthenon Marbles in 2016, the ECtHR deemed the claim inadmissible, amongst others, under referral to the considerable time that had passed since the loss of the marbles.[165] In the light of recent developments in the field of colonial takings and the status of UNDRIP, a claim to sacred cultural objects lost by indigenous people might be another matter. Obviously, a problem is that this system is meant for states parties to the European Convention.

The African human rights system acknowledges in the African Charter the right to culture and expressly refers to communal traditional values and communal rights, which implicates that respect for indigenous customs and laws is guaranteed by this human rights system, as underlined by the *Endorois*

161 Optional Protocol to the International Covenant on Economic, Social and Cultural Rights (adopted 10 December 2008) UN Doc A/RES/63/117 art 2: 'Communications may be submitted by or on behalf of individuals or groups of individuals, under the jurisdiction of a State Party, claiming to be victims of a violation of any of the economic, social and cultural rights set forth in the Covenant *by that State Party.*'

162 European Convention for the Protection of Human Rights and Fundamental Freedoms (adopted 4 November 1950) 213 UNTS 222 (ECHR). In the case law, rights that may fall under the notion of 'cultural rights' were recognised. Jakubowski (2016) 158.

163 Ibid. 178-79. First Protocol to the European Convention for the Protection of Human Rights and Fundamental Freedoms (adopted 20 March 1952) ETS 9 art 1: 'Every natural or legal person is entitled to the peaceful enjoyment of his possessions. No one shall be deprived of his possessions except in the public interest and subject to the conditions provided for by law and by the general principles of international law'.

164 *Nowakowski v Poland* (Jugdment, 2012) Application No 55167/11, discussed by Jakubowski (2016) 176.

165 *Syllogos ton Athoinon against the United Kingdom* (n. 113). The court held that the claim for the United Kingdom (UK) government to engage in mediation was inadmissable, *ratione tempore* as well as *ratione materiae*, as none of the invoked articles 'would give rise to any right for an association in the postion of the applicant to have the Marbles returned to Greece or to have the UK engage in international mediation.'

case mentioned above.[166] And, although the inter-American human rights system has no direct relevance, the jurisprudence of the Inter-American Court of Human Rights – including the 2015 case *Kaliña and Lokono Peoples v Suriname* – is noteworthy in its recognition of pre-existing indigenous peoples' collective property rights and the participatory solutions found.[167] However, as in the African example, these cases dealt with indigenous peoples' land rights, not with cultural property.

Lastly, an interesting roadmap for indigenous peoples on how to proceed with claims regarding cultural objects in foreign museums was given by the Colombian Constitutional Court in a 2017 case concerning the 'Quimbaya Treasure.'[168] In its ruling, the court ordered the Columbian government to pursue restitution from Spain of a treasure of 122 golden objects, taken at the close of the nineteenth century, on behalf of the indigenous Quimbaya people. The court argued that, by today's standards of international law – and, here, it was referring to human rights law (UNDRIP) as well as cultural property law (the 1995 UNIDROIT Convention and other conventions) – indigenous peoples are entitled to the restitution of their lost cultural heritage. How such a claim is pursued by the Colombian government is left to the discretion of the government. In the first reaction to the subsequent request by the Colombian authorities for a dialogue on the return of the Quimbaya Treasure, the Spanish authorities declined on the grounds that the Quimbaya Treasure has become Spanish patrimony and is inalienable.[169] As seen earlier, this is not an uncommon European reaction. The 2018 decision by President Macron to return statues and regalia taken during a punitive colonial expedition from the Kingdom of Dahomey to Benin,[170] for example, had earlier been denied by French authorities according to the inalienability of French public collections.[171]

Notwithstanding the uncertain state of the law, developments in the field of human rights law do unmistakably point in a certain direction. That direction is toward the acknowledgement of heritage interests of communities – and their rights – with regard to certain categories of involuntarily lost cultural objects, irrespective of a proven illegality of the acquisition at the time.

---

166 African Charter (n. 148) art 17(2): 'Every individual may freely take part in the cultural life of his community, and 17 (3) The promotion and protection of morals and traditional values recognized by the community shall be the duty of the State.'

167 E.g., *Kalina and Lokono Peoples v Suriname* (Merits, Reparations and Costs) (2015) Inter-American Court of Human Rights, Series C, No 309. Within the scope of the right to property and political rights. Implementation of these rulings by state parties is problematic.

168 Judgment SU-649/17 (2017) (Republic of Colombia, Constitutional Court).

169 For a critical discussion, see D. Mejia-Lemos, 'The 'Quimbaya Treasure,' Judgment SU-649/17' (2019) 113 American Journal of International Law 122. Indeed, basing such a right on UNESCO 1970 or 1995 UNIDROIT, Conventions that were explicitly not meant for losses before implementation by states parties, is remarkable.

170 'Remise du Rapport Savoy/Sarr sur la Restitution du Patrimoine Africain' (n. 5).

171 Dagen (2017).

5 Concluding remarks

> With German colonial rule the chiefs began their subservience to an outside authority. ... Gone was their invincibility. ... Gone too, were many of the royal ancestor statues which formed a link with the past and were an essential feature of the Lefem. [T]oday they stare glumly from their pedestals in the alien Lefems of European and American museums.[172]

This chapter has analysed the legal framework for a claim regarding an African ancestral sculpture known as the Bangwa Queen that was taken in the course of colonial annexation of the Bangwa territory in 1899. Often it is argued that, according to the law at the time, such acquisitions were lawful, a conclusion that has been challenged for the present case. Nevertheless, even if one could argue that a specific loss was unlawful, the traditional legal framework is not well suited for claims like the Bangwa case. An important reason is that former colonial powers, on the whole, did not acknowledge a legal obligation to return cultural objects taken from their former colonies, as it was in similar instances in the European context.

In the meantime, views on the possession of 'tainted' cultural objects have changed, resulting in the adoption of soft law instruments and professional guidelines. These instruments promote equitable solutions for claims regarding artefacts looted in the past, even in the absence of a clear basis for claims in positive law and notwithstanding later acquired ownership rights by new possessors. The rationale of such norms lies in the intangible 'heritage' value of the artefacts for individuals or communities: as symbols of an identity. Evolving human rights law, was argued, mirrors this development. In this sense, international cultural property law can be said to be evolving from a property framework towards a human rights framework.[173] A human rights law approach to restitution claims can be understood as the acknowledgement of a right to possess, access, or control involuntarily lost cultural objects on the grounds of their intangible heritage value for specific people, independent of ownership. It relies, in other words, on a continuing human rights violation of remaining separated from certain objects (and therefore being denied access), as opposed to a focus on the unlawfulness of the acquisition in the past in an ownership-focused approach. A noteworthy element is that communities may be collective right holders.

As discussed in this chapter, a human rights law approach as adopted in the UNDRIP provides useful tools to address claims to cultural objects lost in the course of colonization. The UNDRIP contains a right of redress with respect

172 Lockhart (1998) 29. The part '[t]hese the Germans looted' is left out given that the exact circumstances of the loss are unclear.

173 See also K.L. Alderman, 'The Human Right to Cultural Property' (2011) 20 Michigan State University College of Law International Law Review 81.

to cultural objects taken without the 'free, prior and informed consent' of indigenous peoples. Depending on the cultural importance of the artefact at stake, redress may vary from a right to 'access and control' to a straightforward right to repatriation of human remains. To fulfil this aim, states are expected to provide assistance – 'effective mechanisms in conjunction with indigenous peoples' – in addressing claims. States might want to consider, in this light, adopting policy measures and setting up claims procedures.[174] Given the strong legal status of the UNDRIP, such human rights claims may also find their way to regular courts of law.

For claims such as the one involving the Bangwa Queen, this approach would mean that her present-day spiritual importance to the Bangwa people is a point of focus, instead of the legality of the events in the past. This is important for cases where present possessors could hardly be held accountable for acts in the past. In this respect, the 2015 study by the Expert Mechanism in the field of Indigenous cultural rights underlines that states should work toward a general acceptance of the UNDRIP's aims beyond collections under their direct authority.[175] A human rights law approach may thus also pave the way to creative solutions, beyond an all-or-nothing-outcome in a property focused approach.

Summarising the findings in this chapter, the following arguments would seem to support the Bangwa people in their quest for their lost Bangwa statues:

- Cultural objects have a protected status under international law and pillage of such objects is prohibited by customary international law, arguably since the end of the nineteenth century.
- Pillage of cultural objects in the course of colonial (military) expeditions falls under the scope of this prohibition and was unlawful.
- Sacred objects of ceremonial importance to a living culture have an enhanced protected status under these rules.
- The UNDRIP is considered to be an interpretation of the right to culture in the ICESCR insofar as it concerns indigenous peoples' cultural property, and provides a legal basis for claims if these were taken 'without their free, prior and informed consent or in violation of their laws, traditions and customs.'
- States that adopted the UNDRIP have committed themselves to its aims and should provide assistance – 'effective mechanisms in conjunction with indigenous peoples' – in addressing claims, which implies that state authorities should support equitable solutions that honour the rights of indigenous peoples to access and control their ceremonial objects.

---

174 As the German government announced its recent policy framework.

175 Reiterated in 'Eckpunkte zum Umgang mit Sammlungsgut aus Kolonialen Kontexten' (n. 4).

Usually, it is said that such cases are a matter of ethics and not law. Indeed, an ethical approach and alternative dispute resolution may provide for a constructive non-adversarial setting for culturally and politically sensitive claims. Nevertheless, general standards are needed to see that similar cases are dealt with similarly. For this reason – and as a guarantee for access to justice for less powerful parties – this chapter proposes a human rights law approach to claims that often are set aside as being merely moral in nature.

Fon Asunganyi, reigning Chief of Fontem in the 1890s (deceased 1951). Image taken in the 1940s, courtesy royal family through Chief C. Taku.

6 Cross-border trade and claims: A synthesis

ABSTRACT

Chapter 6 elaborates on the insights of chapters 2, 3, 4, and 5 in a search for a model in answer to the central research question (how the interests of former owners can be addressed more effectively). It approaches the topic of looted cultural objects – including more recently looted objects – from the wider perspective of heritage protection, the international art trade and the system of the 1970 UNESCO Convention. It analyses the interrelation (and disconnect) between private and public law in this field and puts forward proposals for the notion of 'heritage title' and a human rights law approach as legal tools to bridge gaps. Sub-questions addressed in this chapter are: What interests are at stake in cultural heritage protection, on the one hand, and in the art trade, on the other hand? What are the blind spots in this system? Furthermore: is international human rights law equipped to clarify standards in this regard, and how can such standards be transposed into a private law setting of title claims?

Cultural objects have a special, protected, status because of their intangible 'heritage' value to people, as symbols of an identity. This has been so since the first days of international law and, today, there is an extensive legal framework to protect cultural objects and to prohibit looting. Despite this, for as long as demand exists and profits are high, cultural objects continue to be looted, smuggled and traded. At some point, their character tends to change from protected heritage in an original setting to valuable art and commodity in the hands of new possessors. In this new setting, the legal status of such objects will most likely be a matter of ownership and the private law regime in the country where they happen to end up. This chapter suggests that, irrespective of the acquired rights of others, original owners should still be able to rely on a 'heritage title' if there is a continuing cultural link. The term aims to capture the legal bond between cultural objects and people, distinct from ownership, and is informed by international cultural heritage and human rights law norms.

*Whose cultural objects? Introducing heritage title for cross-border cultural property claims**

'It has been claimed that culture is central to man and that without it no rights are possible since it is the matrix from which all else must spring. Culture is the essence of being human.'[1]

1 Introduction

Cultural objects have a special, protected, status because of their intangible 'heritage' value to people, as symbols of an identity. This has been so since the first days of international law and, today, there is an extensive framework to protect cultural objects and to prohibit looting. Despite this, for as long as demand exists and profits are high, cultural objects continue to be looted, smuggled and traded. At some point, their character tends to change from protected heritage in an original setting to valuable art and commodity in the hands of a new possessor. In this new setting, the legal status of such an object will be a matter of ownership and the private law regime in the country where it happens to end up. This chapter suggests that, irrespective of the acquired rights of new possessors, original owners should still be able to rely on a 'heritage title' if there is a continuing cultural link. The term aims to capture the legal bond between cultural objects and people, distinct from owner ship, and is informed by international cultural heritage and human rights law norms.

A recent Dutch case concerning a Chinese Buddha statue containing the human remains of a mummified monk may serve as an illustration.[2] In 1995

---

* Published in the *Netherlands International Law Review* (Vol. 67 (2): 257-295) in August 2020.

1 UNESCO Secretariat (1970), p. 10, quoted by A.F. Vrdoljak 'Human rights and cultural heritage in international law' in F. Lenzerini, A.F. Vrdoljak (eds) *International law for common goods: normative perspectives on human rights* (2014) Hart Publishing, Oxford, p. 139. Vrdoljak's pioneering work on the interrelation between human rights and cultural heritage law has been a source of inspiration.

2 Discussed in, e.g., Z. Liu 'Will the god win? the case of the Buddhist mummy' (2007) 24 *International Journal of Cultural Property* 221; J. Hooper and T. Plafker, 'The body in the Buddha' (4 May 2017) *The Economist* <www.1843magazi ne.com/features/the-body-in-the-buddha> accessed 29 Apr 2020.

the statue, dating back to the Song Dynasty (eleventh century) and revered as 'Master Zhang Gong' by the Chinese community which it came from, was stolen from a temple. It was acquired in Hong Kong by a Dutch collector who, in 2014, loaned the statue to a Hungarian museum where it was recognised by Chinese villagers as their sacred Master Zhang Gong.[3] They instigated a restitution claim before the Amsterdam District Court.[4] The collector, however, argued that he had bought the statue in good faith and was the lawful owner under Dutch law, claiming that at the time it was not common practice to ask for provenance details (the ownership history). Indeed, the Netherlands only issued implementation legislation for the 1970 UNESCO Convention on the Means of Prohibiting and Preventing the Illicit Import, Export and Transfer of Ownership of Cultural Property after the theft in 2009.[5] For disputes concerning artefacts that were misappropriated before that time – i.e., nearly all of today's cases – the rule applies that a new possessor gains valid title after a good faith acquisition or merely by the passing of time. Whilst the regulation of ownership differs widely per country, this is the situation in a civil law jurisdiction like the Netherlands.[6] The Dutch court denied the claim in its December 2018 ruling.[7] In other words, the application of private law rules prevented the admissibility of a claim by those for whom the statue means the most, the holders of the right to practise their own religion.

The case resembles French litigation brought on behalf of the Hopi Native Americans to stop the auction of their sacred Katsina – masks representing incarnated spirits of ancestors that are referred to as 'friends' and according to Hopi law cannot be privately owned or traded.[8] The Katsina were lost longer ago, in the 1930s and 1940s, but litigation stranded in a similar way: the French court observed that the claim that the Katsina were (inalienable)

3 NB During the procedure some key facts, such as the location of the statue, were not clarified.

4 *Village Communities of Yangchun and Dongpu v Van Overveem, Design & Consultancy BV, Design Consultancy Oscar van Overveem B.V.* (Judgment of 12 December 2018) Amsterdam District Court, Case No. C/13/609408, ECLI:NL:RBAMS:2018:8919.

5 UNESCO Convention on the Means of Prohibiting and Preventing the Illicit Import, Export and Transfer of Ownership of Cultural Property (adopted 14 November 1970) 823 UNTS 231 (1970 UNESCO Convention). See the '*Uitvoeringswet UNESCO-verdrag 1970*,' *Staatsblad* 2009, no. 255, this law was integrated in the Dutch Heritage Act of 9 December 2015.

6 For the Dutch situation, see also *Autocephalous Greek Orthodox Church in Cyprus v Lans* (Judgment of 7 March 2002) The Hague Court of Appeal, Case No. 99/693, ECLI:NL:GHSGR:2002:6, a denial of a claim to icons looted in the 1970s from Cyprus due to prescription. Discussed, amongst others, in E. Campfens, 'Whose cultural heritage? Crimean treasures at the crossroads of politics, law and ethics' (2017) 22 *Art Antiquity and Law* 193 and E. Campfens, 'Bridging the gap between ethics and law: the Dutch framework for Nazi looted art' (2020) 25 *Art Antiquity and Law* 1.

7 Above, n. 4. In a short verdict, the claim was held inadmissible on the ground that the status of the village committees as owner of the statue was unclear.

8 *Association Survival International France v S.A.R.L. Néret-Minet Tessier Sarrou* (2013) Tribunal de Grande Instance de Paris, No. RG 13/52,880 BF/No. 1.

patrimony of the Hopi has no legal basis in French property law.[9] Again, such an approach solely from the perspective of national private law is clearly at odds with the principles and *rationale* of heritage protection on the international level and the rights of indigenous peoples to use and control their (lost) ceremonial objects. To widen the scope: the field of Nazi-looted art is also typified by a striking imbalance between international (soft law) regulations that prescribe 'fair and just solutions' for disputes over family heirlooms lost as a result of racial persecution, on the one hand, and possibilities under national private law, on the other.[10]

Such cases highlight a tension between cultural objects as heritage – symbolic of an identity – and cultural objects as possessions – representing economic interests and exclusive rights. They also illustrate a disconnect between norms on various levels. This disconnect, it is argued, is an incentive for the trade in looted artefacts – resulting in the destruction of cultural heritage –[11] and a cause for legal insecurity in the art world. These tensions will be evaluated in the following sections in a search for tools to bring the various levels more into line.

It will do so by starting out with an overview of different interests and levels of law in this field (Sect. 2), and an analysis of the international regime for the art trade based on the 1970 UNESCO Convention and the notion of 'national treasures' (Sect. 3). This will be followed by a discussion of blind spots in this regime, such as losses that predate the UNESCO Convention or entitlement of communities or individuals to 'their' lost cultural objects, and the proliferation of soft law in that regard (Sect. 4). Section 5 elaborates on a human rights law approach to further develop this field through the notion of heritage title.

The proposition underlying this chapter is that, whilst ownership interests are accounted for in national private law, legal tools are lacking to address

9 In France individual property is the known format as defined by Art. 544 of the French Civil Code. See also K. Kuprecht, *Indigenous peoples' cultural property claims* (2014) Springer International Publishing, pp. 111-112; L. Nicolazzi et al., 'Case Hopi masks – Hopi tribe v Néret-Minet and estimations & ventes aux enchères' (2015) Platform ArThémis, Art-Law Centre, University of Geneva.

10 The US being the exception. For a discrepancy between the US and Western Europe see E. Campfens, 'Nazi-looted art: a note in favour of clear standards and neutral procedures' (2018) 22 *Art Antiquity and Law* 315.

11 On the looting from the MENA region from 1990 to 2015 '[a] large if not the major cause of damage [...] was theft from cultural institutions and illegal digging of archaeological sites to feed the voracious demand of the international market in cultural objects' rather than damage cause during military activities or fanatic of ideologues'. N. Brodie, 'Protecting not preventing: the failure of public policy to prevent the looting and illegal trade of cultural property from the MENA Region (1990-2015)' in J. Anderson, H. Geismar (eds) *The Routledge companion to cultural property* (2017) Routledge, New York, p. 89, cited by P. Gerstenblith, 'The disposition of movable cultural heritage' in A.M. Carstens, E. Varner (eds) *Intersections in international cultural heritage law* (2020) Oxford University Press, p. 19.

heritage interests and identity values that are acknowledged in international law. The notion of 'heritage title' acts as a bridge in that regard.

2 Ownership versus heritage

Cultural objects have a dual nature, as is illustrated by the two ways they are referred to: either as 'cultural property' or as 'cultural heritage'.[12] Similarly, disputes over lost cultural objects can be approached as a matter of stolen property or as lost heritage: this activates different norms. Whereas property and its ownership are mainly regulated by national private law, norms protecting heritage are predominantly of a public international law nature. What follows is an outline of how the international framework accounts for this.

2.1 Ownership

On the one hand, cultural objects can be seen as possessions. As such, they can be traded and owned, and are subject to property law regimes and international trade law regulations. The regulation of property and ownership, traditionally, is a matter of national sovereignty.[13]

Ownership can be defined as 'the greatest possible interest in a thing which a mature system of law recognises'.[14] Apart from this common feature, major differences exist, most notably between common and civil law jurisdictions, with many variations on the theme of whether and how title over a (stolen)

---

12 F. Fiorentini et al., Editorial (2016) 2 *Santander Art and Culture Law Review* 9, p. 11; L.V. Prott and P.V. O'Keefe, 'Cultural heritage or cultural property?' (1992) 1 *International Journal of Cultural Property* 307. The term 'cultural heritage' was first introduced in the Hague Convention for the Protection of Cultural Property in the Event of Armed Conflict (adopted 14 May 1954), 249 UNTS 240, and ever since then has been used in legal texts alongside the term 'cultural property'. Much has been written on these terms. T.V. Hafstein and M. Skrydstrup, 'Heritage vs. Property: Contrasting regimes and rationalities in the patrimonial field' in J. Anderson, H. Geismar (eds) *The Routledge Companion to Cultural Property* (2017) Routledge, New York, for example argue that 'property is associated with technologies of sovereignty and heritage with technologies of reformation'. In the author's view, heritage protection will remain problematic as long as the private law aspects of cultural property are not sufficiently addressed from an international perspective.

13 For example, even within the EU Art. 345 of the Treaty on the Functioning of the European Union (TFEU) regulates that: 'The Treaties shall in no way prejudice the rules in Member States governing the system of property ownership'. TFEU Consolidated version [2012] OJ C 326, p. 194. For an analysis of how international law increasingly influences property relations, see J.G. Sprankling, *The International Law of Property* (2014) Oxford University Press, New York.

14 S. Dromgoole, *Underwater Cultural Heritage and International Law* (2013) Cambridge University Press, Cambridge, p. 96.

good can be transferred to a new possessor.[15] Where misappropriated *cultural* property is concerned, the situation becomes even more fragmented as stolen artefacts tend to surface only years or decades later, by which time they may have crossed many borders. At that point, private international law should guide judges to a just outcome. Two problems occur at this level. First, ownership disputes regarding movable goods are regulated by the law of the country where the object is located at the time of a transaction (*lex rei sitae*).[16] This enables (invites) the 'laundering' of looted objects through jurisdictions that allow for a transfer of the ownership title of stolen goods after a *bona fide* acquisition or merely by the passage of time. A second stumbling block is that foreign public law will not generally be applied in another jurisdiction. Export laws or laws that render certain cultural objects inalienable in their original setting – as a *res extra commercium* –, however, often form the basis of the unlawfulness of a taking.[17] These complications are addressed in international instruments – most notably the 1995 UNIDROIT Convention on Stolen or Illegally Exported Cultural Objects – that promote the harmonisation of private law on the following points:[18]

---

15 Whereas civil law countries opt for security of transactions and a new possessor may gain title after a *bona fide* transfer, in common law countries a thief cannot transfer title (the '*nemo dat (quod not habet)*' rule). These differences surface in cross-border disputes, e.g. in a case concerning a Pissarro painting, lost by its Jewish owners during the Second World War, that has been pending before the US courts for over fifteen years. After several transfers across various jurisdictions, the Pissarro is now in the possession of a Spanish museum which gained lawful ownership title under Spanish private law. (*Cassirer v Thyssen-Bornemisza Collection Foundation*, No. 05-CV-03459 (C.D. Cal. 2019)). For further analysis, E. Campfens, 'Restitution of looted art: what about access to justice?' (2019) 4 *Santander Art and Culture Law Review* 185.

16 J. Gordley, 'The enforcement of foreign law: Reclaiming one's nation's cultural heritage in another nation's courts' in F. Francioni, J. Gordley (eds) *Enforcing International Cultural Heritage Law* (2013) Oxford University Press, New York, p. 110; A. Chechi, *The Settlement of International Cultural Heritage Disputes* (2014) Oxford University Press, New York, pp. 90-96; K. Siehr, 'Private international law and the difficult problem to return illegally exported cultural property' (2015) 20 *Uniform Law Review* 503, pp. 503-515.

17 Chechi (2014), p. 92: '[I]n the absence of inter-State agreements, the domestic norms prohibiting or restricting the export of cultural materials are not enforced in foreign States'. In the UK, e.g., *Attorney General of New Zealand v Ortiz* (1982) 3 All ER 432. Recent UK and US case law in the category of antiquities circumvent this by accepting State ownership as a sufficient basis for a claim: *Government of the Islamic Republic of Iran v The Barakat Galleries Ltd.* (2007) EWCA Civ. 1374; *United States v Schultz*, 178 F. Supp. 2d445 (SDNY 3 January 2002).

18 UNIDROIT Convention on Stolen or Illegally Exported Cultural Objects (adopted 24 June 1995, entered into force 7 July 1998) 2421 UNTS 457 (1995 UNIDROIT Convention). The 1970 Convention does not regulate private law issues. More in Sect. 3.

- The law of the source country – the *lex originis* – should determine the (un)law fulness of a transfer;[19]
- Extension of limitation periods for title claims;[20] and
- Invalidation of a title transfer to a new possessor, who may be entitled to compensation insofar as it can prove to have been duly diligent at the time of acquisition.[21]

This would support a smooth and licit international art trade in the future. However, Western 'market countries' mostly did not accede to the 1995 UNIDROIT Convention (precisely because it deals with ownership) and have only recently become party to the 1970 UNESCO Convention (that is implemented in different ways), and today's restitution claims deal with past losses. As a result, the fragmented situation continues. To retroactively declare that the lawfully acquired ownership title of a new possessor is invalid is problematic – mostly for civil law countries where ownership over stolen goods may pass –, as that would implicate expropriation.[22] It is unlikely that states would ever change their laws in that way,[23] hence the preference for the extra-legal 'ethical' model and alternative dispute resolution for claims to Nazi-looted art.[24]

There are two more reasons why an ownership approach is problematic. Firstly, the zero-sum outcome of ownership disputes may at times obstruct rather than assist dispute resolution while other forms of entitlement may exist,

---

19 1995 UNIDROIT Convention, Art. 3(2); cf., Arts. 2, 3 and 4 of the resolution on the International Sale of Works of Art from the Angle of the Protection of the Cultural Heritage (1991) in *Institute of International Law Yearbook 64 II* (1991 IDI Basel Resolution). See also the new EU import regulation (Regulation (EU) 2019/880 of 17 April 2019 on the introduction and the import of cultural goods [2019] OJ L 151), Recital at (8). As Chechi observed, however, there is no convergence (as yet) over the primacy of the *lex originis*. Chechi (2014), pp. 92 and 97.

20 1995 UNIDROIT Convention, Art. 3(3), (4), (5) and (8), Art. 5(5); 1991 IDI Basel Resolution, Art. 4(1) on this: '[...] may claim, within a reasonable time [...]'.

21 1995 UNIDROIT Convention, Arts. 4 and 6; 1970 UNESCO Convention, Art. 7(b)(ii) that sees to the return of documented objects stolen from a public institution; 1991 IDI Basel Resolution, Art. 4(2), (3).

22 And this could violate the human right to property and would require compensation. Universal Declaration of Human Rights (UDHR), Art. 17; First Protocol to the European Convention for the Protection of Human Rights and Fundamental Freedoms, adopted 20 March 1952, ETS 9. Art. 1: 'Every natural or legal person is entitled to the peaceful enjoyment of his possessions. No one shall be deprived of his possessions except in the public interest and subject to the conditions provided for by law and by the general principles of international law'.

23 G. Robertson, *Who Owns History? Elgin's Loot and the Case for Returning Plundered Treasure* (2019) Knopf Australia, Melbourne, p. 312, proposes a Convention for the Repatriation of Important Cultural Heritage that should retroactively apply with time limitations set at 275 years. In the view of the author such a time period will remain arbitrary, underscoring the need for an alternative approach.

24 On the ethical model for Nazi-looted art claims, Campfens (2017) and (2020).

such as rights to access, control, custody and the like.[25] An open view, beyond an outcome in terms of exclusive and absolute ownership rights, may well pave the way to cooperative solutions.[26] Secondly, in an ownership approach the (un)lawfulness of the loss in the past will be the central point of reference, whereas today's interests may be more relevant, such as the (continuing) spiritual importance of cultural objects.[27]

In other words, there are limitations to a strict ownership approach to solve cultural property disputes – as cases that concern stolen property – and this is a consequence of the special nature of cultural objects. How this is accounted for in the legal framework will be discussed next.

2.2 Heritage

From a heritage point of view, cultural objects are valued because of their intangible value to people: as symbols of an identity. Throughout history and in most cultures, objects that are meaningful to the (own) community enjoy special legal status. Illustrative in this respect is a 1925 Indian court ruling holding that a contested Hindu family idol 'could not be seen as a mere chattel which was owned'.[28]

This intangible heritage value has been the rationale underlying the protected status of cultural objects in international law since its foundation.[29] In the much cited words of Justice Croke in 1813, by which he released artefacts that had been seized (as war booty) during the Anglo-American War:

> 'The arts and sciences are admitted amongst all civilized nations, [...] as entitled to favour and protection. They are considered not as the peculium of this or that nation, but as the property of mankind at large, and as belonging to the common interests of the whole species'.[30]

---

25 Given that ownership could be seen as a 'bundle of rights': the right to control, including the right to exclude others; the right to alienate; the right to exploit; and the right to destroy. Dromgoole (2013), p. 97.

26 Further to be discussed in Sect. 5.3.

27 Ibid.

28 *Mullick v Mullick* (1925) LR LII Indian Appeals 245, cited in Prott and O'Keefe (1992), p. 307. However, as shown in the examples in the introduction, when it comes to the protection of *foreign* heritage interests such special treatment is not a given.

29 On the historical development, e.g. E. Campfens, 'The Bangwa Queen: Artefact or Heritage?' (2019) 26 *International Journal of Cultural Property* 75.

30 Vice-Admiralty Court of Halifax, Nova Scotia Stewart's Vice-Admiralty Reports 482 (1813), reproduced in J.H. Merryman, 'Note on the Marquis de Somerueles' (1996) 5 *International Journal of Cultural Property*, p. 321.

Cultural objects, in other words, deserve protection and immunity, even in times of war, and this is a matter of universal concern as they are 'the property of mankind'.

2.2.1 *Property of mankind?*

The interest of 'mankind' or 'humanity' is often invoked in declarations or preambles in the field of heritage protection.[31] It underlines a shared, universal interest and responsibility to safeguard cultural objects. But what does this mean? It may give the impression that some international authority is in place to oversee the protection and just dissemination of cultural objects (like the global commons).[32] That, however, is not the case. States are appointed as custodians in this regard and no specialised authority or international compliance mechanism is in place.[33]

This does not mean, on the other hand, that the legal status of cultural objects is solely a matter of national sovereignty. Binding international norms do influence their legal status, as illustrated by the role that the UN Security Council has recently adopted in this field. In the name of peace and security it has introduced a ban on the trade in and possession of looted cultural objects

31 E.g. Preamble to the 1954 Hague Convention: 'Being convinced that damage to cultural property belonging to any people whatsoever means damage to the cultural heritage of all mankind, since each people makes its contribution to the culture of the world'.

32 I.e. the legal frameworks for resources of the ocean floor, Antarctica, outer space and the Moon that aim at cooperation and sharing by all, instead of appropriation by some. The Convention on the Law of the Sea, 10 December 1982, 1833 UNTS 397 (UNCLOS), in Art. 137, establishes such an international authority to oversee the equitable sharing of mineral resources on the deep seabed of the high seas – the 'Area' in UNCLOS terms: 'All rights in the resources of the Area are vested in mankind as a whole, on whose behalf the [International Seabed] Authority shall act'. See also the Agreement Governing the Activities of States on the Moon and Other Celestial Bodies, 1979, 1363 UNTS 3, Art. 4. See N.J. Schrijver, 'Managing the global commons: common good or common sink?' (2016) Vol 37 Third World Quarterly, 1252.

33 In fact, even cultural objects found in shipwrecks in the high seas do not fall under the competency of the International Seabed Authority but are linked to States. Arts. 133(a) and 136 of UNCLOS limit the concept of 'Heritage of Mankind' to minerals. In the UNESCO Convention on the Protection of the Underwater Cultural Heritage of 2 November 2001 (entered into force on 2 January 2009), 2562 UNTS 3, nevertheless, a coordination system is set up to ensure the safeguarding of underwater cultural heritage. In this system, States with a verifiable link have 'preferential rights', see Art. 11: 'Any State Party may declare to the Director-General its interest in being consulted on how to ensure the effective protection of that underwater cultural heritage. Such declaration shall be based on a verifiable link to the underwater cultural heritage concerned, particular regard being paid to the preferential rights of States of cultural, historical or archaeological origin'. For a discussion, see Dromgoole (2013), p. 120.

from Syria and Iraq.[34] In more general terms, in its 2017 Resolution the Security Council calls upon states to adopt measures to curb the 'trade and trafficking in cultural property and other items of archaeological, historical, cultural, rare scientific, and religious importance originating from a context of armed conflict' as this 'can fuel and exacerbate conflict and hamper post-conflict national reconciliation, thereby undermining the security, stability, governance, social economic and cultural development of affected states'.[35] These Resolutions are a further confirmation of the binding status of the prohibition on looting cultural objects in times of armed conflict.[36] On the other hand, as Gerstenblith points out, the fact that such *ad hoc* and directly binding action by the Security Council is necessary to ensure not only that the act of looting is unlawful but that the illegality 'sticks' to the object, highlights the weaknesses of the regular regime for the art trade.[37] This will be further discussed in Sect. 3.

Also beyond the category of armed conflict international norms exist that overrule national interests. In this respect, the key principle in the 1970 UNESCO Convention that the unauthorised transfer of cultural objects is illicit may be contrary to the interests of so-called market states. In all its ambiguity, it has been invoked by national courts as international public policy.[38]

The notion 'property (or: heritage) of mankind' may therefore, in the present context, best be understood to underline that the protection of cultural objects in terms of *preservation* and *accessibility* is a matter of international public policy.

---

34 As a matter of peace and security these resolutions contain obligations imposed on all States, aimed at the return of objects to the people they came from: UNSC Res. 2199 (2015) UN Doc S/RES/2199, para. 17: 'decides that all Member States shall take appropriate steps to prevent the trade in Iraqi and Syrian cultural property and other items of archaeological, historical, cultural, rare scientific, and religious importance illegally removed from Iraq since 6 August 1990 and from Syria since 15 March 2011, including by prohibiting cross-border trade in such items, thereby allowing for their eventual safe return to the Iraqi and Syrian people [...]'; UNSC Res 1483 (2003) UN Doc S/RES/1483, para. 7. These are both based on Arts. 39 and 41 of Chapter VII of the UN Charter.

35 UNSC Res. 2347 (2017) UN Doc S/RES/2347.

36 E.g. F. Francioni, 'General principles applicable to international cultural heritage law' in M. Andenas, M. Fitzmaurice, A.Tanzi, J. Wouters (eds) *General principles and the coherence of international law* (2019) Brill, Leiden, p. 406: as general principles of law or customary law; K. Hausler, 'The UN Security Council, the Human Rights Council, and the protection of cultural heritage: a matter of peace and security, human rights, or both?' in A.M. Carstens, E. Varner (eds) *Intersections in International Cultural Heritage Law* (2020) Oxford University Press, Oxford, p. 204.

37 P. Gerstenblith, 'The disposition of movable cultural heritage' in A.M. Carstens, E. Varner (eds) *Intersections in International Cultural Heritage Law* (2020) Oxford University Press, pp. 37-43.

38 The ambiguous character of this term will be discussed in the next sections.

2.2.2 *Preservation and accessibility*

The traditional concern of international law in cultural heritage has been its *preservation*: to protect it from harm.[39] The destruction of cultural heritage has been prohibited since the early days of international law and perpetrators have been convicted by international tribunals: Rosenberg after the Second World War for his part in wide scale Nazi looting and destruction of monuments, and more recently Al Mahdi for the destruction of cultural heritage in Timbuktu.[40] In the context of this research it is important to realise that the allowance of a market for looted cultural objects is an incentive for the destruction of sites of cultural importance.

Apart from preservation, *accessibility* for the public is also acknowledged as a valid interest that may limit the rights of owners. In that sense, the European Court of Human Rights in the *Beyeler* case held that it is legitimate for states to take measures that limit private property rights, in order to facilitate wide public access to works of art lawfully on its territory.[41] The case concerned a complaint against the Italian government by a private owner of a Van Gogh painting that he acquired in Rome and wished to export. The Italian government denied permission and intended to use its right of pre-emption to the painting under Italian heritage law: the owner argued that this was a violation of the right to property under Article 1 of the First Protocol to the European Convention on Human Rights.[42] Although the Court indeed found a violation due to the lack of a fair balance in the way in which the right of pre-emption was exercised (creating a situation of uncertainty), it held that control of the art market by a state is a legitimate aim for the purposes of protecting a country's cultural and artistic heritage.[43] As to the question of how this relates to *foreign* artefacts – the Van Gogh being a painting by a Dutch artist –, the Court referred to the concept of the 'cultural heritage of all nations' and linked it to the public's right to have access to it. In other words, restrictions on property rights may well be justified to uphold the (cultural)

39 Destruction in the context of armed conflict constitutes a violation of international humanitarian law, but, beyond the context of armed conflict, it may affect human rights. See UNHRC, Res. 6/11 on Protection of Cultural Heritage as an Important Component of the Promotion and Protection of Cultural Rights (28 September 2007) UN Doc. A/HRC/RES/6/11, Preamble. See also the UNESCO Declaration Concerning the Intentional Destruction of Cultural Heritage Paris (17 October 2003), and the UNSC Resolutions mentioned above.

40 *Prosecutor v Ahmad al Faqi al Mahdi*, Judgment and Sentence, ICC-01/12-01/15-171, 27 September 2016.

41 *Beyeler v Italy*, App no. 33202/96 (ECtHR, 5 January 2000).

42 Above n. 22.

43 Above n. 41 (§ 112) and Council of Europe, Research Division, 'Cultural rights in the case-law of the European Court of Human Rights' (2011), p. 19.

rights of others, in this case the wider public.[44] Similarly, in a 2019 appeals procedure in Canada the export prohibition of a French painting that an English buyer had acquired from a private Canadian collector was deemed legitimate, since the aim was to enable Canadian museums to acquire the painting.[45] As in many other countries, the Canadian Heritage Act enables such measures if an object is of 'outstanding significance' and of 'national importance'. If no offer by a Canadian museum is made within a certain period, the export permit will be issued.[46] Whereas such measures are justified in the name of wide accessibility to 'universal heritage', a prerequisite is that the artefact is 'lawfully' within that country, in other words that there are not others with a stronger (heritage) title.

2.2.3 *Preservation and accessibility: For whom?*

Where should cultural objects be preserved and *who* is most entitled to access them is not answered by reference to preservation and accessibility alone. On the one hand, the preservation of cultural heritage *in situ* is increasingly acknowledged as important for the sustainable development of societies.[47] The integrity of monuments and archaeological sites deserves special attention in this regard. On the other hand, this does not mean that cultural objects ought always to remain in, or be returned to, their original setting: the *dissemination of culture* is also widely recognised as important 'for the well-being of humanity and the progress of civilisation'.[48]

---

44 Maltese law provides for an export prohibition and a right of pre-emption with regard to *any* 'object of cultural, artistic, historical, ethnographic, scientific or industrial value, even if contemporary, that is worth preserving' that has been brought onto Maltese territory, even with regard to (foreign) artefacts that were recently imported into Malta. This would seem to overstretch the public interests at stake. In the UK and France, e.g., the threshold is a 50-year period of being within the country. See N. De Gaetano, 'On the right of the government of Malta to restrict the movement of cultural objects situated in Malta' (2019) 24 *Art Antiquity and Law* 79.

45 *Canada (Attorney General) v Heffel Gallery Limited*, 2019 FCA 82 (CanLII), https://canlii.ca/t/hzt66 (accessed 30 July 2020). Overruling an earlier verdict that held the measure to be unreasonable as it concerned a French painting that had never been on public display in Canada.

46 Ibid., para. 56.

47 'Safeguarding of the world's cultural and natural heritage' is listed as Sustainable Development Goal no. 4, target 7, UNGA 70/1 (25 September 2015) UN Doc A/RES/70/1, *Transforming Our World: the 2030 Agenda for Sustainable Development*, paras. 4.7 and 11.4; see, e.g., also the SC Resolutions discussed above (n. 34) aiming at return 'to the Iraqi and Syrian people'.

48 In the preamble to the 1995 UNDROIT Convention this tension is noticeable: 'Convinced of the fundamental importance of the *protection of cultural heritage* and of cultural exchanges for promoting understanding between peoples, and the *dissemination of culture* for the well-being of humanity and the progress of civilization [emphasis added]'. This touches upon cultural diversity on which the Universal Declaration on Cultural Diversity (2 November 2001) UNESCO Doc. 31C/Res 25, states in Art. 1: 'As a source of exchange, innovation

The so-called cultural property internationalists – a term introduced by John Henry Merryman – take it a step further.[49] They advocate a liberal trade in cultural objects and argue that physical preservation and wide accessibility are *the* public interests at stake in heritage protection as this serves humanity as a whole, wherever the objects may be. This argumentation has long been used by Western museums to deny return claims by source communities, claiming that these interests are best guaranteed in a 'universal' museum.[50] It has also been widely criticised as one-sidedly favouring the art trade and holding states.[51] Indeed, such an outlook fails to acknowledge another important interest: the significance of cultural objects to people who identify with them, the social and identity-forming value of cultural objects, and their interests in preserving their culture. The notion of heritage title aims to capture that aspect and addresses the legal bond that people may have with specific cultural objects. As will be seen in the next section, the conventional (UNESCO) regime for the art trade appoints source states as exclusive 'right holders' in this respect, whereas more recent instruments focus on communities and individuals (to be discussed in Sects. 4 and 5).

---

and creativity, cultural diversity is as necessary for humankind as biodiversity is for nature'.

49 J.H. Merryman, 'Two ways of thinking about cultural property' (1986) 80 *Am J Int Law* 831 and J.H. Merryman, 'Cultural property internationalism' (2005) 12 *International Journal of Cultural Property* 11. Set against 'cultural nationalists' with reference to protectionism.

50 See the 2002 Declaration on the Importance and Value of the Universal Museum, undersigned by 18 major Western museums. Reproduced in L.V. Prott, *Witnesses to History: A compendium of documents and writings on the return of cultural objects* (2009) UNESCO, Paris, p. 116 and still available through <https://www.hermitagemuseum.org/wps/portal/hermitage/news/news-item/news/1999_2013/hm11_1_93/?lng> accessed 30 July 2020. Lately, several of these museums have implicitly denounced this position by adopting policies acknowledging the rights of source communities to their lost artefacts.

51 E.g. A.A. Bauer, 'New ways of thinking about cultural property: a critical appraisal of the antiquities trade debates' (2007) 31 *Fordham International Law Journal* 690; G. Abungu, 'The Declaration: a contested issue' in L.V. Prott (ed) *Witnesses to history: a compendium of documents and writings on the return of cultural objects* (2009) UNESCO, Paris; I.A. Stamatoudi, *Cultural Property Law and Restitution. A Commentary to International Conventions and European Union Law* (2011) Edward Elgar Publishing Limited, pp. 19-30; R. Peters, 'Nationalism versus internationalism. New perspectives beyond state sovereignty and territoriality in the protection of cultural heritage' in A.M. Carstens, E. Varner (eds) *Intersections in international cultural heritage law* (2020) Oxford University Press, p. 368. J.A.R. Nafziger, 'Cultural heritage law: the international regime' in *The Cultural Heritage of Mankind* (2008) Centre for studies and research in international law and international relations, Académie de droit international de La Haye/Brill Nijhoff, pp. 202-203: 'What the 'cultural property internationalists' seem to have in mind, […], is a generally free trade in cultural heritage unfettered by co-operation among States. At the intergovernmental level, ironically, this interpretation of internationalism turns out to be fundamentally a disguised form of nationalism to protect a country's own collectors and collections. What is more, the rationale for 'cultural international ism' turns out to be essentially commercial.'

3 INTERNATIONAL FRAMEWORK FOR THE ART TRADE

Cultural objects can be traded and owned but are also protected as heritage. Viewed through this lens, the regulation of the art trade is about finding a balance between the interests of free circulation and private ownership on the one hand, and heritage interests worthy of protection on the other. What follows is an overview of the international framework for the art trade and how it accounts for heritage interests by linking cultural objects to states.

3.1 A system of 'national treasures'

That framework relies on the 1970 UNESCO Convention, introducing a system of national export licences; the 1995 UNIDROIT Convention, aiming at the harmonisation of private law to implement the principles of the 1970 Convention, and the 'national treasure' exception in both the GATT[52] and TFEU free trade systems. In broad terms it provides for a system where states designate protected cultural objects that cannot be freely traded (their 'national treasures', 'national heritage' or 'patrimony'), and interstate cooperation after unauthorised export.

3.1.1 GATT and TFEU

Cultural objects deserving protection from free circulation are simply defined as 'national treasures' in the text of the GATT and the TFEU.[53] Article XX (sub. f) of the GATT on General Exceptions allows for national measures that are 'imposed for the protection of national treasures of artistic, historic or archaeological value', that is subject to the requirement 'that such measures are not applied in a manner which would constitute a means of arbitrary or unjustified discrimination between countries [...], or a disguised restriction on international trade'.[54] Within the European Union Article 36 of the TFEU similarly allows for 'prohibitions or restrictions on imports, exports or goods

52 General Agreement on Tariffs and Trade 1994, 1867 UNTS 154, Art. XX sub. (f).

53 NB the official texts of TFEU, Art. 36 vary: in English and French 'national treasures', vs. the Italian and Spanish 'national patrimony' vs. the German 'national cultural property'. R. Peters, 'The protection of cultural property: recent developments in Germany in the context of new EU law and the 1970 UNESCO Convention' (2016) 2 *Santander Art and Culture Law Review* 85, p. 89. The Dutch resembles the 'dry' German version in 'national (artistic, historical or archaeological) property' [in Dutch: *'nationaal artistiek historisch en archeologisch bezit'*].

54 Now part of WTO law. Art. XX. This rule has not been the subject of analysis by a GATT or WTO panel or WTO Appellate Body, so its precise scope remains unclear. J.A.R. Nafziger and R.K. Paterson, 'International trade in cultural material' in J.A.R. Nafziger, R.K. Paterson (eds) *Handbook on the law of cultural heritage and international trade* (2014) Edward Elgar Publishing, p. 22.

in transit' insofar as this concerns 'national treasures possessing artistic, historic or archaeological value'.[55]

3.1.2 UNESCO Convention

In terms of the 1970 UNESCO Convention such national treasures are defined as 'property, which on religious or secular grounds, is specifically designated by each State as being of importance for archaeology, prehistory, history, literature, art or science'.[56] Article 4 of the 1970 Convention sets out five categories of objects that can qualify as national cultural heritage. The first two categories bear a clear territorial link: objects created by nationals or others *within that territory* or objects found *within that territory*.[57] The other three categories cover artefacts that were the subject of a 'freely agreed exchange' or acquired 'with the consent of the authorities of the country of origin'.[58]

The main rule of the 1970 Convention is that the unauthorised transfer of cultural property from the territory of a Member State is illicit, and states should cooperate for their return. What qualifies as national heritage to which return obligations apply after unlawful export, however, is a matter of interpretation. Article 7(b) obliges the return of objects that are documented in an inventory of a public institution. On the other hand, Article 13(d) affirms the 'indefeasible right of each State Party to this Convention to classify and declare certain cultural property as inalienable which should therefore *ipso facto* not be exported', and the obligation of other Member States 'to facilitate recovery

55 TFEU, Art. 36: 'The provisions of Articles 34 and 35 shall not preclude prohibitions or restrictions on imports, exports or goods in transit justified on grounds of [...]; the protection of national treasures possessing artistic, historic or archaeological value; [...]. Such prohibitions or restrictions shall not, however, constitute a means of arbitrary discrimination or a disguised restriction on trade between Member States'; the notion of this term has been partly defined by two other EU instruments in the area, a Regulation on the export of cultural goods out of the territory of the EU (Council Regulation No 3911/92 of 1992, Codified version No 116/2009 of 2009), and a Directive (Directive 2014/60/EU of 1994, Recast of the Directive 93/7/EEC of 2013) on the return of cultural goods illegally exported from the territory of a Member State: these, however, equally refer to the national regime. See also Stamatoudi (2011), pp. 119-120.

56 1970 UNESCO Convention, Art. 1, listing 11 types of objects ranging from objects of historical, archaeological, ethnological or artistic interest (e.g., pictures, paintings, drawings and sculpture) to furniture and antiquities of more than 100 years old, rare stamps and archival material.

57 Art. 4: '[...] property which belongs to the following categories forms part of the cultural heritage of each State: (a) cultural property created by the individual or collective genius of nationals of the State concerned, and cultural property of importance to the State concerned created *within its territory* of that State by foreign nationals or stateless persons resident *within such territory*; (b) cultural property found within the national *territory* [emphasis added]'.

58 Art. 4, sections (c)-(e).

of such property'.[59] In other words, states are free to decide what they designate as national cultural heritage that cannot be freely traded.

The Convention is non-self-executing and is non-retroactive: it only applies after both states are party to the Convention and only to the extent that the principles are translated into national law.[60] This adds up to a system in which the legal status of contested cultural objects depends on the *moment* they were lost, on the *ratification* by both states, on the *designation* in the source country, and on the *implementation* of the principles in the private law of the destination (or transfer) country.[61]

On the other hand, the 1970 Convention has been widely ratified,[62] is referred to in many later instruments,[63] and its main principle that the unauthorised transfer of cultural objects is unlawful has been invoked by national courts as international public policy also in disputes where the states involved had not acceded to the Convention at the time.[64]

3.1.3 UNIDROIT *Convention*

Whereas the 1970 Convention relies on cooperation between states, the 1995 UNIDROIT Convention aims to harmonise the private law of Member States to ensure the return of unlawfully removed objects. It has not been widely ratified, however.[65]

---

59 1970 UNESCO Convention, Art. 13.
60 1970 UNESCO Convention, Art. 21.
61 Various methods of implementation exist, on which Gerstenblith (2020), pp. 31-35.
62 140 Member States on 8 July 2020. Amongst these are the major art market States: the US (1983), China (1989), France (1997), the UK (2002), Japan (2002), Switzerland (2003) and Sweden (2003). The Netherlands ratified in 2009, see above n. 5.
63 The 2019 EU Import Regulation, introducing a uniform licensing system for cultural objects onto EU territory for objects of a certain age (200 years) confirms the basic principle of the 1970 Convention: (Art. 3) 'The introduction of cultural goods referred to in Part A of the Annex which were removed from the territory of the country where they were created or discovered in breach of the laws and regulations of that country shall be prohibited'; For museums, the ICOM Code of Ethics for Museums (under 7.2) presents the 1970 Convention as a minimum standard for museum practice. As the 'ICOM Code of Professional Ethics', the Code was adopted by the 15th General Assembly of the International Council of Museums on 4 November 1986, and was renamed and revised in 2004. See https://icom.museum/wp-content/uploads/2018/07/ICOM-code-En-web.pdf (accessed 30 July 2020).
64 E.g., in Germany: *Allgemeine Versicherungsgesellschaft v EK*, BGHZ 59, 82 (1972); in Switzerland: *L. v Indictment Chamber of the Canton of Geneva* (First Public Law Division, 1 April, 1997), both partly reproduced in Prott (2009), pp. 33-36; more examples in Chechi (2014), p. 281, and see the cases discussed in Sect. 5.4 (n. 168). The Chinese Buddha case, amongst others, underlines that State practice even with regard to recent looting is not uniform.
65 48 States have done so, but excluding Western market States such as the US, the UK, Switzerland, Germany, France and the Netherlands (status 12 July 2020).

The way the Convention classifies claims is interesting: it differentiates between rules for the *restitution* of stolen objects[66] – such a claim can be made by any deprived owner – and standards for the *return* of unlawfully exported cultural objects if these are of 'significant cultural importance to that state'.[67] Claims based on ownership ('restitution'), in other words, can be distinguished from claims based on heritage title ('return'). In Article 5(3) hints are given as to what types of objects may be of 'significant cultural importance', namely if the removal significantly impairs one or more of the following interests:

a) the physical preservation of the object or its context,
b) the integrity of a complex object,
c) the preservation of scientific or historic information,
d) traditional or ritual use of the object by indigenous or tribal communities.[68]

In the Convention a choice is made for the common law principle that title cannot be transferred with regard to stolen property: stolen or unlawfully exported cultural objects should be returned, and only a new possessor who 'neither knew or ought reasonably to have known' of the unlawful provenance of an object can claim compensation.[69] It elaborates on this in Article 4(4):

> In determining whether the possessor exercised due diligence, regard shall be had to all the circumstances of the acquisition, including the character of the parties, the price paid, whether the possessor consulted any reasonably accessible register of stolen cultural objects, and any other relevant information and documentation which it could reasonably have obtained, and whether the possessor consulted accessible agencies or took any other step that a reasonable person would have taken in the circumstances.

66 1995 UNIDROIT Convention, Art. 3, extending the rules to unlawfully excavated cultural objects – usually States vest ownership in archaeological objects in their heritage laws – and private losses, that were not accounted for in the 1970 UNESCO Convention.

67 1995 UNIDROIT Convention, Art. 5(3), in particular (d) last sentence. The 1991 IDI Basel Resolution proposes a similar definition: artefacts 'most closely linked from the cultural point of view' may be claimed by that country if 'the absence of such property would significantly affect its cultural heritage'.

68 This listing is obviously open to a myriad of interpretations. Nevertheless, the general idea is 'cultural significance'. The separate mentioning of the interests of communities in (d) is noteworthy, as this implicates a step away from the paradigm of one national culture underlying the 1970 UNESCO Convention that has in its preamble: 'Considering that cultural property constitutes one of the basic elements of civilization and *national culture*, [...]' (emphasis added).

69 1995 UNIDROIT Convention, Art. 4(1): 'The possessor of a stolen cultural object required to return it shall be entitled, at the time of its restitution, to payment of fair and reasonable compensation provided that the possessor neither knew nor ought reasonably to have known that the object was stolen and can prove that it exercised due diligence when acquiring the object'. Such right to compensation should be seen as a concession to the civil law countries that tend to protect good faith new possessors.

These due diligence standards are repeated in other legal instruments and national laws of countries that have not acceded to the Convention, and thus have gained importance in their own right.[70] Furthermore, the Convention sets a limitation period for filing a claim of three years after the location and possessor of the object are known, with a maximum of fifty years after the theft.[71] Objects forming an integral part of an identified monument or archaeological site, or belonging to a public collection, and sacred or communally important cultural objects used by tribal or indigenous communities, are under enhanced protection.[72]

3.2 Rules for the art trade in practice

The conventional regime thus aims to control the movement of cultural objects. Since market countries have only recently started implementing the 1970 UNESCO Convention – and do so in a number of different ways –, and the 1995 UNIDROIT Convention has not been widely ratified, the fragmented situation continues.[73] As Lixinski observes: 'One of the problems of the licit market is that, because it is largely unregulated by international law [...] it ends up regulated by the private sphere'.[74]

To counter legal insecurity, two rules have surfaced in practice: new possessors need to ascertain that objects have no 'unlawful provenance' (due diligence standards); and the second rule takes a practical approach to the ambiguous question of what exactly constitutes 'unlawful provenance'.

3.2.1 Due diligence standards

The importance of due diligence standards and provenance research for the art market as introduced in the 1995 UNIDROIT Convention is confirmed in

70 E.g., the Netherlands has not ratified the 1995 UNIDROIT Convention, however did include this element in its Heritage Act of 9 December 2015 (*Staatsblad* 2016, no. 14).

71 1995 UNIDROIT Convention, Art. 3.

72 1995 UNIDROIT Convention, Art. 3, paras. (4), (7) and (8). A maximum of 75 years can be set by States. This means that cases that – for whatever reason – take long to surface such as Nazi-looted art or colonial takings, would not be covered. This is the downside of an ownership approach.

73 The 'patchwork quilt of ratifications and implementation of the 1970 UNESCO Convention and of the 1995 UNIDROIT Convention and the limited provisions of the 1954 Hague Convention with respect to stolen or looted cultural objects translate into an international treaty regime that is weak in controlling the movement of illegally obtained cultural objects'. Gerstenblith (2020), p. 37.

74 L. Lixinski, *International Heritage Law for Communities: Exclusion and Re-Imagination* (2019) Oxford University Press, p. 132.

many later legal instruments.[75] The 2017 UN Security Council Resolution, for example, requests states to take

> 'appropriate steps to prevent and counter the illicit trade and trafficking in cultural property [...] including by prohibiting cross-border trade in such illicit items where states have a reasonable suspicion that the items originate from a context of armed conflict, [...] *and which lack clearly documented and certified provenance*, thereby allowing for their eventual safe return'.[76]

The Resolution calls upon states to adopt measures

> 'Engaging museums, relevant business associations and antiquities markets participants *on standards of provenance documentation*, differentiated due diligence and all measures to prevent the trade of stolen or illegally traded cultural property'.[77]

Beyond the context of armed conflict, the new EU Import Regulation similarly relies on the importers' documentation that should support the lawful ownership history (provenance) before an object can be imported.[78] Moreover, the 2017 Council of Europe Nicosia Convention, which has yet to enter into force, replicates these due diligence standards.[79] State parties should take measures to ensure that the acquisition or 'placing on the market' of stolen or unlawfully transferred cultural property is a criminal offence, not only if the person knowingly acquires such objects but 'also in the case of a person who should have known of the cultural property's unlawful provenance if he or she had exercised due care'.[80]

Such regulations clearly underscore the importance of provenance research for the international art world. Buyers, dealers, auction houses and museums must assure themselves not only of the authenticity of an object (is it real?) but also of its provenance (who were the previous owners and was it lawfully acquired?). At the same time, this implies that artefacts with an incomplete

75 Above, n. 70, and the UNESCO International Code of Ethics for Dealers in Cultural Property, UNESCO Doc. CLT/CH/INS.06/25 REV, basically stating that dealers shall not deal in objects with an 'unlawful' provenance.

76 UNSC Res. 2347 (2017) S/RES/2347, para. 8. Emphasis added.

77 Ibid., under 17(g). Emphasis added.

78 2019 EU Import Regulation.

79 Council of Europe Convention on Offences relating to Cultural Property (adopted 3 May 2017) CETS No. 221. The Convention aims to prevent and combat the illicit trafficking and destruction of cultural property, and falls within the Council of Europe's action to fight terrorism and organised crime. It is open to non-members (Mexico is one of the two ratifying States). NB On 28 October 2019, 10 states had signed and 2 had ratified/acceded, thus it has not yet entered into force.

80 Ibid., Arts. 7 and 8.

provenance will surface as 'tainted', whereas the question of what is exactly '(un)lawful' is anything but clear.[81]

3.2.2 *The 1970 watershed rule on provenance*

What, exactly, is an 'unlawful provenance' is a key question in regulating the art trade. The answer, however, depends on the perspective one takes: unlawful according to what law? As discussed, national laws on the transfer of ownership vary widely in time and place, while international rules are neither retroactive nor clearly defined. In this regard, the '1970 watershed rule' has surfaced as a 'proxy to legality'.[82] It is a touchstone used by auction houses, the art trade and museums, implying that artefacts should have a documented provenance as of the entry into force of the 1970 UNESCO Convention (24 April 1972), either as being outside the country of origin before that date or otherwise with an export licence.[83] This rule is confirmed in soft and hard law instruments.[84] The new EU Import Regulation, for example, allows for the importation of cultural objects *without* an export licence as long as the object was outside its source country before 24 April 1972.[85]

The 1970 watershed rule (which in fact is *1972*) operates, in other words, as a time lock for a new international order of controlled trade. In spite of its apparent attraction (legal security), such a time lock has a serious downside. Source countries may not be able to prove that a specific object was still on their territory: cultural objects are not always documented in an inventory – e.g. freshly (illicitly) excavated archaeological objects by definition are not documented and (sacred) items in use by a community may not be listed either. Besides, objects unlawfully taken longer ago may be more important from

81 Problematic is that no publicly managed and accessible database for stolen artefacts exists, whereas some databases that do exist solely focus on provenance between 1933-1945. See also Campfens, 'Restitution of looted art' (2019).

82 To cite P. Gerstenblith, 'Enforcement by domestic courts, criminal law and forfeiture in the recovery of cultural objects' in F. Francioni, J. Gordley (eds) *Enforcing international cultural heritage law* (2013) Oxford University Press, p. 153. See also V. Négri, 'Legal study on the protection of cultural heritage through the resolutions of the Security Council of the United Nations' (2015) UNESCO, p. 10.

83 The 1970 UNESCO Convention entered into force on 24 April 1972; this time lock is also used as simply 'before or after 1970'.

84 E.g., the 2013 Guidelines on the Acquisition of Archaeological Material and Ancient Art of the US Association of Art Museum Directors (AAMD), under 'E', prescribe that 'Member museums normally should not acquire a Work unless provenance research substantiates that the Work was outside its country of probable modern discovery before 1970 or was legally exported from its probable country of modern discovery after 1970'. See: <https://aamd.org/sites/default/fles/document/AAMD%20Guidelines%202013.pdf> (accessed 30 July 2020).

85 Above n. 63.

a heritage perspective, although these are lawfully owned somewhere else.[86] At the same time, provenance research has not always been an issue and many artefacts lack information on their ownership history: this does not necessarily mean that an object was unlawfully taken. Leaving such nuances aside, one noticeable effect of this rule is that artefacts offered on the market remarkably often are presented with a provenance in terms of a 'private (Western) collection' followed by a date before 1970.[87] These blind spots will be further addressed in the next section.

4 Blind spots and the rise of soft law

To curb illicit trade, the 1970 UNESCO Convention aims to prevent the unauthorised export of cultural objects and preservation *in situ*. That, however, does not solve title issues over cultural objects that left their original setting at one point in their existence. Contesting parties may be states, but also communities or private individuals. This is an important blind spot in the legal regime for the art trade, that has caused an increase in soft law to 'mend' gaps: a sign of changing morality and the need for new rules. These points will be further explored hereunder.

4.1 Nationality?

A question that arises in dispute resolution is what 'national cultural heritage' in the 1970 UNESCO Convention – and 'national treasure' in the GATT and TFEU – exactly means in terms of entitlement. It gives the impression that states are exclusive right holders (owners) of cultural objects. What, however, is the basis for such title?

As mentioned in the preceding section, the 1970 UNESCO Convention is not clear on this point and essentially leaves it up to states to decide what they designate as their cultural heritage. In practice, this is done either according to a model of listing a limited number of items of national and/or outstanding importance (the 'liberal' model from the point of view of trade), or according to a model under which broad categories of objects are appointed

86 In jurisdictions allowing for the transfer of title which will be unlawful from the perspective of source communities' laws or international law (above n. 15 and the accompanying text).

87 Observation by the author. Cf., e.g., Lixinski (2019), p. 132: 'The black market in antiquities exploits this loophole through creating mechanisms to prove that the objects left the territories of the states in question before the Convention's entry into force, thus laundering the cultural artefacts'. See also P.B. Campbell, 'The illicit antiquities trade as a transnational criminal network: characterizing and anticipating trafficking of cultural heritage' (2013) 20 *International Journal of Cultural Property* 113.

in blanket legislation (the 'retentionist' model from the point of view of the trade).[88]

In that respect, states may also designate cultural objects to underline a territorial claim, such as the Russian law that, since 2015, considers Crimean collections to be Russian patrimony.[89] Ongoing litigation in the Netherlands over archaeological objects that were on loan in Amsterdam from Crimea at the time of the Russian annexation in 2014 confirms that conflicting claims to the same 'national treasure' occur. The Ukrainian State, on the one side, claims that these artefacts belong to its national patrimony and should be sent to Kiev. On the other side, the Crimean museums claim that it concerns cultural heritage of the Crimean people, having been there since the excavation, and should be returned to them.[90] In the meantime, the contested objects are also designated as Russian cultural property.

A model linking cultural objects to states without clear standards as to what qualifies as such causes tensions. The *Institut de Droit international* advised in this respect that a 'country of origin' should be understood to be the country with which the object is 'most closely linked from a cultural point of view'.[91] The 1995 UNIDROIT Convention similarly gives as a criterion 'significant cultural importance' as a ground for return requests.[92] Lastly, the (more recent) 2001 UNESCO Convention for Underwater Cultural Heritage may serve as inspiration where it introduces a 'verifiable link', based on identification, as a basis for responsibilities and limited rights (but not as a basis for exclusive rights).[93] In sum, a verifiable cultural link between people and objects, that may be called 'heritage title', should underlie a claim to national heritage.

Whereas archaeological finds and ethnological objects are clearly linked to a territory and its people – but not *per se* to a nation state after a change of borders –, artefacts that were destined for the market will not easily pass this test. This is reflected in the US case *Jeanneret v Vichy*.[94] In this case the court denied a claim by the Italian government to a Matisse painting that was exported in violation of Italy's export laws (but obviously lacks a strong

88 As a rule of thumb: culturally rich 'source countries' apply the second form – aiming at wide protection – and importing 'market countries' apply the first. For a discussion on designation as 'national treasures', see above n. 45 and the accompanying text.

89 Russian Federal Law (Feb. 12, 2015) No. 9-FZ 'On regulation of relations in the matter of culture and tourism as related to the annexation of the Republic of Crimea to the Russian Federation [...]'. See: <https://cis-legislation.com/document.fwx?rgn=73149> (accessed 5 May 2020).

90 In 2016, the Amsterdam District Court honoured the claim by Ukraine on the basis of the 1970 UNESCO Convention, *Rechtbank Amsterdam*, Judgment of 14 December 2016, Case No. C/13/577586/HA ZA 14-1179, ECLI:NL:RBAMS:2016:8264. The verdict is subject to an appeal at the time of writing (Spring 2020). The case is discussed in Campfens (2017).

91 1991 IDI Basel Resolution, above n. 19.

92 1995 UNIDROIT Convention, Art. 5(3); see above n. 67 and 68.

93 Above n. 33 and Dromgoole (2013), p. 127.

94 *Jeanneret v Vichy*, 693 F2d 259, 267 (2d Cir. 1982).

cultural link with Italy), which contrasts with judicial practice in the US that tends to award claims by source countries to antiquities.[95]

A more correct interpretation of 'nationality' appears therefore that this primarily serves as a means to allocate responsibilities. States should not be seen as exclusive and absolute 'right holders' to cultural heritage, but act as stewards of the public interest and, in that regard, take measures to preserve cultural objects and make these accessible (the notion of the heritage of mankind). This also means that restrictions on the transfer of cultural objects in national laws to control the market should ideally not only regulate the *export* of cultural objects of local importance, but also the *import* of objects that are important to other people.[96] On the other hand, if a state claims entitlement to an object as its 'national heritage' after it left its territory, it acts in another capacity, namely as a right holder to heritage title. It may do so on behalf of the people on its territory and such a claim should depend on a verifiable and continuing cultural link.

4.2 Sub-state right holders

The UNESCO framework is an interstate affair: only national states are treated as 'right holders' to cultural objects, as seen above. Although the idea of one 'national' culture may reflect reality in a few states, nationality as a criterion for entitlement is insufficient. This mostly becomes relevant when communities or individuals do not (any longer) feel represented by a specific state. The Crimean case discussed above is a clear example, but this may also surface in cases that concern Nazi-looted art. Such disputes, not seldomly, concern artefacts lost by the hands of authorities of states of which the families were once nationals. The *Altmann* case (depicted in the Hollywood movie 'Lady in Gold'), that deals with paintings by the Austrian painter Gustav Klimt that were protected as national Austrian patrimony, may serve as an illustration.[97] The paintings were claimed by a US citizen, Maria Altmann, the niece and heir to the Austrian Jewish collector who lost the works due to Nazi persecution. After attempts to regain the works in Austria failed, litigation in the US was initiated, where the Supreme Court held that it had jurisdiction over the case

95 A well-known example of a claim by a source country to antiquities, *United States v Schultz* (SDNY, 3 January 2002) 178 F. Supp. 2d445.

96 For the European Union, therefore, the introduction of the 2019 EU Import Regulation is important (see above n. 78).

97 *Maria V. Altmann v Republic of Austria et al.*, 142 F. Supp. 2d 1187 (CD Cal. 2001); *Maria V. Altmann v Republic of Austria et al.*, 317 F. 3d 954 (9th Cir. 2002), as amended, 327 F. 3d 1246 (2003); *Republic of Austria et al. v Maria V. Altmann*, 541 US 677 (US 2004). For an overview, Renold et al., 'Case six Klimt paintings – Maria Altmann and Austria' (2012) Platform ArThemis, Art-Law Centre, University of Geneva.

as the loss was considered a violation of fundamental rights.[98] After this victory, international arbitration was set up that resulted in the restitution of the paintings to Altmann. In this particular case, in other words, the interests of the persecuted and dispossessed family outweighed the interests of a national state in preserving its national heritage. Similarly, in a French case concerning a Mokomokai (a mummified tattooed head of a Maori) held in a museum in Rouen, after the initial denial of the claim for repatriation because the 'museum piece' was protected under French patrimony laws, a special law was enacted to enable repatriation and the eventual ritual burial by the Maori.[99] Also here, the interests of the French State in keeping its 'national heritage'(public collections) were outweighed by the interests of the indigenous community. The prevalence of such interests was confirmed by the adoption of the UNDRIP, to be discussed in the next section.[100]

For the category of Nazi-looted art the 1998 Washington Conference Principles on Nazi-Confiscated Art form the basis for a widespread international practice of returns and settlements.[101] It concerns a set of principles supported by over forty states and other stakeholders, stating the right of families of deprived former owners to a 'fair and just solution' with regard to Nazi-looted artefacts.[102] Also for other categories soft law instruments focus on sub-state right holders. Besides informal (non-binding) instruments on the interstate

98 In spite of the immunity provided by the Foreign Sovereign Immunities Act (FSIA), Nazi confiscations fall under an exception that 'abrogates sovereign immunity in any case where *rights in property taken in violation of international law* are in issue and that property [...] is owned or operated by an agency or instrumentality of the foreign state and that agency or instrumentality is engaged in a commercial activity in the United States'. Explained in *David L. de Csepel et al. v Republic of Hungary et al.*, No. 10-1261 (ESH), Memorandum Opinion, US Dist. (C.D. Columbia, 14 March 2016), at p. 28 (emphasis added).

99 For a discussion see F. Lenzerini, 'Reparations for wrongs against indigenous people's cultural heritage' in A. Xanthaki, S. Valkonen (eds) *Indigenous peoples' cultural heritage: rights, debates, challenges* (2017) Brill, p. 339.

100 UNGA Res. 61/295 (13 September 2007) UN Doc. A/RES/61/295, United Nations Declaration on the Rights of Indigenous Peoples (UNDRIP). The introduction of 'the traditional or ritual use by indigenous or tribal communities' as a separate ground in Art. 5(3) of the 1995 UNIDROIT Convention is also an acknowledgement that national States should not be seen as sole right holders.

101 Washington Conference Principles on Nazi-Confiscated Art, in J.D. Bindenagel, Washington Conference on Holocaust-Era Assets (1999) US Government Printing Office.

102 This is contrasted by efforts to arrange this field by UNESCO in the traditional interstate way. See UNESCO, Draft of the Declaration of Principles Relating to Cultural Objects Displaced in Connection with the Second World War (2009), 35 C/24. After years of negotiations the UNESCO Declaration was not adopted and never heard of again, perhaps unsurprisingly given the historical background of the looting. It relied on a traditional intergovernmental model and objects should have been claimed by the country from where these were lost on behalf of the deprived owners. The inefficiency of such a model where individual claimants would have to rely on cooperation with the governments of States that were responsible for the dispossession and persecution in the first place, may be obvious.

level, the ICOM Ethical Code for Museums – an important instrument of self-regulation for museums around the world – prioritises cooperation and dialogue over 'action on a governmental or political level' where return requests are concerned.[103]

Whilst the binding force and practical follow-up of these instruments vary, they signal a preference for the sub-state level over dealing with claims on the interstate level.

4.3 Non-retroactive?

The field of Nazi-looted art also highlights the most poignant blind spot of the conventional framework: that it does not regulate earlier losses.[104] Losses by persecuted Jewish families obviously occurred long before the 1970 UNESCO Convention and are 'stale' under (most) national private laws due to limitation periods for claims, or the acquired ownership rights of new possessors.[105] Nevertheless, since the end of the 1990s such claims have been widely supported by states and participants in the art world, albeit often as a matter of 'morality' through extra-legal procedures. In this regard, a discrepancy has emerged between European and US jurisdictions – where most art cases occur due to the scale of the art market and where the *adage* that a thief cannot transfer good title is inherent in the legal system and such cases can be litigated on their merits.[106] Given the international character of the art market, this discrepancy leads to forum-shopping and legal insecurity. As will be discussed in the next section, a human rights approach and the notion of heritage title may enable access to justice also for such cases.

Increasingly, also countries or communities that have been victims of looting and illicit export in the past reclaim their heritage irrespective of the 1970 threshold.[107] Litigation in the US between the Greek Government and Sotheby's over the (intended) auction of an eighth century BC bronze statuette of a horse – that was part of a Swiss collection in 1967 – is an example.[108]

103 ICOM Code of Ethics for Museums (above, n. 63), Principle 6.2.

104 The 1970 UNESCO Convention, the 1995 UNIDROIT Convention, as well the 1991 IDI Basel Declaration provide for the proactive application of norms (see above Sect. 3). In terms of the last, '*to all future cases* where a work of art has been stolen or otherwise taken away illegally from its owner or holder, or illegally exported'. Emphasis added.

105 After the Second World War, most European countries enacted special restitution laws to restore the rights of victims of Nazi persecution with regard to their lost possessions; however, due to limitation periods in such laws these (mostly) lost their importance. See Campfens (2018).

106 Resulting in a situation where many European restitution claims are brought before American courts. Campfens (2017) and Campfens, 'Restitution of looted art' (2019).

107 These countries include, e.g., China, Turkey, Mexico, Columbia, Egypt and India.

108 See P. Chrysopoulos, 'Greek ministry of culture in legal dispute over return of 8th century BC antiquity' (25 September 2019) *Greek Reporter*.

The Greek Government statement was that 'the owners of stolen property and auction houses cannot trade objects belonging to a country's cultural heritage'.[109] In its June 2020 ruling the US Court of Appeals denied Sotheby's claim for a declaratory judgment that the bronze horse was 'acquired lawfully and in good faith', cutting short the expectations of the 1970 threshold to provide legal security.[110] Another example that underscores the confusion in this field can be found in the Ukrainian heritage law that specifically includes, as national patrimony 'subject to return', works that were pillaged during past wars.[111] Also in China artefacts pillaged in the past are considered to be national treasures that should not be traded.[112] Accordingly, in 2018 the Chinese government objected to the auction in the UK of a bronze vessel that was looted from the Old Summer Palace in 1860 by Anglo-French forces. While the auction eventually went ahead, the vessel was donated to China, to feature in a 2019 exhibition dedicated to 'reclaimed national treasures from abroad'.[113]

This trend may be seen as the result of a failure of the international community to address cultural losses before 1970. During the negotiations of the 1970 UNESCO Convention the return of cultural objects lost as a result of (post)-colonial looting practices had clearly been at stake for formerly colonised states. Yet, the issue was not resolved at the time but was left to bilateral negotiations.[114] To accommodate such negotiations, in 1978, the Intergovernmental

---

109 Ibid.

110 *Barnet v Ministry of Culture & Sport of the Hellenic Republic*, No. 19-2171-cv (US Court of Appeals for the 2nd Circuit, 9 June 2020), available at <https://www.govinfo.gov/content/pkg/USCOURTS-ca2-19-02171/pdf/USCOURTS-ca2-19-02171-0.pdf> accessed 27 July 2020. See Brown (2020).

111 Art. 3 of the 1999 Law of Ukraine 'On Exportation, importation and Return of Cultural Values' includes as 'cultural values of Ukraine' lists 'Cultural values, evacuated from the territory of Ukraine during wars, armed conflicts and not being returned', that, according to Art. 4, are subject to a return to Ukraine. Official Bulletin (Vidomosti) of the Verhovna Rada (BBP), 1999, No. 48, p. 405. Translation kindly provided by I. Tarsis, Managing Director Center for Art Law, NY.

112 The Cultural Relics Protection Law of the People's Republic of China, entered into force in 1982, amended in 2017 [CLI.1.304324(EN)], provides in Art. 5 for ownership by the State of five very broadly formulated categories of (Chinese) 'cultural relics'. Chinese scholars have argued for amendments to include 'lost cultural relics' as a legal basis for return claims. See L. Zhen, 'Examining the recovery of Yuanmingyuan cultural property from the perspective of international law' (2009) Legal System and Society 4, and D. Tao, 'Issue on conflict law in overseas litigation for the recovery of lost cultural relics – Iranian government v. Barakat Art Museum and its enlightenment' (2009) Comparative Law Study 2, both in Chinese. Information and translation kindly provided by Dr. Yue Zhang, visiting fellow at the Max Planck Institute for Comparative Public Law and International Law, Heidelberg, Germany.

113 Global Times, 'Looted 3,000-year-old 'Tiger Ying' bronze vessel donated by mysterious buyer returns to China' (11 December 2018) *Global Times*.

114 Prott (2009), p. 13. A Chinese proposal to include a provision on older losses in the 1970 UNESCO Convention was not accepted by Western States.

Committee for Promoting the Return of Cultural Property to Its Countries of Origin or Its Restitution in Case of Illicit Appropriations (ICPRCP) was established by UNESCO.[115] The political setting of this committee, however, has proven unfavourable to actually solve disputes.

Recent developments underscore that denying victims of past plundering access to justice does not solve the problem. Over time, cultural objects may maintain – or even gain – their symbolic value, especially if they were lost as a result of historical injustices such as colonial oppression or racial persecution. Although such claims may lack legal force from a private law perspective, it should be born in mind that norms prohibiting plundering were in existence long before the entry into force of the 1970 UNESCO Convention.[116]

Meanwhile, international practice and the legal argumentation used in claims signal a new paradigm. The Chinese statement in the case discussed above, for example, refers to the 'cultural rights of the Chinese people', while French President Macron in his famous 2017 speech announcing the return of African artefacts, refers to the right of Africans to access their own culture.[117] Likewise, a 2019 German government policy instrument, facilitating the return of colonial takings by German museums, provides as a rationale that 'all people should have the possibility to access their rich material culture [...] to connect with it and to pass it on to future generations'.[118] Such quotes refer, in other words, to the (human) right of access to one's own culture. The question of how a human rights approach could help regulate this field will be further discussed hereafter.

5 A HUMAN RIGHTS APPROACH AND HERITAGE TITLE

As has emerged in the preceding sections, neither regular ownership law nor the conventional regime for the art trade are particularly suited to solve title

115 Statutes of the ICPRCP (adopted 24 October-28 November 1987, amended October 2005) UNESCO Doc. CLT/CH/INS-2005/21. See <https://unesdoc.unesco.org/ark:/48223/pf0000145960?posInSet=1&queryId=1e02e2a2-fd0d-46bd-8ebe77ad27eb0433> accessed 13 August 2020.

116 This is of importance for booty taken during armed conflict. E.g. K. Siehr, 'International art trade and the law' in *Collected courses of the Hague academy of international law*, vol. 243 (1993) Brill, p. 131: 'It has now been well established that for 150 years any kind of pillage, capture or acquisition of works of art as booty during times of war, armistice or occupation is prohibited by public international law'. For a thorough evaluation of the binding status of the obligation to return colonial booty Zhang (2018). See also Campfens, 'The Bangwa queen' (2019), pp. 88-91.

117 Emmanuel Macron, President of the French Republic, Speech at the University of Ouagadougou (Ouagadougou, 28 November 2017) <https://www.elysee.fr/emmanuel-macron/2017/11/28/discours-demmanuel-macron-a-luniversite-de-ouagadougou> accessed 20 April 2020.

118 *'Erste Eckpunkte Zum Umgang Mit Sammlungsgut Aus Kolonialen Kontexten'* (2019) <https://www. kmk.org/fleadmin/pdf/PresseUndAktuelles/2019/2019-03-25_Erste-Eckpunkte-Sammlungsgut-koloniale-Kontexte_fnal.pdf> accessed 23 July 2020.

issues with regard to contested cultural objects. In the meantime, the proliferation of soft law interstate instruments and private regulations indicate that new standards are needed. In that regard, a human rights approach deserves further examination. The apparent advantages of such an approach are that human rights law is particularly equipped to address heritage and identity values; that human rights are of a universal nature, and penetrate and shape how private law is being interpreted and adjudicated. Which human rights notions can exactly be used, how these can inform the contents of heritage title, and how such title can be made operational will be addressed next. As the law is evolving, this should be read as an invitation for further debate on a human rights-inspired concept of cultural property.

A paragraph on the increasing interrelation between cultural heritage and human rights law will serve as an introduction.

5.1 Humanization of cultural heritage law

International cultural heritage law has rapidly expanded and evolved over the last decades. Regulations may be binding or non-binding, but a common denominator is the increased attention for the intangible and social aspects of cultural heritage, away from an understanding solely in terms of exclusive rights or the intrinsic value of objects for mankind at large, and a shift in focus from state interests to the interest of communities and individuals: the 'humanization' of cultural heritage law.[119]

The increased attention of the Human Rights Council and the Security Council in resolutions on cultural heritage protection, voicing concerns over destruction, looting and illicit trade, highlights not only the scale and urgency of the problems – mostly but not only in conflict areas – but also the impact this has on the affected communities in terms of the realisation of their human (cultural) rights.[120] In this sense, in a 2007 resolution that is dedicated to the protection of cultural heritage, the Human Rights Council affirms that 'cultural heritage is an important component of the cultural identity of communities, groups and individuals, and of social cohesion, so that its intentional destruction may have adverse consequences on human dignity and human

119 See, e.g. Francioni (2011), p. 14: '[B]ringing the focus from the protection of the cultural object to the social structures and cultural processes that have created and developed the 'intangible' heritage. States remain the contracting parties to the Convention but the substantive addressees are the cultural communities and human groups, including minorities, whose cultural traditions are the real object of the safeguarding under international law'.

120 Above n. 34, 35, and 39. See also Hausler (2020).

rights'.[121] As Hausler observes, this initiated a 'human rights based approach' to cultural heritage protection developed by the Council in subsequent resolutions, in which protection is linked to the right of everyone to take part in cultural life.[122] Apart from concerns about the act of looting and the destruction this causes, the Council also addresses the illicit trade and return of looted objects. In this regard, it 'invites' states to adopt measures at the national level.[123]

On the European level, the 2005 Council of Europe Framework Convention on the Value of Cultural Heritage for Society (Faro Convention) also clearly illustrates this 'humanization'. The Convention does not create enforceable rights, but rather voices policy aims for governments, opening the door to a new understanding of cultural heritage and its title holders.[124] It defines cultural heritage as 'a group of resources inherited from the past which people identify, *independently of ownership*, as a reflection and expression of their constantly evolving values, beliefs, knowledge and traditions'.[125] As 'right holders' it introduces the notion of a 'heritage community', defined as 'people who value specific aspects of cultural heritage which they wish, within the framework of public action, to sustain and transmit to future generations'.[126] In as far as it concerns competing claims to heritage, the Faro Convention proposes 'equitable solutions' – similar to the norm in soft law instruments. In this regard, the Convention calls on states to: (a) encourage refection on the ethics and methods of presentation of the cultural heritage and respect for diversity of interpretations; and (b) establish processes for conciliation to deal equitably with situations where contradictory values are placed on the same cultural heritage by different communities.[127]

Given this shift in thinking about values that should underly cultural heritage policies – and thus entitlement to cultural object –, the next question is which binding human rights norms could further inform heritage title.

---

121 UNHRC, Res. 6/11 on Protection of Cultural Heritage as an Important Component of the Promotion and Protection of Cultural Rights (28 September 2007) UN Doc A/HRC/RES/6/11, Preamble.

122 Hausler (2020), pp. 207-213.

123 UNHRC, Res. 33/20 on Cultural rights and the protection of cultural heritage (6 October 2016) UN Doc. A/HRC/RES/33/20 at p. 4; repeated in UNHRC Res. 37/17 on Cultural rights and the protection of cultural heritage (9 April 2018) UN Doc A/HRC/RES/37/17 at p. 4: '*Calls for* enhanced international cooperation in preventing and combating the organized looting, smuggling and theft of and illicit trafficking in cultural objects and in restoring stolen, looted or trafficked cultural property to its countries of origin, and invites States to take measures in this regard at the national level'.

124 E.g., the Netherlands is not yet a signatory, but it has introduced the Faro Convention's definition of cultural heritage in Art. 1(1) of its new Heritage Act (Relating to the Combining and Amendment of Rules Regarding Cultural Heritage) of 2015.

125 Framework Convention on the Value of Cultural Heritage for Society (adopted 27 October 2005), CETS No. 199 (Faro Convention) (emphasis added), Art. 6.

126 Faro Convention, Art. 2(b).

127 Faro Convention, Art. 7(b).

5.2 A human right to cultural property?

5.2.1 *The right of access to (one's own) culture*

Of key importance in this respect is the evolution of the right of 'access to one's culture', as it developed from the right to culture in the International Covenant on Economic, Social and Cultural Rights (ICESCR).[128] According General Comment 21 that deals with the 'right of everyone to take part in cultural life' in Article 15(1)(a) of the ICESCR, this has come to include 'access to cultural goods'.[129] Furthermore, the 2011 report of the independent expert in the field of cultural rights, Farida Shaheed, sheds further light on the content of this right, where she concludes that:

> The right of access to and enjoyment of cultural heritage forms part of international human rights law, finding its legal basis, in particular, in the right to take part in cultural life, the right of members of minorities to enjoy their own culture, and the right of indigenous peoples to self-determination and to maintain, control, protect and develop cultural heritage.[130]

Similar to the concept of 'heritage communities' in the Faro Convention, Shaheed notes that 'varying degrees of access and enjoyment may be recognized, taking into consideration the diverse interests of individuals and groups according to their relationship with specific cultural heritages'.[131] She notes the following hierarchy:
- 'source communities', people who are keeping cultural heritage alive and/ or have taken responsibility for it;
- individuals and communities [...] who consider the cultural heritage in question an integral part of the life of the community, but may not be actively involved in its maintenance;
- scientists and artists; and
- members of the general public accessing the cultural heritage of others.

Although this list is of a general nature and not *per se* aimed at lost cultural objects, this hierarchy underscores that, at times, there may be more than one right holder, and that the weighing of interests should depend on the specific

---

128 Art. 15 of International Covenant on Economic, Social and Cultural Rights (adopted 16 December 1966), 993 UNTS 3 (ICESCR). See also Art. 27 of the UDHR.

129 Committee on Economic, Social and Cultural Rights, General Comment No. 21 (2009), UN Doc E/C.12/GC/21, under 'Normative content', para. 7.

130 Human Rights Council, Report of the independent expert in the field of cultural rights, Farida Shaheed, 21 March 2011, UN Doc A/HRC/17/38, p. 20, para. 78.

131 Ibid., p. 16, para. 62.

social function of cultural objects. This resurfaces in the UNDRIP and NAGPRA[132] models discussed further on.[133]

5.2.2 *The right to (cultural) property*

Heritage title may also be addressed from the perspective of the (human) right to property, given that this protection is not only aimed at the right of *ownership* of things.[134] Of course, if owners lose their artefact as a result of unjustified expropriation, that loss in itself may constitute a violation of the human right to property.[135] Beyond the loss of ownership, however, other interests may qualify as 'property' in a human rights' sense. For example, the Inter-American Court of Human Rights has on several occasions recognised pre-existing collective property rights by indigenous peoples to ancestral lands (owned by others) within the scope of the right to property (and political rights).[136]

According to the European Court of Human Rights (ECtHR) 'the notion of 'possessions' in Article 1 of the First Protocol indeed has an autonomous meaning which is not limited to ownership of physical goods: certain other rights and interest constituting assets can also be regarded as 'property rights''.[137] In that spirit, although the European Convention on Human Rights does not include a right to culture, rights to cultural objects (beyond ownership) have been addressed from the perspective of the right to property in

132 US Native American Graves Protection and Repatriation Act of 16 November 1990 (25 USC paras. 3001-13) (NAGPRA).

133 Janet Blake observes that if we wish to ensure a human rights-based approach to cultural heritage protection, local and cultural communities have an overriding interest, over and above national interests, because of their connection with their heritage. J. Blake, *International Cultural Heritage Law* (2015) Oxford University Pres, p. 289.

134 Above n. 22.

135 E. Jayme ('Narrative norms in private international law, the example of art law' in *Collected courses of the Hague academy of international law*, vol. 375 (2015) Brill) argues that the *Altmann* case, litigated in the US, proves the retroactive effect of the human right to property to losses predating human rights instruments (in that case, a loss in the 1940s). In a common law system, this may be easier than in civil law systems.

136 E.g. *Kaliña and Lokono Peoples v Suriname*, Merits, Reparations and Costs, Inter-Am. Ct HR, Series C, No. 309, 25 November 2015. Furthermore, in the Charter of Fundamental Rights of the European Union (2012) OJ C 364, the protection of possessions also covers *intellectual* property (Art. 17(2)).

137 *Gasus Dosier- und Fördertechnik v the Netherlands*, no. 15375/89, ECtHR 23 February 1995, Series A vol. 306-B, § 53. See H.D. Ploeger and C. Stolker, 'In search of the importance of Article 1 Protocol no. 1 ECHR to private law' in J.P. Loof, H.D. Ploeger, A. Van der Steur (eds) *The right to property: the influence of Article 1 Protocol no. 1 ECHR on several fields of domestic law* (2000) Shaker.

Article 1 of the First Protocol by the ECtHR.[138] An example is the 2012 *Nowakowski* case in which the ECtHR acknowledged the 'sentimental' value of a cultural object to a certain person – in this case, a collection of firearms in private property that had been confiscated by Polish authorities – and gave that preference over other interests.[139]

Whether (human rights) courts would be ready to acknowledge an infringement of human rights with regard to cultural property lost in the (far) past, remains to be seen. In 2016 the ECtHR rejected the application brought by an Athenian association with regard to the Parthenon Marbles – important sculptures from the Acropolis in Athens that the British Ambassador to the Ottoman Empire, Lord Elgin, hacked of and took with him to London at the beginning of the nineteenth century –, due to the time that had passed since the loss.[140] The court held that the claim was inadmissible, *ratione tempore* as well as *ratione materiae*, as none of the invoked articles 'would give rise to any right for an association in the position of the applicant to have the Marbles returned to Greece or to have the UK engage in international mediation'.[141] Nevertheless, given that morality in this field is rapidly changing – whether it concerns present-day looting, Nazi-looted art or colonial losses –, this path should not be dismissed too soon.

5.2.3 *Other human rights norms*

Potentially, many other human rights qualify to inform heritage title, such as the freedom of religion;[142] respect for private and family life;[143] the rights of minorities to enjoy their own culture,[144] or the right to self-determination.[145]

---

138 European Convention for the Protection of Human Rights and Fundamental Freedoms (adopted 4 November 1950, entered into force 3 September 1953) 213 UNTS 221 (ECHR). In the case law, rights that may fall under the notion of 'cultural rights' have been recognised. A. Jakubowski, 'Cultural heritage and the collective dimension of cultural rights in the jurisprudence of the European Court of Human Rights' in Jakubowski A (ed) *Cultural rights as collective rights, an international law perspective* (2016) Brill, pp. 158 and 178-179.

139 *Nowakowski v Poland*, no. 55167/11, ECtHR 24 July 2012, discussed by Jakubowski (2016), p. 176.

140 *Syllogos ton Athinaion against the United Kingdom*, no. 48259/15, ECtHR 31 May 2016.

141 Ibid.

142 E.g. Art. 18 UDHR; Art. 18 International Covenant on Civil and Political Rights (adopted 16 December 1966, entered into force 23 March 1976) 999 UNTS 171 (ICCPR); Art. 9 ECHR.

143 E.g. Art. 8 ECHR.

144 Art. 27 ICCPR: 'In those States in which ethnic, religious or linguistic minorities exist, persons belonging to such minorities shall not be denied the right, in community with the other members of their group, to enjoy their own culture, to profess and practise their own religion, or to use their own language'; Art. 9 ECHR.

145 Which specifically mentions culture, see e.g. Art. 1 ICESCR: 'All peoples have the right of self-determination. By virtue of that right they freely determine their political status and freely pursue their economic, social and *cultural development*'. Emphasis added.

This last right has been invoked and accepted in a 2008 Italian ruling dealing with a sculpture (the 'Venus of Cyrene') taken by Italian colonial agents from what is now Libyan soil. In this ground-breaking (albeit not exemplary) case the Italian Council of State confirmed the view that the return of cultural objects taken during colonial rule is inherent in the right of self-determination of newly independent states.[146] The right to self-determination, in other words, may include the right to the cultural heritage linked to the territory or peoples of that state.

5.2.4 *Cultural rights of indigenous peoples*

While the right of 'access to culture' in the binding ICESCR may seem vague and unspecified, the 2007 United Nations Declaration on the Rights of Indigenous Peoples (UNDRIP) is clear and specific in its obligations. The UNDRIP entitles indigenous peoples to rights with regard to their cultural heritage, including their lost cultural property.[147] In Article 11(2), this is defined as a right of 'redress through effective mechanisms, which may include restitution, developed in conjunction with indigenous peoples, with respect to their cultural, intellectual, religious and spiritual property taken without their free, prior and informed consent or in violation of their laws, traditions and customs'.[148] Article 12 deals with rights to objects of special importance – providing for a right to 'use and control' where lost ceremonial objects are concerned and a straightforward right to repatriation for objects containing human remains.[149]

Since these provisions are acknowledged as part of the (binding) right of access to culture of Article 15(1)(a) ICESCR insofar as the cultural heritage of

146 *Consiglio di Stato*, 23 June 2008, No. 3154, *Associazione nazionale Italia Nostra Onlus c. Ministero per i beni e le attività culturali et al.*, discussed by A. Chechi, 'The return of cultural objects removed in times of colonial domination and international law: the case of the Venus of Cyrene' (2008) 18 Italian Yearbook of International Law 159. For a discussion of the importance of the right to self-determination to restitution issues, see A.F. Vrdoljak, *International law, museums and the return of cultural objects* (2006) Cambridge University Press.

147 See also International Labour Organization (ILO) Convention no. 169 Concerning Indigenous and Tribal Peoples in Independent Countries (adopted 27 June 1989) 28 ILM 1382. It requests States to take special measures to 'safeguard' the cultures of indigenous peoples (Art. 4). The UNDRIP is more specific.

148 UNDRIP, Art. 11(2).

149 UNDRIP, Art. 12(1): 'Indigenous peoples have the right to manifest, practice, develop and teach their spiritual and religious traditions, customs and ceremonies; [...] the right to the use and control of their ceremonial objects; and the right to the repatriation of their human remains. (2) States shall seek to enable the access and/or repatriation of ceremonial objects and human remains in their possession through fair, transparent and effective mechanisms developed in conjunction with indigenous peoples concerned'.

indigenous peoples is concerned, this is an important instrument.[150] That it is more than 'just' a non-binding declaration is also illustrated by the fact that the UNDRIP was adopted after 20 years of negotiations and by now is supported almost universally.[151] States, in other words, are under the obligation to assist indigenous peoples in providing 'redress through effective mechanisms' and to 'enable the access and/or repatriation of ceremonial objects and human remains in their possession through fair, transparent and effective mechanisms developed in conjunction with indigenous peoples concerned'.[152]

As to the question of what exactly constitutes an indigenous people, the UNDRIP deliberately abstains from a definition to allow for the flexible evolution of the concept.[153] In general terms the link between people, their land and culture, and self-identification as a distinct community, are decisive factors.[154]

5.3 Heritage title

Beyond direct applicability in specific cases, the approach followed in UNDRIP highlights three elements that shape the content of heritage title.

150 According to General Comment No. 21 the right of 'access to culture' includes the rights as listed in the UNDRIP. See also A. Xanthaki, 'Culture: Articles 11(1), 12, 13(1), 15, and 34' in Hohmann J, Weller M (eds) *The UN Declaration on the Rights of Indigenous Peoples: a commentary* (2018) Oxford University Press, p. 275. With reference to Res. 5/2012 of the International Law Association, Lenzerini concludes that the right of indigenous peoples to reparation for the wrongs suffered has today crystallized into a principle of customary international law. Lenzerini (2017), p. 336. See also W. Van Genugten and F. Lenzerini, 'Legal implementation and international cooperation and assistance: articles 37-42' in J. Hohmann, M. Weller (eds) *The UN declaration on the rights of indigenous peoples: a commentary* (2018) Oxford University Press.

151 It was adopted by a majority of 144 States in favour, 11 abstentions (Azerbaijan, Bangladesh, Bhutan, Burundi, Colombia, Georgia, Kenya, Nigeria, the Russian Federation, Samoa and Ukraine) and four votes against. These objectors all reversed their vote: on 3 April 2009, Australia's government endorsed it; on 19 April 2010, New Zealand's support became official; on 16 December 2010, the United States declared it would 'lend its support', and in 2016, Canada officially adopted the declaration.

152 UNDRIP, Art. 12(2).

153 Following the advice of Special Rapporteur Daes, Commission on Human Rights, Subcommission on Prevention of Discrimination and Protection of Minorities, 'Discrimination against Indigenous Peoples: Protection of the Heritage of Indigenous People', Final Report (1995), Doc. E/Cn.4/Sub.2/1995/26. Also Campfens, 'The Bangwa queen' (2019), p. 101.

154 See *Centre for Minority Rights Development (Kenya) and Minority Rights Group International (on Behalf of Endorois Welfare Council) v Kenya* (2010) ACHPR, Communication No. 276/2003, discussed in A.F. Vrdoljak, 'Standing and collective cultural rights' in Jakubowski A (ed) *Cultural rights as collective rights, an international law perspective* (2016) Brill, p. 281.

5.3.1 *Basis for entitlement*

First of all, such entitlement is not *per se* based on the unlawfulness of a loss of ownership in the past, but on the *continuing injustice* of remaining separated from objects with a specific meaning for people who identify with them.

In many of today's restitution cases, the unlawfulness of the taking at the time is not a given. If a loss occurred during times of historical injustice, such as the Holocaust or colonial rule, often a changing notion of justice and legality is at the core of claims: In some instances the original taking can indeed be classified as unlawful, but in other cases the loss was legal at the time.[155] In other words, such cases rely on present-day norms that aim to reunite people with cultural objects that have a specific symbolic meaning, and to provide redress for a continuing injustice.

A continuing cultural link and entitlement without regard to the proven unlawfulness of the loss at the time, similarly underlies UNDRIP. In this sense, the notion of 'cultural affiliation' introduced in the American Graves Protection and Repatriation Act is also noteworthy.[156] It is used to allocate rights to (lost) cultural property of Native Americans of 'ongoing historical, traditional or cultural importance' on the basis of a shared group identity and the (continued) existence of an identifiable group. Likewise, as discussed above (in Sect. 4.1), a continuing cultural link is the rationale for entitlement of states to their lost cultural patrimony. In sum, heritage title depends on a (verifiable) continuing cultural link between people and objects.

5.3.2 *Classification of objects*

The second element of heritage title is that it enables the *classification* of objects depending on their social function and identity value for the people involved. UNDRIP differentiates for example between ceremonial objects, objects containing human remains and a general category of cultural objects 'taken without free, prior and informed consent'. Objects that contain human remains or are sacred to a living community, such as the Chinese Buddha statue (Master Zhang Gong) and the Hopi masks (Katsina) in the examples in the intro-

155 The sale of artefacts by Jewish collectors in the early thirties, before racial laws were enacted by the Nazis, could for example hardly be qualified as unlawful at the time. Still such losses qualify for reparations under the system of the Washington Principles. See e.g. Campfens (2018), p. 325. Likewise, in the 2018 French policy report – Sarr and Savoy, The Restitution of African Cultural Heritage. Toward a New Relational Ethics – the term 'restitution' is deliberately used to underline the authors' views on the injustice of colonial acquisition practices, not their unlawfulness.

156 NAGPRA recognises the inalienability of cultural objects with an 'ongoing historical, traditional or cultural importance central to the Native American Group'. See Kuprecht (2012). Obviously, NAGPRA is only binding in the US.

duction, clearly stand out.[157] Regalia or other objects symbolic to the identity of people are other obvious examples. The way in which objects were lost may enhance that symbolic meaning. For example, this was key in the repatriation of a kris (an Indonesian dagger) that belonged to the 'rebel prince' Diponegoro, who led an uprising against Dutch colonial rule, by the Netherlands, and that of the Witbooi Bible that had once belonged to the Namibian hero Hendrik Witbooi by Germany.[158] Likewise, also family heirlooms that were lost in the course of racial persecution stand out, as tangible symbols of a (lost) family life. As discussed above (in Sect. 4.1) archaeological objects and elements of a monument form another separate category as these are strongly, and often intrinsically, connected with a territory.[159]

5.3.3 Rights

The third element is that the rights involved are defined in terms of access, return or equitable solutions, not in terms of (the restitution of) exclusive ownership rights. Rights, in other words, tailored to the heritage interests involved, and this enables remedies that take account of the interests of other right holders, such as new possessors.

The jurisprudence of the Inter-American Court of Human Rights is noteworthy in this regard, apart from its acknowledgement of pre-existing rights of the indigenous peoples (to their ancestral lands, not cultural objects), in its choice for participatory solutions. In the 2015 *Kaliña and Lokono Peoples v Suriname* case the Court held that the right of access can be compatible with the rights of other title holders.[160]

This reflects soft law and (best) practice in the field. The 1998 Washington Principles on Nazi-Confiscated Art, for example, prescribe 'fair and just solutions, depending on the circumstances of the case'.[161] In a similar spirit,

---

157 A number of soft law instruments underscore this classification. See also Campfens, 'The Bangwa Queen' (2019), para. 2.3.

158 See: <https://www.rijksoverheid.nl/actueel/nieuws/2020/03/04/nederland-geeft-dolk-van-javaanse-verzetsheld-terug-aan-indonesie> and H. Neuendorf, 'Germany is returning artefacts stolen from a Namibian freedom fighter during its colonial rule' (2019) Artnet News.

159 E.g. see also the argumentation in the UNSC Resolutions, above n. 34 and 35.

160 The Court ruled with respect to ancestral land that was now owned by third parties that 'the State must establish, by mutual agreement with the Kaliña and Lokono peoples and the third parties, rules for peaceful and harmonious coexistence in the lands in questions, which respect the uses and customs of these peoples and ensure their access to the Marowijne River'. *Kaliña and Lokono Peoples v Suriname,* Merits, Reparations and Costs, Inter-Am. Ct HR, Series C, No. 309, 25 November 2015, para. 159.

161 These solutions often involve a financial settlement, but recognition by addressing the ownership history (e.g. in a plaque in a museum) also features as a 'fair solution'. In the words of a claimant at the Dutch Restitutions Committee: 'Our objective is not to recover every stolen work of art. For us it's about recognition. The most important issue for us is that the name of our great-grandfather is restored into the work's provenance', in A. Marck and M. Schoonderwoerd, 'We want to honour the memory of our great-grand-

the 2015 Operational Guidelines to the 1970 UNESCO Convention suggest cooperative solutions in the event of competing claims of states 'to realize [...] interests in a compatible way through, inter alia, loans, temporary exchange of objects [...], temporary exhibitions, joint activities of research and restoration'.[162] Such creative solutions are not uncommon in practice as it is. For example, when France returned looted scriptures to (South) Korea on a renewable long-term loan – to circumvent laws prohibiting French museums to deaccession national patrimony –, it separated ownership rights from rights to access, use and control.[163] A solution mirrored by the Korean example is the transfer of title of (presumably looted) Nok and Sokoto statuettes by France to Nigeria, whereas they physically remained in France under the terms of a 25-year loan in the Quai Branly Museum.[164] In the Korean example physical possession, whereas in the Nigerian example rehabilitation and a formal recognition appear to have been key.

The notion of heritage title that thus emerges relies on a (verifiable) continuing cultural link between people and an object. Dependent on the type of object and the values it represents, it entitles people to an equitable solution. The specific circumstances and interests involved, including the interests of other right holders, should determine what is 'equitable'.

5.4 Operationalisation of heritage title

The last question that needs to be addressed is how to make heritage title operational. Having established that former owners may be entitled to rights with regard to their lost cultural objects, how can they claim such rights? Alternative dispute resolution and cultural diplomacy on the interstate level are often promoted as being best equipped to solve disputes in this field.[165]

parents' – and interview with Ella Andriesse and Robert Sturm in Campfens E (ed) *Fair and just solutions, alternatives to litigation in Nazi-looted art disputes: status quo and new developments* (2015) Boom, pp. 147-148.

162 Operational Guidelines for the Implementation of the Convention on the Means of Prohibiting and Preventing the Illicit Import, Export and Transfer of Ownership of Cultural Property, adopted at the UNESCO Meeting of States Parties, 18-20 May 2015 (C70/15/3.MSP/11), para. 19.

163 *Décret No.2011-527 Portant publication de l'accord entre le Gouvernement de la République Française et le Gouvernement de la République de Corée relatif aux manuscrits royaux de la Dynastie Joseon (ensemble une annexe)* (adopted 7 February 2011) <https://www.legifrance.gouv.fr/jorf/id/JORFTEXT000024022738?r=g7YcXLuG3d>

164 M. Cornu and M.A. Renold, 'New developments in the restitution of cultural property: alternative means of dispute resolution' (2010) 17 *International Journal of Cultural Property* 1, pp. 20-21.

165 E.g. the International Law Association's Principles for Co-operation in the Mutual Protection and Transfer of Cultural Material: 'If the [... parties, EC] are unable to reach a mutually satisfactory settlement [...] both parties shall submit the dispute to good offices, consultation, mediation, conciliation, ad hoc arbitration or institutional arbitration'. International Law

However valid this may be in specific cases, access to justice is eventually key, not only in the recognition of unequal power relations, but also for the development of standards in a field that is hindered by legal insecurity.[166]

The question *if* norms can be made operational obviously depends on the binding force of norms that a party invokes for its heritage title before a specific forum. Here, hurdles exist as the law is evolving. Nevertheless, even if the mentioned norms – e.g. the right to culture – would not be directly applicable in a court of law, heritage title may operate as a 'narrative norm'.[167] Heritage title should thus instruct judges on the interpretation of open norms that exist in all jurisdictions, for example through the application of concepts such as 'public policy', 'public order', 'general principles of (international) law' or 'reasonableness and fairness'. In fact, courts in various countries have already prevented 'unjust' outcomes to cultural property disputes in a strict private law approach in that way, for example by accepting as the international standard (international public policy) that looted cultural objects should be returned, even though no directly binding treaties applied to the case – and in spite of general (international) private law rules that would point at another direction.[168]

In a setting of dispute resolution before national courts, the notion that the private sector should adhere to human rights standards, as advocated by the UN, may be relevant in cases where auction houses, art dealers or private museums are involved.[169]

Association, Report of the Seventy-second Conference (2006), Principle 9. Annex to Nafziger (2007), p. 159; cf. M. Frigo, 'Methods and techniques of dispute settlement in the international practice of the restitution and return of cultural property' (2017) Rivista di Diritto Internazionale Privato e Processuale 569.

166 Campfens, 'Restitution of looted art' (2019). See also Shyllon (2017).

167 Jayme (2015), p. 41: 'These norms speak, but they are flexible and not very precise. They describe certain policies without giving answers in a single case'. As an example, he refers to the 1998 Washington Principles that judges should take into account.

168 Above n. 64, examples from Switzerland (relying on 'international public policy') and Germany (relying on 'the morality of the international trade'). Two UK examples, relying on 'public policy' and 'public order': (1) *City of Gotha and Federal Republic of Germany v Sotheby's and Cobert Finance SA* (1998) No. 1993 C 3428; 1997 G 185, where Judge Moses observed that he would have invoked the public order exception if the application of foreign (German) law had necessitated a ruling in favour of a new possessor who was aware of the painting's tainted provenance (it was stolen in the aftermath of WWII); and (2) *Government of the Islamic Republic of Iran v The Barakat Galleries Ltd.* (2007) EWCA Civ. 1374: '[I]n our judgment it is certainly contrary to *public policy* for such claims [by a State to recover antiquities which form part of its national heritage] to be shut out […]. There is international recognition that States should assist one another to prevent the unlawful removal of cultural objects including antiquities'.

169 See the UN Guiding Principles on Business and Human Rights: Implementing the United Nations 'Protect, Respect and Remedy' Framework. Report of the Special Representative of the Secretary-General on the issue of human rights and transnational corporations and other business enterprises, John Ruggie, presented to the seventeenth session of the Human Rights Council of the United Nations, A/HRC/17/31 (21 March 2011).

In terms of a straightforward human rights claim, the question is whether a forum could evaluate a claim based on the argument that the continued deprivation of a specific cultural object is an infringement of the right to 'access to culture'. In this respect, the Optional Protocol to the ICESCR offers a complaints procedure. This procedure, however, appears limited to nationals or groups in the state responsible for the alleged violation, whereas claimants are not usually nationals of a holding state, and is subject to ratification of the Protocol by that state.[170] Within the European human rights system, while a stumbling block is that the European Convention on Human Rights does not include a right to culture, claims may be addressed through the right to property of the First Protocol, or other rights, as mentioned above.[171]

An interesting roadmap on how a community may proceed in its claim to a long lost treasure in a foreign museum, is given by the Colombian Constitutional Court in a 2017 case concerning the 'Quimbaya Treasure'.[172] In its ruling, the Court ordered the Colombian government to pursue – on behalf of the indigenous Quimbaya people – the return from Spain of a treasure of 122 golden objects lost at the close of the nineteenth century. The Court argued that under today's standards of international law, referring to human rights law and UNDRIP – but interestingly also to the 1970 UNESCO Convention –, indigenous peoples are entitled to their lost cultural objects. *How* such a claim is pursued is left to the discretion of the government, but according to the Court *the fact that* governments should work towards this goal is clear.[173] In a first reaction to the subsequent request by the Colombian authorities for the return of the Quimbaya Treasure, the Spanish authorities, however, declined on the grounds that today the Quimbaya Treasure has become Spanish patrimony and is inalienable.

As discussed above, that has long been a common European reaction to restitution requests by former colonised people.[174] It is also reminiscent of the (initial) position that the Austrian government took in the *Altmann* case: due to national administrative law (patrimony laws) the Klimt paintings that were lost during the Nazi era were inalienable. In that case, however, after US Supreme Court established a violation of international human rights law,

170 Optional Protocol to the International Covenant on Economic, Social and Cultural Rights (adopted 10 December 2008, entered into force 5 May 2013) UN Doc A/RES/63/117, Art. 2: 'Communications may be submitted by or on behalf of individuals or groups of individuals, under the jurisdiction of a State Party, claiming to be victims of a violation of any of the economic, social and cultural rights set forth in the Covenant *by that State Party*'. Emphasis added.

171 Above n. 22.

172 Judgment SU-649/17 (2017) (Republic of Colombia, Constitutional Court).

173 For a critical discussion, see Mejia-Lemos (2019).

174 See above Sect. 4.2 for a similar argumentation.

the Austrian government accepted to abide by an arbitral award that the rights of Altmann should prevail.[175]

It illustrates the difficulties in this field and the clash of laws on various levels, but also highlights the potential of the human rights framework as a universal language to further develop this field.

6 Conclusion

'Hard cases make bad law', so the maxim goes. A question at the conclusion of this chapter is whether cases such as those mentioned in the introduction are indeed hard and exceptional – which no law can address – or whether the law is in need of change. The analysis in the previous sections illustrates that title disputes about contested cultural objects are indeed complex: international and domestic, public and private laws of different places and times, as well as soft law, meet and not seldom clash. On the other hand, if claims to cultural heritage cannot be addressed on their merits in our courts of law due to the inflexibility of private law, the law is up for a change.

Given the rhetoric on the importance of heritage protection for humanity at large, not only on account of the intrinsic value of cultural objects but because destruction and looting are detrimental to the sustainable development of societies and the realisation of human rights, one would expect that the trade and possession of looted cultural objects would be more difficult than it is today. The illegality of the act of looting simply does not 'stick' to the objects. This, in spite of the introduction fifty years ago of the 1970 UNESCO Convention to curb the one-way traffic of cultural objects from culturally rich source countries to Western market countries. Through trade and acquisition ownership title is passed on, or 'laundered' in civil law countries. Often, the provenance of a specific object (its ownership history) is omitted or unknown by new possessors along the line. A first step to counter the illicit trade is therefore to oblige actors in the art world to abide by clear due diligent standards: to only trade, buy and possess objects that have a documented lawful provenance. The need for measures in that regard resonates even in the UN Security Council.[176] Nevertheless, this will still not solve title issues in a private law setting for objects that already circulate: who should be seen as legitimate 'title holders' when ownership laws differ per jurisdiction?

As demonstrated in this chapter, neither traditional ownership concepts nor the conventional regime for the art trade are particularly suited to solve title issues with regard to contested cultural objects. The 1970 UNESCO Convention operates on the interstate level and was primarily set up as a means to control the movement of cultural objects, not to provide answers for competing

175 Above n. 97.
176 UNSC Res 2347 (24 March 2017) UN Doc S/RES/2347.

claims. Moreover, the 1995 UNIDROIT Convention, meant to harmonise private law, has not been ratified by market states, and none of the conventions cover earlier losses. This adds up to a highly fragmented framework where states implement standards in different ways, not seldom primarily to protect their own heritage. That is not surprising, given that the 1970 UNESCO Convention appoints states as exclusive right holders ('owners') of their national cultural heritage. Nationality alone, however, is insufficient to decide the matter of title, as it fails to acknowledge that the value of cultural objects may change in time and place. Such blind spots surface in dispute resolution over artefacts that left their original setting, where parties claiming 'their' heritage may be states, but also communities or private individuals. Mostly if communities or individuals do not (or no longer) feel represented by a state, nationality proves insufficient.

To disentangle the matter of title, the notion of heritage title was introduced. It is based on a (verifiable) continuing cultural link that entitles people with rights defined in terms of access and control, not in terms of absolute and exclusive ownership. Although we are used to define relations between objects and people by way of exclusive ownership rights, this exclusivity does not fit cultural property. Owners of certain 'outstanding' artefacts are not free to destroy, or alienate such objects, as this could be contrary to the (heritage) interests of the wider public: preservation and accessibility are well accepted public interests that limit private ownership. Similarly, and more directly, the interests of specifically interested people beyond the wider public, such as former owners or creators who are tied to the objects on the basis of a continuing cultural link, limit the rights of (new) owners. International human rights law apprears particularly suited to further develop this field: it addresses identity values, is of a universal nature and may penetrate and shape private law. As such, it can act as a bridge for internationally acknowledged heritage interests onto national private law settings. Various human rights may inform heritage title, depending on the facts of a case. The right of access to culture, as developed in the realm of the right to culture in Article 15(1) ICESCR, is of key importance in this respect. Furthermore, the rights provided in UNDRIP are relevant for indigenous peoples' lost cultural objects, whereas the human right to property is the logical basis to further develop heritage title of dispossessed private former owners (e.g. the field of Nazi-looted art).

Heritage title that thus surfaces is based on a continuing cultural link and three elements shape its content. In the first place, not to be able to have access to or control over objects over which one has heritage title – after removal without free consent – implicates a continuing injustice of remaining separated from those objects. Such an outlook brings with it a shift in focus from past events – the unlawfulness of the loss that is decisive in an ownership approach – to present-day interests. In the second place, the rights involved are defined in terms of access, control, return or 'equitable solutions', as opposed to the restitution of full ownership rights. This enables the weighing, and ideally conciliation, of competing interests that parties may have in the same object by aiming at creative and participatory solutions. A third element is the classification of cultural objects depending on their specific social function and heritage value. In that sense, for example, sacred or other highly symbolic objects stand out on account of their identity value for the people involved, whereas an artefact produced for the market will not easily pass the test for heritage title unless such artefact turned into a tangible symbol for a (lost) family or community life.

Obviously, heritage title may coincide with ownership title and, where this is the case, there is no need to rely on heritage title in dispute resolution. Furthermore, where no heritage title in terms of a continuing cultural link can be proven, cases fall under regular ownership laws. However, in all those cases in the 'grey' categories of lawfully possessed but unlawfully taken artefacts, heritage title could be invoked. In the case concerning 'Master Zhang Gong', introduced at the start of this chapter, the Chinese communities could rely on a strong heritage title with regard to their lost sacred statue irrespective of the ownership situation in a specific jurisdiction. This implicates a right of access and control that, given the religious function for the local community, would mean a return in its original setting. And what about the owner of an object that, on closer examination, is encumbered with heritage title? According to rules already operative in the art world, that owner's position should depend on its due diligence on acquisition, most notably the provenance research performed.

7 Concluding observations

1 Introduction

This dissertation aimed to shed light on the legal framework for cross-border claims to involuntarily lost cultural objects. Are such claims a matter of justice and the law, or merely of ethics and politics? Moreover, if we take a legal perspective, should we approach the objects as property, or as heritage? The guiding question throughout this study was how the interests of former owners in their lost cultural objects can be addressed more effectively. To that end, a critical analysis was needed to identify blind spots and clashes in the law that obstruct such claims at present. The preceding chapters have attempted to provide this analysis. The main finding was that although the heritage value of cultural objects, as symbols of an identity, mostly lies at the core of claims, adequate legal tools to address these interests are lacking.

Chapters 2 and 3 addressed the two main models that currently exist for claims to contested artefacts: private restitution claims to lost possessions, and interstate return claims to national cultural heritage. The subsequent Chapters 4 and 5 were studies of two types of historical claims: Chapter 4 covered the field of Nazi-looted art, with a focus on claims by dispossessed private owners; Chapter 5 explored the category of colonial looting, with a focus on claims by indigenous communities. Chapter 6, written as the substantive conclusion of this dissertation, revisited the legal framework from the wider perspective of heritage protection and the international art trade. It analysed the interrelation (and disconnect) between private and public law in this field and put forward proposals to bridge the gaps. The analysis in Chapter 6 included more recently looted antiquities. Although referred to here as 'chapters', these were written as independent publications, not as a subsequent set of chapters of a book.

These concluding observations summarise the findings in the separate chapters and the replies to the research questions defined in the introduction. In section 3 some further observations and proposals will be made.

2 Summary of findings

2.1 Private title claims

Claims to lost cultural objects are generally perceived as title claims over lost possessions. As such these are covered by private law rules. The second chapter gave an overview of this model, evaluated its limits and reflected on the emergence of the 'ethical model' for claims.

'What is stolen should be returned' may sound so simple, the reality for dispossessed owners to regain their lost cultural objects lost is more complex. Artefacts cross borders and are meant to be kept over time, meaning that the laws of different times and places may be relevant to their legal status. Regulation of property and ownership is traditionally a matter of state sovereignty and domestic law and, consequently, the legal framework is typified by major differences amongst jurisdictions. Dispute settlement in this field is complex and the outcomes are often unpredictable. According to private international law rules in most countries, the law of the country where the cultural objects is located at the time of the claim or where it was last traded governs title issues over lost cultural objects (the *lex rei sitae*), although that rule may be interpreted differently. The main obstructions for cross-border title claims in a private law approach that were identified are: the transfer of ownership title to a new possessor; limitation periods for claims; the non-applicability of foreign administrative law in court proceedings; and the non-retroactivity of treaties that contain return obligations.

In common law countries, the basic rule is that a thief cannot convey good title over stolen possessions - a choice for security of title. In countries with a civil law tradition, however, ownership title can pass after an acquisition in good faith or simply by the passage of time - a choice for security of transactions and a smooth market. Since most European countries have a civil law tradition, former owners here have a relatively weak starting position in comparison to common law jurisdictions like (most states of) the US and the UK. These last countries, nevertheless, are important trendsetters due to their dominant position on the international art market.

Claims by former owners are often barred by limitation periods. At a certain point, the law tends to adjust itself to the situation as it appears and if that is not challenged within a specific time, a new possessor will *be* the legitimate owner. Nonetheless, the moment when that time period starts differs widely. It may start to run from the moment of the loss, or only from the moment of discovery of the object by the dispossessed owner, with many variations. Generally, time limitations will not run in favour of a bad faith possessor, who is or reasonably could be aware that the artefact was stolen. Then again, in some jurisdictions this *may* be possible.[1]

Another obstacle to claims is that courts will generally not apply foreign public law, whilst export restrictions or rules on their inalienability typically lie at the basis of claims that regard antiquities or communally owned (sacred) objects.[2] This is reason why states increasingly vest state-ownership over (undiscovered) archaeological objects.[3]

Given this fragmented situation, attempts have been undertaken to harmonise private law. In that regard, the UNIDROIT Convention on Stolen or Illegally Exported Cultural Objects[4] was adopted in 1995 to clarify and further elaborate on the principles underlying the 1970 UNESCO Convention.[5] The Convention's main rule is that cultural objects that were stolen or unlawfully exported - according to the law in the country of origin - should be returned upon a claim by the deprived owner or the state or origin.[6] This implicates a shift from the *lex rei sitae* (the law where the cultural objects is located upon a claim or was last traded) towards the 'lex originis' - the law of the country of origin -, as the law that should govern cross-border title disputes over unlawfully exported cultural objects.

Under the 1995 UNIDROIT Convention claims should be filed within three years from the moment the object was located with the option to set a maximum of 75 years also if it concerns objects that qualify for enhanced protection (public collections, elements of monuments or archaeological sites or indigenous peoples cultural object). Although countries such as the Netherlands and Germany did not accede to the 1995 UNIDROIT Convention, in their implementation legislation of the 1970 UNESCO Convention they did introduce such

1 E.g. in the Netherlands a new possessor in bad faith may gain lawful ownership title, a reason for some controversial rulings in this field (Chapter 1, section 2.2.1 and Chapter 2, section 2.2). As discussed in Chapter 1 (section 2.2.1), in the light of recent Dutch case law, today such outcomes could (should) be different. Moreover, it is out of line with the international standard that only innocent new possessors deserve protection.

2 E.g. (UK) *Attorney General of New Zealand v Ortiz* (1982) 3 All ER 432. More recently, courts in the US and the UK have accepted and endorsed state ownership over antiquities in two seminal cases: *Government of the Islamic Republic of Iran v The Barakat Galleries Ltd.* (2007) EWCA Civ. 1374 and *United States v Schultz*, 178 F. Supp. 2d445 (SDNY 3 January 2002).

3 As promoted in the UNESCO-UNIDROIT Model Provisions on State's Ownership of Undiscovered Cultural Objects, drafted by the Expert Committee on State Ownership of Cultural Heritage (1 July 2011), CLT-2011/CONF.208/COM.17.5.

4 UNIDROIT Convention on Stolen or Illegally Exported Cultural Objects (adopted 24 June 1995, entered into force 7 July 1998) 2421 UNTS 457 (1995 UNIDROIT Convention).

5 Convention on the Means of Prohibiting and Preventing the Illicit Import, Export and Transfer of Ownership of Cultural Property (adopted 14 November 1970, entered into force 24 April 1972) 823 UNTS 231 (1970 UNESCO Convention). See Chapter 1, section 2.2 and Chapter 2, section 2.2.1.

6 Arts. 3 and 5, 1995 UNIDROIT Convention. The return of unlawfully exported cultural objects depends on their cultural significance to the source states (art. 5 (3)).

a maximum period of 75 years.[7] An observation in this regard is that, whilst this is a considerable extension compared with regular limitation periods, the time span that currently separates us from the Nazi era is over 80 years (i.e. more than the maximum time limit provided for in the 1995 UNIDROIT Convention). This highlights that a model based on the moment of a loss of ownership in the past does not fit all cases we currently believe should be addressed.

Furthermore, a new possessor, upon return, may be entitled to 'fair and reasonable' compensation if it can prove it exercised due diligence upon acquisition. 'Due diligence', as introduced in the 1995 UNIDROIT Convention, implicates that 'regard shall be had to all the circumstances of the acquisition, including the character of the parties, the price paid, whether the possessor consulted any reasonably accessible register of stolen cultural objects, and any other relevant information and documentation which it could reasonably have obtained, and whether the possessor consulted accessible agencies or took any other step that a reasonable person would have taken in the circumstances'.[8] Although most market states did not accede to the 1995 UNIDROIT Convention, these due diligence standards gained legal importance in their own right as *the* international standard, and are replicated in many later instruments in this field. Accordingly, a new possessor who was not duly diligent upon acquisition – i.e. did not perform (solid) provenance research –, should be unprotected.

The 1995 UNIDROIT Convention on itself is not widely adopted and, most importantly in the present context, it is not retroactive. Even if all countries were to adopt the UNIDROIT Convention today, in other words, this would not affect the legal status of artefacts that are already circulating. Such objects, nevertheless, *will* surface as 'tainted' as a result of the more stringent due diligence standards and required provenance research in the market. The non-retroactivity of international conventions, in sum, proves to be the major obstacle to claims by dispossessed owners.

In the last decades, a vast body of international soft law and transnational private regulation has emerged in support of return claims by former owners, reflecting a new morality and normativity on the possession of looted art, also if such losses occurred in the past and are inadmissible under positive private law. Thus, grey categories have emerged where expectations have been raised that 'justice' will be done, expectations that often cannot be fulfilled by relying on regular legal channels for claims, especially in civil law countries. Such non-binding instruments generally promote equitable solutions (not *per se* restitution of full ownership) after an 'unjust' loss in the past (not *per se* an

7 E.g., countries such as The Netherlands (see art 3:310 (a) of the Dutch Civil Code) and Germany (art 55 (2) Cultural Property Protection Act of 31 July 2016) introduced such an (extended) limitation periods of 75 years as the absolute maximum for most categories in their implementation legislation of the 1970 UNESCO Convention.

8 Art. 4 (4) 1995 UNIDROIT Convention. See Chapter 2, section 2.1.

unlawful loss) and voluntary settlement of claims through alternative dispute resolution (ADR).

The traditional private law model for title claims to looted art as a model to guide judges to a 'just' outcome on the basis of domestic private law, has thus clearly come under pressure. Mostly in civil law countries and mostly for older losses the 'ethical' model for claims has come in its place. Given that soft law is not binding, compliance depends on the willingness of the parties and on ADR to 'clear' the title of tainted objects. A lack of transparent neutral procedures to implement and clarify soft-law norms has proven problematic in terms of access to justice.

2.2 The interstate model

Cultural objects that were removed from the territory of a state may be subject to interstate return claims. This model reflects the long-standing protected status of cultural objects in international law, not merely as possessions (of an individual or a state) but as the 'intellectual patrimony' of communities of origin.[9] This means, in the first place, that cultural objects may not be seized in times of war. The protection of cultural objects in international law developed through the law of wars. To cite an 1813 verdict that condemns the seizure of artefacts during the Anglo-American War as war booty:

> '(t)he arts and sciences are admitted amongst all civilized nations, [...] as entitled to favour and protection. They are considered not as the peculium of this or that nation, but as the property of mankind at large, and as belonging to the common interests of the whole species.'[10]

The first multilateral treaty dedicated to cultural heritage, the 1954 UNESCO Convention for the Protection of Cultural Property in the Event of Armed Conflict, confirmed this rule and provides that states should 'prohibit, prevent and [...] put a stop to any form of theft, pillage or misappropriation of, and any acts of vandalism directed against, cultural property', and 'refrain from requisitioning movable cultural property'.[11] Its (1954) First Protocol obliges states to take into their custody cultural objects removed from an occupied territory with the aim of their return to the territory previously occupied: these should never be retained as war reparations. Its (1999) Second Protocol further

9 Chapter 3, section 4; The term was used in the Treaty of Peace of Saint-Germain (1919) 226 CTS 8.

10 Ibid.; Vice-Admiralty Court of Halifax, Nova Scotia Stewart's Vice-Admiralty Reports 482 (1813).

11 Art. 4, Hague Convention for the Protection of Cultural Property in the Event of Armed Conflict (adopted 14 May 1954, entered into force 7 August 1956) 249 UNTS 240 (1954 Hague Convention).

strengthens such obligations with regard to cultural objects misappropriated in times of armed conflict.[12]

The 1970 UNESCO Convention on the Means of Prohibiting and Preventing the Illicit Import, Export and Transfer of Ownership of Cultural Property is the second multilateral treaty in this field. Its aim was to curb the ever-growing trade in looted cultural objects, also beyond a situation of armed conflict or foreign occupation. This treaty provides for a system where states designate protected 'national cultural heritage' (and declare that inalienable), set up a system of export licences, and cooperate in the return after the unauthorised export.

Chapter 3 explored the interstate model for return claims on the basis of a dispute under litigation in the Netherlands. At stake in this dispute are archaeological objects from various Crimean museums that had been sent to Amsterdam for a temporary exhibition. The period of this exhibition coincided with the Russian occupation and the subsequent secession of Crimea from the Ukraine in March 2014. This change of borders, however, is generally not recognised.[13] At the close of the exhibition, the Allard Pierson Museum, in custody of the artefacts, was confronted with two competing claims. The Ukrainian State claims the objects as national patrimony and state property; the Crimean museums seek their return on the basis of the loan agreements that stipulated their return after the exhibitions, and entitlement as 'operational manager' under Ukrainian law. They argue, moreover, that Crimea is the genuine home of these antiquities as they were discovered and preserved there over time.

In 2016, the Amsterdam District Court ruled that the objects should be returned to Ukraine, unsurprisingly perhaps in light of the political situation. The Court argued that the non-return after a temporary loan adds up to the 'unlawful' export within the meaning of the 1970 UNESCO Convention, and that the issue of return is an interstate affair. The Amsterdam Appeals Court in its 2019 interlocutory judgment, however, rejected that view: neither the export nor the import of the artefacts can be seen as unlawful behaviour the 1970 UNESCO Convention aims to reverse.[14] Instead, it qualified the dispute as a matter of private law and asked the parties to further clarify the matter of title.[15]

Two questions relevant to the present study arise in the Crimean case. First, what is the basis for entitlement of states to their national cultural heritage

---

12 See Chapter 1, section 2.3.

13 See the condemning UNGA Res. 68/262 (27 March 2014) UN Doc A/RES/68/262, entitled 'Territorial Integrity of Ukraine', adopted by 100 states in favour, 11 against and 58 abstentions.

14 *The Travida Central Museum et al. v the State of Ukraine v University of Amsterdam* (Judgment of 16 July 2019) Amsterdam Court of Appeal, Case No. 200.212.377/01, ECLI:NL:GHAMS:2019:2427. Chapter 3, section 6.

15 Ibid. The appeals procedure is ongoing at the moment of writing.

(patrimony)? And, second, what is the position of sub-state actors such as communities or individuals with regard to 'their' lost cultural objects?

Neither the 1954 UNESCO Convention nor the 1970 UNESCO Convention are clear on the matter of entitlement. The 1954 UNESCO Convention seems to propagate territoriality by providing for the 'return to ... the territory after cessation of hostilities.' The 1970 UNESCO Convention, however, is based on nationality. National cultural heritage is defined as 'property, which on religious or secular grounds, is specifically designated by each State as being of importance for archaeology, prehistory, history, literature, art or science'.[16] Article 4 sets out five categories of objects that can qualify as national cultural heritage. The first two categories bear a clear territorial link: objects created by nationals or others *within that territory* or objects found *within that territory*.[17] The other three categories cover artefacts that were the subject of a 'freely agreed exchange' or acquired 'with the consent of the authorities of the country of origin'.[18] *What* states designate as their national patrimony, from that point on, is open to their own discretion as they have the 'indefeasible right ... to classify and declare certain cultural property as inalienable', and other member states should then 'facilitate recovery of such property'.[19] That this may result in clashes is for example illustrated by the fact that, since 2015, a Russian law also designates the Crimean collections as Russian cultural heritage.[20]

Clues as to what may serve as a basis for entitlement do however exist. The *Institut de Droit international* advised for example that a 'country of origin' should be understood as the country with which the object is 'most closely linked from a cultural point of view'.[21] Likewise, the 1995 UNIDROIT Convention uses the criterion 'significant cultural importance' as a ground for return requests by states.[22] Clues as to what objects may qualify as such are given in article 5 (3), namely if the removal significantly impairs (a) the physical preservation of the object or its context; (b) the integrity of a complex object; (c) the preservation of scientific or historic information; or (d) the traditional or ritual use of the object by indigenous or tribal communities. Although this listing is open to a myriad of interpretations, the general idea is 'cultural significance'. That this is not *per se* tied up to nation states follows from the acknowledgement of the interests of communities separately: this illustrates

---

16 1970 UNESCO Convention, Art. 1, listing 11 types of objects ranging from objects of historical, archaeological, ethnological or artistic interest (e.g., pictures, paintings, drawings and sculpture) to furniture and antiquities of more than 100 years old, rare stamps and archival material.

17 Ibid, Art. 4, section (a)-(b).

18 Ibid, Art. 4, sections (c)–(e).

19 Ibid, Art. 13, 1970 UNESCO Convention; Chapter 6, section 3.1.2.

20 Chapter 3, section 3.3.

21 Chapter 3, section 4.2.1; Chapter 6, section 4.1.

22 Ibid.; Art. 5(3), 1995 UNIDROIT Convention.

a step away from the paradigm of one national culture that underlies the 1970 UNESCO Convention.[23]

The more recent 2001 UNESCO Convention for Underwater Cultural Heritage can also serve as inspiration where it introduces a 'verifiable link' as the basis for responsibilities and limited rights by states (but not for exclusive right).[24] In sum, a verifiable cultural link between objects and people in my opinion should underly entitlement of a state to its national patrimony. Archaeological objects or elements of a built monument would, in this outlook, normally follow the territory.

With regard to the 'nationality' prong in the 1970 UNESCO Convention, it should be kept in mind that that treaty's primary goal was to set up a system to preserve cultural heritage *in situ* and protect it from illicit trade. Against that background, states can be seen, and are appointed, as custodians of the cultural heritage within their borders, for the benefit of all mankind. This should not be confused with entitlement of states as exclusive and absolute right holders ('owners'). Normally such a state-oriented framework works well, but tensions arise if communities or individuals do not, or no longer, feel represented by a specific state they were part of, like in the Crimean case. This also applies to claims that concern Nazi-looted art: private (Jewish) dispossessed owners are often no longer citizens of the state from which the objects were looted.

Increasingly communities and individuals are acknowledged as independent right holders in other (soft law) instruments and this is reflected in recent practice. For example, in the *Altmann* litigation and subsequent international arbitration about a number of paintings by the Viennese painter Gustav Klimt, claimed by Austria as its national patrimony, were overruled by the interests of the individual family of the pre-war owner who no longer resided in Austria but in the US.[25] Another example is the United Nations Declaration for the Rights of Indigenous Peoples that attributes independent rights to indigenous communities to their (lost) cultural objects.[26]

The analysis in this chapter highlighted that the UNESCO treaty system – the 1954 and 1970 UNESCO Conventions – focus on the preservation of cultural objects but do not provide tools for competing claims. Entitlement by states to their national heritage should, in my view, depend on a verifiable cultural link, as follows from more recent legal instruments. In Chapter 6 of this thesis, this was developed into the notion of 'heritage title'.

23 This paradigm surfaces in the preamble of the 1970 UNESCO Convention 'Considering that cultural property constitutes one of the basic elements of civilization and *national culture*, [...]' (emphasis added).

24 Chapter 6, section 4.1.

25 Chapter 6, section 4.2.

26 UNGA Res. 61/295 (13 September 2007) UN Doc A/RES/61/295, arts. 11 and 12. Chapter 5, section 4.5.

2.3 Nazi looting

Chapter 4 addressed the normative framework for claims to Nazi-looted art. The background to this category is the wide-scale looting by the Nazis, both in occupied territories and within Germany. Public collections as well as private collections were systematically seized or acquired under duress, and in neighbouring 'Aryan' countries suitable art was also acquired on the market through regular (but prohibited) sales.

The post-War restitution framework aimed to reverse all these different types of looting.[27] It relied on a process of 'external restitution' of artefacts to the countries from where they had last been removed – irrespective of the grounds for removal – and a process of 'internal restitution' to dispossessed owners at the local (national) level. To organise the process of internal restitution, states enacted special regulations that suspended regular private law rules. Typically, such laws declared void (*ab initio*) confiscations on the basis of discriminatory Nazi regulations, whilst other transactions were voidable if the loss was a result of persecution by the Nazis.[28] Within Germany, the Allies imposed laws that aimed to reverse the deprivation of property 'for reasons of race, religion, nationality, ideology or political opposition to National Socialism'.[29] Their aim was 'to remedy wrongs caused by the failure of a government to observe minimum international standards for the treatment of human beings' by rearranging ownership relations, a field generally considered to be an internal affair of states.[30] Besides, even neutral countries like Switzerland where looted art had come on the market, were to enact special restitution laws. Contemporary legal scholars explained this interference in national private law by pointing at the 'more comprehensive idea of interstate law'.[31] In other words, it was a matter of international human rights law (emerging at the time). Another point of interest is the distinction that was made between regular possessions and possessions such as artefacts or personal

27 Based on the Inter-Allied Declaration against Acts of Dispossession committed in the Territories under Enemy Occupation or Control (5 January 1943) *The Department of State Bulletin*, vol. 8 (1943) US Government Printing Office. Chapter 4, section 2.1.

28 Chapter 4, section 2.2.

29 Art. 1 (1) 'Law No. 59, Restitution of Identifiable Property' of the Military Government for Germany, US in United States Courts of the Allied High Commission for Germany, *Court of Restitution Appeals Reports* (1951) 499-536. See Chapter 4, section 2.2.

30 N. Bentwich, 'International Aspects of Restitution and Compensation for Victims of the Nazis', in *BYIL (1955/1956)* Oxford University Press. See also A.F. Vrdoljak, 'Gross Violations of Human Rights and Restitution: Learning from Holocaust Claims' in L.V. Prott, *Realising Cultural Heritage Law: Festschrift for Patrick O'Keefe* (2013) Institute for Art & Law. Chapter 4, section 2.2.

31 G. Weiss, 'Beutegueter aus besetzten Laendern und die privatrechtliche Stellung des schweizerischen Erwebers' (1946) 42 *Schweizerische Juristen-Zeitung* 274. See Chapter 4, section 2.2. Further elaboration in E. Campfens, *Fair and Just Solutions? Alternatives to Litigation in Nazi-Looted Art Disputes* (2015) Eleven International Publishing, p. 15-27.

property with sentimental value for the dispossessed owners.[32] This underscores the special interests involved in claims over cultural objects.

Due to the lapse of the often short limitation periods, post-War restitution laws hardly play a role in today's practice. At times they do, as in French litigation about a Pissarro painting that had been confiscated from a Jewish collector and, eventually, was found in the hands of an American collector who had acquired it in the 1990s, unaware of its provenance.[33] Since the original confiscation was void, under application of French law legal title had remained with the pre-War owner and, thus, the claim by the heirs for restitution could be awarded. At the time of writing, this outcome is being challenged before the European Court of Human Rights by the American collectors for a violation of their right to property, not having received any compensation.[34] This underscores the potential for human rights law to develop this field further. At the same time, it highlights the weakness of the zero-sum outcome in an ownership approach – as it caters for only one absolute right holder (the lawful owner) whilst, over time, more parties may surface with legitimate interests.

Under positive private law, claims to Nazi-looted art are usually 'stale' due to the time that passed since their loss. In reaction to the apparent injustice this causes for deprived families whose paintings re-appeared on museum walls, in 1998 over 40 states adopted the non-binding Washington Conference Principles on Nazi-Confiscated Art. They introduced the, by now, internationally recognised standard for claims that former owners or their heirs are entitled to a 'just and fair solution', recognising this may vary according to the 'facts and circumstances surrounding a specific case'.[35] Along with later instruments, they furthermore stress the importance of ADR for resolving claims: the ethical model for claims.

Whilst it is clear that the 'just and fair' rule calls for redress for dispossessed families that lost their artefacts as a result of Nazi-looting, what it means *exactly* is less clear, even - or perhaps even more so - after almost twenty-five years. My hypothesis is that the rule has two pillars. First, the fact that it concerns personal *cultural* property justifies a special, favourable, treatment. Looted heirlooms that symbolise a (lost) family life are not merely stolen possessions or commodities, and therefore impediments under regular private law to claims should not apply equally. Second, the rule for Nazi-looted art

32 At least in some of the laws. Chapter 4, section 1; Further elaboration in Campfens (2020), p. 10.

33 *Bauer et al v B and R Toll* (2017) *Tribunal de Grande Instance de Paris*, No RG 17/58735 No 1/FF; confirmed *Cour de Cassation*, No B 18-25.695. Chapter 4, section 1.

34 Under Article 1 of the First Protocol to the European Convention on Human Rights. See <https://www.theartnewspaper.com/news/pissarro-european-court>.

35 Washington Conference Principles on Nazi-Confiscated Art (3 December 1998) released in connection with the Washington Conference on Holocaust-Era Assets, Washington, DC (Washington Principles) Principle VIII.

sees to *looted* art, implicating that it concerns involuntary losses such as confiscation, theft or sales under duress with a direct causal relationship with Nazi persecution. If these two elements are fulfilled, an equitable solution should follow; if not, a claim should be dismissed. What that equitable solution should entail – restitution of full ownership or another solution – depends on the circumstances of the case, most notably the due diligence of the new possessor on acquisition of the artefact (the provenance research performed) and compensation received for the loss at an earlier stage.

Nevertheless, international practice in this field is inconsistent and not transparent. Often, claims are settled confidentially on the occasion of an intended sale, which puts market parties at the fore. Settlements will then depend on the power relations between parties. Besides, the standards applied by European governmental panels differ considerably. Even where it concerns artefacts from the same collection that were lost in the exact same manner, outcomes are inconsistent.[36] An explanation for such differences by a comprehensible argumentation is also often lacking. This is problematic from the perspective of justice since 'just' would imply that similar cases are treated similarly, and disparities are comprehensible.

Given that private laws in most jurisdictions do not support ownership claims based on a loss so long ago, alternative procedures are often the *only* way to settle title claims. Around the turn of the millennium, several European countries installed governmental panels to review claims to Nazi-looted art in public collections. In countries such as France and the Netherlands, the focus originally was on so-called 'heirless art' collections, a term for artefacts left in the custody of governments since the post-War 'external restitution' programme. In such cases the interests of the present possessor (i.e. the state that received these as a custodian) obviously are not, or should not be, an issue.[37] Yet, in other instances the interests of new possessors would seem legitimate if these new possessors were unaware of the 'tainted' provenance upon acquisition and they gained valid ownership title under domestic private law. The Dutch Restitutions Committee upon weighing the interests of new possessors,

36 This mostly surfaces in the categories of 'early' sales or so-called *Fluchtgut*, see Chapter 4, sections 3.2.2 and 3.2.3. See also M. Weller 'In search of 'just and fair' solutions: Towards the future of the Washington Principles of Nazi-confiscated art' and C. Woodhead 'Action towards consistent 'just and fair' solutions', both in the publication *Guide to the work of the Restitutions Committees* (2019) CIVS.

37 The agreement for delivery reads: 'the said Government hereby agrees … as custodians, pending the determination of the lawful owners …'; NARA M1941, Records Covering the Central Collecting Points, (OMGUS Headquarters Records 1938-1951). See Chapter 4 section 1; further elaboration in Campfens (2020); E. Campfens, 'Sources of Inspiration: Old and New Rules for Looted Art' in E. Campfens (ed) *Fair and Just Solutions? Alternatives to Litigation in Nazi-Looted Art Disputes* (2015) Eleven International Publishing, p. 17.

nevertheless, came under strong criticism for doing so.[38] Also the German governmental panel, the *Beratende Kommission*, seems under constant criticism. Interventions by politicians in individual cases pending before these panels in both countries highlight the political dimension of these procedures.[39] From the point of view of justice, this also illustrates that an extra-legal model based on morality has its limits.

In terms of access to justice, the US system serves as the exception. As mentioned above, the US legal system is more open to claims by former owners. Besides, a law was introduced that extends limitation periods for claims to Nazi-looted art – enabling litigation on the merits even though under regular limitation periods claims would be stale.[40] This discrepancy has led to an increasing number of typically 'European' cases (that concern artefacts in European museums) being litigated before US courts.[41] By comparison to the European panels, however, US courts appear to use a narrower notion of what loss qualifies as 'Nazi loot'. Accordingly, claims to artefacts lost as a result of sales that were not under direct Nazi threat (i.e. without a direct causal relation) are denied by US courts, whilst similar claims are honoured by European panels.[42]

This appears to reflect the different settings. With the exception of the UK Spoliation Panel, the European governmental panels were primarily installed to compensate families of Nazi victims for injustice that the specific governments can be held responsible for, either by being the successor to a Nazi (affiliated) government or by a failure to return the repatriated artefacts that became part of state collections to the rightful owners in time. In other words, different *rationales* for redress operate in this field. On the one hand, for example in the case law in the US, it concerns the recognition and reparation of the dispossessed owner's (or their heirs') lawful title with regard to a specific artefact, irrespective of in whose hands it is found (i.e. a right *in rem*). On the other hand, in the Dutch or German setting, this reparation extends to com-

38 Heavily criticised was the recommendation regarding a Kandinsky where the outcome relied on the value of the painting for the museum (RC 3.141). See Chapter 4, section 3.4.2. Subsequently, in 2020, a new policy was introduced that basically denounces the weighing of interests. See <https://www.raadvoorcultuur.nl/english/documenten/adviezen/2020/12/07/striving-for-justice>. See also T. Oost 'From "Leader to Pariah"? On the Dutch Restitutions Committee and the inclusion of the public interest in assessing Nazi-spoliated art claims', *International Journal of Cultural Property* (2021), 1-31.

39 E.g. Letter of the Mayor and Aldermen to the Amsterdam Municipal Council of 19 February 2021, see <https://amsterdam.raadsinformatie.nl/modules/1/Berichten%20uit%20het%20college/651069>, acc. 5 August 2021. As to political interference in individual cases in Germany, see <https://www.sueddeutsche.de/kultur/limbach-kommission-raubkunst-monika-gruetters-restitution-1.5218083>.

40 The Holocaust Expropriated Art Recovery Act of 2016, see Chapter 4, section 4.3.1.

41 Chapter 4, section 4.3.2. More cases have followed since.

42 Chapter 4, sections 3.2.2 and 3.2.3. Litigation in the US often then revolves around technical issues such as jurisdiction and immunity, prescription and the equitable defense of latches (requiring a dispossessed owner to be duly diligent in searching for their artefacts).

pensation for injustices afflicted on the persecuted owners that is not specifically related to the cultural object at stake. In these countries the governmental panels honoured, for example, claims regarding artefacts that were not even owned by the family to whom these were 'returned',[43] or that were sold in a neutral country for market value in seemingly voluntary transactions,[44] losses that can hardly be qualified as 'Nazi loot'. Since the focus in this dissertation is on the (legal) status of cultural objects in relation to their former owners – not on reparation for victims of historical injustices more generally – the conclusions and proposals made in Chapter 6 and hereafter in section 3.1 relate to the first objective.

Apart from such differences, a general principle of law can be deducted from this practice of national courts and panels, namely that dispossessed owners of Nazi-looted art are entitled to equitable solutions with regard to their lost family heirlooms.[45] This rule increasingly resonates in (binding) domestic legislation that singles out Nazi-looted art as a special category (for which regular law does not equally apply),[46] has been embraced by the private sector in ethical codes, and is generally supported by legal scholars.[47]

---

43 E.g. *Beratende Kommission*, Recommendation of the Advisory Commission in the case of heirs of A. B. vs. Bavarian State Painting Collections (1 July 2020) concerning the restitution of the painting The Lemon Slice, that had been the collateral for a loan. Although it had never been owned by the predecessor in rights of the claimants, a Jewish banker, the claim was awarded 'to make a contribution toward the recognition and amendment of historical injustice'.

44 Chapter 4, sections 3.2.3. for Dutch and German restitutions concerning so-called *Fluchtgut.*

45 Lubina concludes that no rule of customary rule for the return of Nazi spoliated art (respectively human remains) exists, although she admits to 'a general trend to facilitate returns.' KRM Lubina, *Contested Cultural Property. The Return of Nazi Spoliated Art and Human Remains from Public Collections* (2009) (doctoral thesis) Maastricht, p. 460. Cf. B. Schönenberger (2009), p. 285. Ten years later, state practice has intensified. For a customary rule, however, the threshold is high. *Opinio juris* that this rule concerns a legal obligation, arguably, is still insufficient.

46 See Chapter 4, section 4.3.1 on the US HEAR Act and other US laws exempting Nazi looted art from other movable goods in order to allow access for justice for claimants. Other examples are the UK *Holocaust (Return of Cultural Objects) Act 2009* - allowing for the de-accessioning of Nazi looted art from public museums -; and section 44 of the *German Cultural Property Protection Act* of 31 July 2016, that provides for enhanced due diligence standards to ascertain artefacts were not lost due to Nazi persecution.

47 E.g. E. Jayme, 'Human Rights and Restitution of Nazi-Confiscated Artworks from Public Museums: The Altmann Case as a Model for Uniform Rules?' (2006) 11 *Uniform Law Review* 393. Van Woudenberg takes the view that cases involving Holocaust confiscated art involve a 'serious breach of an obligation arising under a peremptory norm of general international law' (N. van Woudenberg, 'Developments Concerning Immunity from Seizure for Cultural State Property on Loan' in A.M. Carstens, E. Varner (eds) *Intersections in international cultural heritage law* (2020) OUP, p. 363). Since domestic takings (i.e. Nazi-confiscations of Jewish property in Germany or in France by the Vichy Government) are generally 'off limits' under (traditional) international law, an obligation, in my view, can only be based on international human righs law. The rule that Nazi-looted art should be returned is mostly taken for granted, at times under referral to the 1943 Interallied Declaration. As discussed in Chapter

Without doubt, such practices contribute to the emergence of a general principle of international law. However, caution is needed as it does *not* extend to an obligation of restitution in full ownership, is mostly limited to Western-Europe and the US, and is often presented as merely 'moral' in nature. In that vein for example, Weller concludes that, usually, no legal claims exist, and, moreover, that this cannot be remedied by (retroactive) legislation.[48] Whilst that may be the correct view in as far as it concerns a right to the restitution of full ownership under private law, legal obligations or rights (not to full ownership but to an equitable solution) may also follow from other norms such as international human rights law – the view advocated in this dissertation.

In summary, from Chapter 4 it became clear that, at least in Western Europe, the legal model for dispute resolution in the field of Nazi-looted art (both the interstate and the post-War model for private claims) has been mostly superseded by the ethical model, at least in Western-European civil law countries. Market forces and politics set the tone in that model. To address the interests of former owners more efficiently, standards need to be clarified and neutral claims procedures – with guarantees in terms of due process – should be more widely available.

2.4 Colonial looting and indigenous peoples' lost cultural objects

Chapter 5 addressed colonial looting, a category with similarities to Nazi-looted art: neither category is covered by modern-day treaties in this field. For Nazi-looted art, however, the rule that cultural objects removed from the territory of an occupied state should be returned was (and is) widely acknowledged. Moreover, on the sub-state level, private claims were covered by special restitution laws in the post-War period and, today, by the ethical model. This contrasts sharply with the framework for cultural losses in a colonial setting. In order to understand these differences, this chapter took a closer look at the development of international law in the field of heritage protection. Given the broad notion of 'colonial looting', the discussion in Chapter 5 focussed on a case example concerning the loss of an ancestral statue by the indigenous Bangwa people in the course of the colonial annexation of an area in West Africa in today's Cameroon in 1899.

---

4 this declaration was an official warning that acquisitions by the Nazis in occupied territories (not in Germany) *would* be voided, and be seen as a legal basis for internatonal law obligations with regard to confiscated private property in Germany.

48 As this would violate other fundamental rights (and the prohibition to expropriate new owners without compensation). M. Weller,'Study … (2017), p. 100. He therefore proposes stricter due diligence standards and a refinement of the 'ethical model' by EU funding of a restatement of restitution principles. However useful, in my view an extra-legal model based on morality fails to address the problem of access to justice.

Cultural objects have a protected status in international law because of their intangible value to people, as symbols of an identity. Precisely that identity is often targeted in looting practices. That was the case with Nazi looting, and similarly racial discrimination instigated the looting in colonial settings.[49] Looting may be as old as history, the notion that harming other people's cultural objects is 'uncivilized', is also remarkably old. Cicero in his Verrines argues, for example, that while pillage was allowed, an honourable Roman should show respect for the material culture of defeated people. Through the writings of Grotius, De Vattel, and others, and through a series of peace treaties, this notion gained legal importance. The 1815 Treaty of Paris, arranging for the restitution of artefacts after Napoleon's defeat on the basis of territoriality, is generally seen as a key moment in this development. On that occasion, return of cultural objects on the basis of territoriality after their removal in times of foreign occupation was acknowledged as a 'principle of justice amongst civilized nations'.

This process continued in the 19th century, to be codified in the Hague Regulations concerning the Laws and Customs of War on Land of 1899 that prescribed that 'All seizure of [...] works of art or science, is prohibited, and should be made the subject of proceedings'.[50] Eventually, the 1954 UNESCO Convention confirmed that cultural objects removed in violation of the prohibition to seize cultural objects in times of armed conflict may never be retained, as also discussed in Chapter 3.

This means that seizure of artefacts in the course of military actions at the close of the 19th century was unlawful by contemporary (European) standards of international law. When *exactly* this rule is to be considered as having status of customary international law is a matter of scholarly debate; some argue this was the case at the close of the 18th century, others later.[51] Nevertheless, such standards were only applied among a small group of 'civilized nations'. Yet territories such as those in West Africa were considered 'terra nullius'.[52] In that vein, colonial powers had arranged for the division of Africa at the Berlin Conference on West Africa in 1884-85, justifying the appropriation of land and resources by relying on their religious duty to spread the 'blessings of civilization'.[53] Although this may explain the events at the time, that line

49 Chapter 5, section 3.2.

50 Convention (II) with Respect to the Laws and Customs of War on Land and its annex: Regulations Concerning the Laws and Customs of War on Land (1899) 32 Stat. 1803. Repeated in the 1907 version of the Regulations (Convention (IV) respecting the Laws and Customs of War on Land and its annex: Regulations concerning the Laws and Customs of War on Land 205 CTS 277).

51 Chapter 5, section 3.5.

52 Chapter 5, section 2.2.

53 General Act of the Berlin Conference on West Africa (1885), Art. 6: 'All the Powers ... bind themselves ... to care for the improvement of the conditions of their moral and material well-being. ... They shall ... protect and favour all religious, scientific or charitable institutions and undertakings ... which aim at instructing the natives and bringing home to them the

of argumentation can hardly be used as justification for acts with a continuing effect today – such as looting and holding on to cultural objects.[54] For cultural objects that were taken in violation of international law and are still in the hands of the state responsible for that violation (e.g. booty taken during colonial punitive actions at the close of the 19th century), reparations are warranted. In this respect, Article 14(2) ARSIWA clarifies that a 'breach of an international obligation by an act of a state having a continuing character extends over the entire period during which the act continues and remains not in conformity with the international obligation.'[55] Nevertheless, as discussed in Chapter 5, claims based on the unlawfulness of the taking in the past will encounter many legal obstacles in terms of access to justice, for source communities.

Return of cultural objects after decolonisation may also fit in with concepts of state succession and self-determination, as argued by Vrdoljak and Jakubowski.[56] After the dissolution of the Austrian-Hungarian empire in Europe, for example, cultural objects were redistributed to successor states on the basis of territorial provenance. In that spirit, the 1973 UN General Assembly Resolution 'on restitution of works of art to countries victim of expropriation' seemed indeed promising for former colonies that had gained independence.[57] It linked the return of cultural objects to the right to self-determination, as a necessary element for the cultural development of new states. The 1975 Dutch-Indonesian agreement to return certain cultural objects 'directly linked with persons of major historical and cultural importance or with crucial historical events' may be seen in that light.[58] Similarly, the 2008 Italian return to Libya of the so-called Venus of Cyrene confirms that outlook. The return was based on a ruling by the Italian supreme administrative court, stating that the right of self-determination of former colonies implicates that cultural objects removed from these territories should be returned to the people they came from.[59]

On the whole, however, former colonial powers did not accept legal obligations in this respect, and did not return dispersed cultural objects. Hence, a separation between two scenarios of return of dispersed cultural objects became the legal reality. Colonial losses were to be discussed as a matter of 'return'

blessings of civilization.'

54 See *Western Sahara* (Advisory Opinion) ICJ Rep 1975, 79; Chapter 5, section 3.5.

55 See Chapter 1, section 2.3.3.

56 Chapter 5, section 3.6.

57 UNGA Res. 3187 (18 December 1973) UN Doc A/RES/3187 (XXVIII); Chapter 5, section 3.6.

58 Joint Recommendations by the Dutch and Indonesian Team of Experts concerning Cultural Cooperation in the Field of Museums and Archives including Transfers of Objects (22 November 1975, Archive of the Ministry of Foreign Affairs 1975-1984, inv. No. 10266); Chapter 5, section 3.2.

59 *Associazione nazionale Italia Nostra Onlus c Ministero per i beni e le attività culturali et al.* (23 June 2008) Consiglio di Stato, No. 3154; Chapter 5, section 3.6.

on moral grounds – in the setting of the UNESCO Intergovernmental Committee for Promoting the Return of Cultural Property to its Countries of Origin or Its Restitution in Case of Illicit Appropriation (ICPRCP) – as opposed to restitution on legal grounds in the European context (e.g. the external restitution process after the Second World War). The 2002 Declaration on the Value and Importance of Universal Museums highlights the long-prevailing paradigm that it is in the best interest of civilisation that former colonial powers remain in custody of the cultural objects of their former colonies.[60]

Over the last years, this status quo is being challenged by a change in public opinion reflected in soft-law and museum policy guidelines. The 2015 UNESCO Museum Declaration for example urges member states to take appropriate measures to encourage and facilitate dialogue between museums and indigenous peoples concerning the management of those collections and, where appropriate, facilitate return or restitution.[61] This trend extends to non-indigenous source communities.

Human rights law instruments mirror this development. Of particular importance to the category of colonial losses is the 2007 UN Declaration on the Rights of Indigenous Peoples (UNDRIP).[62] It contains a right of redress with respect to cultural objects taken without the 'free, prior and informed consent' of indigenous peoples.[63] Depending on the cultural importance of the object at stake, redress may vary from a right to 'access and control' to a straightforward right to repatriation of human remains.[64] To fulfil this aim, states are expected to provide assistance – 'effective mechanisms in conjunction with indigenous peoples' – in addressing claims. These provisions of the UNDRIP are considered the implementation of the human right to culture in Article 15(1)(a) of the International Covenant on Economic, Social and Cultural Rights in as far as it concerns indigenous peoples' cultural heritage.[65] Though the UNDRIP started out as a non-binding declaration, these provisions on the cultural rights of indigenous peoples therefore gained strong legal status. Moreover, they are considered by some to have crystallised into principles of customary international law.[66]

---

60 Chapter 5, section 3.6.

61 UNESCO Museum Recommendation, adopted by the General Conference at its 38th session (17 November 2015) Doc 38 C/25, at 18; Chapter 5, sections 4.1 and 4.2.

62 Chapter 5, section 4.5.

63 Article 11(2) of UNDRIP defines this as 'redress through effective mechanisms, which may include restitution, developed in conjunction with indigenous peoples, with respect to their cultural, intellectual, religious and spiritual property taken without their free, prior and informed consent or in violation of their laws, traditions and customs.'

64 Article 12 deals with rights to objects of special importance – namely, a right to 'use and control' where it concerns lost ceremonial objects, while for human remains a straightforward right to repatriation applies

65 Committee on Economic, Social and Cultural Rights, General Comment No 21 (2009) E/C.12/GC/21.

66 See Chapter 5, section 4.5.2. and Chapter 6, section 5.2.4.

In this light, recent initiatives in Western-European countries to establish procedures in the museum sector to address claims to colonial takings can be seen as the fulfilment of an international obligation in as far as it concerns indigenous peoples' lost cultural objects.[67] For such claims, standards are provided in UNDRIP. This implicates for example that indigenous communities should be allowed to independently file claims - irrespective of the support of governments of their home states.[68]

Notwithstanding the difficulties for indigenous communities to reclaim their lost cultural objects in foreign museums in terms of access to justice, claims do find their way to courts. One roadmap on how to proceed was given in a 2017 Colombian verdict.[69] In its ruling, the court ordered the Colombian government to pursue the return by Spain of a treasure taken at the close of the 19th century, on behalf of the indigenous Quimbaya people. The argumentation was that by today's standards of international law – referring to UNDRIP, but interestingly also to the 1970 UNESCO Convention and the 1995 UNIDROIT Convention – indigenous peoples are entitled to their lost cultural objects.

Such developments, in combination with recent government policies in Western Europe that enable the return of cultural objects to source communities, and (older) policies and laws to that effect in settler states,[70] signal evolving law. Although the law is all but settled, these practices contribute to the emergence of international law obligations: it is evidence of *opinio juris* that the return of cultural objects to indigenous source communities is not merely a matter of political discretion, but a matter of justice and the law.[71]

In summary, contrary to the prevailing paradigm that no legal standards exist for cultural objects looted in a colonial setting, it can be concluded that a variety of standards are in place. A lack of political will by Western holding states is the explanation why claims have generally not been honoured in the past. Also for this category, however, the ethical model is gaining in import-

67 The 2020 Report of the Expert Mechanism on the Rights of Indigenous Peoples (A/HRC/45/35), at 87 and 92, concludes that 'States should enact or reform legislation on repatriation in accordance with [UNDRIP, *EC]* with the full and meaningful participation of indigenous peoples and the safeguard of free, prior and informed consent'; and that 'Museums, universities and other collecting institutions must become partners in ensuring that articles 11, 12 and 31 of the Declaration are respected and upheld. Museums must develop relationships of collaboration and trust, and seek out and respect indigenous peoples' knowledge, protocols, traditional laws and customs regarding items in their collections.'; V.M. Tünsmeyer, *Repatriation of sacred indigenous cultural heritage and the law: Lessons from the United States and Canada* (2020) Maastricht University, proposes the repatriation of indigenous sacred cultural heritage is an obligation following from Art. 27 ICCPR.

68 Especially in situations where national states may be seen as a 'colonial construct' this seems important.

69 *Judgment SU-649/17* (2017) Republic of Colombia, Constitutional Court; Chapter 5, section 4.5.4.

70 Such as NAGPRA in the US, see Chapter 5, section 4.5.3.

71 Cf. Article 38 of the Statute of the International Court of Justice international customary law pre-supposes an established practice and *opinio juris*.

ance. To address the interest of former owners more effectively, the human rights law model of UNDRIP is useful, also beyond the category of indigenous people's lost cultural objects. Since the notion of an indigenous people has (on purpose) not been strictly defined, it could – either directly or indirectly – provide for standards in cases that concern communal (often sacred) cultural objects. In this model, the focus is on: (i) a continuing cultural link (also: cultural affiliation) – not only on a loss in the past; (ii) on sub-state actors as independent right holders (indigenous peoples and communities); and (iii) on differentiated rights – of access, control or return – that depend on the identity value at stake.

2.5 Cross-border trade and claims: A synthesis

The last chapter zoomed out from specific categories and provided an analysis of the international framework for the cross-border trade in cultural objects and how it accounts for interests of former owners. In that sense, Chapter 6 is the synthesis of the preceding chapters. It included examples of more recent looting.

A first observation is that similar obstacles to claims arise in the various categories looked at in this thesis, including present-day looting. A striking example is the denial by a Dutch court of the claim by a Chinese community to a sacred Buddha statue with a mummified monk inside - known and revered to as Zhanggong-zushi –, that was stolen as recently as 1995.[72] It was found in the hands of a Dutch collector in 2014 who claimed ownership title under Dutch private law.[73] This is not unlike the outcomes of litigation over indigenous cultural objects lost in a colonial setting, or litigation over Nazi-looted art in civil law countries. An approach solely from the perspective of national ownership law that typifies such outcomes, nevertheless, is clearly at odds with the principles and *rationale* of heritage protection on the international level. This highlights a tension between cultural objects as heritage – symbolic of an identity – and cultural objects as possessions – representing economic interests and exclusive rights. It also illustrates a disconnect between norms on different levels: where international standards are unequivocal in the rule that title over looted cultural objects should not pass, domestic private law often appears not (yet) to be in line with those standards. This disconnect

72 *Village Communities of Yangchun and Dongpu v Van Overveem, Design & Consultancy BV, Design Consultancy Oscar van Overveem B.V.* (Judgment of 12 December 2018) Amsterdam District Court, Case No. C/13/609408, ECLI:NL:RBAMS:2018:8919.

73 The Netherlands only implemented the 1970 UNESCO Convention recently (2009). For a loss in 1995 regular private law would therefore apply (and a 20-years' period for acquisitive prescription). The claim was denied in a short ruling on the basis of a lack of standing of the Chinese communities. See Chapter 6, section 1.

is an incentive for the trade in looted artefacts and, in my view, the main reason why the interest of former owners are not addressed effectively.

Regulation of the international art trade is about finding a balance between the interests of free trade and the exchange of cultures on the one hand, and heritage interests that are worthy of protection, on the other. This regulation relies on the 1970 UNESCO Convention, introducing a system of export controls, and the 'national treasure' exception in both the GATT and TFEU free trade systems. In broad terms, it provides for a system where states designate protected cultural objects that cannot be freely traded – their national treasures, patrimony or national cultural heritage – and interstate cooperation following unauthorised export.

The most prominent blind spots in this system that were identified are: (1) that nationality is both inefficient and insufficient as a criterion for entitlement – and may have as an undesirable side effect the 'nationalisation' of cultural objects instead of fostering cultural diversity;[74] (2) that the position of sub-state rights holders such as communities and individual owners is not accounted for – and this clashes with other (more recent) regulations; and (3) that it only covers losses *after* their adoption and implementation in all countries involved – whilst claims concern past losses and market states only recently started to adopt the 1970 UNESCO Convention (and mostly did not accede to the 1995 UNIDROIT Convention).

This means that many categories of claims are *not* covered by these international treaties. Through trade and acquisition, ownership title can be (or has been) passed on to a new possessor, and objects are 'laundered' in civil law countries: the illegality of the looting simply does not 'stick' to the objects.[75] Often, the provenance of a specific object (its ownership history) is also omitted or unknown by new possessors along the line: the trade in unprovenanced cultural objects has been the rule rather than the exception for a long time, and is still common practice. With that reality in mind, solutions need to be found.

A first step to counter the illicit trade in the future is therefore to focus on the *possession* of looted artefacts and to oblige actors in the art world to abide by clear standards of due diligence: to only trade, buy, and possess objects that have a documented lawful provenance. The need for measures in that regard resonates even in the UN Security Council.[76] Such measures are indeed being adopted at present. On the regional level, the introduction

74 In this sense K.A. Appiah, 'Whose Culture Is It, Anyway?' in K.A. Appiah (ed) *Cosmopolitanism: Ethics in a World of Strangers* (2006) W.W. Norton & Company, 119. The patriotism involved in repatriation efforts by the Chinese government is also what Ai Wei Wei critiques with his 2010 'Circle of Zodiac Heads'. E. Wong 'Ai Weiwei's Animal Heads Offer Critique of Chinese Nationalism' (10 August 2016) *The New York Times*.

75 Chapter 6, section 2.2.1.

76 UNSC Res. 2347 (24 March 2017) UN Doc S/RES/2347; Chapter 1, section 2.3.1; Chapter 6, sections 2.2.1 and 3.2.1.

of the 2019 EU Import Regulation for example prohibits (as of December 2020) the *im*port of unlawfully *ex*ported cultural objects – independent of implementation of the 1970 UNESCO Convention in the countries in question.[77] This should force art market participants to be transparent and knowledgeable about the former history of objects, not merely as a matter of ethics but as a legal standard that can be enforced under penal law. Nevertheless, this will still not solve title issues: who should be seen as legitimate 'right holders' when ownership laws differ per jurisdiction?

Legitimate ownership under the private law of the country where an object ended up or was acquired as *the* criterion for contested cultural artefacts is being challenged by state practice and soft law instruments. In that respect, international standards slowly but steadily influence how courts adapt domestic private law rules to the specific field of cultural property, also in cases where such standards are not directly binding. The main principle of the 1995 UNIDROIT Convention, that stolen or unlawfully exported cultural objects – according to the law of the country of origin – should be returned and that only a new possessor who was duly diligent upon acquisition deserves (some) protection, is key in this regard.

The contours of such practice, where courts find ways to reach an outcome in line with international standards (that themselves may not be binding), by relying on open norms such as 'public policy' and the like, surfaced in case law discussed in this dissertation.[78] A noteworthy recent example is the 2020 Chinese *Zhanggong-zushi* ruling – a follow-up of the case mentioned above concerning a claim to a stolen sacred Buddha statue that was dismissed by a Dutch court in 2018.[79] After litigation in the Netherlands had stranded, the claim was pursued in China.[80] This time, the claim *was* awarded. Under reference to the object and purpose of the 1970 UNESCO and 1995 UNIDROIT

77 Regulation (EU) 2019/880 of 17 April 2019 on the introduction and the import of cultural goods (2019) OJ L 151. See also Chapter 1, section 2.3.1.

78 See Chapter 1, section 2.2; Chapter 6 sections 1, 3.1.2 and 5.4. Public policy was invoked in two UK cases concerning looted art, namely the *City of Gotha and Federal Republic of Germany v Sotheby's and Cobert Finance SA* (1998) No. 1993 C 3428 (QB) (See Chapter 1, section 2.2.1) and in *Government of the Islamic Republic of Iran v The Barakat Galleries Ltd.* (2007) EWCA Civ. 1374. In this last case the court enforced Iranian patrimony laws as 'it is certainly contrary to public policy for such claims to be shut out. There is international recognition that states should assist one another to prevent the unlawful removal of cultural objects ...' (paras 154-155). Another example is the German ruling *Allgemeine Versicherungs-gesellschaft v EK*, BGHZ 59, 82 (1972), in which an insurance contract (relating to unlawfully exported masks from Nigera) was deemed void on the basis of 'morality of the international trade in cultural goods', though Germany was no party to the 1970 UNESCO Convention at the time. More examples are given by Chechi (2014), p. 281.

79 *The Committee of Yunchun Village and the Committee Dongpu Village v. Oscar Van Overeem, Design & Consultancy B.V. and Design Consultancy Oscar van Overeem B.V.* (Judgment of 4 December 2020) Sanming Intermediate People's Court (2015) Sanmin Chuzi No. 626.

80 *Village Communities of Yangchun and Dongpu v Van Overveem, Design & Consultancy BV, Design Consultancy Oscar van Overveem B.V.* (Judgment of 12 December 2018), above n 29.

Conventions (neither of which applied directly to this case), the court held that in cases that concern cultural property, the law of the country where the object was stolen should govern the issue of ownership.[81] This meant that not Dutch law but Chinese law should apply and, accordingly, ownership could not have passed.[82] This indeed reflects the preferred international standard.[83] A special conflict of law rule for cultural objects, under which the law of the country of origin (the *lex originis*) or the law of the country where the loss occurred (the *lex furti*) governs the question of ownership, is generally acknowledged as an important tool to prevent the laundering of looted cultural objects in civil law countries.[84] In that sense, such practices signal the birth of a specialised conflict of law rule for cross-border title disputes over cultural objects and strengthen the principles containted in the 1995 UNIDROIT Convention.

Still, this does not solve title issues with regard to objects that were lost longer ago in civil law jurisdictions. Since that loss, innocent new possessors may have gained lawful ownership title and to retroactively void such title would challenge other settled rules of international law. More so than in cases that concern present-day looting where all participants of the art market should be aware of the need for due diligence standards before acquisition, in cases that concern older losses the legitimate interest of innocent third parties may be at stake. The proliferation of soft law instruments and private regulations, as discussed in the previous chapters, highlight the need for a legal framework also for these cases. Given that a zero-sum (ownership) approach is not particularly suited to those cases, another model is needed.

The 'humanization' of cultural heritage law, in that regard, offers prospects. Soft law instruments in this field generally aim at equitable solutions, depending on the significance of specific objects for the former owners. This attention for the social dimension of cultural objects and their intangible value for source

81 More precisely: the *lex rei sitae* - generally understood as the place where the object is at the time of the claim or the last transaction - was to be interpreted as the *lex furti* - the place where the misappropriation took place. H. Zhengxin, 'The Chinese villages win a lawsuit in China to repatriate a Mummified Buddha Statue hold by a Dutch Collector – What Role has Private International Law Played?' in *Conflict of Laws.net, Views and News in Private International Law* (12 December 2020). Quite another matter, of course, is how to enforce such a judgment.

82 An appeal is ongoing at the moment of writing. Information kindly provided by dr. Meng Yu from Bejing China University of Political Science and Law.

83 See Chapter 1, section 2.2 and Chapter 6, section 2.2.1. Such instruments are, e.g., the 1995 UNIDROIT Convention, Art. 3(2); Arts. 2, 3 and 4 the 1991 IDI Basel Resolution of the *Institut de Droit international*; Regulation (EU) 2019/880 of 17 April 2019 on the introduction and the import of cultural goods [2019] OJ L 151), Recital at (8); an example of domestic legislation is Article 90 of the Belgian Code of Private International Law (introducing the *lex furti*).

84 E.g. S.C. Symeonidis 'A Choice-of-Law Rule for Conflicts Involving Stolen Cultural Property' (2005) 38 *Vand. J. Transnat'l L.* 1177.

communities is mirrored in international cultural heritage law instruments.[85] In this sense, international cultural heritage law can be said to be evolving from a property-based framework towards a human rights framework. The 2005 Council of Europe Framework Convention on the Value of Cultural Heritage for Society (Faro Convention) is an example of this 'humanization', by defining cultural heritage as 'a group of resources inherited from the past which people identify, *independently of ownership*, as a reflection and expression of their constantly evolving values, beliefs, knowledge and traditions'.[86] As right holders, the Faro Convention introduces the notion of a 'heritage community', defined as 'people who value specific aspects of cultural heritage which they wish, within the framework of public action, to sustain and transmit to future generations'.[87] In as far as it concerns competing claims to heritage, it proposes 'equitable solutions' – similar to the norm in soft law instruments.

Extending a human rights law approach to the issue of contested cultural objects, this can be understood as the acknowledgement that communities or individuals may have rights with regard to cultural objects on the grounds of their specific intangible heritage interests. The right of access to one's culture, as developed in the realm of Article 15(1) ICESCR, plays a central role in this model. Remaining separated from certain objects, in this outlook, may then add up to a continuing human rights violation.

To disentangle the matter of title, the notion of 'heritage title' was introduced. It is based on the idea that specific heritage values – defined as a continuing cultural link – entitle people with rights to their lost cultural objects. On the basis of existing and evolving law, two types of heritage title can be distinguished. In the first place, source states are entitled to national cultural heritage if a continuing cultural link can be established. This type of heritage title is based on the traditional interstate model as codified in the 1954 and 1970 UNESCO Conventions and in the 1995 UNIDROIT Convention, and (directly) only applies after these treaties were adopted and implemented. Indirectly, however, this rule is gaining ground also for instances *not* covered by these treaties, especially where it concerns looted antiquities protected under patrimony laws in source states.[88]

The second type is heritage title that communities or individuals may have with regard to their lost cultural objects. In the context of this dissertation, this is the more important type as it codifies, so to speak, existing practice and soft law addressing sub-state right holders, and covers claims that current-

85 Chapter 6, section 5.1.

86 Framework Convention on the Value of Cultural Heritage for Society (adopted 27 October 2005) CETS No. 199 (emphasis added), Art. 6.

87 Faro Convention, Art. 2(b).

88 Chapter 6, section 4.3. See also *Government of the Islamic Republic of Iran v The Barakat Galleries Ltd.* (2007) EWCA Civ. 1374 and *United States v Schultz*, 178 F. Supp. 2d445 (SDNY 3 January 2002).

ly seem to be floating in a legal void.[89] The distinguishing feature of this model is that the focus is not on (restitution of) ownership rights, but on rights of access and control, depending on the heritage interests at stake – which obviously may add up to a right to return of the object to its original setting.[90]

Various human rights may inform heritage title.[91] Apart from the right to culture as a general basis for this model, the rights provided in UNDRIP are relevant for indigenous communities with regard to their cultural objects lost in a colonial setting, whereas the human right to property and respect for private and family life appear the logical base for heritage title individual owners may have with regard to their lost artefacts. Potentially, other human rights qualify to inform heritage title, depending on the type of object and identity values involved.

Heritage title that thus surfaces is based on a continuing cultural link and three elements shape its content.[92] First, not to be able to have access to, or control over, objects over which one has heritage title, implicates a continuing injustice of remaining separated from those objects. Such an approach brings with it a shift in focus from past events to present-day interests: not the unlawfulness of the loss in the past is decisive, but the continuing cultural affiliation today is key. Second, the rights involved are defined in terms of access, control, return, or 'equitable solutions', not in terms of absolute ownership. This enables the weighing, and ideally reconciliation, of competing (legitimate) interests that parties may have in the same cultural object – by aiming at creative and participatory solutions. It implicates a more social notion of ownership over cultural objects, where the content of ownership depends on possible (cultural) rights of others. A third element is that this focus on heritage interests enables the classification of (looted) cultural objects, depending on their specific social function. This means, for example, that sacred or other highly symbolic objects stand out on account of their identity value for specific people, whereas a painting that was produced for the market will not easily pass the test – unless it concerns a family heirloom that is symbolic for a (lost) family life.

Obviously, heritage title will often coincide with ownership title (of an individual, community or state) and, where this is the case, there is no need

89 Since such claims are often inadmissible in a 'regular' private law approach, mostly in civil law countries, as discussed in Chapter 2.

90 The suggestion of Appiah (elaborating on the notion of 'shared heritage') to constitute 'universal collections' and make these available in places that suffered from colonial looting – at the cost of former colonial powers – might be an example of a creative equitable solution. K.A. Appiah 'Cosmopolitanism and Cultural Heritage. Thomas Thiemeyer in conversation with Kwame Anthony Appiah' in Humboldt Forum *(Post)Colonialism and Cultural Heritage. International Debates at the Humboldt Forum* (2021) Hanser Verlag.

91 Chapter 6, section 5.2.

92 Chapter 6, section 5.3.

to rely on heritage title or human rights in title claims.[93] Conversely, where no heritage title surfaces, cases would fall under regular private law. However, in all those 'grey' categories of lawfully owned but unlawfully – or unjustly – lost cultural objects, heritage title could play a role. Irrespective of the ownership situation in a specific jurisdiction, it entitles former owners at the very least to rights of access to their cultural heritage and information about its provenance. Depending on the identity values involved, this may add up to a right of control or return in its original setting. According to rules already operative in the art world based on the principle set out in the 1995 UNIDROIT Convention, the new owner's position should depend on its due diligence on acquisition, most notably the provenance research performed. Although this model does not pretend to offer solutions for all the complexities that surround the field of looted art, it could be a step towards a more balanced and 'humanized' ownership concept with regard to cultural heritage, and one that takes better stock of the interests of former owners.

3 FURTHER CONSIDERATIONS AND PROPOSALS

3.1 Beyond ownership

This dissertation explored how cross-border claims to cultural objects fit in the wider legal framework, and how the interests of former owners could be addressed more effectively.

In the model developed in Chapter 6 a key insight was taken into account, namely that the intangible heritage value of cultural objects, that distinguishes them from other goods, is not sufficiently covered by a notion of ownership that entitles one right holder with exclusive rights.

Today, a number of treaties are in place that set the norm that looted cultural objects should be returned after involuntary loss. In order for this system to work well, and to avoid that they are passed on in ownership anyway – e.g. by omitting provenance details – the trade and import need to be regulated by a solid licensing system in combination with due diligence standards for the trade. That, however, by no means solves title issues with regard to objects that are already in circulation and were looted before these regulations came into force, or objects of which the exact provenance is unknown. A subsequent possessor, by now, may well have become the legitimate owner of such artefacts under application of private law rules, as has been illustrated throughout this study. Irrespective of such ownership title under domestic private law, soft law instruments and private regulations

93 It has become common for states to vest state ownership over vulnerable categories such as undiscovered (and therefore undocumented) archaeological finds: a claim to future losses may then rely on ownership title.

increasingly support former owners in their claims to their lost cultural objects. As a consequence, grey categories of tainted cultural objects have emerged that today can only be 'cleared' through extra-legal procedures: the ethical model for title disputes. In that approach, claims depend on the willingness of new possessors to relinquish their rights – who may be influenced by market forces or political pressure – whilst norms remain vague. Such a situation is prone to legal insecurity, ad-hoc political decisions and, at times, injustice.

To align the law in this field, it has often been suggested that states should adapt their private laws to ensure the restitution of cultural objects to the former ('rightful') owners.[94] However, it is unlikely that states – especially with a civil law tradition – would ever be willing to retroactively change their ownership laws that way as it would implicate the expropriation of new owners and, thus, the need for compensation of those new owners by these states - in accordance with settled norms of international law. Another obstacle in an ownership approach is that the unlawfulness of the loss is mostly decisive for claims. Although the *injustice* of a loss may be obvious in certain situations, a model that relies on the *unlawfulness* of a loss misses an essential point. Looting practices were at times undeniably unlawful – and in respect of colonial looting practices, this certainly has been insufficiently acknowledged – but not seldom the unlawfulness of a removal is not obvious at all, or simply undocumented. For these and other reasons discussed in this dissertation, a strict ownership approach appears not well suited as a general model for the problems at hand. Although the types of claims in this study vary, they also all share one commonality and that is that the interests at stake go beyond private ownership.

3.2 Heritage title

The better option that *was* explored, therefore, is to focus on the present-day interest of people in specific cultural objects as a base for entitlement. Accordingly, the notion of heritage title was introduced to capture the legal bond between people and cultural objects, apart from ownership. Although we are used to defining relationships between objects and people by way of ownership, its exclusivity and focus on economic aspects appear not to fit *cultural* property. Owners of protected cultural objects are not free to destroy or export these as this could be contrary to the (heritage) interests of the wider public: in international cultural heritage law preservation and accessibility are well accepted public interests that limit private ownership. Owners of cultural objects, in other words, at the same time should be seen as the custodians of cultural objects since these all make up the 'heritage of mankind'. This comes

94 Chapter 6, sections 2.1 and 2.2. Various soft-law declarations on Nazi-looted art suggest this (Chapter 4, section 4.2).

with obligations. Museums, for example, should research the history of their collections and ensure wide access to these collections, ideally also beyond the obvious places where universal museums already allow for such wide access.[95] Similarly, and more immediate, the (heritage) interests of former owners or creators may limit the rights of new owners. Original owners, in that perspective, retain certain rights over their lost cultural objects if there is a continuing cultural link. This notion is not unlike the artist's or author's moral right over its creation.[96] The notion of heritage title – based on a continuing cultural link –, in other words, builds further on the idea that owners of cultural objects are custodians of heritage of mankind, and also fits the (private law) notion that others that are intellectually linked to an object remain entitled to certain rights if it has passed in ownership to a new possessor. From different angles, these notions all centre around an ownership concept that is non-exclusive and comes with obligations.

The humanization of cultural heritage law more in general and the evolution of the right of access to one's culture in particular, appear to provide sufficient ground for the acknowledgement of a legal bond between people and their lost heritage if there is a continuing cultural link. As such, heritage title informed by human rights and internatonal law standards can act as a bridge between international public law and domestic private law.

Depending on the specific (domestic) situation, heritage title may be made operational either by relying on binding human rights, or on open norms that exist in all legal systems. As the *lingua franca*, international human rights law seems suited to further develop this field within the law, as it addresses both identity values as well as the right to property, is universal, and may penetrate and shape private law - the usual setting for title disputes. And although originally human rights law was thought to cover the relationship between a state and its own nationals, its broader scope as a standard for the conduct of a state in its relationship also with others (i.e. foreign claimants), by now seems well accepted.[97] Alternative dispute resolution and cultural diplomacy may at times be best equipped to solve disputes over contested cultural objects, however in the end, access to justice is key. This is not only needed in recognition of unequal power relations that obviously influence outcomes of voluntary procedures, but also in the understanding that precedents are needed to develop and clarify standards.

---

95 Cf., e.g., Appiah (n. 57).

96 See Berne Convention for the Protection of Literary and Artistic Works (1886) 828 UNTS 221, Art. 6 bis. These are linked to the person of the artist. In the proposed model, rights are linked to communities (or families).

97 On extra-territoriality, see e.g. Schuberth S, Tuchtfeld E, Lischewski I, Eschenhagen P, #3 Bindung an Menschenrechte im Ausland: So close, no matter how far?, Podcast (5 March 2021) *Völkerrechtsblog*; see also the acknowledgement that the private sector should adhere to human rights standards, Chapter 6, section 5.4.

3.3 An integrated approach

Since the administration of justice is a public task, governments should ensure that neutral procedures with guarantees in terms of due process are in place to effectively address the rights of dispossessed owners with regard to their lost cultural objects. Apart from the above proposal for conceptual changes that should ensure access to justice also for individuals and communities – which may resonate in the long run – this also calls for solutions in the short run.

As a result of the legislative action of the UN Security Council, protection of cultural heritage and prevention of the illicit trade have become a matter of global public policy. In the words of Jakubowski:

> 'Without doubt the protection of cultural heritage today constitutes a global imperative, calling for political, legal and technical cooperation among transnational actors, […]. However, the value of cultural heritage for global development, the maintenance of peace, and the protection of all human rights is hampered by the weaknesses of the existing legal mechanisms on the one hand, and the evolving multipolar and multilevel initiatives and programmes on the other. A more integrated approach and focused guidance are necessary.'[98]

That this is a widely-shared conviction is highlighted by the first-ever declaration on culture of the G20 of July 2021 that calls for harmonisation of regulation and enforcement to combat illicit trafficking by reference to the importance of cultural heritage for identity, social cohesion, peace and security.[99]

In a relatively short period, cultural heritage protection has thus become a matter of peace and security; of international criminal justice; of human rights; and is also listed as one of the overarching principles of the sustainable development of societies.[100] All this implicates that states are under the obligation to adopt measures to prevent looted cultural objects from freely circulating on their markets. Title issues can therefore no longer be dismissed as an internal matter that concerns domestic private law. One immediate consequence is that stricter (legal) standards for the 'lawful provenance' of cultural objects are being introduced. In that sense, in its 2017 Resolution the UN Security Council calls on states to adopt measures to prevent and counter the illicit trade and trafficking in cultural property 'which lack clearly documented and certified provenance', to allow for their eventual safe return.[101] It also urges states to adopt measures to engage 'museums, relevant business

98 A. Jakubowski, 'Resolution 2347: Mainstreaming the protection of cultural heritage at the global level' (2018) 48 Question of International Law 21, p. 32.
99 Rome Declaration of the G20 Ministers of Culture, adopted 30 July 2021.
100 Chapter 1, sections 1.3.1 and 2.3.4; Chapter 6, sections 2.2 and 5.1.
101 Above, n. 52, para. 8.

associations and antiquities market participants on standards of provenance documentation, differentiated due diligence and all measures to prevent the trade of stolen or illegally traded cultural property'.[102] The EU Import Regulation that prohibits the import of unlawfully exported cultural objects (as of December 2020) indeed relies on documentation to support the lawful provenance before an object may be imported.[103] Such binding regulations underscore the importance of provenance research, not merely as a matter of ethics as is the case in soft law instruments, but as a matter of criminal justice. Buyers, dealers, auction houses and museums must thus assure themselves not only of the authenticity of an object (is it real?) but also of its provenance (who were the previous owners and was it lawfully acquired?).

This has important ramifications for the possession of all sorts of cultural objects, not only antiquities that can be identified as coming from war-torn areas today.[104] Cultural objects with an incomplete provenance will surface as 'tainted', although it is unsettled what exactly a 'lawful' provenance is. Furthermore, no mechanisms are in place where parties can turn to for clarification of title issues as was demonstrated throughout this dissertation.[105]

In the first place, this calls for raising awareness about the illicit trade and (new) regulations, and education in international cultural heritage law. If consumers and professionals in the art world, or even law enforcers, are not aware of such regulations on the international level, it can hardly be expected that these will be followed up or enforced.

Furthermore, in light of the institutional vacuum in European jurisdictions for claims that regard losses that predate the implementation of international treaties, and the rise in litigation concerning 'European' cases in the US, in Chapters 2 and 4 the establishment of a European claims procedure was proposed.[106] This proposal gained urgency in the light of the recent regulations mentioned above: in the EU region, as a result of the 2019 EU Import Regulation. A pragmatic and integrated approach would be to set up an EU agency as a central coordinating office, or embed this task in an existing agency in a related field.[107] Logically, the licensing system envisaged in the 2019

102 Ibid., under 17(g).

103 Above, n. 53. The Regulation introduces a licensing system that will gradually become operational before June 2025. Chapter 1, section 1.3.1; Chapter 6, section 3.2.2.

104 Chapter 6, section 3.2.

105 E.g. Chapter 1 section 2.3.1; Chapter 6, section 3.2.

106 Chapter 2, section 5; Chapter 4, section 5.

107 For similar ideas see N. Palmer 'The best we can do? Exploring a collegiate approach to Holocaust-related claims' in E. Campfens (ed), *Fair and Just Solutions? Alternatives to Litigation in Nazi-Looted Art Disputes* (2015) Eleven International Publishing; M.A. Renold, 'Cross-Border Restitution Claims of Art Looted in Armed Conflicts and Wars and Alternatives to Court Litigations' (2016) European Parliament, Directorate General for Internal Policies, PE 556.947; M. Weller 'Study on the European added value of legislative action on cross-border restitution claims of works of art and cultural goods looted in armed conflicts and wars with special regard to aspects of private law, private international law and civil

EU Import Regulation – that should be operative by 2025 – needs to be accompanied by the establishment of a clearance system to address the problems that will surface with regard to cultural objects without a clear provenance. Such a system should provide for neutral and transparent procedures to assess title and provenance issues. Beyond acting as a clearance institute, such an organisation could serve as a central coordination and administration office for issues relating to due diligence and provenance – for example by setting up a publicly administered and accessible registration system similar to those in place in other fields (e.g. endangered species or precious metals), or even the setting up of a mandatory title insurance system to spread risks that, at times, are unequally divided.[108]

In sum, public guidance is needed for a successful transition from a market with many grey areas to a transparent and licit art market. Measures in that regard would not only serve the interests of former owners but *all* stakeholders. The main message is that the present institutional vacuum needs to be addressed not only by market parties or museums, but also by governments who have obligations in that regard under international law. Experiences in the field of Nazi-looted art underscore that the topic of cultural objects looted in the past is not a temporary 'problem'.

4 In conclusion

> *'One of the most noble incarnations of a people's genius is its cultural heritage. The vicissitudes of history have nevertheless robbed many peoples of this inheritance. They ... have not only been despoiled of ... masterpieces but (were) also robbed of a memory. ... These men and women have the right to recover these cultural assets which are part of their being.'*[109]

These words, spoken by Director General to UNESCO M'Bow in 1978, underline that the current attention for looted cultural objects is no whim of the day. In all places and at all times, cultural objects have inspired people and this was reason for their protected status, even if these were 'foreign'. In that vein, lawyers like Cicero and Grotius already argued that it is uncivilised to take what is of 'great worth' to others, but history has also shown us that rules

---

procedure', *Annex 1 to European Added Value Assessment* (2017) European Parliament Research Service, PE 610.998.

108 E.g. a transparency register for antiquities similar to the EU Transparency register, introduced in 2017 – in the context of the regulation on due diligence requirements for the trade in zinc, tungsten, tantalum and gold – as proposed in the ILLICID Report (2020), p. 12; On a mandatory insurance system, see J. Nathan, 'Mandatory Title Insurance for Cultural Property: A Solution for Claimants and Owners of Looted and Stolen Art' (2018) 23 *Art Antiquity & Law* 247.

109 A.M. M'Bow, 'A Plea for the Return of an Irreplaceable Cultural Heritage to Those Who Created It' (1978) <http://www.unesco.org/culture/laws/pdf/PealforReturn_DG_1978.pdf>.

for their protection do not prevent them from being looted after all. This has always been the case and has gained importance in this era of globalisation. Increased legislation at the international level and a rise of soft law underscore the importance attached to cultural heritage, not only in terms of its intrinsic value for humanity at large but also in terms of its specific value for community and family life, as symbols of an identity. Nevertheless, if tools are lacking to address such values at the level where disputes arise and are addressed – in domestic courts – this aspiration remains mere rhetoric.

The main finding in this dissertation was that although the heritage value of cultural objects generally lies at the core of claims, adequate legal tools to address these values are lacking. Entitlement to cultural objects is not merely a matter of domestic property law, but also a matter of heritage and international (cultural heritage and human rights) law. This means that even though ownership title passed under private law, former owners may still have rights over their lost cultural objects. To bridge the gap that presently exists between private law and public law the notion of heritage title was introduced in a human rights law approach to claims. This notion is based on: (i) the continued injustice of remaining separated from one's cultural heritage; (ii) the classification of cultural objects depending on their identity value to people; and (iii) rights that are defined in terms of access, return or equitable solutions. For quite some time, the traditional private law model to solve title issues over lost cultural objects – with a focus on ownership according to the law in the country where an object is situated – has come under pressure, and the same can be said for the interstate model – with its focus on the nationality of cultural objects. The proposed model reflects soft law, but may be based on binding human rights law norms that can be invoked in a court of law. Especially for historical losses, such a human rights' approach may offer tools to overcome obstacles former owners encounter in traditional approaches. In practice, heritage title may operate by reference to international standards that can enter a private law setting either by reliance on binding human rights law norms or through open norms that exist in all jurisdictions.

Furthermore, to address the shortcomings of the legal framework in the short run, awareness raising and education on cultural heritage law, and the setting up of a regional coordinating and clearance institute for objects that already circulate, are being proposed.

The main challenge throughout the dissertation was to identify rules that operate on different levels. That search was undertaken in various branches of the law and for various categories of looted art. This broad approach has resulted in insights, but also had its limits: certain relevant fields of law to the topic of looted art could not be addressed, such as the legal framework for reparations for historical injustice. The above proposals should therefore be understood as a way forward in the development of the law and as a basis for further legal analysis. An (extra-legal) ethical model, based on morality and a willingness of the parties to find solutions, is not a guarantee for justice.

In that sense, the role of the law is to ensure access to justice and provide a solid and predictable framework in which injustices can be addressed, similar cases can be dealt with similarly, and outcomes can be challenged.

Table of Instruments

List of Treaties and other International Instruments

Treaties

- 1815 Treaty of Paris.
- 1885 General Act of the Berlin Conference on West Africa.
- 1886 Berne Convention for the Protection of Literary and Artistic Works 828 UNTS 221.
- 1899 Convention (II) with Respect to the Laws and Customs of War on Land and its annex: Regulations Concerning the Laws and Customs of War on Land 32 Stat. 1803.
- 1907 Convention (IV) respecting the Laws and Customs of War on Land and its annex: Regulations concerning the Laws and Customs of War on Land 205 CTS 277.
- 1907 Convention (VIII) relative to the Laying of Automatic Submarine Contact Mines 205 CTS 331.
- 1919 Treaty of Versailles 225 CTS 188.
- 1919 Treaty of Peace Between the Principal Allied and Associated Powers and Austria Together With Protocol and Declarations, Saint-Germain-en-Laye, 226 CTS 8.
- 1944 Final Act of the United Nations Monetary and Financial Conference.
- 1945 Charter of the United Nations and Statute of the International Court of Justice 1 UNTS 16.
- 1945 Charter of the International Military Tribunal 82 UNTS 279.
- 1947 Treaty of Peace with Italy 49 UNTS 3.
- 1948 Convention on the Prevention and Punishment of the Crime of Genocide 78 UNTS 277.
- 1950 European Convention for the Protection of Human Rights and Fundamental Freedoms 213 UNTS 221.
- 1952 Protocol to the European Convention for the Protection of Human Rights and Fundamental Freedoms ETS 9.
- 1952 Convention on the Settlement of Matters Arising out of the War and the Occupation, as amended by the 1954 Protocol on the Termination of the Occupation Regime in the Federal Republic of Germany.
- 1954 Hague Convention for the Protection of Cultural Property in the Event of Armed Conflict 249 UNTS 240.
- 1954 First Protocol to the Convention for the Protection of Cultural Property in the Event of Armed Conflict 249 UNTS 358.
- 1966 International Covenant on Economic, Social and Cultural Rights 993 UNTS 3.
- 1966 International Covenant on Civil and Political Rights 999 UNTS 171.

- 1969 Vienna Convention on the Law of Treaties 1155 UNTS 331.
- 1970 UNESCO Convention on the Means of Prohibiting and Preventing the Illicit Import, Export and Transfer of Ownership of Cultural Property 823 UNTS 231.
- 1972 UNESCO Convention concerning the Protection of the World Cultural and Natural Heritage 1037 UNTS 151.
- 1979 Agreement Governing the Activities of States on the Moon and Other Celestial Bodies 1363 UNTS 3.
- 1981 African Charter on Human and Peoples' Rights 21 ILM 58.
- 1982 United Nations Convention on the Law of the Sea 1833 UNTS 397.
- 1989 International Labour Organization (ILO) Convention No 169 Concerning Indigenous and Tribal Peoples in Independent Countries 28 ILM 1382.
- 1994 General Agreement on Tariffs and Trade 1994 1867 UNTS 154.
- 1995 UNIDROIT Convention on Stolen or Illegally Exported Cultural Objects 2421 UNTS 457.
- 1999 Second Protocol to the Hague Convention for the Protection of Cultural Property in the Event of Armed Conflict 2253 UNTS 212.
- 2001 UNESCO Convention on the Protection of the Underwater Cultural Heritage 2562 UNTS 3.
- 2003 UNESCO Convention for the Safeguarding of the Intangible Cultural Heritage 2368 UNTS 3.
- 2005 UNESCO Convention on the Protection and Promotion of the Diversity of Cultural Expressions 2440 UNTS 311.
- 2005 Council of Europe Framework Convention on the Value of Cultural Heritage for Society CETS No. 199.
- 2008 Optional Protocol to the International Covenant on Economic, Social and Cultural Rights UN Doc A/RES/63/117.
- 2009 Consolidated Version of the Treaty on the Functioning of the European Union OJ C 326.
- 2009 Charter of Fundamental Rights of the European Union OJ C 364.
- 2017 Council of Europe Convention on Offences relating to Cultural Property CETS No. 221.

Other International Instruments

United Nations Security Council

- Resolution 1483 (22 May 2003) UN Doc S/RES/1483: The situation between Iraq and Kuwait.
- Resolution 2199 (12 February 2015) UN Doc S/RES/2199: Threats to international peace and security caused by terrorist acts.
- Resolution 2347 (24 March 2017) UN Doc S/RES/2347: Maintenance of international peace and security.

United Nations General Assembly

- Resolution 217 A (III) (10 December 1948): Universal Declaration of Human Rights.

- Resolution 3187 (18 December 1973) UN Doc A/RES/3187 (XXVIII): Restitution of works of art to countries victims of expropriation.
- Resolution 3391 (19 November 1975) UN Doc A/RES/3391 (XXX): Restitution of works of art to countries victims of expropriation.
- Resolution 31/40 (30 November 1976) UN Doc A/RES/31/40: Protection and restitution of works of art as part of the preservation and further development of cultural values.
- Resolution 32/18 (11 November 1977) UN Doc A/RES/32/18: Restitution of works of art to countries victims of expropriation.
- Resolution 33/50 (14 December 1978) UN Doc A/RES/32/18: Protection, restitution and return of cultural and artistic property as part of the preservation and further development of cultural values.
- Resolution 34/64 (29 November 1979) UN Doc A/RES/34/64: Return or restitution of cultural property to the countries of origin.
- Resolutions 35/128 (11 December 1980) UN Doc A/RES/35/128: Return or restitution of cultural property to its countries of origin.
- Resolution 36/64 (27 November 1981) UN Doc A/RES/36/64: Return or restitution of cultural property to the countries of origin.
- Resolution 38/34 (25 November 1983) UN Doc A/RES/38/34: Return or restitution of cultural property to the countries of origin.
- Resolution 40/19 (21 November 1985) UN Doc A/RES/40/19: Return or restitution of cultural property to the countries of origin.
- Resolution 42/7 (22 October 1987) UN Doc A/RES/42/7: Return or restitution of cultural property to the countries of origin.
- Resolution 44/18 (6 November 1989) UN Doc A/RES/44/18: Return or restitution of cultural property to the countries of origin.
- Resolution 46/10 (22 October 1991) UN Doc A/RES/46/10: Return or restitution of cultural property to the countries of origin.
- Resolution 48/15 (2 November 1993) UN Doc A/RES/48/15: Return or restitution of cultural property to the countries of origin.
- Resolution 50/56 (11 December 1995) UN Doc A/RES/50/56: Return or restitution of cultural property to the countries of origin
- Resolution 52/24 (25 November 1997) UN Doc A/RES/52/24: Return or restitution of cultural property to the countries of origin.
- Resolution 54/190 (17 December 1999) UN Doc A/RES/54/190: Return or restitution of cultural property to the countries of origin.
- Resolution 56/97 (14 December 2001) UN Doc A/RES/56/97: Return or restitution of cultural property to the countries of origin.
- Resolution 58/17 (3 December 2003), UN Doc A/RES/58/17: Return or restitution of cultural property to the countries of origin.
- Resolution 60/147 (16 December 2005) UN Doc A/RES/60/147: Basic Principles and Guidelines to a Remedy and Reparation for Victims of Gross Violations of International Human Rights Law and Serious Violations of International Humanitarian Law
- Resolution 61/52 (4 December 2006) UN Doc A/RES/61/52: Return or restitution of cultural property to the countries of origin.

- Resolution 61/295 (13 September 2007) UN Doc A/RES/61/295: United Nations Declaration on the Rights of Indigenous Peoples.
- Resolutionn 64/78 (7 December 2009) UN Doc A/RES/64/78: Return or restitution of cultural property to the countries of origin.
- Resolution 67/80 (12 December 2012) UN Doc A/RES/67/80: Return or restitution of cultural property to the countries of origin.
- Resolution 68/262 (27 March 2014) UN Doc A/RES/68/262: Territorial integrity of Ukraine.
- Resolution 69/196 (18 December 2014) UN Doc A/RES/69/196: International Guidelines for Crime Prevention and Criminal Justice Responses with Respect to Trafficking in Cultural Property and Other Related Offences.
- Resolution 70/76 (9 December 2015) UN Doc A/RES/70/76: Return or restitution of cultural property to the countries of origin.
- Resolution 70/1 (25 September 2015) UN Doc A/RES/70/1: Transforming our world: the 2030 Agenda for Sustainable Development.
- Resolution 73/130 (13 December 2018) UN Doc A/RES/73/130: Return or restitution of cultural property to the countries of origin.

International Law Commission of the United Nations

- Draft Articles on Responsibility of States for Internationally Wrongful Act (2001) UN Doc A/56/10.

United Nations Human Rights Council (resolutions and reports)

- Resolution 6/11 Protection of Cultural Heritage as an Important Component of the Promotion and Protection of Cultural Rights (28 September 2007) UN Doc A/HRC/RES/6/11.
- Shaheed F, 'Report of the independent expert in the field of cultural rights, Submitted Pursuant to Resolution 10/23 of the Human Rights Council' (22 March 2010) UN Doc A/HRC/14/36.
- Ruggie J, 'Guiding Principles on Business and Human Rights: Implementing the United Nations 'Protect, Respect and Remedy' Framework', Final Report (21 March 2011) UN Doc A/HRC/17/31.
- Shaheed F, 'Report of the independent expert in the field of cultural rights' (21 March 2011) UN Doc A/HRC/17/38.
- Expert Mechanism on the Rights of Indigenous Peoples, 'Role of languages and culture in the promotion and protection of the rights and identity of indigenous peoples' (16 August 2012) UN Doc A/HRC/21/53.
- Expert Mechanism on the Rights of Indigenous Peoples, 'Promotion and Protection of the Rights of indigenous Peoples with Respect to Their Cultural Heritage' (19 August 2015) UN Doc A/HRC/30/53.
- Resolution 33/20 on Cultural rights and the protection of cultural heritage (6 October 2016) UN Doc A/HRC/RES/33/20.
- Resolution 37/17 on Cultural rights and the protection of cultural heritage (9 April 2018) UN Doc A/HRC/RES/37/17.

- Expert Mechanism on the Rights of Indigenous Peoples, 'Repatriation of ceremonial objects, human remains and intangible cultural heritage under the United Nations Declaration on the Rights of Indigenous Peoples' (21 July 2020) UN Doc A/HRC/ 45/35.

United Nations Economic and Social Council

- Daes EI, 'Discrimination against Indigenous Peoples: Protection of the Heritage of Indigenous People', Final Report (1995) Doc E/CN.4/Sub.2/1995/26.
- Committee on Economic, Social and Cultural Rights, 'General Comment No. 21' (21 December 2009) UN Doc E/C.12/GC/21.

UNESCO

- Statutes of the Intergovernmental Committee for Promoting the Return of Cultural Property to its Countries of Origin or its Restitution in case of Illicit Appropriation (adopted 24 October-28 November 1978, amended October 2005) UNESCO Doc CLT/CH/INS-2005/21.
- International Code of Ethics for Dealers in Cultural Property (1999) UNESCO Doc CLT/CH/INS.06/25 REV.
- Universal Declaration on Cultural Diversity (2 November 2001) 31 C/Resolutions.
- Declaration Concerning the Intentional Destruction of Cultural Heritage, adopted by the General Conference at its 32nd session (17 October 2003) 32 C/Resolutions.
- Strategy to facilitate the restitution of stolen or illicitly exported cultural property (3-21 October 2005) 33 C/44.
- Draft of the Declaration of Principles Relating to Cultural Objects Displaced in connection with the Second World War (6-23 October 2009) 35 C/24.
- UNESCO-UNIDROIT Model Provisions on State's Ownership of Undiscovered Cultural Objects, drafted by the Expert Committee on State Ownership of Cultural Heritage (1 July 2011) CLT-2011/CONF.208/COM.17.5.
- Operational Guidelines for the Implementation of the Convention on the Means of Prohibiting and Preventing the Illicit Import, Export and Transfer of Ownership of Cultural Property (18-20 May 2015) C70/15/3.MSP/11.
- Recommendation concerning the Protection and Promotion of Museums and Collections, their Diversity and their Role in Society adopted by the General Conference at its 38th session (Paris, 17 November 2015) 38 C/25 (UNESCO Museum Recommendation).

OTHER INTERGOVERNMENTAL STANDARD-SETTING INSTRUMENTS

- International Declaration concerning the Laws and Customs of War (27 August 1874) (Brussels Declaration).
- Declaration of the Allied Nations against Acts of Dispossession Committed in Territories under Enemy Occupation and Control (5 January 1943) (London or Inter-allied Declaration).

- Washington Conference Principles on Nazi-Confiscated Art (3 December 1998) Released in connection with the Washington Conference on Holocaust-Era Assets, Washington, DC.
- Council of Europe, Resolution 1205 on Looted Jewish Cultural Property (5 November 1999) Doc 8563.
- Vilnius Forum Declaration on Holocaust Era Looted Cultural Assets (5 October 2000) (under the auspices of the Council of Europe).
- Terezin Declaration on Holocaust Era Assets and Related Issues (30 June 2009).

Standard-setting instruments of non-governmental organisations

- Institut de Droit international, 'The Laws of War on Land', Manual adopted at Oxford (1880).
- Institut de Droit International, 'The Inter-Temporal Problem in Public International Law', Resolution adopted at the Session of Wiesbaden (1975).
- Institut de Droit International, 'The International Sale of Works of Art from the Angle of the Protection of the Cultural Heritage', Resolution adopted at Basel (1991).
- International Council of Museum, 'ICOM Code of Ethics for Museums' (2004).
- International Law Association, Principles for Co-operation in the Mutual Protection and Transfer of Cultural Material (adopted 4-8 June 2006) Report of the Seventy-second Conference.
- International Law Association, 'Fragmentation of International Law: Difficulties arising from the diversification and expansion of international law' (2006) Report of the Study Group of the ILC, finalized by Koskenniemi M, UN Doc A/CN.4/L.682.
- International Law Association, 'Rights of Indigenous Peoples' (2010) Interim Report.

REGIONAL INSTRUMENTS

EU

- Council Regulation (EC) No 1210/2003 of 7 July 2003 concerning certain specific restrictions on economic and financial relations with Iraq and repealing Regulation (EC) No 2465/96.
- Council Regulation (EC) No 116/2009 of 18 December 2008 on the export of cultural goods (Codified version) OJ L 39.
- Council Regulation (EU) No 1332/2013 of 13 December 2013 amending Regulation (EU) No 36/2012 concerning restrictive measures in view of the situation in Syria.
- Directive 2014/60/EU of the European Parliament and of the Council of 15 May 2014 on the return of cultural objects unlawfully removed from the territory of a Member State and amending Regulation (EU) No 1024/2012 (Recast, 2014) OJ L 1159.
- European Parliament Resolution of 17 January 2019 on Cross-border Restitution Claims of Works of Art and Cultural Goods Looted in Armed Conflicts and Wars, 2017/2023 INI.

- Regulation (EU) 2019/880 of the European Parliament and of the Council of 17 April 2019 on the introduction and the import of cultural goods, OJ L 151.

BILATERAL INSTRUMENTS

- Joint Recommendations by the Dutch and Indonesian Team of Experts concerning Cultural Cooperation in the Field of Museums and Archives including Transfers of Objects (22 November 1975) Archive of the Ministry of Foreign Affairs 1975-1984, inv. No. 10266.
- Federal Republic of Germany/U.S. Department of State Joint Declaration Concerning the Implementation of the Washington Principles from 1998 (26 November 2018).

NATIONAL INSTRUMENTS

Austria

Art Restitution Act (1998) Federal Law Gazette I No. 181/1998.

Belgium

Belgium Code of Private International Law, 2004

China

Law of the People's Republic of China on Protection of Cultural Relics (adopted 19 November 1982, amended on 29 December 2007).

France

- French Civil Code (1804).
- Loi n° 2002-323 relative à la restitution par la France de la dépouille mortelle de Saartjie Baartman à l'Afrique du Sud (adopted 6 March 2002).
- Code du patrimoine (2004).
- Loi n° 2010-501 visant à autoriser la restitution par la France des têtes maories à la Nouvelle-Zélande et relative à la gestion des collections (1) (adopted 18 May 2010).
- Décret No. 2011-527 Portant publication de l'accord entre le Gouvernement de la République Française et le Gouvernement de la République de Corée relatif aux manuscrits royaux de la Dynastie Joseon (ensemble une annexe) (adopted 7 February 2011).

Germany

- 'Guidelines for German Museums. Care of Collections from Colonial Context' (2018) German Museums Association.

- Cultural Property Protection Act of 31 July 2016.
- 'Erste Eckpunkte zum Umgang mit Sammlungsgut aus Kolonialen Kontexten' (13 March 2019) Standing Conference of the Ministers of Education and Cultural Affairs of the Länder in the Federal Republic of Germany.
- *Beratende Kommission*, Guidelines for implementing by Statement by the Federal Government, the Länder and the national associations of local authorities on the tracing and return of Nazi-confiscated art, especially Jewish property, of December 1999 (New edition 2019).

Russia

- Federal Law on Cultural Valuables Displaced to the URSS as a Result of the Second World War and Located on the Territory of the Russian Federation (15 April 1998) No. 64-FZ.
- Federal Law of the Russian Federation of February 12, 2015 No. 9-FZ.

Switzerland

- Decree of 10 December 1945 concerning actions for the recovery of goods taken in occupied territories during the war, 15 Bundesblatt.

The Netherlands

- Besluit Rechtsverkeer in Oorlogstijd (7 June 1940) Staatsblad A6.
- Besluit Herstel Rechtsverkeer (17 September 1944) Staatsblad E100.
- Tractatenblad van het Koninkrijk der Nederlanden (1977) No. 40.
- Besluit Adviescommissie Restitutieverzoeken Cultuurgoederen en Tweede Wereldoorlog (16 November 2001) WJZ/2001/45374(8123).
- Ekkart Committee's Recommendations Regarding the Art Trade (2003).
- Parliamentary Documents, Kamerstuk 25839, No 38, Vergaderjaar 2005-2006.
- Parliamentary Documents, Kamerstuk 31255, No 3, Vergaderjaar 2007-2008.
- Act of 9 December 2015 Relating to the Combining and Amendment of Rules Regarding Cultural Heritage.
- Civil Code.
- Code of Civil Procedure.
- Netherlands Arbitration Institute, NAI Arbitration Rules and AiA/NAI Adjunct Arbitration Rules Combined (30 April 2018).
- Netherlands Arbitration Institute, NAI Mediation Rules and AiA/NAI Adjunct Mediation Rules Combined (1 January 2019).

The United States of America

- Instructions for the Government of Armies of the United States in the Field, General Orders No. 100 (adopted 24 April 1863).
- Law No. 59, Restitution of Identifiable Property of the Military Government for Germany, United States in United States Court of the Allied High Commission for Germany, *Court of Restitution Appeals Reports* (1951).

- Foreign Sovereign Immunities Act of 1976 (28 USC paras. 1330, 1332, 1391(f), 1441(d) and 1602-11).
- Native American Graves Protection and Repatriation Act of 16 November 1990 (25 USC paras. 3001).
- Guidelines on the Acquisition of Archaeological Material and Ancient Art of the US Association of Art Museum Directors (2013).
- Foreign Cultural Exchange Jurisdictional Immunity Clarification Act of 2016, 114th Congress, HR 6477.
- Holocaust Expropriated Art Recovery Act of 2016, 114th Congress, 2nd Session, S.2763.

United Kingdom of Great Britain and Northern Island

- Parliamentary Debates from the Year 1803 to the Present Time (1816) Published under the superintendence of T.C. Hansard, Vol 32.
- UK Holocaust (Return of Cultural Objects) Act 2009.

Ukraine

- Law of Ukraine 'On Museums and Museum Affairs' (29 June 1995) No 249/95-BP.
- Law of Ukraine 'On Exportation, Importation and Return of Cultural Values' (21 September 1999) No 1068-XIV.
- Order of the Cabinet of Ministers of Ukraine No 209 (2 February 2000).
- Law of Ukraine 'On Protection of Cultural Heritage' (8 June 2000) No 1805-III.
- Law of Ukraine 'On Protection of Archeological Heritage' (18 March 2004) No 1626-IV.
- Law of Ukraine 'On Securing the Rights and Freedoms of Citizens and Legal Regime on the Temporarily Occupied Territory of Ukraine' (15 April 2014) No 1207-VII.
- Order on Transfer of Museum Objects to the National Historical Museum of Ukraine No 292 (13 May 2014).

Table of Cases

INTERNATIONAL CASE LAW

- *Permanent Court of International Justice.*
- *Factory of Chorzow (Germany v Poland)*, Merits, 1928 PCIJ Series A No 17.

International Court of Justice

- *Application of the Convention on the Prevention and Punishment of the Crime of Genocide (Bosnia and Herzegovina v Serbia and Montenegro)* Judgment, ICJ Reports 2007, 43.
- *Certain Property (Liechtenstein v Germany)* Judgement, ICJ Reports 2005, 6.
- *Interhandel (Switzerland v United States of America)* Judgment, ICJ Reports 1959, 6.
- *Western Sahara*, Advisory Opinion, ICJ Reports 1975, 12.

International Criminal Court

- *Prosecutor v Ahmad al Faqi al Mahdi* (Judgment and Sentence) ICC-01/12–01/15-171 (27 September 2016).

European Court of Human Rights

- *Beyeler v Italy*, App no. 33202/96 (ECtHR, 5 January 2000).
- *Gasus Dosier- und Fördertechnik v the Netherlands*, App no. 15375/89 (ECtHR, 23 February 1995).
- *Nowakowski v Poland*, App no. 55167/11 (ECtHR, 24 July 2012).
- *Syllogos ton Athinaion v the United Kingdom*, App no. 48259/15 (ECtHR, 31 May 2016).

African Commission on Human and People's Right

- *Centre for Minority Rights Development (Kenya) and Minority Rights Group International (on Behalf of Endorois Welfare Council) v Kenya* (2010) African Commission on Human and People's Right, Communication No 276/2003.

Inter-American Court of Human Rights

- *Kaliña and Lokono Peoples v Suriname*, Merits, Reparations and Costs, Inter-American Court of Human Rights, Series C, No. 309 (Judgment of November 25, 2015).

Other Inter-State Arbitration

- *Island of Palmas (The Netherlands v USA)* (Arbitral Tribunal Award, 4 April 1928).
- *Maria V. Altmann and others v Republic of Austria* (Arbitral Award, 15 January 2004).
- *Maria V. Altmann and others v Republic of Austria* (Arbitral Award, 6 May 2004).

NATIONAL CASE LAW

Canada

- *Canada (Attorney General) v Heffel Gallery Limited* (16 April 2019) Federal Court of Appeal, 2019 FCA 82.

China

- *The Committee of Yunchun Village and the Committee Dongpu Village v. Oscar Van Overeem, Design & Consultancy B.V. and Design Consultancy Oscar van Overeem B.V.* (Judgment of 4 December 2020) Sanming Intermediate People's Court (2015) Sanmin Chuzi No. 626.

Colombia

- Judgment SU-649/17 (2017) Colombian Constitutional Court.

France

- *Association Survival International France v S.A.R.L. Néret-Minet Tessier Sarrou* (2013) *Tribunal de Grande Instance de Paris*, No RG 13/52880 BF/No 1.
- *Bauer et al v B and R Toll* (2017) *Tribunal de Grande Instance de Paris*, No RG 17/58735 No 1/FF.
- *De Keller v Maison de la Pensée Française* (12 July 1954) *Tribunal civil de la Seine*, 82 *Journal du Droit International (Clunet)*.
- *Gentili di Giuseppe et al v Musée du Louvre* (1999) Court of Appeal of Paris, 1st Division, Section A, No RG 1998/19209.

Germany

- *Allgemeine Versicherungsgesellschaft v EK* (1972) Federal Court of Justice, BGHZ 59, 82.
- *Hans Sachs Poster Collection* (2012) *Bundesgerichtshof*, V ZR 279/10.
- *Oberlandesgericht Frankfurt am Main* (2013) 16 U 161/11.
- *Landgericht Frankfurt am Main Urt* (2016) Az: 2-21 O 251/15.
- *Oberlandesgericht Frankfurt am Main* (2018) Az: 1 U 196/16.

German ADR procedures

- *Beratende Kommission*, First Recommendation of the Advisory Commission (12 January 2005) Nr. 19/05.
- *Beratende Kommission*, Recommendation of the Advisory Commission in the case of heirs of A. B. vs. Bavarian State Painting Collections (1 July 2020)
- *Beratende Kommission*, Recommendation of the Advisory Commission in the case of the heirs of Kurt and Else Grawi vs. Landeshauptstadt Düsseldorf (2021).
- *Beratende Kommission*, Recommendation of the Advisory Commission in the Matter of the Heirs of Alfred Flechtheim v Stiftung Kunstsammlung Nordrhein-Westfalen, Düsseldorf (21 March 2016).
- *Beratende Kommission*, Recommendation of the Advisory Commission on the Return of Cultural Property Seized as a Result of Nazi Persecution (9 April 2013).
- *Beratende Kommission*, Recommendation of the Advisory Commission regarding the Welfenschatz (2014).

India

- *Mullick v Mullick* (1925) Privy Council, LR LII Indian Appeals 245.

Italy

- *Associazione nazionale Italia Nostra Onlus c Ministero per i beni e le attività culturali et al.* (23 June 2008) Consiglio di Stato, No. 3154.

South Korea

- Daejeon District Court, 2017.1.26 Judgment, 2016 Gahap102119.

Switzerland

- *L. v Indictment Chamber of the Canton of Geneva* (1 April 1997) First Public Law Division.

The Netherlands

- *Autocephalous Greek Orthodox Church in Cyprus v Lans* (7 March 2002) The Hague Court of Appeal, Case No. 99/693, ECLI:NL:GHSGR:2002:6.
- *Land Sachsen* (8 May 1998) Hoge Raad, Case No. 16546, ECLI:NL:HR:1998:ZC2644.
- *Municipality Heusden v. Plaintifs* (24 Feburary 2017) Supreme Court of the Netherlands, ECLI:NL:HR:2017:309.
- *Plaintiffs v. Municipality of Amsterdam*, (16 December 2020), District Court Amsterdam, ECLI:NL:RBAMS:2020:6277.
- *Plaintiffs v. the Dutch State* (1 October 2019), Court of Appeals the Hague, ECLI:NL:GHDHA:2019:2524.
- Rechtbank Amsterdam (8 April 2015) Amsterdam District Court, Case No. C/13/577586/HA ZA 14–1179, ECLI:NL:RBAMS:2015:2000.

- Rechtbank Amsterdam (Judgment of 14 December 2016) Amsterdam District Court, Case No. C/13/577586/HA ZA 14–1179, ECLI:NL:RBAMS:2016:8264.
- Rechtbank Rotterdam (4 February 1999) District Court, Case No. 44053/HA ZA 96-2403.
- The Travida Central Museum, the Kerch Historical and Cultural Preserve, the Bakhchisaray History and Cultural State Preserve of the Republic of Crimea, the National Preserve of 'Tauric Chersonesos' v the State of Ukraine v University of Amsterdam (Interlocutory Judgment of 16 July 2019) Amsterdam Court of Appeal, Case No. 200.212.377/01, ECLI:NL:GHAMS:2019:2427.
- *Village Communities of Yangchun and Dongpu v Van Overveem, Design & Consultancy BV, Design Consultancy Oscar van Overveem B.V.* (Judgment of 12 December 2018) Amsterdam District Court, Case No. C/13/609408, ECLI:NL:RBAMS:2018:8919.

Dutch ADR procedures

- Amical Settlement between the Municipality of Amsterdam and the Malewicz heirs (24 April 2008) (on file with the author).
- Dutch Restitutions Committee, Binding advice on dispute over the painting Road to Calvary (2010) RC 3.95.
- Dutch Restitutions Committee, Binding opinion in the dispute on restitution of the painting entitled Christ and the Samaritan Woman at the Well by Bernardo Strozzi from the estate of Richard Semmel, currently owned by Museum de Fundatie (2013) RC 3.128.
- Dutch Restitutions Committee, Binding opinion in the dispute on restitution of the painting The Landing Stage by van Maarten Fransz van der Hulst from the estate of Richard Semmel, currently owned by Stichting Kunstbezit en Oudheden Groninger Museum (2013) RC 3.126.
- Dutch Restitutions Committee, Binding opinion regarding the dispute about restitution of the painting Painting with Houses by Wassily Kandinsky, currently in the possession of Amsterdam City Council (2018) RC 3.141.
- Dutch Restitutions Committee, Binding opinion regarding the dispute about the return of the painting Madonna and Child with Wild Roses by Jan van Scorel from the collection of Richard Semmel, currently in the possession of Utrecht City Council (2013) RC 3.131.
- Dutch Restitutions Committee, Binding Advice in the case *Bild mit Häusern* by Wassily Kandinsky (2018) RC 3.141.
- Dutch Restitutions Committee, Recommendation regarding a sculpture in Fritz Gutmann's collection (2011) RC 1.114-B.
- Dutch Restitutions Committee, Recommendation regarding Glaser (2010) RC 1.99.
- Dutch Restitutions Committee, Recommendation regarding Katz-A (2009) RC 1.90-A.
- Dutch Restitutions Committee, Recommendation Regarding Krasicki (2017) RC 1.152.
- Dutch Restitutions Committee, Recommendation regarding Mogrobi II (2015) RC 1.145.
- Dutch Restitutions Committee, Recommendation regarding Semmel (2009) RC 1.75.
- Dutch Restitutions Committee, Recommendation regarding Stern (2010) RC 1.96.

- Dutch Restitutions Committee, Recommendation regarding the application by the Amsterdamse Negotiatie Compagnie NV in Liquidation for the Restitution of 267 Works of Art from the Dutch National Art Collection (2005) RC 1.15.
- Dutch Restitutions Committee, Recommendation regarding the application for the restitution of fifteen objects of applied art from the trading stock of art dealership Kunsthandel Mozes Mogrobi (2007) RC 1.37.
- Dutch Restitutions Committee, Recommendation regarding the application for the restitution of Poultry by M. d'Hondecoeter and Saint Peter repentant by G. Reni (2006) RC 1.28.
- Dutch Restitutions Committee, Recommendation regarding Van Lier (2009) RC 1.87.
- Dutch Restitutions Committee, Recommendation regarding Von Goldschmidt-Rothschild (2012) RC 1.110.

The United States of America

- *Autocephalous Greek-Orthodox Church v. Goldberg & Feldman Fine Arts, Inc.* – 917 F.2d 278 (7th Cir. 1990).
- *Bakalar v Vavra* (17 August 2011) United States District Court for the Southern District of New York, 819 F. Supp 2d 293.
- *Bakalar v Vavra* (11 October 2012) United States Court of Appeals for the Second Circuit, No. 11-4042-cv.
- *Barnet et al. v Ministry of Culture & Sports of the Hellenic Republic* (9 June 2020) United States Court of Appeals, No. 19-2171-cv.
- *Cassirer v Kingdom of Spain* (12 August 2010) United States Court of Appeals for the Ninth Circuit, 616 F. 3d 1019.
- *Cassirer v Thyssen-Bornemisza Collection Foundation* (9 December 2013) United States Court of Appeals for the Ninth Circuit, 737 F. 3d 613.
- *Cassirer v Thyssen-Bornemisza Collection Foundation* (2015) United States District Court for the Central District of California, 153 F. Supp 3d 1148.
- *Cassirer v Thyssen-Bornemisza Collection Foundation* (10 July 2017) United States Court of Appeals for the Ninth Circuit, 862 F. 3d 951.
- *Cassirer v Thyssen-Bornemisza Collection Foundation* (30 April 2019) United States District Court for the Central District of California, No. 05-CV-03459.
- *David L. de Csepel et al. v Republic of Hungary et al.* (Memorandum Opinion, 14 March 2016) United States District Court for the Central District of Columbia, No. 10-1261 (ESH).
- *Detroit Institute of Arts v Ullin, Slip Copy* (31 March 2007) United States District Court for the Eastern District of Michigan, No. 06-10333.
- *Goodman (and Gutmann) v Searle* (1996) United States District Court for the Northern District of Illinois, No. 96C-6459.
- *Green et al v National Gallery of Art, London, American Friends of the National Gallery of Art, London, and Great Britain* (7 September 2016; Memorandum Opinion and Order 21 September 2017) United States District Court for the Southern District of New York, No. 1:16-CV-06978.
- *Hulton et al v Bayerische Gemäldesammlungen* (2016) United States District Court for the Southern District of New York, No. 16-CV-9360.
- *Jeanneret v Vichy* (1982) Court of Appeals for the Second Circuit, 693 F2d 259, 267.

- *Konowaloff v The Metropolitan Museum of Art* (18 December 2012) United States Court of Appeals for the Second Circuit, No. 11-4338.
- *Kunstsammlungen zu Weimar v Elicofon* (5 May 1982) United States Court of Appeals for the Second Circuit, 678 F2d 1150.
- *Lewenstein et al v Bayerische Landesbank* (2017) United States District Court for the Southern District of New York, No. 17-CV-0160.
- *Malewicz v City of Amsterdam* (30 March 2005) United States District Court for the District of Columbia, 362 F. Supp. 2d 298.
- *Malewicz v City of Amsterdam* (27 June 2007) United States District Court for the District of Columbia, 517 F. Supp. 2d 322.
- *Maria V. Altmann v Republic of Austria et al.* (9 May 2001) United States District Court for the Central District of California, 142 F. Supp. 2d 1187.
- *Maria V. Altmann v Republic of Austria et al.* (12 December 2002) United States Court of Appeals, 317 F. Supp. 3d 954, as amended, 327 F. Supp. 3d 1246 (2003).
- *Matter of Peters v Sotheby's Inc* (14 September 2006) Appellate Division of the Supreme Court of New York, First Department, NY Slip Op 6480 (34 AD3d 29).
- *Menzel v List* (10 February 1966) Supreme Court, New York County, 267 NYS 2d 804.
- *Menzel v List and Perls* (26 February 1969) New York Court of Appeals, No. 298 NYS 2d 979.
- *Philipp et al v Federal Republic of Germany et al* (2015) United States District Court for the District of Columbia, No. 1:15-CV-00266.
- *Philipp et al v Federal Republic of Germany* (2017) United States District Court for the District of Columbia, No. 15-266.
- *Philipp et al v Federal Republic of Germany* (2021) United States US Supreme Court, writ for certiorarim No. 19-351.
- *Reif v Nagy* (4 April 2018) Supreme Court of the state of New York County, No. 161799/2015.
- *Republic of Austria et al. v Maria V. Altmann* (7 June 2004) Supreme Court of the United States, 541 US 677.
- *Rosenberg v Seattle Art Museum and Knoedler-Modarco* (1999) United States District Court for the Western District of Washington, 42 F. Supp 2d 1029.
- *Schoeps et al v Freistaat Bayern* (Summary Order, 22 May 2015) United States Court of Appeals for the Second Circuit, No. 14-2739.
- *Schoeps et al v The Museum of Modern Art and The Solomon R Guggenheim Foundation* (Memorandum Order, 2 March 2009) United States District Court for the Southern District of New York, No. 07-Civ-11074 (JSR).
- *Silsbury v McCoon* (1 July 1850) New York Court of Appeals, 3 NY 379.
- *Simon v Republic of Hungary* (29 January 2016) United States Court of Appeals for the District of Columbia Circuit, No. 14-7082.
- *Stroganoff-Scherbatoff v Weldon* (18 May 1976) United States District Court for the Southern District of New York, 420 F. Supp 18.
- *Toledo Museum of Art v Claude George Ullin et al* (28 December 2006) United States District Court for the Northern District of Ohio, No. 3:06 CV 7031.
- *Toren v Federal Republic of Germany and Free State of Bavaria* (5 March 2014) United States District Court for the District of Columbia, No. 1:14-cv-00359-ABJ.

- *Toren v Federal Republic of Germany* (20 September 2016) United States District Court for the District of Columbia, No. 1:16-cv-01885.
- *United States v. McClain* 593 F2d 658 (5th Cir.1979)
- *United States v Portrait of Wally* (30 September 2009) United States District Court for the Southern District of New York, 663 F. Supp. 2d 232.
- *United States v Schultz* (3 January 2002) District Court for the Southern District of New York, 178 F. Supp. 2d445.
- *Von Saher v Norton Simon Museum of Art at Pasadena et al* (2016) United States District Court for the Central District of California, No. 2:07-cv-02866-JFW.
- *Von Saher v Norton Simon Museum of Art at Pasadena et al* (2019) United States Supreme Court, 587 U.S. 18-1057.
- *Zuckerman v The Metropolitan Museum of Art* (Complaint, 30 September 2016) United States District Court for the Southern District of New York, No. 1:16-cv-07665.
- *Zuckerman v The Metropolitan Museum of Art* (26 June 2019) United States Court of Appeals for the Second Circuit, No. 18-634.
- *Zuckerman v The Metropolitan Museum of Art* (2 March 2020) United States Supreme Court, No. 19-942.

United Kingdom of Great Britain and Northern Island

- *Attorney General of New Zealand v Ortiz* (1982) Court of Appeal, 3 All ER 432.
- *City of Gotha and Federal Republic of Germany v Sotheby's and Cobert Finance SA* (1998) High Court of Justice, No. 1993 C 3428; 1997 G 185.
- *Government of the Islamic Republic of Iran v The Barakat Galleries Ltd.* (2007) Court of Appeal, EWCA Civ. 1374.
- *Princess Paley Olga v Weisz* (1929) Court of Appeal, 1 KB 718.

British ADR procedures

- Report of the Spoliation Advisory Panel in Respect of a Painting Now in Possession of the Tate Gallery (18 January 2001) HC 111.
- Report of the Spoliation Advisory Panel in Respect of a renewed claim by the Metropolitan Chapter of Benevento for the return of the Beneventan Missal now in the possession of the British Library (15 September 2010) HC 448.
- Report of the Spoliation Advisory Panel in Respect of a 12th-Century Manuscript Now in the Possession of the British Library (23 March 2005) HC 406.
- Report of the Spoliation Advisory Panel in Respect of Eight Drawings Now in the Possession of the Samuel Courtauld Trust (24 June 2009) HC 757.
- Report of the Spoliation Advisory Panel in Respect of Fourteen Clocks and Watches Now in the Possession of the British Museum (7 March 2012) HC 1839.

Selected Bibliography

Books

Bazyler MJ, *Holocaust Justice: The Battle for Restitution in America's Courts* (2003) New York University Press.

Belder LPC, 'The Legal Protection of Cultural Heritage in International Law and Its Implementation in Dutch Law' (2014) Doctoral thesis, Universiteit Utrecht.

Bindenagel JD, *Washington Conference on Holocaust-Era Assets* (1999) US Government Printing Office, Washington DC.

Blake J, *International Cultural Heritage Law* (2015) Oxford University Press, Oxford.

Brain R, *The Bangwa of West Cameroon: A Brief Account of Their History and Culture* (1967) London University College.

Brain R, Pollock A, *Bangwa Funerary Sculpture* (1971) Gerald Duckworth & Company Limited, London.

Brodie N, Yates D (e.a.), *Illicit trade in cultural goods in Europe Characteristics, criminal justice responses and an analysis of the applicability of technologies in the combat against the trade: final report* (2019), European Commission.

Campfens E (ed), *Fair and Just Solutions? Alternatives to Litigation in Nazi-Looted Art Disputes* (2015) Eleven International Publishing.

Carstens A-M, Varner E (eds), *Intersections in International Cultural Heritage Law* (2020) Oxford University Press, Oxford.

Chechi A, *The Settlement of International Cultural Heritage Disputes* (2014) Oxford University Press, New York.

Cornu M, Fromageau J, Wallaert C, *Dictionnaire comparé du droit du patrimoine culturel* (2012) CNRS Éditions.

De Vattel E, *Le droit des gens ou Principes de la loi naturelle, Appliqués à la conduite et aux affaires des Nations & des Souverains* (1758) London.

De Visscher C, *International Protection of Works of Art and Historic Monuments* (1949) Department of State, Division of Publications, Office of Public Affairs, Washington DC.

Dromgoole S, *Underwater Cultural Heritage and International Law* (2013) Cambridge University Press, Cambridge.

Erdos A (ed), 'Museum. Return and restitution of cultural property' Vol 31, n°1 (1979) UNESCO, Paris.

Francioni F, Gordley J (eds), *Enforcing International Cultural Heritage Law* (2013) Oxford University Press.

Gazzini IF, *Cultural Property Disputes: The Role of Arbitration in Resolving Non-Contractual Disputes* (2004) Transnational Publishers.
Grotius H, *De Jure Belli Ac Pacis (On the Law of War and Peace)* (1625).

Halliday TC, Shaffer G (eds), *Transnational Legal Orders* (2015) Cambridge University Press, New York.
Hemeier B and Hilgert M, *Transparency, Provenance and Consumer Protection. Facts and Policy Recommendations Concerning the Trade in Ancient Cultural Property in Germany. Findings of the Federal Ministry of Education and Research's Collaborative Project «Analysing the Dark Figure as a Basis for Countering and Preventing Crime Using the Example of Ancient Cultural Property»* (ILLICID) (2020).
Henckaerts JM, Doswald-Beck L (eds), *Customary International Humanitarian Law* (2005) International Committee of the Red Cross, Cambridge University Press.
Hickley C, *The Munich Art Hoard: Hitler's Dealer and His Secret Legacy* (2015) Thames and Hudson.

Jakubowski A, *State Succession in Cultural Property* (2015) Oxford University Press.
Jakubowski A (ed), *Cultural rights as collective rights, an international law perspective* (2016) Brill, The Hague.

Kowalski WW, *Art Treasures and War* (1998) Institute of Art and Law.
Kuprecht K, *Indigenous Peoples' Cultural Property Claims* (2014) Springer International Publishing.

Leiris M, *Phantom Africa* (2017) Edwards BH tr, Seagull Books.
Liu Z, *Repatriation of cultural objects: The case of China* (2015), UVA-Dare (doctoral thesis).
Lixinski L, *International Heritage Law for Communities: Exclusion and Re-Imagination* (2019) Oxford University Press, New York.
Loth MA and Van Vliet LPW., *Recht over tijd. Hoever reikt het privaatrecht in het verleden? Preadviezen Nederlandse Vereniging voor Burgerlijk Recht* (2018) Zutphen
Lubina KRM, *Contested Cultural Property. The Return of Nazi Spoliated Art and Human Remains from Public Collections* (2009) (doctoral thesis) Maastricht

Muller E, Schretlen H, *Betwist Bezit* (2002) Waanders.

Négri V, *Legal study on the protection of cultural heritage through the resolutions of the Security Council of the United Nations* (2015) UNESCO #Unite4Heritage
Nicholas L, *The Rape of Europa* (1994) Alfred Knopf, New York.

O'Keefe PJ, *Protecting Cultural Objects: Before and After 1970* (2017) Institute of Art and Law.

Palmer N, *Museums and the Holocaust* (2000) Institute of Art and Law.
Peters R, 'Complementary and Alternative Mechanisms beyond Restitution: An Interest-oriented Approach to Resolving International Cultural Heritage Disputes' (Doctoral Thesis, European University Institute, Florence, 2011).

Prott LV (ed), *Witnesses to History: A compendium of documents and writings on the return of cultural objects* (2009) UNESCO, Paris.

Renold MA, Cross-Border Restitution Claims of Art Looted in Armed Conflicts and Wars and Alternatives to Court Litigations (2016) European Parliament, Directorate General for Internal Policies, PE 556.947.

Retél P, Vugts T (eds), *De Krim: Goud en geheimen van de Zwarte Zee* (2014) WBooks.

Robertson G, *Who Owns History? Elgin's Loot and the Case for Returning Plundered Treasure* (2019) Knopf Australia, Melbourne.

Sandholtz W, *Prohibiting Plunder: How Norms Change* (2007) Oxford University Press

Schönenberger B, *The Restitution of Cultural Assets* (2009) Eleven International Publishing.

Sjouke PS, *Het behoud van cultuurgoederen, twee werelden, twee visies* (1999) Ars Aequi Libri.

Sprankling JG, *The International Law of Property* (2014) Oxford University Press, New York.

Stamatoudi IA, *Cultural Property Law and Restitution. A Commentary to International Conventions and European Union Law* (2011) Edward Elgar Publishing Limited, Massachusetts.

Tünsmeyer VM, *Repatriation of sacred indigenous cultural heritage and the law: Lessons from the United States and Canada* (2020) Maastricht University.

Vadi V, Schneider H EGS (eds), *Art, Cultural Heritage and the Market. Ethical and Legal Issues* (2014) Springer.

Van Beurden JM, *Treasures in Trusted Hands: Negotiating the Future of Colonial Cultural Objects* (2017) Sidestone Press.

Van Mierlo AIM, Van Nispen CJJC (eds), *Tekst & Commentaar: Burgerlijke Rechtsvordering, zesde druk* (2014) Wolters Kluwer.

Van Woudenberg N, *State immunity and cultural objects on loan* (2012) Martinus Nijhoff Publishers, Leiden/Boston.

Veraart WJ, *Ontrechting en rechtsherstel in Nederland en Frankrijk in de jaren van bezetting en wederopbouw* (2005) Kluwer.

Vrdoljak AF, *International law, museums and the return of cultural objects* (2006) Cambridge University Press, Cambridge.

Weller M, *Study on the European added value of legislative action on cross-border restitution claims of works of art and cultural goods looted in armed conflicts and wars with special regard to aspects of private law, private international law and civil procedure, Annex 1 to Study European Added Value Assessment* (2017) European Parliament Research Service PE 610.998.

Xanthaki A, Valkonen S (eds), *Indigenous peoples' cultural heritage. Rights, debates, challenges* (2017) Brill Nijhof.

Yeide NH, Walsh A, Akinsha K, *The AAM Guide to Provenance Research* (2001) American Association of Museums, Washington DC.

Zeidler K, *Resitution of cultural property. Hard case, theory of argumentation, philosophy of law* (2016) Wolters Kluwer.

JOURNAL ARTICLES

Adler A, 'Expanding the Scope of Museums' Ethical Guidelines With Respect to Nazi-Looted Art: Incorporating Restitutions Claims Based on Private Sales Made as a Direct Result of Persecution' (2007) 14 International Journal of Cultural Property 57.

Alderman KL, 'The Human Right to Cultural Property' (2011) 20 Michigan State University College of Law International Law Review 69.

Bandle AL, Theurich S, 'Alternative Dispute Resolution and Art-Law – A New Research Project of the Geneva Art-Law Centre' (2011) 6 Journal of International Commercial Law and Technology 28.

Bauer AA, 'New ways of thinking about cultural property: a critical appraisal of the antiquities trade debates' (2007) 31 Fordham International Law Journal 690.

Campbell PB, 'The illicit antiquities trade as a transnational criminal network: characterizing and anticipating trafficking of cultural heritage' (2013) 20 International Journal of Cultural Property 113.

Campfens E, 'Nazi-looted art: a note in favour of clear standards and neutral procedures' (2017) 22 Art Antiquity and Law 315.

Campfens E, 'Whose cultural heritage? Crimean treasures at the crossroads of politics, law and ethics' (2017) 22 Art Antiquity and Law 193.

Campfens E, 'Restitution of looted art: what about access to justice?' (2019) 4 Santander Art and Culture Law Review 185.

Campfens E, 'The Bangwa Queen: Artefact or Heritage?' (2019) 26 International Journal of Cultural Property 75.

Campfens E, 'Bridging the gap between ethics and law: the Dutch framework for Nazi looted art' (2020) 25 Art Antiquity and Law 1.

Chamberlain K, 'Claude Cassirer v. Kingdom of Spain: The US Foreign Sovereign Immunity Act and its application to Nazi-expropriated works of art' (2006) 11 Art Antiquity and Law 371.

Chechi A, 'The return of cultural objects removed in times of colonial domination and international law: the case of the Venus of Cyrene' (2008) 18 Italian Yearbook of International Law 159.

Chechi A, 'Evaluating the establishment of an international cultural heritage court' (2013) XVIII Art, Antiquity and Law 31.

Chechi A, 'Some reflections on International Adjudication of Cultural Heritage-related Cases' (2013) 10(5) Transnational Dispute Management.

Chilver EM, 'The Bangwa and the Germans: A Tailpiece' (1967) 4 Journal of the Historical Society of Nigeria 156.

Cornu M, Renold MA, 'New developments in the restitution of cultural property: alternative means of dispute resolution' (2010) 17 International Journal of Cultural Property 1.

De Gaetano N, 'On the right of the government of Malta to restrict the movement of cultural objects situated in Malta' (2019) 24 Art Antiquity and Law 79.

Desmarais F (ed.) 'Countering illicit traffic in cultural goods. The global challenge of protecting the world's heritage' (2015) ICOM International Observatory on Illicit Traffic in Cultural Goods.

Dunstan E, 'A Bangwa Account of Early Encounters with the German Colonial Administration' (1965) 3 Journal of the Historical Society of Nigeria 403.

Fincham D, 'The rescue, stewardship, and return of the Lysi frescoes by the Menil Foundation' (2015) 22 International Journal of Cultural Property 1.

Fiorentini F, Hausler K, Jagielska-Burduk A, Jakubowski A, Editorial (2016) 2 Santander Art and Culture Law Review 9.

Francioni F, 'Au-dela des traits: l'emergence d'un nouveau droit coutumier pour la protection du patrimoine culturel' (2007) CXI Revue Generale de Droit International Public 19

Francioni F, 'The human dimension of international cultural heritage law: an introduction' (2011) 22 European Journal of International Law 9.

Francioni F, 'Public and Private in the International Protection of Global Cultural Goods' (2012) 23 European Journal of International Law 719.

Françozo M, Strecker A, 'Caribbean Collections in European Museums and the Question of Returns' (2017) 24 International Journal of Cultural Property 451.

Frigo M, 'Methods and techniques of dispute settlement in the international practice of the restitution and return of cultural property' (2017) Rivista di Diritto Internazionale Privato e Processuale 569.

Ganslmayr H, Landais H, Lewis G, Makambila P, Perrot P, Pré J, Vistel J, 'Study on the principles, conditions and means for the restitution or return of cultural property in view of reconstituting dispersed heritages' (1979) 31 Museum International 62.

Goodwin PS, 'Mapping the Limits of Repatriable Cultural Heritage: A Case Study of Stolen Flemish Art in French Museums' (2008) 157 University of Pennsylvania Law Review 673.

Grimsted PK, 'Nazi-Looted Art from East and West in East Prussia: Initial Findings on the Erich Koch Collection' (2015) 22 International Journal of Cultural Property 7.

Hausler K, 'Cultural heritage and the Security Council: Why Resolution 2347 Matters' (2018) QIL, Zoom-in 48, 5.

Hébié M, 'The Role of the Agreements Concluded with Local Political Entities in the Course of French Colonial Expansion in West Africa' (2016) 85 British Yearbook of International Law 21.

Hillgenberg H, 'A Fresh Look at Soft Law' (1990) 10 European Journal of International Law 499.

Jakubowski A, 'State responsibility and the international protection of cultural heritage in armed conflicts' (2015) 2 Santander Art and Culture Law Review.
Jakubowski A, 'Resolution 2347: Mainstreaming the protection of cultural heritage at the global level' (2018) 48 Question of International Law 21.
Jayme E 'Globalization in art law: clash of interests and international tendencies' (2005) 38 Vanderbilt Journal of Transnational Law 927.
Jayme E, 'Human Rights and Restitution of Nazi-Confiscated Artworks from Public Museums: The Altmann Case as a Model for Uniform Rules?' (2006) 11 Uniform Law Review 393.

Kreder JA 'Reconciling individual and group justice with the need for repose in Nazi-looted art disputes. Creation of an international tribunal' (2007) 73 Brooklyn Law Review 155.
Kuprecht K, 'The concept of 'cultural affiliation' in NAGPRA: its potential and limits in the global protection of indigenous cultural property rights' (2012) 19 International Journal of Cultural Property 33.

Liu Z, 'Will the god win? the case of the Buddhist mummy' (2007) 24 International Journal of Cultural Property 221.
Lockhart V, 'A Social-Historical Study of Social Change among the Bangwa of Cameroon' (1994) Occasional Papers No 52, Centre of African Studies, Edinburgh University.

Mejia-Lemos D, 'The 'Quimbaya treasure' judgment SU-649/17' (2019) 113 American Journal of International Law 122.
Merryman JH, 'Note on the Marquis de Somerueles' (1996) 5 International Journal of Cultural Property 321.
Merryman JH, 'Cultural property internationalism' (2005) 12 International Journal of Cultural Property 11.
Miles MM, 'Cicero's Prosecution of Gaius Verres: A Roman View of the Ethics of Acquisition of Art' (2002) 11 International Journal of Cultural Property 33.
Monreal L, 'Problems and Possibilities in Recovering Dispersed Cultural Heritages' (1979) 31 Museum 49 (Reprinted in Museum international, No. 212, 2001).

Nafziger JAR, 'The principles for cooperation in the mutual protection and transfer of cultural material' (2007) 8 Chicago Journal of International Law 147.
Nahlik SE, 'International Law and the Protection of Cultural Property in Armed Conflicts' (1976) 27 Hastings Law Journal 1069.
Nathan J, 'Mandatory Title Insurance for Cultural Property: A Solution for Claimants and Owners of Looted and Stolen Art' (2018) 23 Art Antiquity & Law 247.
Nudelman M, 'Who Owns the Scythian Gold? The Legal and Moral Implications of Ukraine and Crimea's Cultural Dispute' (2015) 38 Fordham International Law Review 1261.

O'Donnell NM, 'The Holocaust Expropriated Art Recovery Act. A Sea Change in US Law of Restitution' (2017) 22 Art Antiquity and Law 273.

Oost T, 'From "Leader to Pariah"? On the Dutch Restitutions Committee and the inclusion of the public interest in assessing Nazi-spoliated art claims' (2021) International Journal of Cultural Property 1-31.
Ottone Ramirez E, Editorial (October 2020) The UNESCO Courier.

Palmer N, 'Unclaimed art and the duty of active pursuit: Cornelius Gurlitt and the hidden hoard' (2014) 19 Art Antiquity and Law 41.
Peters R, 'The protection of cultural property: recent developments in Germany in the context of new EU law and the 1970 UNESCO Convention' (2016) 2 Santander Art and Culture Law Review 85.
Pott PH, Sutaarga MA, 'Arragments Concluded or in Progress for the Return of Objects: The Netherlands-Indonesia' (1979) 31 Museum International 38.
Prott LV, 'The international movement of cultural objects (2005) 12 IJCP 225.
Prott LV, 'The ethics and law of returns' (2009) 61 Museum International 101.
Prott LV, O'Keefe PJ, 'Cultural heritage or cultural property?' (1992) 1 International Journal of Cultural Property 307.

Renold MA, 'Cultural Co-Ownership: Preventing and Solving Cultural Property Claims' (2015) 22 International Journal of Cultural Property 163.
Robinson N, 'War Damage Compensation and Restitution in Foreign Countries' (1951) 16 Law and Contemporary Problems 347.
Ross SG, 'Res extra commercium and the barriers faced when seeking the repatriation and return of potent cultural objects' (2017) 4 American Indian Law Journal 299.

Schlothauer A, 'Gustav Conrau's Cameroon Collection in the Berlin Ethnological Museum' (2015) 9 Kunst & Kontext Humboldt-Forum 20.
Schrijver NJ, 'Managing the global commons: common good or common sink?' (2016) Vol 37 Third World Quarterly, 1252.
Shyllon F, 'The rise of negotiation (ADR) in restitution, return and repatriation of cultural property: moral pressure and power pressure' (2017) 22 Art Antiquity and Law 130.
Siehr K, 'Private internartional law and the difficult problem to return illegally exported cultural property' (2015) 20 Uniform Law Review 503.
Symeonidis SC, 'A Choice-of-Law Rule for Conflicts Involving Stolen Cultural Property' (2005) 38 Vand. J. Transnat'l L. 1177.

Tao D, 'Issue on conflict law in overseas litigation for the recovery of lost cultural relics – Iranian government v. Barakat Art Museum and its enlightenment' (2009) Comparative Law Study 2.

Vliet LPW, 'The Dutch Postwar Restoration of Rights Regime Regarding Movable Property' (2019*) Legal History Review* 87, pp. 651-673
Van Woudenberg N, Nafziger JAR, 'The Draft Convention on Immunity from Suit and Seizure for Cultural Objects Temporarily Abroad for Cultural, Educational or Scientific Purpose' (2014) 21 International Journal of Cultural Property 481.
Von Lintig B, 'On the Bangwa collection: formed by Gustav Conrau' (2017) 86 Tribal Art 94.

Vrdoljak AF, 'Genocide and Restitution: Ensuring Each Group's Contribution to Humanity' (2011) 22 European Journal of International Law 17.

Weiss G, 'Beutegueter aus besetztend Laendern. Die privatrechtlichte Stellund des schweizerischen Erwerbens' (1946) 42 Schweizerische Juristen-Zeitiung 274.

Wolfrum R, 'Cultural Property, Protection in Armed Conflict' (2010) Max Planck Encyclopedia of Public International Law.

Woodhead C, 'Nazi Era Spoliation: Establishing Procedural and Substantive Principles' (2013) 18 Art Antiquity and Law 167.

Zhang Y, 'Customary international law and the rule against taking cultural property as spoils of war' (2018) 17 Chinese Journal of International Law 943.

Zhen L, 'Examining the recovery of Yuanmingyuan cultural property from the perspective of international law' (2009) Legal System and Society 4.

Zhengxin, H, 'The Chinese villages win a lawsuit in China to repatriate a Mummified Buddha Statue hold by a Dutch Collector – What Role has Private International Law Played?' (2020) Conflict of Laws.net, Views and News in Private International Law (12 December 2020)

Contributions to edited volumes

Abungu G, 'The Declaration: a contested issue' in Prott LV (ed), *Witnesses to history: a compendium of documents and writings on the return of cultural objects* (2009) UNESCO, Paris.

Appiah KA, 'Whose Culture Is It, Anyway?' in Appiah KA, *Cosmopolitanism: Ethics in a World of Strangers* (2006) W.W. Norton & Company.

Appiah KA, 'Cosmopolitanism and Cultural Heritage. Thomas Thiemeyer in conversation with Kwame Anthony Appiah' in Humboldt Forum *(Post)Colonialism and Cultural Heritage. International Debates at the Humboldt Forum* (2021) Hanser Verlag.

Bentwich N, 'International Aspects of Restitution and Compensation for Victims of the Nazis' in *British Yearbook of International Law (1955/1956)* Oxford University Press.

Boyle A, 'Soft Law in International Law-making' in Evans M (ed), *International Law* (4th edition, 2014) Oxford University Press.

Brodie N, 'Protection not Prevention: The Failure of Public Policy to Prevent the Looting and Illegal Trade of Cultural Property from the Mena Region (1990-2015) in Anderson J, Geismar H (eds), *The Routledge companion to cultural property* (2017) Routledge, New York.

Campfens E, 'Sources of Inspiration: Old and New Rules for Looted Art' in Campfens E (ed), *Fair and Just Solutions? Alternatives to Litigation in Nazi-Looted Art Disputes* (2015) Eleven International Publishing.

Carstens AM, 'The Swinging Pendulum of Cultural Heritage Crimes in International Criminal Law' in Carstens AM, Varner E (eds), *Intersections in International Cultural Heritage Law* (2020) Oxford University Press, Oxford.

Chechi A, 'Plurality and coordination of dispute settlement methods in the field of cultural heritage' in Francioni F, Gordley J (eds), *Enforcing International Cultural Heritage Law* (2013) Oxford University Press, Oxford.

Donders Y, 'Foundations of Collective Cultural Rights in International Human Rights Law' in Jakubowski A (ed), *Cultural rights as collective rights, an international law perspective* (2016) Brill, The Hague.

Esterling SE 'Under the umbrella: the remedial penumbra of self-determination, retroactivity and the restitution of cultural property to indigenous peoples' in Xanthaki A, Valkonen (eds), *Indigenous peoples' cultural heritage. Rights, debates, challenges* (2017) Brill Nijhof.

Fiorentini F, 'A legal pluralist approach to international trade in cultural objects' in Nafziger JAR, RK Paterson (eds), *Handbook on the Law of Cultural Heritage and International Trade* (2014) Edward Elgar Publishing.

Francioni F, 'A dynamic Evolution of Concept and Scope: From Cultural Property to Cultural Heritage', in Yusuf AA (ed), *Standard Setting in UNESCO, Vol. I: Normative Action in Education, Science and Culture* (2007) Martinus Nijhoff, Leiden.

Francioni F, 'Reparation for indigenous peoples: Is international law ready to ensure redress for historical injustices?' in Lenzerini F (ed), *Reparations for Indigenous Peoples: International and Comparative Perspectives* (2008) Oxford University Press, Oxford.

Francioni F, 'General principles applicable to international cultural heritage law' in Andenas M, Fitzmaurice M, Tanzi A, Wouters J (eds), *General principles and the coherence of international law* (2019) Queen Mary Studies in International Law. Brill, Leiden.

Gerstenblith P, 'Enforcement by domestic courts, criminal law and forfeiture in the recovery of cultural objects' in Francioni F, Gordley J (eds), *Enforcing international cultural heritage law* (2013) Oxford University Press, Oxford.

Gerstenblith P, 'The disposition of movable cultural heritage' in Carstens A-M, Varner E (eds), *Intersections in International Cultural Heritage Law* (2020) Oxford University Press, Oxford.

Gordley J, 'The enforcement of foreign law: Reclaiming one's nation's cultural heritage in another nation's courts' in Francioni F, Gordley J (eds), *Enforcing International Cultural Heritage Law* (2013) Oxford University Press, New York.

Hafstein TV, Skrydstrup M, 'Heritage vs. Property: Contrasting regimes and rationalities in the patrimonial field' in Anderson J, Geismar H (eds), *The Routledge Companion to Cultural Property* (2017) Routledge, New York.

Hausler K, 'The UN Security Council, the Human Rights Council, and the protection of cultural heritage: a matter of peace and security, human rights, or both?' in Carstens A-M, Varner E (eds), *Intersections in International Cultural Heritage Law* (2020) Oxford University Press, Oxford.

Jakubowski A, 'Cultural heritage and the collective dimension of cultural rights in the jurisprudence of the European Court of Human Rights' in Jakubowski A (ed), *Cultural rights as collective rights, an international law perspective* (2016) Brill, The Hague.

Jayme E 'Narrative norms in private international law, the example of art law' in *Collected courses of the Hague academy of international law*, vol. 375 (2015) Brill Nijhoff, Leiden.

Kowalski WW, 'Restitution of works of art pursuant to private and public international law' in *Collected courses of the Hague academy of international law*, vol. 288 (2002) Brill Nijhoff.

Kunert F, Marck A, 'The Dutch Art Market 1930-1945 and Dutch Restitution Policy Regarding Art Dealers' in Blimlinger E, Mayer M (eds), *Kunst sammeln, Kunst handeln : Beiträge des Internationalen Symposiums in Wien* (2012) Böhlau Verlag.

Lenzerini F 'Reparations for indigenous peoples in international and comparative law: an introduction', in Lenzerini F (ed), *Reparations for Indigenous Peoples: International and Comparative Perspectives* (2008) Oxford University Press, Oxford.

Lenzerini F, 'The Role of International and Mixed Criminal Counts in Enforcement of International Norms concerning the Protection of Cultural Heritage' in Francioni F, Gordley J (eds), *Enforcing International Cultural Heritage Law* (2013) Oxford University Press, Oxford.

Lenzerini F, 'Reparations for wrongs against indigenous people's cultural heritage' in Xanthaki A, Valkonen S (eds), *Indigenous peoples' cultural heritage: rights, debates, challenges* (2017) Brill Nijhoff, Leiden/Boston.

Marck A, Muller E, 'National Panels advising on Nazi-Looted Art in Austria, France, the United Kingdom, the Netherlands and Germany. A brief Overview' in Campfens E (ed), *Fair and Just Solutions? Alternatives to Litigation in Nazi-Looted Art Disputes* (2015) Eleven International Publishing.

Marck A, Schoonderwoerd M, 'We want to honour the memory of our great-grandparents' – and interview with Ella Andriesse and Robert Sturm in Campfens E (ed), *Fair and just solutions, alternatives to litigation in Nazi-looted art disputes: status quo and new developments* (2015) Boom, The Hague.

Nafziger JAR, 'Cultural heritage law: the international regime' in *The Cultural Heritage of Mankind* (2008) Centre for studies and research in international law and international relations, Académie de droit international de La Haye. Brill Nijhoff, Leiden/Boston.

Nafziger JAR, Paterson RK, 'International trade in cultural material' in Nafziger JAR, Paterson RK (eds), *Handbook on the law of cultural heritage and international trade* (2014) Edward Elgar Publishing, Cheltenham.

O'Keefe R, 'Tangible Cultural Heritage and International Human Rights Law' in O'Keefe PJ, *Protecting Cultural Objects: Before and After 1970 (2017)* Institute of Art and Law.

Palmer N, 'Waging and Engaging: Reflections on the Mediation of Art and Antiquity Claims' in Bandle AL, Chechi A, Renold MA (eds), *Resolving Disputes in Cultural Property* (2012) Schulthess Verlag, Zürich.

Palmer N, 'The best we can do? Exploring a collegiate approach to Holocaust-related claims' in Campfens E (ed), *Fair and Just Solutions? Alternatives to Litigation in Nazi-Looted Art Disputes* (2015) Eleven International Publishing.

Pauwelyn J, 'Informal International Lawmaking: Framing the concept and research questions' in Pauwelyn J, Wessel RA and Wouters J (eds) *Informal International Lawmaking* (2012) OUP.

Pell OC, 'Using Arbitral Tribunals to Resolve Disputes Relating to Holocaust-Looted Art' in International Bureau of the Permanent Court of Arbitration (ed), *Resolution of cultural property disputes* (2004) Kluwer Law International.

Peters R, 'Nationalism versus internationalism. New perspectives beyond state sovereignty and territoriality in the protection of cultural heritage' in Carstens AM, Varner E (eds), *Intersections in international cultural heritage law* (2020) Oxford University Press, Oxford.

Ploeger HD, Stolker CJJM, 'In search of the importance of Article 1 Protocol no. 1 ECHR to private law' in Loof JP, Ploeger HD, Van der Steur A (eds), *The right to property: the influence of Article 1 Protocol no. 1 ECHR on several fields of domestic law* (2000) Shaker, Maastricht.

Prott LV, 'Responding to WWII Art Looting' in International Bureau of the Permanent Court of Arbitration (ed), *Resolution of cultural property disputes* (2004) Kluwer Law International.

Salomon A.F., 'National Report on the Transfer of Ownership of Movables in The Netherlands', in W. Faber, B. Lurger (eds) National Reports on the Transfer of Movables in Europe, Vol. 6 (Sellier, Munich, 2011)

Schrijver NJ, 'UNESCO's Role in the Development and Application of International Law: An Assessment', in Yusuf AA (ed), *Standard-setting in UNESCO. Normative action in Education, Science and Culture, Essays in Commemoration of the Sixtieth Anniversary of UNESCO*, Vol. I (2007) UNESCO, Paris.

Shelton D, 'Reparations for Indigenous Peoples: The Present Value of Past Wrongs' in Lenzerini F (ed), *Reparations for Indigenous Peoples: International and Comparative Perspectives* (2008) Oxford University Press.

Shelton D, 'International Law and Relative Normativity' in Evans M (ed), *International Law*, 4th edition (2014) Oxford University Press.

Shyllon F, 'Collective Cultural Rights as Human Rights Simpliciter: The African and African Charter Example' in Jakubowski A (ed), *Cultural Rights as Collective Rights, An International Law Perspective* (2016) Brill Nijhoff.

Siehr K, 'International art trade and the law' in *Collected courses of the Hague academy of international law*, vol. 243 (1993) Brill Nijhoff.

Slimani S, Theurich S, 'The New ICOM-WIPO Art and Cultural Heritage Mediation Program' in Bandle AL, Chechi A, Renold MA (eds), *Resolving Disputes in Cultural Property* (2012) Schulthess Verlag, Zürich.

Stoll PT, 'Where Should Nefertiti Go? Reflections on International Cultural Law' in Hestermeyer HP and others (eds), *Coexistence, Cooperation and Solidarity* (2012) Martinus Nijhoff Publishers.

Van Genugten W, Lenzerini F, 'Legal implementation and international cooperation and assistance: articles 37-42' in Hohmann J, Weller M (eds), *The UN declaration on the rights of indigenous peoples: a commentary* (2018) Oxford University Press, Oxford.

Veraart W, 'Contrasting Legal Concepts of Restitution in France and the Netherlands', in Veraart W and Winkel L (eds), *The Post War Restitution of Property Rights in Europe: Comparative Perspectives* (2011) Scientia Verlag.

Vrdoljak AF, 'Reparations for Cultural Loss' in Lenzerini F (ed), *Reparations for Indigenous Peoples: International and Comparative Perspectives* (2008) Oxford University Press.

Vrdoljak AF, 'Enforcement of Restitution of Cultural Heritage through Peace Agreements' in Francioni F, Gordley J (eds), *Enforcing International Cultural Heritage Law* (2013) Oxford University Press.

Vrdoljak AF, 'Gross Violations of Human Rights and Restitution: Learning from Holocaust Claims' in Prott LV, *Realising Cultural Heritage Law: Festschrift for Patrick O'Keefe* (2013) Institute for Art & Law.

Vrdoljak AF, 'Human rights and cultural heritage in international law' in Lenzerini F, Vrdoljak AF (eds), *International law for common goods: normative perspectives on human rights*, 1st edn. (2014), Hart Publishing, Oxford.

Vrdoljak AF, 'Standing and collective cultural rights' in Jakubowski A (ed), *Cultural rights as collective rights, an international law perspective* (2016) Brill, Leiden.

Vrdoljak AF and Meskell L, 'Intellectual cooperation organisation, Unesco, and the culture conventions' in Francioni F and Vrdoljak AF (eds) *The Oxford Handbook of International Cultural Heritage Law* (2020), OUP.

Weller M, 'Key Elements of Just and Fair Solutions: The Case for a Restatement of Restitution Principles' in Campfens E (ed), *Fair and Just Solutions? Alternatives to Litigation in Nazi-Looted Art Disputes* (2015) Eleven International Publishing.

Weller M 'In search of 'just and fair' solutions: Towards the future of the Washington Principles of Nazi-confiscated art' in *Guide to the work of the Restitutions Committees* (2019) CIVS.

Woodhead C 'Action towards consistent 'just and fair' solutions' in *Guide to the work of the Restitutions Committees* (2019) CIVS.

Van Woudenberg, N 'Developments Concerning Immunity from Seizure for Cultural State Property on Loan' in Carstens AM, Varner E (eds), *Intersections in international cultural heritage law* (2020) Oxford University Press, Oxford.

Xanthaki A, 'Culture: Articles 11(1), 12, 13(1), 15, and 34' in Hohmann J, Weller M (eds), *The UN Declaration on the Rights of Indigenous Peoples: a commentary* (2018) Oxford University Press, Oxford.

Other resources

International organisations' documents

- De Clercq W CEH, Report on a legal framework for free movement within the internal market of goods whose ownership is likely to be contested (26 November 2003) European Parliament, Committee on Legal Affairs and the Internal Market, A5-0408/2003.
- Council of Europe, Research Division, 'Cultural rights in the case-law of the European Court of Human Rights' (January 2011).
- International Military Tribunal, *Trials of the Major War Criminals Before the International Military Tribunal*, vol. 22 (1948) Nuremberg.
- Rome Declaration of the G20 Ministers of Culture (30 July 2021).
- UNESCO Database of National Cultural Heritage Laws.
- UNESCO Secretariat, 'Working paper' in Cultural rights as human rights (1970) UNESCO Studies and documents on cultural policies, No 3. SHC.68/XIX.3/A.

Other documents

- Cadman H, 'An Assessment Report on the Bangwa Tribal Area in the Mamfe Division of the Cameroon Province' (1922) Buea Archive File No. Af 13.
- Conrau G, Letters to Felix von Luschan (11 June and 1 October 1899) *Acta Africa*, vol. 21, file E1015/99-49.
- Atem G, 'Account on the Looting of the Bangwa King and Queen by the Germans' (2017) Statement (on file with the author).
- Bugnion F, 'The Origins and Development of the Legal Protection of Cultual Property in the Event of Armed Conflict', Speech at the Fiftieth Anniversary of the 1954 Hague Convention for the Protection of Cultural Property in the Event of Armed Conflict (Geneva, 2004).
- Commission for the Compensation of Victims of Spoliation Resulting from the Anti-Semitic Legislation in Force during the Occupation, Key Figures (June 2017).
- Conference on Jewish Material Claims Against Germany and the World Jewish Restitution Organization, 'Looted Art and Cultural Property Initiative'
- Cummins A, President of ICOM, 'Promoting the use of Mediation in Resolution of disputes over the Ownership of objects in Museum Collections', Statement (January 2006).
- Declaration on the Importance and Value of the Universal Museum (December 2002) <https://www.hermitagemuseum.org/wps/portal/hermitage/news/news-item/news/1999_2013/hm11_1_93/?lng> accessed 30 July 2020.

- DeFabo JL, 'The Bangwa Queen: Interpretations, Constructions, and Appropriations of Meaning of the Esteemed Ancestress Figure from the Cameroon Grassfields' (2014) Senior Project Spring 2014, Paper 14.
- Fisher WA, Weinberger R, 'Holocaust-Era Looted Art: A Current World-Wide Overview', presented at the ICOM Museum & Politics Conference in St Petersburg (September 2014).
- French Ministry of Culture, 'France's new organization for the restitution of cultural property spoliated due to national socialism' (2018) <http://www.civs.gouv.fr/images/pdf/documents_utiles/autres_documents/UK-FLYER-pageApage.pdf> accessed 30 April 2019.
- Letter of the Mayor and Aldermen to the Amsterdam Municipal Council (19 February 2021), <https://amsterdam.raadsinformatie.nl/modules/1/Berichten%20uit%20het%20college/651069>, accessed 10 May 2021.
- Macron E, President of the French Republic, Speech at the University of Ouagadougou (28 November 2017) <https://www.elysee.fr/emmanuel-macron/2017/11/28/discours-demmanuel-macron-a-luniversite-de-ouagadougou> accessed 20 April 2020.
- M'Bow AM, 'A Plea for the Return of an Irreplacable Cultural Heritage to those who Created It' (1978) Address Secr-Gen UNESCO <http://www.unesco.org/culture/laws/pdf/PealforReturn_DG_1978.pdf>.
- Note delivered by Viscount Castlerough to the Allied Ministers, and Placed upon their Protocol, Respecting the Restitution of the Works of Art (Paris, 11 September 1815).
- Oxford University Museum, 'Procedures for claims for the return of Cultural Objects from Oxford University Museums and Libraries' (2020) <https://www.glam.ox.ac.uk/procedures-for-return-of-cultural-objects-claims>.
- Report of the German Consul in Leningrad Following the Ceremonial Return (1973) Political Archive of the German Foreign Minstry, B 86, Bd 1596.
- Sarr F and Savoy B, 'The Restitution of African Cultural Heritage. Toward a New Relational Ethics' (2018) <http://restitutionreport2018.com/sarr_savoy_en.pdf> accessed 23 April 2019.
- Schmiegelt U, 'A Hostage of the Cold War? The Return of the Monastery Treasure of Pechory', Conference paper presented at the conference 'From Refugees to Restitution: The History of Nazi Looted Art in the UK in Transnational Perspective', Cambridge (May 2017).
- World Intellectual Property Organization, 'ICOM-WIPO Art and Cultural Heritage Mediation' <https://www.wipo.int/amc/en/center/specific-sectors/art/icom/>.

Blogs

- Bandle AL, Chechi A, Renold MA, 'Case Note – Afo-A-Kom – Furman Gallery and Kom People' (2012) Platform ArThémis, Art-Law Centre, University of Geneva.
- Bandle AL, Contel R, Renold MA, 'Case Note – Ancient Manuscripts and Globe – Saint-Gall and Zurich' (2012) Platform ArThémis, Art-Law Centre, University of Geneva.

- Bursey L, Velioglu Yildizci E, Renold MA, 'Case Christ Carrying the Cross Dragged by a Rascal – Gentili Di Guiseppe Heirs v. Italy' (2015) Platform ArThémis, Art-Law Centre, University of Geneva.
- Chechi A, Velioglu E, Renold MA, 'Case Note – 14 Artworks – Malewicz Heirs and City of Amsterdam' (2013) Platform ArThémis, Art-Law Centre, University of Geneva.
- Neuendorf H, 'Germany is returning artefacts stolen from a Namibian freedom fighter during its colonial rule' (2019) *Artnet News*.
- Nicolazzi L, Chechi A, Renold MA, 'Case Hopi Masks – Hopi Tribe v. Néret-Minet and Estimations & Ventes aux enchères' (2015) Platform ArThémis, Art-Law Centre, University of Geneva.
- O'Donnell NM, Art Law Report (13 May 2015).
- O'Donnell NM, Art Law Report (29 September 2016).
- Renold C, Chechi A, Bandle AL, Renold MA, 'Case six Klimt paintings – Maria Altmann and Austria' (2012) Platform ArThemis, Art-Law Centre, University of Geneva.
- Schuberth S, Tuchtfeld E, Lischewski I, Eschenhagen P, #3 Bindung an Menschenrechte im Ausland: So close, no matter how far?, Podcast (5 March 2021) *Völkerrechtsblog*.
- Wuerth I, 'An Art Museum Amendment to the Foreign Sovereign Immunities Act' (2017) *Lawfare* <https://www.lawfareblog.com/art-museum-amendment-foreign-sovereign-immunities-act>.

Media reports & Press releases

- Baranovskaya M, Klymchuck O, 'Ukraine seeks to bring home Renaissance artworks sold under false pretenses' (27 October 2020) *Deutsche Welle*.
- Brown K, 'Sotheby's just lost its lawsuit against Greece over an 8th-century BC horse statue – and the decision may have lasting implications for the trade' (10 June 2020) *ArtNet News* <https://news.artnet.com/artworld/barnet-case-sothebys-1883349> accessed 27 July 2020.
- Cheon-yeol L, Article from the 13 March 2017, *Seoul Metropolitan Governement* <http://www.seoul.co.kr/news/newsView.php?id=20170314016002&wlog_tag3=naver>.
- Chrysopoulos P, 'Greek ministry of culture in legal dispute over return of 8th century BC antiquity' (25 September 2019) *Greek Reporter* <https://greece.greekreporter.com/2019/09/25/greek-ministry-of-culture-in-legal-dispute-over-return-of-8th-century-bc-antiquity/> accessed 20 April 2020.
- Cohan WD, 'A Suit Over Schiele Drawings Invokes New Law on Nazi-Looted Art' (27 February 2017) *The New York Times* <https://www.nytimes.com/2017/02/27/arts/design/a-suit-over-schiele-drawings-invokes-new-law-on-nazi-looted-art-html>.
- Commission for the Compensation of Victims of Spoliation Resulting from the Anti-Semitic Legislationin Force during the Occupation, Establihsment of a Network of European Restitution Committees, Press Release (29 January 2019) <http://www.civs.gouv.fr/news/establishment-of-a-network-of-european-restitution-committees/> accessed 30 April 2019.

- Dagen P, 'La restitution d'œuvres d'art : « Une question de dignité » (17 August 2017) *Le Monde* <https://www.lemonde.fr/festival/article/2017/08/17/la-restitution-d-uvres-d-art-une-question-de-dignite_5173397_4415198.html> accessed 23 April 2019.
- *Deutsche Kolonialzeitung* (8 February 1900) Vol 17.
- Dutch National Museum of World Cultures, 'Return of Cutlural Objects: Principles and Process' (7 March 2019) Press Release <https://www.volkenkunde.nl/en/about-volkenkunde/press/dutch-national-museum-world-cultures-nmvw-announces-principles-claims> accessed 23 April 2019.
- *Elysée*, 'Remise du Rapport Savoir/Sarr sur la Restitution du Patrimoine Africain' (23 November 2018) <https://www.elysee.fr/emmanuel-macron/2018/11/23/remise-du-rapport-savoy-sarr-sur-la-restitution-du-patrimoine-africain>.
- Global Times, 'Looted 3,000-year-old 'Tiger Ying' bronze vessel donated by mysterious buyer returns to China' (11 December 2018) *Global Times* <https://www.globaltimes.cn/content/11313 43.shtml> accessed 23 July 2020.
- Gropp RM, 'Wirklich Fair Une Gerecht' (26 July 2017) *Frankfurter Allgemeine Zeitung* <https://www.faz.net/aktuell/feuilleton/kunstmarkt/restitution-paul-klees-sumpflegende-bleibt-in-muenchen-15123237.html>.
- Häntzschel J, '*Ärger ums 'Zitronenscheibchen''* (26 February 2021) *Süddeutsche Zeitung* <https://www.sueddeutsche.de/kultur/limbach-kommission-raubkunst-monika-gruetters-restitution-1.5218083>.
- Heath EA, 'Korean Court Rules Statue Stolen from Japan Can Remain in the Country (January 26, 2017)' (2017) *American Society of International Law* <https://www.asil.org/blogs/korean-court-rules-statue-stolen-japan-can-remain-country-january-26-2017> accessed 10 August 2017.
- Hickley C, 'After 26 Years, Munich Settles Case Over a Klee Looted by the Nazis' (26 July 2017) *The New York Times* <https://www.nytimes.com/2017/07/26/arts/design/after-26-years-munich-settles-case-over-a-klee-looted-by-nazis.html>.
- Hickley C, 'Dutch policy on Nazi-loot restitutions under fire' (21 December 2018) *The Art Newspaper* <https://www.lootedart.com/news.php?r=TETJ4L309041> accessed 23 April 2019.
- Hooper J, Plafker T, 'The body in the Buddha' (4 May 2017) *The Economist* <www.1843magazine.com/features/the-body-in-the-buddha> accessed 29 April 2020.
- Jaeger T, '*Gemeente Amsterdam wil Kandinsky uit het Stedelijk wellicht toch teruggeven aan erven*' (22 February 2021) *NRC Handelsblad* <https://www.nrc.nl/nieuws/2021/02/22/bild-mit-hausern-van-wassily-kandinsky-wellicht-toch-terug-naar-de-erven-a4032716>.
- Jewish Voice, *JVP News* (28 September 2016).
- Kazakina K, 'Oprah Said to Snag $150 Million Selling Klimt to Chinese Buyer' (8 February 2017) *Bloomberg News* <https://www.bloomberg.com/news/articles/2017-02-08/oprah-said-to-snag-150-million-selling-klimt-to-chinese-buyer>.
- MDM Newswire, 'Nazi art looting restitutions settlement agreement leads to Christie's auction of rare artworks' (16 October 2014) *MDM Newswire* <https://www.lootedart.com/news.php?r=QVXQRY760781>.
- Muchnic S, '$3.4-Million Sculpture Sale Sets Record for African Art' (22 April 1990) *Los Angeles Times* <https://www.latimes.com/archives/la-xpm-1990-04-22-mn-392-story.html>.

- Noce V, 'Paris court orders US collector to turn over Pissarro painting' (3 October 2018) *The Art Newspaper* <https://www.theartnewspaper.com/news/paris-court-orders-us-collector-to-turn-over-pissarro-painting> accessed 30 April 2019.
- Parzinger H, President of the Stiftung Preusssischer Kulturbesitz, Speech at the conference of the German Lost Art Foundation 'New Perspectives of Provenance Research in Germany' (27 November 2015) <https://www.preussischer-kulturbesitz.de/fileadmin/user_upload_SPK/documents/reden_p/151126_Provenienzforschung_Rede-P-FINAL_eng.pdf>.
- Parzinger H, 'Bauen wir Museen in Afrika!' (25 January 2018) *Frankfurter Allgemeine Zeitung*.
- Petterson E, 'Spanish Museum Can Keep Nazi-Looted Masterpiece, Judge Rules' (30 April 2019) *Bloomberg News* <https://www.bloomberg.com/news/articles/2019-04-30/spanish-museum-can-keep-nazi-looted-masterpiece-judge-rules>.
- Prussian Cultural Heritage Foundation, 'Ethnologisches Museum Returns Objects to Alaska Natives' (16 May 2018) Press Release <http://www.preussischer-kulturbesitz.de/fileadmin/user_upload_SPK/documents/presse/pressemitteilungen/2018/180516_Restitution-Chugach-Ceremony_EN.pdf>.
- Quinn A, 'French Court Orders Return of Pissarro Looted by Vichy Government' (8 November 2017) *The New York Times* <https://www.nytimes.com/2017/11/08/arts/design/french-court-pissarro-looted-nazis.html?searchResultPosition=1> accessed 16 January 2019.
- Rathaus Landeshauptstadt München, Umschau 140/2017: Vergleich zur Beilegung der Auseinandersetzung im Falle des Gemäldes 'Sumpflegende' von Paul Klee (2017) Press Release, Municipality of Munchen <https://ru.muenchen.de/>.
- *Stiftung Preußischer Kulturbesitz*, "Stiftung Preußischer Kulturbesitz Findet Erneut Faire Und Gerechte Lösung Mit Den Erben von Prof. Dr. Curt Glaser' (2016) *Stiftung Preußischer Kulturbesitz* <http://www.preussischer-kulturbesitz.de/pressemitteilung/article/2016/04/20/pressemeldung-stiftung-preussischer-kulturbesitz-findet-erneut-faire-und-gerechte-loesung-mit-den-erb.html> accessed 1 April 2019.
- Taylor A, 'To Understand Crimea, Take a Look Back at Its Complicated History' (27 February 2014) *The Washington Post* <https://www.washingtonpost.com/news/worldviews/wp/2014/02/27/to-understand-crimea-take-a-look-back-at-its-complicated-history/?utm_term=.d9b8bef3486c>.
- The British Museum, 'Long-term loans' <https://www.britishmuseum.org/our-work/national/exhibitions-and-loans/long-term-loans> accessed 8 August 2017.
- UNESCO, 'Mutual Presentation of Cyprus and the Netherlands on the return of 4 icons from the Netherlands to Cyprus under the Protocol of the Hague Convention of 1954', 10th meeting of the High Contracting Parties to the Hague Convention (16 December 2013) <http://www.unesco.org/culture/laws/1954/NL-Cyprus-4icons_en>.
- Van Bergh GJ, Attorney of the Lewenstein heirs, Press Release (27 December 2018) <https://www.lootedart.com/web_images/pdf2019/PRESS%20RELEASE%2027%20December%202018.pdf> accessed 1 April 2019.
- Watt H, 'Bank's Kandinsky painting was looted by Nazis, says family' (3 March 2017) *The Guardian*.
- Wong E, 'Ai Weiwei's Animal Heads Offer Critique of Chinese Nationalism' (10 August 2016) *The New York Times*.

Annex
Original sources

An overview of the original sources of the various chapters is provided below:

Chapter 2 was published previously 'Restitution of Looted Art: What About Access to Justice?' in the *Santander Art and Culture Law Review* (Vol. 2/2018 (4): 185-220) in May 2019. To avoid major overlaps with other chapters, some sections have been shortened and some ongoing cases were updated.

Chapter 3 was published previously as 'Whose Cultural Heritage? Crimean Treasures at the Crossroads of Politics, Law and Ethics' in the journal *Art Antiquity and Law* (Vol. XXII, Issue 3/2017) in November 2017 and is reprinted with permission. A few changes have been made and a new section (3.6) has been added to take stock of the preliminary outcome (interlocutory judgement) of the appeals procedure in the Crimean Gold case in 2019.

Chapter 4 was published previously as 'Nazi-looted art: A note in favour of clear standards and neutral procedures' in the journal *Art Antiquity and Law* (Vol. XXII, Issue 4/2017) in January 2018 and is reprinted with permission. It has been amended, most notably to take account of new rulings in ongoing cases discussed in this publication.

Chapter 5 was published previously as 'The Bangwa Queen: Artefact or Heritage?' in the *International Journal of Cultural Property* (Volume 26 (1): 75-110) in April 2019. It was reprinted in M. Weller, N.B. Kemle, Th. Dreier, K. Kuprecht (Ed.) 'Zwischen Kolonialzeit und Washington Principles. Tagungsband des Dreizehnten Heidelberger Kunstrechtstags am 18. und 19. Oktober 2019' in 2020 (p. 167-209). A few corrections have been made in the original text.

Chapter 6 was published previously as 'Whose cultural objects? Introducing Heritage Title for Cross-Border Cultural Property Claims' in the *Netherlands International Law Review* (Vol. 67 (2): 257-295) in August 2020. This article is licensed under a Creative Commons Attribution 4.0 International License, which permits use, sharing, adaptation, distribution and reproduction in any medium or format (visit http://creative commons.org/licenses/by/4.0/). One editorial correction was made.

Curriculum vitae

Evelien Campfens was born in Amersfoort and attended secondary school at the Gemeentelijk Gymnasium in Hilversum. She was awarded a master's degree in law from the University of Amsterdam in 1990 with a thesis on the delimitation of the Aegean Sea between Greece and Turkey. She lived in Greece from 1990 until 1998 where she was a trainee at Kantoros Lawyers in Athens, and manager of Hotel Kavos on the island of Naxos. Back in the Netherlands, between 1999 and 2001 she was a lawyer at the Inspectorate of Cultural Heritage in The Hague working on the 'Origins Unknown' project on the provenance history of works of art in the Dutch state collection. Since its establishment in 2001 until 2015, she served as the general secretary to the Dutch Restitutions Committee for Nazi-looted art (*Adviescommissie Restitutieverzoeken Cultuurgoederen en Tweede Wereldoorlog*). She started her PhD research at Leiden Law School in 2016 under the supervision of prof. N.J. Schrijver and prof. W.J. Veraart, and joined the Grotius Centre for International Legal Studies that same year. Since 2020, she is senior researcher at the Museums, Collections and Society research group based at the Leiden University Centre for the Arts in Society. Since 2019, she also is research coordinator of the Heritage Under Threat group of the LDE Centre for Global Heritage and Development, and sat on the Board of Trustees of the German Lost Art Foundation from 2015 to 2020. She is a member of the Ethics Committee of the Dutch Museum Association (*Ethische Codecommissie*) and of the Committee on Participation in Global Cultural Heritage Governance of the International Law Association.

In de boekenreeks van het E.M. Meijers Instituut van de Faculteit der Rechtsgeleerdheid, Universiteit Leiden zijn in 2020 en 2021 verschenen:

MI-338 F. Jiang, *Greening' the WTO Ban on China's Export Duties. Should WTO law allow China to use export duties to protect the environment and, if so, in what manner?*, (diss. Leiden), Amsterdam: Ipskamp Printing 2020
MI-339 M.J.R. Broekema, *Cognitive Bias in the Judgment of Business Valuations and Valuators. How Systematic Patterns of Irrationality Affect Entrepreneurs, Legal Professionals and Business Valuators*, (diss. Leiden), Amsterdam: Ipskamp Printing 2020
MI-340 H. Horii, *Child Marriage as a Choice. Rethinking agency in international human rights*, (diss. Leiden), Amsterdam: Ipskamp Printing 2020
MI-341 R. de Graaff, *Concurrence in European Private Law*, (diss. Leiden), The Hague: Eleven International Publishing 2020, ISBN 978 94 6236 134 8
MI-342 J.M.M. van der Vliet, *The International Legal Protection of Environmental Refugees. A human rights-based, security and State responsibility approach*, (diss. Leiden), The Hague: Eleven International Publishing 2020, ISBN 978 94 6236 139 3
MI-343 M. Samadi, *Normering en Toezicht in de Opsporing. Een onderzoek naar de normering van het strafvorderlijk optreden van opsporingsambtenaren in het voorbereidend onderzoek en het toezicht op de naleving van deze normen*, (diss. Leiden), Den Haag: Boom juridisch 2020, ISBN 978 94 6290 816 1
MI-344 D.J. Verheij, *Credit rating agency liability in Europe. Rating the combination of EU and national law in rights of redress*, (diss. Leiden), The Hague: Eleven International Publishing 2020, ISBN 978 94 6236 144 7
MI-345 P. Rustenburg, *Een algemene normtheorie toegepast op open normen in het belastingrecht*, (diss. Leiden), Amsterdam: Ipskamp Printing 2020
MI-346 J.V.O.R. Doekhie e.a., *Invoering jeugdstrafrecht in Caribisch Nederland: een verkenning naar een jeugdstrafrechtmonitor*, Den Haag: Boom criminologie 2020, ISBN 978-94-6236-151-5
MI-347 A. Varga, *Establishing State Responsibility in the Absence of Effective Government*, (diss. Leiden), Amsterdam: Ipskamp Printing 2020
MI-348 M. Darouei, *Managing a Sustainable Career in the Contemporary World of Work: Personal Choices and Contextual Challenges*, (diss. Leiden), Amsterdam: Ipskamp Printing 2020
MI-349 N. Strohmaier, *Making Sense of Business Failure. A social psychological perspective on financial and legal judgments in the context of insolvency*, (diss. Leiden), Amsterdam: Ipskamp Printing 2020
MI-350 S. Kouwagam, *How Lawyers Win Land Conflicts for Corporations. Legal Strategy and its Influence on the Rule of Law in Indonesia*, (diss. Leiden), Amsterdam: Ipskamp Printing 2020
MI-351 A.D. Sarmiento Lamus, *The proliferation of dissenting opinions in international law. A comparative analysis of the exercise of the right to dissent at the ICJ and the IACtHR*, (diss. Leiden), Amsterdam: Ipskamp Printing 2020
MI-352 B. Ribeiro de Almeida, *Building land tenure systems. The political, legal, and institutional struggles of Timor-Leste*, (diss. Leiden), Amsterdam: Ipskamp Printing 2020
MI-353 K.A.M. van der Zon, *Pleegrechten voor kinderen. Een onderzoek naar het realiseren van de rechten van kinderen die in het kader van de ondertoezichtstelling in een pleeggezin zijn geplaatst* (diss. Leiden), Den Haag: Boom juridisch 2020
MI-354 E.G. van 't Zand e.a., *Bestuurlijke boetes en de Verklaring Omtrent het Gedrag. Een onderzoek naar de realiseerbaarheid en wenselijkheid van het betrekken van bestuurlijke boetes bij de VOG-screening aan de hand van een casestudy naar handhaving en integriteit in de financiële sector*, Den Haag: Boom juridisch 2020, ISBN 978 94 6290 843 7
MI-355 J. Boakye, *Understanding Illegal Logging in Ghana. A Socio-Legal Study on (non)Compliance with Logging Regulations*, (diss. Leiden), Amsterdam: Ipskamp Printing 2020
MI-356 N. Sánchez, *International law and the sustainable governance of shared natural resources. A principled approach*, (diss. Leiden), Amsterdam: Ipskamp Printing 2020, ISBN 978 94 0282 145 1

MI-357 S.S. Arendse, *De uiterlijke verschijningsvorm in het strafrecht. Een analyse van de jurisprudentie van de Hoge Raad*, (diss. Leiden), Den Haag: Boom juridisch 2020, ISBN 978 94 6290 844 4

MI-358 J. Reef, M. Jeltes & Y.N. van den Brink, *De PIJ-maatregel doorgelicht. Juridische grondslagen, populatiekenmerken, gedragsverandering en recidive*, Nijmegen: Wolf Legal Publishers 2020, ISBN 978 94 6240 608 7

MI-359 S. Guo, *Recognition of Foreign Bank Resolution Actions*, (diss. Leiden), Amsterdam: Ipskamp Printing 2020

MI-360 B. Muscat, *Insolvency Close-out Netting: A comparative study of English, French and US laws in a global perspective*, (diss. Leiden), Amsterdam: Ipskamp Printing 2020

MI-361 J.M. ten Voorde, S.V. Hellemons & P.M. Schuyt, *Discriminatie als strafbeïnvloedende omstandigheid bij strafbare feiten, Een rechtsvergelijkende studie*, Den Haag: Boom juridisch 2020, ISBN 978 94 6290 8710

MI-362 F. Afandi, *Maintaining Order: Public Prosecutors in Post-Authoritarian Countries, the Case of Indonesia*, (diss. Leiden), Amsterdam: Ipskamp Printing 2020

MI-363 R.M. Koenraadt, M.M. Boone, S.E. Rap & S. Kappert, *Financieel toezicht binnen het (jeugd)strafrecht. Een onderzoek naar het verloop, de resultaten en mogelijke uitbreiding van verplicht financieel toezicht binnen het (jeugd)strafrecht*, Den Haag: Boom juridisch 2020, ISBN 978 94 6290 933 5

MI-364 J.J. Asscher, Y.N. van den Brink, H.E. Creemers, E. Huls, E.K. van Logchem, N. Lynch & S.E. Rap, *De strafmaat voor jeugdige daders van ernstige gewelds- en zedenmisdrijven in internationaal perspectief*, Den Haag: Boom juridisch 2020, ISBN 978 94 6290 943 4

MI-365 M.P.A. Spanjers, *Belastingbudget. Onderzoek betekenis budgettaire impact belastingen bij parlementaire vaststelling belastingwetgeving* (diss. Leiden), Den Haag: Flosvier 2021, ISBN 978 90 8216 072 7

MI-366 J. Zhang, *The Rationale of Publicity in the Law of Corporeal Movables and Claims. Meeting the Requirement of Publicity by Registration?* (diss. Leiden), Den Haag: Boom juridisch 2021

MI-367 B.C.M. van Hazebroek, *Understanding delinquent development from childhood into early adulthood in early onset offenders* (diss. Leiden), Amsterdam: Ipskamp Printing 2021, ISBN 978 94 6421 2723

MI-368 M.R. Manse, *Promise, Pretence and Pragmatism – Governance and Taxation in Colonial Indonesia, 1870-1940* (diss. Leiden), Amsterdam: Ipskamp Printing 2021

MI-369 M.E. Stewart, *Freedom of Overflight: – A Study of Coastal State Jurisdiction in International Airspace* (diss. Leiden), Amsterdam: Ipskamp Printing 2021

MI-370 M.T. Beumers, *De bescherming van immateriële contractuele belangen in het schadevergoedingsrecht* (diss. Leiden), Den Haag: Boom juridisch 2021, ISBN 978 94 6290 962 5

MI-371 C.M. Sandelowsky-Bosman, T. Liefaard, S.E. Rap & F.A.N.J. Goudappel, *De rechten van ongedocumenteerde kinderen in Curaçao – een gezamenlijke verantwoordelijkheid*, Den Haag: Boom juridisch 2021, ISBN 978-94-6290-965-6

MI-372 G.J.A. Geertjes, *Staatsrecht en conventie in Nederland en het Verenigd Koninkrijk*, (diss. Leiden), Zutphen, Uitgeverij Paris bv 2021, ISBN 978 94 6251 270 2

MI-373 L. Noyon, *Strafrecht en publieke opinie. Een onderzoek naar de relatie tussen de strafrechtspleging en het publiek, met bijzondere aandacht voor het Openbaar Ministerie*, (diss. Leiden), Den Haag: Boom juridisch 2021, ISBN 978 94 6290 978 6

MI-374 F. Behre, *A European Ministry of Finance? Charting and Testing the National Constitutional Limits to EU Fiscal Integration*, (diss. Leiden), Amsterdam: Ipskamp Printing 2021

MI-375 R. Spence, *Collateral transactions and shadow banking* (diss. Leiden), Amsterdam: Ipskamp Printing 2021

MI-376 B.H.M. Custers, F. Dechesne & S. van der Hof (red.), *Meesterlijk. Liber amicorum ter gelegenheid van het emeritaat van prof. dr. Jaap van den Herik*, Amsterdam: Ipskamp Printing 2021

MI-377 E. Campfens, *Cross-border claims to cultural objects. Property or heritage?*, (diss. Leiden), The Hague: Eleven 2021, ISBN 978 94 6236 250 5

www.ingramcontent.com/pod-product-compliance
Ingram Content Group UK Ltd.
Pitfield, Milton Keynes, MK11 3LW, UK
UKHW051240300926
15471UKWH00015B/1112

9 789462 362505